Peter Bloom, Rok Kranjc
Introduction to the Social Economy

Peter Bloom, Rok Kranjc

Introduction to the Social Economy

Commons, Cooperation and Sustainability

DE GRUYTER

ISBN 978-3-11-107963-9
e-ISBN (PDF) 978-3-11-108014-7
e-ISBN (EPUB) 978-3-11-108021-5

Library of Congress Control Number: 2025935117

Bibliographic information published by the Deutsche Nationalbibliothek
The Deutsche Nationalbibliothek lists this publication in the Deutsche Nationalbibliografie;
detailed bibliographic data are available on the internet at http://dnb.dnb.de.

www.degruyter.com
Questions about General Product Safety Regulation:
productsafety@degruyterbrill.com

Acknowledgments

We would like to express our heartfelt gratitude to the many people and communities who contributed to the development of this book.

First and foremost, we extend our thanks to the members of our research centre for Commons Organizing, Values, Equalities, and Resilience (COVER) at the University of Essex. In particular, we are deeply grateful to Stevphen Shukaitis, Phoebe Moore, Rodrigo Nunes, and Olimpia Burchiellaro for their insightful contributions, collegiality, and ongoing support.

Peter would also like to thank his collaborators in the SE 4Ces project – *Social Economy 4Ces: Joining Social Economy Forces towards Community Development, Connected Societies, Co-creation of Knowledge, and Collaborative Education Practices*. Special thanks go to George Kokkinidis, Effie Amanatidou, Martin Parker, and Valerie Fournier, whose dedication and critical engagement have been invaluable.

Peter is profoundly thankful to his incredible partner, Sara Gorgoni, for her unwavering support and love, and to his son, Tomas Bloom-Gorgoni, whose joy and curiosity continue to motivate and inspire him.

Rok would like to thank his parents, Saša Fux and Miha Kranjc, for their lifelong support and encouragement.

https://doi.org/10.1515/9783111080147-202

Contents

Chapter 1
The Social Economy: Core Perspectives and Concepts

Introduction

Economies are fundamentally shaped by the values, goals, and assumptions underpinning economic activities. Mainstream economic models prioritize growth, individualism, and efficient allocation driven by self-interest. But across history, groups marginalized or disillusioned by the status quo have imagined and constructed alternative economic systems centered on different values like cooperation, sustainability, democracy, and community benefit. The social economy encompasses these diverse experiments striving to organize economic activities to better serve human and ecological well-being.

This chapter provides an introductory overview of the social economy, spanning its historical evolution, core concepts and values, contemporary models and debates, and transformative possibilities. It aims to empower readers to engage critically and creatively with alternatives to dominant capitalist paradigms.

What is the Social Economy?

The social economy refers to organizations and enterprises oriented toward social goals and community benefit rather than profit maximization. It includes cooperatives, mutual associations, foundations, social enterprises, certain public programs, community groups, and non-profit initiatives motivated by social missions and ethical values, not just revenue. These organizations address issues like healthcare, education, housing, job training, social services, cultural activities, ecosystem restoration, fair trade, microfinance, food security, worker rights, and community development. They aim to meet common needs, spread benefits equitably, and nurture sustainability and solidarity.

The social economy has roots stretching back to cooperative and mutual aid movements that emerged in Europe and North America alongside industrialization in the late eighteenth century and nineteenth. As capitalist markets created dislocations and inequities, cooperative banks, worker cooperatives, social clubs, friendly societies, trade unions, and self-help groups formed to pool resources and provide mutual social insurance lacking under laissez-faire policies.

Over the twentieth century, the social economy continued evolving with the welfare state, rise of non-profit organizations, social activism spurring community-based initiatives, public–private partnerships, and creative social enterprises combining business methods with social missions. It came to be seen as a "third sector" distinct from private enterprise and state apparatus.

https://doi.org/10.1515/9783111080147-001

The global financial crisis of 2008 and ongoing ecological crises have spurred new interest and experimentation in the social economy, seen as providing more ethical, sustainable, and democratic economic models. Momentum has grown around concepts like the solidarity economy, sharing economy, collaborative economy, circular economy, and green economy, aiming to re-embed markets and capital within social (and ecological) values.

Key Values and Principles

Certain core values tend to motivate and shape organizations within the social economy:

Cooperation—collective, democratic coordination of efforts and resources to meet shared needs, in contrast to competition.

Solidarity—bonding within and across groups that enables unified action despite differences. Builds social capital.

Sustainability and regeneration—stewarding ecological, social, economic, and cultural capital holistically to maintain balance across generations.

Mutuality—voluntary reciprocal exchange of knowledge and resources on the basis of mutual benefit and shared interests.

Equity—spreading benefits, wealth, and decision-making power broadly rather than concentrating it. Commitment to social justice.

Ethics—embedding transparent, democratic accountability and moral values like honesty and sustainability into governance and operations.

Pluralism—supporting a diversity of organizational models and enterprise types.

These values shape behaviors of sharing, cooperation, and collective action motivated by the public good. They spur innovations in economic organization and help build solidaristic cultures, enabling grassroots agency.

Key Organizational Forms

The social economy encompasses a mosaic of organizational forms hybridizing aspects of for-profit, non-profit, cooperative, and public enterprises. Some key models include:

Cooperatives—member-owned and governed businesses that generate member and community benefit through democratic participation. Prevalent across sectors like agriculture, finance, retail, utilities, housing, healthcare, arts, and education.

Mutual associations—member-owned and governed organizations providing insurance, finance, benefits, or professional services without external shareholders. Examples include credit unions, mutual insurance firms, and guilds.

Social enterprises—organizations using business techniques to achieve a social mission while generating revenue to become self-sufficient. Often combine aspects of non-profits and businesses.

Peer-to-peer platforms—online platforms enabling decentralized, peer-to-peer economic activities like crowdfunding, sharing, and collaborative production using virtual social networks.

Community development organizations—local organizations owned by and serving disadvantaged communities through vehicles like housing cooperatives, land trusts, social programs, community centers, job training, and commercial development.

Solidarity economy—networks of grassroots initiatives aimed at transforming capitalism based on principles of cooperation, equity, ethics, democracy, and ecological sustainability. Generally locally based.

These models enable collective economic action that diverges sharply from the institutional norms of impersonal commodity markets and shareholder corporations.

Transformative Possibilities

Proliferation of social economy organizations applies transformative pressures on mainstream capitalism in several ways, including by:
- demonstrating possibilities for embedding social values like transparency, sustainability, and democracy into economic structures
- promoting pluralism and diversity of enterprise types, diluting monolithic corporate dominance of markets
- circumventing profit-maximizing logics by orienting production and exchange to fulfill social needs
- generating surplus under stakeholder control rather than siphoning it to external shareholders
- redistributing resources and control more equitably through democratic participation mechanisms
- re-personalizing economic transactions based on reciprocity and ethics instead of impersonal commodification
- cultivating solidaristic cultures and social capital underlying risk-taking, collaboration, collective action, and grassroots innovation

A thriving social economy thus fosters the capabilities, norms, expectations, behaviors, and relationships needed to transform capitalism from within toward more ethical, sustainable, and democratic systems centered on social welfare.

History of the Social Economy

The social economy refers to economic activities oriented toward social goals and community benefits rather than solely toward profit maximization. It encompasses organizations and enterprises with social missions, such as cooperatives, mutual organizations, associations, foundations, and social enterprises (Moulaert & Ailenei, 2005). While the social economy has existed in various forms throughout history, it has gained increasing prominence and attention over the past few decades (Defourny & Develtere, 2009).

The roots of the modern social economy can be traced back to the cooperative movements that emerged in Europe and North America in the eighteenth and nineteenth centuries (Quarter, Mook & Richmond, 2003). As the Industrial Revolution brought rapid urbanization and often exploitative working conditions, groups of workers, farmers, and consumers began forming cooperatives to provide goods and services in a more equitable manner. Some of the earliest cooperatives were consumer food cooperatives started by workers in England known as the Rochdale Society of Equitable Pioneers, established in 1844. The Rochdale Pioneers outlined principles of democratic governance and open membership that became foundations for the cooperative movement. In 1865, Friedrich Wilhelm Raiffeisen founded the first rural credit union in Germany, pioneering a cooperative model for providing credit and savings services to rural populations. The success of early cooperatives led to a wave of new cooperative formations in banking, agriculture, retail, housing, healthcare, and other sectors across industrializing countries.

In the late nineteenth century and early twentieth, the social economy expanded beyond its early cooperative roots with the emergence of mutual aid societies, social service organizations, community development associations, and charitable foundations (Watrin, 1979). Many of these organizations were seeded by faith groups and religious organizations aiming to support vulnerable populations through services like healthcare, education, childcare, and disability benefits. Community foundations, pioneered in the early 1900s, allowed philanthropists to establish and grow local endowments for charitable causes. The settlement house movement, spearheaded by Jane Addams and others in low-income neighborhoods, established multi-purpose community centers offering social, educational, and artistic programs to community members.

In the aftermath of World War II, the social economy continued to evolve in response to new social needs. Across Europe, governments began funding non-profit organizations to deliver social welfare services previously provided by churches and charities (Amin et al., 2002). This included services like healthcare, education, and housing. The rise of the welfare state and public funding for social services stimulated growth in many non-profit organizations. In the 1960s and 1970s, a new wave of social activism led to alternative, community-based organizations providing services around issues like environmental protection, women's rights, and racial equality. These new social movements brought about new formations in the social economy.

The 1980s brought new challenges and changing political and economic contexts. The debt crisis in Latin America and structural adjustment policies decreased public spending on social services. To fill these gaps, non-profit organizations stepped in to provide healthcare, education, housing, and other services, often with support from international foundations and aid agencies. In Europe and the United States, rollbacks of some government welfare programs and new contracting out of public services created space for non-profits and other social economy organizations to deliver social services (Kay, 2006). The rise of new public management led to increasing collaboration between government agencies and non-profit service providers.

More recently, the social economy has continued to adapt to new needs and issues. One major trend is the growth of social enterprises—businesses that integrate social missions into their economic activities. Social enterprises adopt business models to address social problems in creative ways, recycling profits back into their social missions. They often target issues around poverty, healthcare, education, and environment. The emergence of new hybrid organizational forms at the intersection of business and charity has opened new frontiers for the social economy.

Another important trend is the rise of the solidarity economy—informal community groups organized around principles of cooperation, sustainability, democracy, and mutualism. The solidarity economy encompasses things like community gardens, barter networks, community-supported agriculture, peer-to-peer lending circles, and alternative local currencies. These grassroots initiatives aim to strengthen social ties and community resilience.

The global financial crisis of 2008 and its economic fallout brought renewed attention to the social economy. With rising inequality, decline of public services, and distrust of large corporations, interest has grown in community-based and democratically run alternatives centered on social welfare rather than profit maximization. This has created new opportunities for expansion of the social economy.

In summary, the social economy has continually evolved across history in response to changing economic conditions, social needs, demographic shifts, and ideological currents. From its origins in the cooperative movements of the Industrial Revolution era to today's proliferation of social enterprises and grassroots solidarity networks, the social economy represents economic activities oriented around social aims and community benefit. As new social and economic challenges emerge in the twenty-first century, the social economy will continue developing innovative organizational forms and enterprises to create more equitable, sustainable, and democratic alternatives to conventional profit-maximizing firms.

Social Economy Pioneer: José María Arizmendiarrieta, Catalyst of Mondragon

Basque priest, educator, and social innovator José María Arizmendiarrieta (1915–1976) played a pivotal role incubating the Mondragon federation of cooperatives that became one of the world's largest and most successful examples of cooperative economics. Arizmendiarrieta's vision and tireless efforts empowering Basque youth and working-class community members were foundational to demonstrating possibilities for scaled worker-owned enterprise.

Born in the Basque region of Spain, Arizmendiarrieta entered seminary and was ordained a Catholic priest in 1941. Assigned to the town of Mondragón, he became deeply immersed in the lives of struggling working-class families laboring in the town's factories and farms. Arizmendiarrieta grew determined to use education and community action to alleviate local poverty and lack of agency.

In 1943, Arizmendiarrieta established a technical high school based on active student participation and experiential learning. This soon evolved into a full polytechnic college providing technically skilled graduates opportunities to gain middle-class jobs and social mobility. But Arizmendiarrieta had bigger ambitions than just individual advancement. He saw potential to organize empowered graduates into democratically governed cooperatives, owned and run by workers to generate community wealth and jobs.

To realize this cooperative vision, Arizmendiarrieta brought on graduates of his school as collaborators. In 1956 they formed the first Mondragon cooperative producing paraffin heaters. This planted the seeds of what became the Mondragon Corporation, today a network of approximately 250 cooperatives and subsidiary companies with more than 70,000 worker-owners and 14 billion euro revenue.

Arizmendiarrieta continued teaching to spread cooperative principles and provided ongoing mentorship to the nascent cooperatives. Reflecting his vision, the firms promoted participatory management and profit sharing among members to actualize end goals of community betterment, not just business gains. Arizmendiarrieta fostered connections between the autonomous coops to catalyze local economic synergies.

The humanistic educational philosophy and community orientation instilled by Father Arizmendiarrieta became pillars of Mondragon's shared culture, undergirding its commitment to cooperative solidarity. While the specifics evolved over time, his seminal ideas shaped principles prioritizing sovereignty of labor over capital, subsidiary support for member cooperatives, inter-cooperation, social responsibility, and reinvestment in community.

By empowering motivated youth with knowledge and community consciousness, then guiding implementation of cooperatively owned livelihoods, Arizmendiarrieta pioneered a replicable pathway for community development through cooperative economics. The scale and longevity of Mondragon pays tribute to the power of Arizmendiarrieta's vision of human dignity realized through democratic participation in economic self-determination.

While not without imperfections and challenges, Mondragon stands as one of history's most influential demonstrations of cooperative economics. It continues as an evolving experiment focused on equitable wealth distribution, sustainability, and participatory self-governance. The improbable roots of this now global enterprise reveal the potentially generative power of education and cooperative culture in transforming local economic life.

The story of José María Arizmendiarrieta leaves a legacy of what impassioned teaching, mentoring, and community institution-building can achieve. It remains an inspiration for creating economies centered on nurturing human and community capacities rather than extracting financial profits. For catalyzing cooperative possibilities, Arizmendiarrieta deserves recognition as a key pioneer of community-driven development through social economic innovation.

The Importance of the Social Economy

The social economy plays several important roles in society. First, it provides goods, services, and employment opportunities that address social issues and community needs (Amin et al., 2003). Social enterprises and non-profits often deliver social services left underserved by government or private sectors, reaching disadvantaged and marginalized populations (Evans & Syrett, 2007). They provide services like affordable housing, microfinance, fair trade, social assistance for the elderly and disabled, drug rehabilitation, and youth development programs (Abele, 2009). The social economy also creates inclusive employment for people with disabilities, minorities, and other groups facing labor market barriers (Monzón Campos & Chaves Ávila, 2008).

In addition, organizations within the social economy can drive social innovation (Cardoso et al., 2012). By adopting alternative governance models oriented around shared social missions, they are uniquely positioned to develop and diffuse new approaches to tackling complex social problems (Mendell, 2009). Social innovation refers to new strategies, concepts, ideas, and organizations that aim to meet social needs in better ways than existing solutions (Chaves Ávila & Monzón Campos, 2012). Because they do not have to maximize shareholder value or revenues, social economy organizations have flexibility to experiment, take risks on innovative ideas, and share knowledge (Chui et al., 2012). Fields like microfinance, fair trade, social enterprise, and participatory democracy structures grew through experimentation by non-profits and cooperatives looking for better ways to fulfill social goals (Carpi, 1997).

The social economy can strengthen civil society and community engagement as well (Bauer et al., 2012). Democratic participation and membership in associations provide ways for citizens to come together, build trust and relationships, and exercise agency over decisions affecting their lives. Social economy organizations are often rooted in grassroots community activism and voluntary citizen participation. Membership in a food cooperative, credit union, or community land trust fosters social capital and empowerment. By mobilizing collective community resources to meet local needs, the social economy fosters active democratic processes and civic involvement.

The social economy also provides organizational diversity within market economies. Having a mix of enterprise types—public, for-profit, cooperative, mutual, and non-profit—creates a more pluralistic and resilient economic system (Amin et al., 2003). Different ownership structures and missions produce unique organizational behaviors and innovations. Cooperatives and mutuals bring member voice, patient capital, and concern for community impact (Monzón Campos & Chaves Ávila, 2008). Nonprofits often pioneer new approaches that governments and for-profits later adopt (Chaves Ávila & Monzón Campos, 2012). This diversity of organizational forms allows economies to tap a wider range of motivations, resources, and innovations.

Moreover, the social economy can promote more sustainable business practices (Evans & Syrett, 2007). Organizations driven by social missions tend to prioritize long-term benefits for society and the environment over short-term profits. They embed broader ethical values—like transparency, democracy, solidarity, and stewardship of community assets—into their models. Studies suggest social enterprises are more likely than conventional businesses to adopt practices like eco-friendly production, transparent supply chains, higher labor standards, democratic decision-making, and equitable profit-sharing (Villalba-Eguiluz et al., 2023). In this way, proliferation of social economy enterprises applies pressure for responsible business conduct across the entire market.

The diverse array of organizations and activities grouped under the concept of the social economy have major significance for building fairer, more inclusive, and more democratic economies (Abele, 2009). The social economy provides mechanisms to re-embed market activities within social relations and community values, creating more humane pathways for production, exchange, and redistribution (Chui et al., 2012). By harnessing associative power and civic engagement, the social economy offers potential solutions as strains of capitalism generate rising inequality and social dislocation (Carpi, 1997).

Social Economy Profile: Brazilian Landless Workers' Movement

The Brazilian Landless Workers' Movement (Movimento dos Trabalhadores Rurais Sem Terra or MST) has become one of Latin America's largest and most influential social movements through its mass mobilization of landless peasants to advocate for agrarian reform and establish cooperative farms. Emerging in the 1980s, MST has won land titles for more than 350,000 families and pioneered alternative models of ecological agriculture and cooperative community living.

Origins

MST originated in Brazil's impoverished rural areas where centuries of colonialism and oligarchic power concentrated land ownership among a wealthy elite. By the 1960s, just 3 percent of landowners controlled approximately two-thirds of arable lands. Imposed modernization exacerbated inequities, displacing small tenant farmers toward swelling slums around urban factories. But a culture of grassroots Catholic activism cultivated capacities for resistance.

In the 1970s and 1980s, community organizers helped landless peasants form associations to pressure the government and occupy unused lands. This coalesced into MST, bound by shared identity as landless workers. Tens of thousands joined "encampments" on sites demanded for cooperative farming. MST framed land redistribution as fulfilling both social justice and food security aims.

Strategies and Impact

MST organizes mass mobilizations of peasants to pressure government authorities to provide legal entitlements and support for cooperative farmland while protesting latifundia land concentration. Settlements emerge from strategic organization by MST of encampments on unproductive estates that are then legally compelled to allocate acreage for redistribution to landless peasants.

But MST involves more than just land occupations. Organizers build leadership capacities and cooperative culture within encampments. Settlements are governed through collective decision-making assemblies aimed at empowering marginalized groups like women. Once legally secured through concessions, donated lands are developed into productive, ecologically managed cooperative farms, with proceeds funding community needs like health and education.

MST has built a broad support base through public campaigns conveying the moral urgency of land reform. Marches, rallies, and demonstrations keep pressure on politicians and large landholders. Partnerships with trade unions, academics, and the Catholic Church coalesce wider backing. Settlement cooperatives strengthen food sovereignty and model sustainability.

While repressive responses by elite interests persist, MST has broken longstanding marginalization of the rural poor by asserting landless identity and capacity for self-organized mobilization. Settlements enact alternatives to hierarchical economic relations. The movement continues advancing agroecology and food justice while opening spaces for popular participation and gender equity.

Significance

MST is credited with contributing to policies securing land, credit, and support for approximately one million landless families, benefiting in the region of 4.5 million people. Settlement farms have pioneered agroecological techniques like water harvesting, organic polyculture, and participatory guarantee systems. MST eco-regions showcase family farming as a path to sustainability.

On a symbolic level, MST has instilled a sense of pride, dignity, and possibility among disenfranchised rural populations often treated as backward. The movement reflects a rising peasant class consciousness and articulation of an autonomous political identity. In rallying for "land to the tiller," MST ties livelihood struggles to larger transformations of exclusionary systems.

MST demonstrates the potent force of grassroots social movements in catalyzing structural reforms and consciousness shifts through sophisticated strategies combining protest, organization, education, communication, and the creation of prefigurative cooperative models reflecting alternative possibilities. The movement continues working toward new solidaristic economies advancing community development, food sovereignty, and environmental justice across the countryside.

Overview of Core Concepts of the Social Economy

The social economy encompasses a diverse range of organizations and activities, however there are some core concepts that unify and distinguish this sector (Westlund, 2003):

Social aims—The fundamental orienting purpose of social economy organizations is creating social value rather than maximizing profits (Asiminei & Soitu, 2014). Social aims can include things like providing affordable housing, recycling waste, training unemployed youth, supplying fair trade goods, delivering social services, revitalizing distressed communities, and stewarding community assets and heritage (Lewis & Swinney, 2007). These organizations measure impact in terms of fulfilling social missions rather than financial returns.

Democratic governance—Most social economy entities embrace democratic and participatory governance structures that allow members or stakeholders to have a voice in decision-making (Moulaert & Nussbaumer, 2005). Members of a cooperative or non-profit organization elect boards of directors. Associations and foundations have memberships whose participation steers activities. These democratic mechanisms, rooted in member ownership and open membership, contrast with corporate governance models focused on returns to shareholders (Quarter, Mook & Armstrong, 2017).

Social capital—The social economy relies on associative relationships and social networks built on trust and reciprocity (Young, 2008). Face-to-face interactions, shared values, and community ties foster the social capital needed for collective action. Social capital lowers transaction costs and provides a basis for innovating informal, community-based economic models rooted in social solidarity (Lakatos et al., 2016).

Hybridity—Many social economy organizations have blended characteristics that do not fit neatly into traditional for-profit, non-profit, or public sector categories (O'Boyle, 2005). For example, social enterprises adopt business strategies to achieve social missions, mixing aspects of businesses and charities. Cooperatives generate member benefits through market transactions. The social economy inhabits a fertile space between public, private, and non-profit spheres (Hulgård, 2011).

Social innovation—In pursuing their social aims, organizations in the social economy often pioneer new strategies and models that get diffused through networks of cooperatives, voluntary associations, and community activists (McMurtry, 2004). Social innovation happens through knowledge sharing and experimentation by values-driven organizations seeking better ways to address social problems.

Solidarity economy—At the grassroots level, the social economy encompasses informal community initiatives based on principles of cooperation, mutualism, sustainability, and democratic participation (Fasenfest et al., 1997). Things like community gardens, barter networks, peer lending circles, and local currencies provide avenues for expressing solidarity values through economic activities embedded in social relationships.

Pluralism—The diversity of organizational forms within the social economy—cooperatives, mutuals, associations, non-profits, social enterprises, etc.—contributes to a more pluralistic economic landscape (Dees et al., 2002). This diversity results in a wider variety of motivations and innovative approaches than a monoculture of capitalist firms. A thriving social economy decentralizes economic power.

Reciprocity—Social economy entities often rely on reciprocal exchange through mechanisms like volunteering, donation, lending, and community self-help (Connelly et al., 2011). Reciprocity leverages altruism, civic duty, social recognition, and other non-financial motivations to mobilize resources and labor toward collective aims, reducing reliance on monetary exchange.

Self-help—Many social economy organizations emerge from grassroots self-help initiatives in response to unmet needs. Groups facing exclusion, disadvantage, or discrimination come together in self-help associations to provide mutual social services or economic opportunities. This capacity for mutual aid fosters community agency, resilience, and empowerment.

Social justice—The social economy seeks to address root causes of marginalization and inequality. It provides social assistance, opportunities, and voice to disadvantaged groups. The social economy model offers ways for these groups to take greater control over decisions, assets, and activities affecting their well-being. Promoting social justice is both a means and an end.

Sustainability—Organizations in the social economy often integrate social, economic, and environmental aims in a holistic fashion. Their community orientation compels stewardship of collective assets for long-term well-being. A triple bottom line approach balances financial, social, and ecological sustainability. This contrasts with a narrow corporate focus on returns to shareholders.

The concepts outlined above point to some defining strengths of the social economy: capacity to build social capital and community cohesion, harness collective resources for mutual self-help, pioneer grassroots economic innovations, provide inclusive opportunities to marginalized groups, and integrate ethical values into economic structures. These distinguishing features empower the social economy to correct imbalances and inequities generated by mainstream capitalist markets.

At the same time, the social economy has its own challenges and limitations. Democratic governance mechanisms can sometimes be inefficient and slow. A reliance on volunteerism and intrinsic motivations may limit scaling. Hybridity can create confusing identities. Values like inclusion and reciprocity can be difficult to maintain over time as organizations grow. Significant variation exists across regions and cultures in how the social economy evolves and interrelates with other sectors.

Nonetheless, the array of activities and organizational forms grouped under the umbrella of the social economy represent fundamental building blocks for creating economies that better balance economic, social, and environmental aims. The social economy opens paths for re-embedding economic activities within social values and community ties. And it empowers ordinary citizens to come together in pursuit of common goals that enhance collective well-being. The social economy ultimately provides living examples of economic democracy and humanistic development.

The Different Meanings of the Social Economy

The term social economy has been defined and interpreted in varied ways by different schools of thought, disciplines, and geographic contexts (Vidal, 2010). This definitional plurality reflects the diversity of economic forms and social movements encompassed under the concept (Bouchard, 2009). Some key perspectives include:

Cooperatives and mutuals—One common usage equates the social economy with cooperatives, mutuals, and related organizational forms based on member ownership and benefit (Ismail, 2009). These democratically governed enterprises distinguish themselves from extractive capitalist firms by emphasizing service to members over profit maximization. This meaning has roots in the cooperative movements of the nineteenth century (Emelianoff, 1948). UN agencies often take this organizational approach, defining the social economy as cooperatives, mutuals, and associations with explicit social objectives (Nalebuff & Brandenburger, 1997).

Third sector—Some definitions focus on tax-exempt, philanthropic, and voluntary organizations that are neither private businesses nor public institutions (Booth & Fortis, 1984). This includes charities, foundations, social enterprises, associations, and non-profit service providers. It positions the social economy as a third distinct sector alongside private and public. This meaning prevails in countries like the United States and United Kingdom that have large non-profit sectors.

Social enterprises—In certain contexts, primarily enterprises that combine business methods with social missions get classified under social economy, social entrepreneurship, or social business (Mooney, 2004). While taking different legal forms, they mix aspects of non-profit missions and market-based approaches. This meaning gained popularity in the 1990s with the rise of hybrid entrepreneurial models.

Solidarity economy—Concepts of solidarity economy originated in Latin America to describe grassroots economic activities embedded in social relations and community values instead of profit motives (Petropoulou, 2013). Local exchanges, fair trade groups, self-help networks, and cooperative complexes get framed as elements of an alternative solidarity-based economy. This meaning contrasts capitalist markets with community-oriented economies.

Social movements—Some civil society activists and scholars define the social economy as a social movement for economic alternatives to capitalism (Altman, 2015). It encompasses organizations, enterprises, networks, and behaviors aligned with ideals of co-operation, sustainability, equity, and democracy. This frames the social economy as a counter-hegemonic bloc aiming to transform economic structures and blurring boundaries between economy, society, and polity.

Informal sector—In developing countries, the social economy sometimes includes the informal sector of micro-enterprises, livelihood activities, communal support systems, and subsistence practices partially or fully outside of regulated markets and state policies (Rothschild, 2016). Scholars have examined ways that informal community economies create solidarity, reciprocity, and collective self-help systems.

Community development—Grassroots groups engaged in participatory processes to improve social, economic, ecological, and cultural conditions in marginalized communities get included under a community development vision of the social economy (Spicer, 2022). It encompasses things like participatory budgeting, neighborhood planning councils, community development corporations, land trusts, and eco-villages.

New social movements—Some link the social economy to activist networks mobilizing around identity politics, ecology, indigenous rights, feminism, peace, and other causes that surged in the 1960s (Brzustowski & Caselli, 2021). These new social movements challenge dominant institutions and inject new social values into economic debates. Their disruptive ideas help seed alternative economic models.

Partner state—One radical discourse positions the social economy in an adversarial relationship with both capitalism and the welfare state (Lewis & Conaty, 2012). In this view, social economy organizations provide seeds for a "partner state" model where government supports autonomous, democratically managed enterprises to meet needs, while avoiding top-down bureaucracy.

As evident above, the social economy concept has been defined in diverse and sometimes contradictory ways. This definitional plurality has pros and cons. It allows the concept to encompass a rich array of organizational forms, activities, movements, and ideological currents. This provides an expansive framework for collaboration across sectors, disciplines, and schools of thought on building more just, sustainable, and democratic economies. But it also creates ambiguity, diffusion, and conceptual stretching.

For analytic clarity, it can help to delineate levels of the social economy—micro level of organizations and enterprises, meso level of networks and supply chains, macro level of broad political-economic eco-systems. Different definitions focus on different levels. But all the approaches recognize the social economy as opening spaces for economic activities oriented toward collective benefit rather than maximizing profits for a small group of shareholders. This unifying aim of democratizing economic participation and embedding reciprocity and social values into economic structures binds together the plural meanings.

Going forward, the social economy concept will likely continue refracting into multifaceted meanings tailored to different contexts. This definitional plurality can be viewed as a strength, not a weakness, of the concept. It reflects the diversity of histories, cultures, ideologies, and socioeconomic conditions that stimulate community-oriented and democratizing economic innovations. The social economy takes different organizational forms as it evolves within varied environments. But at its core, it represents initiatives that enlarge economic democracy, socialize economic returns, decommodify core aspects of livelihood, and re-embed markets into social relations—providing meso-level connective tissue between micro-level organizations and macro-level systemic change.

CASE STUDY: Open Co-Op

Open Co-op is a collaborative network focused on developing open-source technological infrastructure to facilitate more ethical, cooperative economic systems. Formed in the UK in 2011, Open Co-op convenes technologists, designers, cooperators, commoners, scholars, and activists around a shared mission of democratizing the economy through open-source, decentralized technologies and an ethos of transparency, autonomy, inclusivity, and democratic governance.

Open Co-op facilitates grassroots innovation communities prototyping tools and platforms aimed at bypassing extractive intermediaries and strengthening peer-to-peer economic collaboration. The broader aim is seeding an "open collaborative economy" centered on common good over profit maximization.

Background

Open Co-op emerged out of crossover between the cooperative movement and open-source technology subcultures in the early 2010s, catalyzed by pioneering organizations like Enspiral, P2P Foundation, Sensorica, and Fairmondo. These experiences demonstrated potential for open-source tools and peer governance models to advance cooperative aims. Initiators saw an opportunity for self-organized communities developing technological infrastructure for cooperative ecosystems beyond dependence on the proprietary platforms increasingly mediating economic exchange.

An initial convening occurred in Berlin in 2014, which led to the formation of an international working group. Open Co-op crystallized into an active network of contributive members facilitated by lightweight democratic governance structures. Alongside an online community platform and tools, physical "Hubs" support localized collaboration, mutual learning, and grassroots economic experiments. Regional chapters formed from San Francisco to Manchester, finding ways to adapt the Open Co-op model across cultures.

Activities and Impacts

–   Developing free/open platforms and software for collaborative economic activities and decentralized organization: Examples include modules for resource sharing, collaborative decision-making, value flow mapping, decentralized peer-to-peer (P2P) trade, reputation systems, cryptocurrency social wallets, and platform cooperativism. Offerings include stand-alone tools, application programming interfaces (APIs), guides, and white papers.
–   Facilitating participatory design processes and workshops bringing end-users together with developers, designers, cooperators, and technologists to co-create solutions grounded in real economic needs.
–   Hosting hackathons, skill shares, work sprints, unconferences, and other collaborative events to cultivate sharing cultures and grassroots innovation communities around open-source economic tools.
–   Providing fiscal sponsorship and incubator support for pioneering open, collaborative initiatives like Sensorica, Backfeed, Commons Engine, and Resonate Cooperative to help these vulnerable early stage projects grow sustained footing.
–   Functioning as an open cooperative itself, practicing transparent, democratic self-governance while developing the processes and digital systems to enable decentralized organizational autonomy for the broader cooperative ecosystem.
–   Inspiring replication of regional Open Co-op chapters and autonomous project teams spontaneously forming around open-source economic ideas and tools. The decentralized, viral spread of the Open Co-op model manifests the viability of open collaborative organizing logics and peer governance.

The Open Co-op case reveals potential for open digital infrastructure and decentralized organizational models to facilitate proliferation of more ethical, cooperative, community-centric economic relationships beyond dependence on extractive corporate intermediaries. It pioneers processes and tools to empower grassroots collaborative agency over essential economic functions like production, consumption, funding, and governance.

Social Economy Management

Social economy management must balance financial constraints and sustainability with participatory, democratic processes, and public service missions (Cardoso et al., 2012). This requires adapting models to facilitate stakeholder inclusion, transparent communication, and member consent while maintaining coherence and efficiency (Dunn, 1988). Fostering integrated sustainability across social, economic, and ecological dimensions is crucial through equitable programs, self-sufficient funding models, conservation practices, and supply chain ethics (Zeuli, Cropp & Schaars, 2004). Strategic revenue management involves prudent reserves, commercial optimization, diversified income streams, and demonstrating social returns on investment (Peterson & Anderson, 1996). While demanding, incorporating principles of democracy, sustainability, and mission-driven resourcing provides a management framework tailored to the contexts and aims of social economy organizations (Porter & Scully, 1987). The unique blend of participation, adaptation, and strategic financing equips social economy entities to effectively pursue their public benefit missions (Harris et al., 1996).

Democratic Management

A defining feature of many social economy entities like cooperatives, associations, and membership non-profits is their democratic governance structure. This presents unique management challenges compared to top-down, hierarchical firms (De Peuter & Dyer-Witheford, 2010). Democratic management in the social economy involves:
- Facilitating participatory decision-making through member assemblies, boards elected by members, staff input channels, and collaborative deliberation processes. This requires investing time in communication, relationship-building, and consensus-oriented processes.
- Managing the organization on behalf of a broad base of members and stakeholders, not just shareholders or executives. This entails transparent flows of information to sustain trust and accountability.
- Navigating complex dynamics between professional managers, elected board members, and engaged memberships. Clarifying roles and duties while allowing representative oversight is key.

- Developing member engagement through education, two-way communication, and participatory committees. This empowers member voice and development of shared goals.
- Fostering a culture of dialogue, inclusion, and collective responsibility for the organization's sustained success.
- Instilling a sense of ownership and solidarity among stakeholders despite potentially divergent interests between different member groups.

While demanding, democratic practices enable social economy entities to better embody public benefit values (Birchall, 2004). The involvement, oversight, solidarity, and consent generated sustains commitment to the social mission.

Sustainability-Based Management

Many social economy organizations integrate social, economic, and ecological sustainability into their models. This triple bottom line approach requires management strategies tailored to these multifaceted aims. Key aspects include:
- Incorporating social justice, community development, and equitable distribution of benefits into programs and operations. This ensures the organization generates broad social returns.
- Building economically self-sustaining models less dependent on scarce grants and donations. Earned income streams give flexibility to adapt.
- Minimizing ecological footprints by conserving energy, recycling waste, procuring green inputs, and assessing life cycle impacts of activities. Modeling sustainability practices also educates.
- Supporting sustainable and ethically produced supply chains through fair trade purchasing or local sourcing. Bring visibility to upstream impacts.
- Developing participatory processes that engage staff, volunteers, partners, and community in applying sustainability vision. This creates shared responsibility.
- Using sustainability criteria in planning, budgets, operations, reporting, and audits. Embed it into systems, not an add-on.
- Collaborating with networks and partners to scale up innovations and advocate for policy frameworks supporting sustainable development.

Pursuing integrated social, economic, and ecological sustainability aligns well with public service missions of social economy entities. It instills values of stewardship, justice, and resilience.

Revenue-Based Management

Many social economy organizations face resource constraints and funding uncertainties. This requires management strategies focused on:

- Diversifying revenues through a hybrid mix of commercial income, government contracts, grants, fees, and donations. This reduces dependence on limited funding streams.
- Optimizing enterprise activities to maximize both social returns and surpluses for reinvestment. Managing business lines to balance both goals is crucial.
- Prudently managing reserves and retained surpluses to weather funding shortfalls is key for resilience. But accumulation should balance current community needs.
- Deploying surplus revenues for the social mission through subsidized services, inclusion programs, community reinvestment, and solidarity funds demonstrates public benefit principles.
- Exploring participatory capital models that pool member savings and patient capital willing to accept capped returns in exchange for social value creation. This expands self-reliant financing.
- Adopting social accounting, impact assessment, and transparent reporting to give funders evidence that the organization provides strong social returns on investment.
- Collaborating with peer organizations on joint revenue-generating initiatives, bulk purchasing, shared services, and synchronized advocacy helps stretch resources further.

Mobilizing revenues in service to society differentiates social economy management from profit-maximizing firms. It requires strategic management of hybrid funding streams guided by both financial prudence and community stewardship.

Social Economy Profile: Fannie Lou Hamer and "Cooperative Economics for Civil Rights"

Fannie Lou Hamer was a civil rights activist and social entrepreneur who helped launch the Freedom Farm Cooperative (FFC) in 1967 as a pioneering attempt at African American economic self-determination through cooperative ownership. This experiment in the Mississippi Delta region presaged later efforts at building community wealth and the social economy amid ongoing marginalization.

Hamer grew up the youngest of twenty children in a poor Black sharecropping family in rural Mississippi in the 1920s and 1930s. After being sterilized without consent in 1961 while seeking medical care, she became more outspoken about injustices facing Black communities. Hamer joined the Student Nonviolent Coordinating Committee (SNCC) in 1962 as a recruit and field secretary.

While traveling in 1963 to register people to vote, police detained and savagely beat Hamer for her activism. This galvanized Hamer's leadership. She co-founded the Mississippi Freedom Democratic Party (MFDP) in 1964 to advocate for inclusion of African Americans in the unrepresentative Democratic Party system. She courageously testified before the Democratic National Convention about racist intimidation and violence inflicted on rural Black communities trying to exercise basic civil rights like voting.

Despite MFDP's exclusion from the convention, Hamer's stirring testimony brought national attention to racial inequities in the Jim Crow South. This raised her profile as a movement leader. But she became increasingly focused on grassroots community development for economic empowerment as crucial to securing civil rights aims.

In 1969, Hamer launched the Freedom Farm Cooperative with assistance from the SNCC, the National Council of Negro Women, and others. This pioneering cooperative sought to leverage collective land ownership, resources, and market access to build sustainable livelihoods and financial independence for African American families in Sunflower County, Mississippi.

FFC coordinated group purchases of farmland for member families to cultivate. Members pooled resources for supplies and equipment. The cooperative enabled members to set favorable prices, access markets, and develop agricultural expertise. Profit distributions aimed to guarantee basic income so families could meet needs without depending on white-owned businesses. FFC envisioned food processing facilities allowing farmers to capture more value from crops.

Hamer described cooperatives like FFC as giving the people who have no voice a voice. The cooperative model offered a vehicle for asserting agency in contexts of racial and economic exclusion. It sought to build community wealth under local ownership to provide security and unlock greater political participation.

Despite raising initial capital, FFC struggled to access ongoing financing and sustain operations. Many white-run banks refused loans as racist intimidation persisted. Tensions within the Black freedom movement over goals and strategies also impacted FFC. Hamer continued advocating for cooperative economic development but died in 1977 before her visions could be fully realized.

FFC was one of many civil rights era initiatives focused on cooperative and community-driven economic models as pathways to financial security and political power for marginalized groups. This laid foundations for the social economy sphere emerging decades later.

Hamer's instrumental role spearheading FFC demonstrated her foresight on economic independence as crucial to securing civil rights. Her cooperative solution drew on both Black self-help traditions and New Deal era cooperative precedents. Though short-lived, FFC became an inspiring forerunner of African American cooperative economics advancing community development, food justice, and sustainable livelihoods in the Mississippi Delta. It reflected Hamer's long-term vision of participatory economic democracy as integral to social and political equity.

Reimagining the Economy and Management

While the social economy encompasses pragmatic reforms to current systems, it also represents transitional steps toward more radical transformation of economic structures in a post-capitalist direction (Armitage, 2008). Several currents within the social economy align with more disruptive visions of commons ownership, reduced labor, and cooperative, abundant economies:

Commons Resource Management

Many social economy initiatives revolve around community management of shared resources or "commons" (Berkes et al., 1989). Things like fisheries, groundwater, forests, grazing lands, seeds, and even knowledge get framed as commons needing collective governance (Villamayor-Tomas & García-López, 2018). Social economy organizations like land trusts, water boards, open-source networks, seed banks, and wiki platforms provide avenues for democratic stewardship of these resources for community benefit rather than private profits.

Commons discourses view elements of human livelihood and shared heritage as inappropriate for enclosure and commodification by markets. Bringing such common pool resources under participatory management re-embeds economy in social relations aligned with values of inclusion, sustainability, and collective agency (Gronlund, 1965). This prefigures post-capitalist expansion of non-market procurement, allocation, and production governed through participatory democratic processes.

Post-Work Visions

Cooperatives, unions, and civil society networks within the social economy have increasingly engaged with debates on the future of work in the face of technology, automation, precarity, environmental limits, and changing aspirations (Naylor, 2016). Social economy provides organizational models to implement post-work policies like universal basic income and reduced work weeks that recognize social contribution beyond employment (Restakis, 2020).

Transitioning from economies centered on full-time wage labor to ones embracing plurality of work modes with shared, sustainable prosperity requires new social contracts and power balances (Gronlund, 1892). Democratized economic participation through social economy organizations provides tools to reframe notions of work, value, reciprocity, and welfare as technological disruptions reduce the need for human labor (MacLeavy & Lapworth, 2020). The solidarity, agency, and security fostered through associations provides foundations for just transitions in a post-work society (Aronowitz & Cutler, 2013).

Cooperative Commonwealth

The cooperative movement holds a vision of displacing capitalist shareholder firms with a "cooperative commonwealth" where enterprises are owned and governed democratically by workers, consumers, and communities (Cohen, 2019). By embedding ethics of solidarity, sustainability, and economic democracy into the core of production and exchange, cooperatives represent living experiments scaling up participation, distributing surplus more equitably, and anchoring the economy in social relations.

A thriving ecosystem of cooperatives interlinked across sectors and regions illustrates possibilities for pluralistic markets populated by democratically managed firms (Chase, 1934). This they envision not just alleviating capitalism's ills but transcending it altogether toward an economy organized around meeting human needs equitably and sustainably, not maximizing private profits and accumulation.

Abundance Frameworks

The capitalist logic of scarcity compels competition and individualistic gain-seeking. But emergent digital technologies and automation enable dramatically increased production of certain goods and services with reduced labor (Auty, 2001). Open design, maker spaces, creative commons, and peer-to-peer networks facilitate low-cost, decentralized production, and sharing. Elements of a more abundant economy are visible.

Social economy organizations like FabLabs, hackerspaces, open hardware enterprises, collaborative design, and maker communities pioneer institutional innovations around open-source, decentralized production, and sharing (Dugger & Peach, 2015). This cultivates norms and logics of abundance, collective agency, access over ownership, and mutualism over competition. Their cultural shift toward embracing the possibilities in abundance reorients economic imagination beyond market scarcity.

Non-Monetary Exchange

Informal exchanges through social economy entities provide avenues for non-monetary transactions embedded in social relations. Local exchange trading systems (LETS), time banks, food swaps, open knowledge and maker communities engage in reciprocal non-cash flows centered on social contribution not financial return. Peer-to-peer gift economies sustain themselves through shared social values and norms.

By elevating social logic over market pricing mechanisms and reasserting reciprocity, these experiments provide living examples of community resource flows following a social calculus rather than financial calculus. Their embeddedness in social relations seeds more cooperative post-capitalist systems no longer mediated principally through impersonal markets and cash.

These wide-ranging experiments in re-embedding economies within democratic social relations provide living illustrations that other worlds are attainable beyond capitalism. The possibilities seeded within the social economy suggest it represents not just pragmatic reforms, but also transitional steps on the path toward fundamentally transforming economic systems to be more equitable, democratic, and sustainable.

References

Abele, F. (2009). The state and the northern social economy: Research prospects. *Northern Review*, (30), 37–56.

Altman, M. (2015). Cooperative organizations as an engine of equitable rural economic development. *Journal of Co-operative Organization and Management, 3*(1), 14–23.

Amin, A., Cameron, A., & Hudson, R. (2002). *Placing the Social Economy*. London: Routledge.

Amin, A., Cameron, A., & Hudson, R. (2003). The alterity of the social economy. In A. Leyshon, R. Lee, & C. Williams (Eds.), *Alternative Economic Spaces*, 27–54.

Armitage, D. (2008). Governance and the commons in a multi-level world. *International Journal of the Commons, 2*(1), 7–32.

Aronowitz, S., & Cutler, J. (2013). *Post-work*. London: Routledge.

Asiminei, R., & Şoitu, C. (2014). Social economy: A shifting paradigm. *Journal of Social Economy, IV*(1), 17–30.

Auty, R. M. (ed.). (2001). *Resource Abundance and Economic Development*. New York: Oxford University Press.

Bauer, C. M., Guzmán, C., & Santos, F. J. (2012). Social capital as a distinctive feature of Social Economy firms. *International Entrepreneurship and Management Journal, 8*, 437–448.

Berkes, F., Feeny, D., McCay, B. J., & Acheson, J. M. (1989). The benefits of the commons. *Nature, 340*(6229), 91–93.

Birchall, J. (2004). *Cooperatives and the Millennium Development Goals*. Geneva: International Labour Organization.

Booth, D. E., & Fortis, L. C. (1984). Building a cooperative economy: A strategy for community based economic development. *Review of Social Economy, 42*(3), 339–359.

Bouchard, M. J. (ed.). (2009). *The Worth of the Social Economy: An International Perspective* (No. 2). Peter Lang.

Brzustowski, T., & Caselli, F. (2021). *Economic Growth in a Cooperative Economy*. Centre for Economic Policy Research.

Cardoso, L., Meireles, A., & Ferreira Peralta, C. (2012). Knowledge management and its critical factors in social economy organizations. *Journal of Knowledge Management, 16*(2), 267–284.

Carpi, J. A. (1997). The prospects for the social economy in a changing world. *Annals of Public and Cooperative Economics, 68*(2), 247–279.

Chase, S. (1934). *The Economy of Abundance*. New York: Macmillan.

Chaves Ávila, R., & Monzón Campos, J. L. (2012). Beyond the crisis: The social economy, prop of a new model of sustainable economic development. *Service Business, 6*(1), 5–26.

Chui, M., Manyika, J., Bughin, J., Dobbs, R., & Roxburgh, C. (2012). *The Social Economy: Unlocking Value and Productivity through Social Technologies*. McKinsey Global Institute.

Cohen, M. J.(2019). From worktime reduction to a post-work future: Implications for sustainable consumption governance. In Mont, O. (Ed.), *A Research Agenda for Sustainable Consumption Governance* (pp. 185–200). Glos and Massachusetts: Edward Elgar Publishing.

Connelly, S., Markey, S., & Roseland, M. (2011). Bridging sustainability and the social economy: Achieving community transformation through local food initiatives. *Critical Social Policy, 31*(2), 308–324.

De Peuter, G., & Dyer-Witheford, N. (2010). Commons and cooperatives. *Affinities: A Journal of Radical Theory, Culture, and Action,* 4(1), 30–56.

Dees, J. G., Emerson, J., & Economy, P. (2002). *Enterprising Nonprofits: A Toolkit for Social Entrepreneurs.* New York: John Wiley & Sons.

Defourny, J., & Develtere, P. (2009). The Social Economy: The Worldwide Making of a Third Sector. In J., Defourny, P., Develtere, B., Fonteneau, & M., Nyssens (Eds.), T*he Worldwide Making of the Social Economy. Innovations and Changes* (pp. 15–40). Leuven and The Hague: ACCO.

Dugger, W. M., & Peach, J. T. (2015). *Economic Abundance: An Introduction.* New York and London: Routledge.

Dunn, J. R. (1988). Basic cooperative principles and their relationship to selected practices. *Journal of Agricultural Cooperation, 3,* 83–93.

Emelianoff, I. V. (1948). *Economic Theory of Cooperation: Economic Structure of Cooperative Organizations* (No. 1567-2016-133427). Center for Cooperatives, University of California.

Evans, M., & Syrett, S. (2007). Generating social capital? The social economy and local economic development. *European Urban and Regional Studies, 14*(1), 55–74.

Fasenfest, D., Ciancanelli, P., & Reese, L. A. (1997). Value, exchange and the social economy: Framework and paradigm shift in urban policy. *International Journal of Urban and Regional Research, 21*(1), 7–22.

Gronlund, L. (1892). *The Co-operative Commonwealth: An Exposition of Modern Socialism* (Vol. 7). London: Swan Sonnenschein & Company.

Gronlund, L. (1965). *The Cooperative Commonwealth.* Cambridge: Harvard University Press.

Harris, A., Stefanson, B., & Fulton, M. E. (1996). New generation cooperatives and cooperative theory. *Journal of Cooperatives, 11*(1142-2016-92720), 15–28.

Hulgård, L. (2011). Social economy and social enterprise: An emerging alternative to mainstream market economy? *China Journal of Social Work, 4*(3), 201–215.

Ismail, M. (2009). Corporate social responsibility and its role in community development: An international perspective. *Journal of International Social Research, 2*(9), 199–209.

Kay, A. (2006). Social capital, the social economy and community development. *Community Development Journal, 41*(2), 160–173.

Lakatos, E. S., Bercea, O. B., & Bacali, L. (2016). The concept of innovation in social economy. A review and a research agenda. *Review of Applied Socio-Economic Research, 11*(1), 32–50.

Lewis, M., & Conaty, P. (2012). *The Resilience Imperative: Cooperative Transitions to a Steady-state Economy.* Gabriola: New Society Publishers.

Lewis, M., & Swinney, D. (2007). *Social Economy? Solidarity Economy?: Exploring the Implications of Conceptual Nuance for Acting in a Volatile World.* Canadian Centre for Community Renewal (CCCR).

MacLeavy, J., & Lapworth, A. (2020). A "post-work" world: Geographical engagements with the future of work. *The Political Quarterly, 91*(2), 310–316.

McMurtry, J. J. (2004). Social economy as political practice. *International Journal of Social Economics, 31*(9), 868–878.

Mendell, M. (2009). The three pillars of the social economy: The Quebec experience. In A. Amin (Ed.), *The Social Economy: International Perspectives on Economic Solidarity,* London and New York: Zed Press, 176–207.

Monzón Campos, J. L., & Chaves Ávila, R. (2008). The European Social Economy: concept and dimensions of the third sector. *Annals of Public and Cooperative Economics, 79*(3–4), 549–577.

Mooney, P. H. (2004). Democratizing rural economy: Institutional friction, sustainable struggle and the cooperative movement. *Rural Sociology, 69*(1), 76–98.

Moulaert, F., & Ailenei, O. (2005). Social economy, third sector and solidarity relations: A conceptual synthesis from history to present. *Urban Studies, 42*(11), 2037–2053.

Moulaert, F., & Nussbaumer, J. (2005). Defining the social economy and its governance at the neighbourhood level: A methodological reflection. *Urban Studies, 42*(11), 2071–2088.

Nalebuff, B. J., & Brandenburger, A. M. (1997). Co-opetition: Competitive and cooperative business strategies for the digital economy. *Strategy & Leadership, 25*(6), 28–33.

Naylor, J. (2016). *The Fate of Labour Socialism: The Co-operative Commonwealth Federation and the Dream of a Working-Class Future*. Toronto: University of Toronto Press.

O'Boyle, E. J. (2005). Homo socio-economicus: Foundational to social economics and the social economy. *Review of Social Economy, 63*(3), 483–507.

Peterson, H. C., & Anderson, B. L. (1996). Cooperative strategy: Theory and practice. *Agribusiness: An International Journal, 12*(4), 371–383.

Petropoulou, C. C. (2013). "Alternative Networks of Collectivities" and "Solidarity-Cooperative Economy" in Greek cities: Exploring their theoretical origins. *Journal of Regional & Socio-economic Issues, 3*(2), 61–85.

Porter, P. K., & Scully, G. W. (1987). Economic efficiency in cooperatives. *The Journal of Law and Economics, 30*(2), 489–512.

Quarter, J., Mook, L., & Armstrong, A. (2017). *Understanding the Social Economy: A Canadian Perspective*. Toronto: University of Toronto Press.

Quarter, J., Mook, L., & Richmond, B. J. (2003). *What counts: Social accounting for non-profits and cooperatives*. Upper Saddle River, NJ: Prentice Hall.

Restakis, J. (2020). Cooperative commonwealth and the Partner State. In Gustave Speth, J. & Courrier, K. (Eds.), *The New Systems Reader* (pp. 362–384). New York: Routledge.

Rothschild, J. (2016). The logic of a co-operative economy and democracy 2.0: Recovering the possibilities for autonomy, creativity, solidarity, and common purpose. *The Sociological Quarterly, 57*(1), 7–35.

Spicer, J. (2022). Cooperative enterprise at scale: Comparative capitalisms and the political economy of ownership. *Socio-Economic Review, 20*(3), 1173–1209.

Vidal, I. (2010). Social economy. In Taylor, R. (Ed.), *Third Sector Research* (pp.61–71), New York: Springer.

Villalba-Eguiluz, U., Sahakian, M., González-Jamett, C., & Etxezarreta, E. (2023). Social and solidarity economy insights for the circular economy: Limited-profit and sufficiency. *Journal of Cleaner Production*, 418, 138050. https://doi.org/10.1016/j.jclepro.2023.138050

Villamayor-Tomas, S., & García-López, G. (2018). Social movements as key actors in governing the commons: Evidence from community-based resource management cases across the world. *Global Environmental Change*, 53, 114–126.

Watrin, C. (1979). The principles of the social market economy—Its origins and early history. *Zeitschrift Für Die Gesamte Staatswissenschaft/Journal of Institutional and Theoretical Economics*, 135(3), 405–425.

Westlund, H. (2003). Form or contents? On the concept of social economy. *International Journal of Social Economics, 30*(11), 1192–1206.

Young, K. G. (2008). The minimum core of economic and social rights: A concept in search of content. *Yale J. Int'l L., 33*, 113.

Zeuli, K. A., Cropp, R., & Schaars, M. A. (2004). *Cooperatives: Principles and Practices in the 21st Century*. Madison: Cooperative Extension Publishing.

Chapter 2
Commons Ownership: Principles and Histories

Introduction

Commons ownership refers to a model where resources are owned or managed collectively by a community, rather than by individuals or private firms. Examples of commons include public parks, fisheries, forests, knowledge commons, and even the air we breathe. The concept has seen renewed interest in recent years as a potential alternative to both state control and private ownership of resources (Ostrom, 1990).

The theoretical foundations for commons ownership can be traced back to the seventeenth century English Enclosure Acts, which privatized commonly held farmland. Political economist William Forster Lloyd highlighted the potential tragedy of the commons in 1833 (Lloyd, 1833), noting that individuals may act in their own self-interest in a way that depletes commonly held resources over time. Garrett Hardin popularized this term in his influential 1968 essay (Hardin, 1968), though later work has noted that self-governed commons can often sustainably manage resources through communication and shared rules (Ostrom, 1990). Elinor Ostrom was awarded the 2009 Nobel Prize in Economics for showing how groups work together to manage natural resources as commons, challenging assumptions that either state control or privatization are the only effective options (Ostrom, 1990).

There are various examples of successful commons governance today. Lobster fisheries in Maine have been sustainably harvested from coastal waters for more than 150 years through collaborative rules and monitoring (Acheson & Gardner, 2004). Switzerland's alpine grazing lands have been managed collectively by local farmers since the thirteenth century. Indonesia's Subak irrigation system that sustains rice cultivation has operated for more than 1,000 years (Lansing, 2006). Spain's Huerta irrigation institutions have governed water sharing for more than 500 years (Glick, 1970). However, achieving effective self-governance of a commons is often complex in practice. Ostrom (1990) outlined core design principles, noting that commons typically require participation freedom, community monitoring, graduated sanctions, fast and fair conflict resolution, local rule making, and nested enterprises (when part of a larger system).

In recent decades, new types of "knowledge commons" have also emerged. These are institutionalized community approaches for governing the production, use, application, sharing, and preservation of information and knowledge resources (Frischmann, Madison & Strandburg, 2014). Prominent examples include free and open-source software projects like Linux and Wikipedia, sharing economy platforms, and genomic databases. These commons are built around digital resources that are non-rival (use by one person does not diminish others' use) and partially non-excludable (difficult to limit access, but some controls may apply) (Hess & Ostrom, 2007). Knowl-

https://doi.org/10.1515/9783111080147-002

edge commons can enable decentralized innovation that is not limited to proprietary models or traditional intellectual property rights (Benkler, 2006).

Several factors help explain growing interest in commons-based approaches. First is the recognition of limitations around privatization and state control in managing societal resources effectively (Ostrom, 1990). Private goods may generate externalities that harm communities when narrow corporate interests dominate governance. State centralized planning also has limitations in responding to diverse local needs. Second, digital networks now enable new models of decentralized, self-organized governance at scale (Benkler, 2006). Peer production through networks can be coordinated through shared protocols and social norms. Finally, commons provide an alternative model for ecological sustainability and shared prosperity amid growing environmental and economic pressures (Bollier & Helfrich, 2019). Commons shift value creation from individual extraction to collective stewardship that can balance conservation and human well-being.

However, successfully governing resource commons involves overcoming various social dilemmas. There are inherent tensions between individual interests and collective needs (Ostrom, 1990), especially when dealing with scarce or depletable resources. Rational individuals may be incentivized to overuse or under-contribute to a commons in pursuit of self-gain. Commons thus require building trust, shared purpose, community monitoring, and perceived legitimacy around rules and distribution decisions (Ostrom, 1990). Clear expectations around usage rights, responsibilities, entitlements, and contributions are crucial. This points to design principles noted earlier around participation, monitoring, graduated sanctions, fast and fair conflict resolution, and local rule making.

In practice there is a spectrum of commons ownership models today, ranging from more government-driven to fully grassroots-driven approaches:

- State-supported commons have significant government involvement, whether in initial funding, ongoing subsidies, beneficial regulation, or other entitlements. Examples include public libraries, parks (Hess et al., 2014), wireless spectrum (Benkler, 2006), and the BBC.
- Co-governed/managed commons have a blend of government and community stewardship. Examples include coastal fishery co-management (Acheson & Gardner, 2004), land trusts with public agency involvement (Frischmann, 2012), and ecosystem service markets (Muradian & Rival, 2012).
- Self-governed commons are driven through bottom-up voluntary action. This includes Wikipedia (Ayers et al., 2008), open software, makerspaces (Aryan et al., 2021), and grass-fed beef consortiums (Welsh & MacRae, 1998). They may still interact with state policies and markets around them.

There are also different types of rights and resource bundles that can be managed as commons:

- Use rights provide access/withdrawal from a resource (e.g., using a shared workshop; harvesting fish stocks).
- Contribution rights require giving time, money, or materials to maintain a resource (e.g., contributing to Wikipedia).
- Authority rights enable participation in decisions over rules, membership, and access.
- Exclusion rights control who can access or join a commons (Hess & Ostrom, 2007).

In essence, commons provide an institutional framework for collective action around shared resources. They enable sustainable access, use, contribution to, and control over resources to achieve shared purposes. Challenges remain, however, around ensuring equitable participation, monitoring use, avoiding free ridership, and handling disagreement. Ostrom's design principles provide guidance here. There are also open questions regarding interaction with state policies and markets, financing mechanisms given lack of direct price signals, and scalability.

The business implications are noteworthy, too. Commons present an alternative framing to traditional corporate ownership models (Bollier & Helfrich, 2019). Shared infrastructure or platforms can stimulate innovation and new value creation. Open models can also challenge incumbent competitive advantages, as seen in cases like Linux, Wikipedia, and web browsers. Companies may therefore sponsor internal knowledge commons. Some scholars describe Google's approach this way (Cook, 2008), enabling employees to spend 20 percent of their time on passion projects that sometimes lead to new products. Companies may also participate in and co-govern natural resource commons like fisheries to aid sustainability (Acheson & Gardner, 2004). Partnerships across sectors can govern common pool resources as well to align private and public interests, such as the Marine Stewardship Council's sustainable seafood certification program (Ponte, 2012). However, there are risks if commons are managed loosely without accountability. Finding the right governance balance is key.

The commons have, thus, shown promise as an alternative model of ownership and governance in select areas, particularly where shared use/interest exists around natural resources or knowledge resources. They offer ways to balance sustainability and access, providing counterpoints to excessive privatization (Bollier & Helfrich, 2019). However, commons ultimately depend on the cooperation of their participants. Overcoming individual self-interests and finding equitable and accountable governance mechanisms remain ongoing challenges. Further research is still needed on the design, financing, and interaction of commons with markets and states. But the success cases demonstrate the viability of commons-based models under certain conditions (Ostrom, 1990). Their unique governance merits wider study among business and economics students as we navigate issues around conservation, climate change, inequality, and digital transformation today. They offer insight into shared approaches to value creation and highlight the potentials of decentralized, grassroots innovation through networks (Benkler, 2006).

Definitions of the Commons

The concept of the commons refers to shared resources that are collectively managed or owned by a community of users, rather than being privately controlled or state-owned. Examples include public parks, community forests, open-source software, and creative works in the public domain. Commons are characterized by principles of stewardship, use rights, participation, and sustainability (Ostrom 1990). Defining the commons involves understanding key principles that distinguish them from private or state regimes, theoretical foundations, and ongoing debates about their limitations.

Garrett Hardin's 1968 article, "The tragedy of the commons," argued that open-access resources would be overexploited due to individuals' self-interest. His example described herders adding more livestock to a shared pasture to gain individually while overgrazing would be a cost shared by all, thus incentivizing overuse. Elinor Ostrom challenged this view through her extensive research on communities that had sustainably shared natural resources like pastures, forests, and fisheries. Ostrom showed that effective rules, monitoring, graduated sanctions, and conflict resolution within communities could prevent the overexploitation of resources (Ostrom, 1990; Cox et al., 2010). Her work has demonstrated demonstrated that localized, self-governed commons could be viable alternatives to privatization or state control.

Four attributes distinguish true commons:
- Common-pool resources: These are resources that are non-excludable (difficult to exclude users) and rivalrous (one person's use diminishes availability for others), such as fish stocks or grazing lands (Anderies and Janssen, 2016).
- Community of users: There is a defined group with shared access, use, management, and ownership rights, creating a direct stake in sustainable resource management (Ostrom, 1990).
- Institutionalized rules and norms: Expectations around resource use and contributions to sustainability are established, often through formal governance systems or social norms (Cox et al., 2010).
- Non-state authority: Governance is driven by user participation rather than state mandates alone, enabling a degree of autonomy (Ostrom, 1990).

Economic explanations help account for the viability of self-governed commons, countering Hardin's tragedy scenario. Restricted access and effective rules prevent free-riding and overexploitation. Governance participation fosters shared purpose and legitimacy that encourage sustainable behaviors (Anderies & Janssen, 2016).

Commons exist in natural, cultural, social, and digital domains. Classic examples include Swiss alpine pastures, Spanish irrigation systems, Nepalese community forests, and Maine lobster fisheries (Berkes, 1989). The concept has expanded to urban parks, seed banks, and even global public goods like air quality and climate stability (Foster, 2011). Knowledge commons such as open-source software, Wikipedia, and Creative Commons licenses reflect the idea of sharing intellectual and cultural resources

(Frischmann, Madison and Strandberg, 2014). Urban commons include community gardens and participatory budgeting initiatives. The solidarity economy movement uses commons frameworks to promote equitable and eco-friendly business models (Utting, 2018).

Despite the promise of commons, several challenges and limitations persist:

- Social dilemmas: The risk of overuse or free-riding is high if rules and oversight are weak. Rational users might overharvest or fail to contribute to maintenance costs, making commons vulnerable to congestion, pollution, inequality, or collapse (Nightingale, 2019).
- Equity concerns: Elite capture can occur if privileged groups dominate governance, excluding marginalized or disadvantaged populations. Women and minorities often struggle for influence in male-dominated policymaking environments (Agarwal, 2001).
- Scalability: Many local commons rely on dense social ties, trust, and ecological knowledge that cannot be easily replicated at larger scales. Critics argue that small-scale commons lack the capacity or legitimacy to manage infrastructure systems or global issues like climate change (Meinzen-Dick & Mwangi, 2009; Dolšak & Ostrom, 2003).

Ostrom's core design principles for successful commons governance include clearly defined boundaries, participatory rule-making, effective monitoring, conflict resolution, and graduated sanctions (Cox et al., 2010). These principles guide the creation of sustainable self-governance systems that balance individual and collective interests.

Commons can fill governance gaps left by state and market failures. Over-centralized state bureaucracies or privatization often struggle to accommodate diverse local needs. By contrast, commons emphasize inclusivity, participation, and social purpose, making them effective at managing shared resources (Ostrom, 1990; De Moor, 2013). Digital networks enable new forms of large-scale commons governance for non-rival information resources. For instance, Wikipedia and open-source software projects show that digital commoning can succeed through modularized tasks, granular transparency, and non-monetary signals of purpose-driven work (Benkler, 2006).

Commons governance challenges assumptions that resources must be either privatized or state-driven. Instead, it proposes that some goods may be best managed through collective action with dynamic, democratic input from participating users (Harvey, 2011). Context-sensitive rules, transparency, and grassroots engagement can enable sustainable management of shared resources at various scales, from local fisheries to global climate governance (De Angelis, 2017).

While the diversity of commons types and scales complicates the search for universal models, the underlying logic—emphasizing shared purpose, community capabilities, and humane values around justice and inclusion—continues to inspire innovative governance experiments.

History of Commons Ownership

The concept of shared communal resources held in stewardship for collective use and benefit rather than private gain has deep historical roots across cultures. Forms of commons governance emerged thousands of years ago and evolved across ancient civilizations. Understanding this long legacy provides context to contemporary manifestations.

Shared hunting and foraging grounds: Among hunter-gatherer bands and nomadic pastoralist tribes, critical survival resources like forests, grazing lands, or watering holes were treated as common pool assets open to all tribal members rather than any one person's private property. However, boundaries, harvesting limitations, and norms around resource use between different tribes were strictly maintained through rituals, threats of force, and reciprocal respect (Bollier 2014). Violations risked conflict. Protection and sustainability depended greatly on ancestral customs and spiritual injunctions against overuse.

Village granaries: After the transition to sedentary agriculture, early small-scale village farming communities developed collective storage facilities managed by elders or spiritual authorities to even out seasonal food scarcity through crop contributions from all households, for redistribution in lean times, or emergencies based on need (Scott, 2017). Such granaries constituted commons infrastructure balancing self-reliance, sharing, and survival needs holistically rather than atomized market transactions during precarious years.

Medieval European commons: In the feudal era, serfs and free peasants across Western and Central Europe shared rights to use common pasturelands, forests, lakes, waste, and stubble farmland between growing seasons for livestock grazing, gathering wood, hunting small game, fishing, and other productive activities mitigating individual poverty (Linebaugh, 2008). Village councils and manorial courts oversaw rules on resource usage bounds. Nobles and church authorities held territorial control, but villagers retained subordinate use rights. Peasant communities co-managed these vital economic commons over generations.

Swiss alpine commons: Alpine meadows and forests have been shared among Swiss peasant villages to graze dairy cattle and gather wood fuel for hundreds of years, regulated by cooperative agreements. Boundaries, seasonal usage turns, and maintenance responsibilities are collectively governed at the village and canton level based on traditional and current use levels (Netting, 1981). Swiss herding and grazing commons continue surviving today.

Spanish irrigation huertas: Farmer managed irrigation commons have had long continuity in arid regions of Spain to sustain agriculture and villages. The thousand-year-old huertas in the Valencia region feature intricate infrastructure, including canals, dams, tunnels, and systems for water allocation. These structures are collectively constructed, maintained, and managed by the farmers. Governing councils regulate usage and maintenance work. Similar farmer-built, farmer-run irrigation commons prevail in the Philippines.

Inca land stewardship: In the Andes, Inca civilization had state infrastructure like roads and storage but farmland was collectively cultivated by peasant clans without land sales. The ayllu system allocated plots across varied microclimates for crop rotations and fallowing sustainably. Stewardship norms structured solidarity economy relations rather than commodified land or calculating profitability. Ayllu communal principles faded under Spanish feudal haciendas but indigenous remnants persist in the Andes.

Ocean and forest commons: Coastal seas, large lakes, and vast forest regions have also functioned as commons where access and use by fisherfolk, mobile pastoralists, or foraging tribes have been open rather than limited to a state or single community. However, protectionist norms against overuse prevailed through restraints on technology, spiritual codes, and customary rules on sharing natural abundance through parts of Africa and Asia over generations (Berkes, 1989).

Globalization pressures on traditional commons: However, the spread of capitalist property relations and growth imperatives from sixteenth-century European colonialism imposed strains on many subsistence-oriented commons in indigenous societies. Privatizing land and resources for commercial export and elite profit generated dispossession and inequality across Asia, Africa, and Americas over centuries, enclosing what tribes had held in common. Customary commons came under threat even as some European peasant commons also eroded under agrarian capitalism.

Yet settled agricultural villages were better able to resist commercial pressures through cooperative structures like Peru's contemporary Potato Park retaining a rotational farming commons or Indian tribal regions upholding customary gathering from forest commons despite modern legal efforts to curtail use. Small-scale community oversight persisted in pockets whereas diffuse ocean and forest commons without bounded membership proved harder to protect from commercial harvesting technologies.

Modern revival of commons ideas: By the late twentieth century amidst growing concerns around environmental sustainability and inequality, scholars revived interest in commons models against excessive privatization. Elinor Ostrom's landmark 1990 work highlighted self-organized groups successfully managing communal forests, fisheries, and pastures themselves through cooperative rules and norms evolved over generations without state or market mechanisms. This fueled policy interest in supporting community-based conservation commons instead of simply designating parks or industries owned by governments or private entities (Agrawal, 2003).

Digitally networked twenty-first century commons like Wikipedia and open-source software have also enabled large-scale collaborative production and knowledge sharing within managed internet platforms. Groups of users create public good infrastructure and information without individual profit motives or state control (Benkler, 2006). The internet has propagated an explosion of such digital commons even as extractive capitalist structures still dominate its political economy. Questions around sustaining non-commercial, non-exploitative paths persist (De Angelis, 2017).

A spectrum of collectively held and produced commons now thrives from heritage seed banks to cryptocurrency platforms to city parks; some small-scale and self-organized, others interacting heavily with government agencies and programs or regulated by public bodies to preserve public access. Inequality, climate pressures, and technology keep generating new enclosures of resources once freely shared as common pool goods from genomes to even outer space orbits (Bollier, 2002). This fuels commoning movements struggling to retain elements of sharing economies vital for social reproduction and sustainability against commodification. Understanding the deep but fragile lineage of the commons through changing historical phases and geographies informs both threats and possibilities to retain non-commercialized spaces for community in our marketized world.

Commons Governance

Governing shared resources sustainably requires overcoming inherent collective action problems around individual interests versus the common good. Commons governance involves creating institutions enabling participants to collaborate rather than selfishly defect. Key elements include defining boundaries, membership rights, usage limits, monitoring procedures, sanctioning processes, conflict resolution methods, decision-making rules, and mechanisms for adapting policies over time as conditions change.

Foundational governance scholarship emerged from Nobel laureate Elinor Ostrom's field studies of long-enduring commons. She outlined core design principles in *Governing the Commons* (1990) based on cases like Swiss grazing meadows and Spanish irrigation systems surviving for centuries. These principles remain touchstones for commons governance today, supplemented by later research on digital commons, urban commons, and global commons.

Ostrom's principles derived inductively from cases are:

1. Clearly defined boundaries—The identities of both the shared resource system and its user community are clearly delineated, with specified resource zones and participating members. For example, an irrigation canal community with associated farmer beneficiaries is bounded unlike a regional watershed or ocean. This aids defining usage and contribution rights and duties.

2. Congruence—Appropriation and provision rules limiting water or fish harvests match local conditions. Governance ties usage rights to requirements like contributing labor for infrastructure maintenance reflecting ecological realities.

3. Collective-choice arrangements—Users participate in modifying operational rules over time through transparent democratic processes without external authorities dictating policies. Distribution of decision-making powers aids adaptation.

4. Monitoring—Responsible monitors keep track of resource conditions and user behaviors. Water guards assess flows and infractions in huertas. Lobster gangs cross-check trap counts. Monitoring deters overuse.

5. Graduated sanctions—Violating rules leads to accountability measures increasing in severity for continued noncompliance, ranging from warnings to fines to temporary loss of usage rights and ultimately permanent expulsion as the worst penalty. But initial light punishments allow learning.

6. Fast and fair conflict resolution—Rapid, low cost, locally accessible conflict adjudication systems exist for disputes over rule violations before higher-level authorities. Neighbor to neighbor resolution maintains community bonds better than dependency on external legal procedures.

7. Local rule-making—Acknowledging context, rules come from participatory decisions by users tailored to local needs, reflecting past learning and changing current realities, supporting compliance and solution fit. Alien policies often fail.

8. Nested enterprises—When a common pool resource system is embedded within a larger social-ecological system like a river section within a broader watershed, governance should also be organized in nested tiers appropriately linked across system levels for coherent reinforcement.

These core design features facilitate trust, reciprocity, and shared purpose against more extractive self-interest. Variations suit different contexts—more complex irrigation systems require multi-tier participation platforms than lobster gangs (Meinzen-Dick, 2007). But inclusion aids legitimacy and compliance.

Challenges facing groups lacking such designed institutions help explain failures managing shared resources sustainably, whether congested city parks degrading without rules and responsibilities or online networks overrun by spam and harassment absent oversight mechanisms protecting against abuse. Hardin's tragedy scenario reflects this absence of governance more than inherent flaws in commoning itself (Feeny, 1992).

However, Ostrom's principles constituted a beginning framework, not rigid requirements or panacea guarantees against resource degradation, inequality, and conflict in restless open systems (Cox, 2010). Creating participatory, culturally legitimate rules remains an evolutionary challenge. Continuing research contributes further dimensions like knowledge commons principles, integrative frameworks on legal-social diversity, and polycentric governance ideas.

Contemporary Commons Governance Advances

Digital commons governance: Governing digitally shared non-rival, less depletable re-sources like software code or Wikipedia still requires contribution incentives and platform rules against potential chaos or dominance by subsets of users. But digital transparency tools enable faster policy adaptation through usage data analysis. Modular technical architectures allow decentralized innovation and task coordination. Domain-specific rules can dynamically balance open access for public benefit against sustaining quality, reliability, and civility, avoiding congestion or hijacking.

Urban commons governance: Cities involve dense contested spaces with neighborhoods competing over resources like vacant land but also facing problems better solved collectively like pollution, homelessness, or disaster resilience (Dellenbaugh et al., 2015). Urban commons require appropriate governance between grassroots self-management, partnerships with authorities, and public oversight for interventions balancing localism and equity across fragmented groups lacking strong solidarities.

Global commons governance: International environmental regimes try governing globally shared ecosystems like oceans, the atmosphere, and Antarctic but face high inter-state bargaining costs, uncertainty, and geostrategic conflicts (Dietz et al., 2003). Fragmented authorities, inadequate science, monitoring weaknesses, North–South equity conflicts, and free rider disincentives hinder stronger cooperation. Yet some architectures like the Montreal Protocol on limiting ozone-depleting substances or the International Whaling Commission model overcoming tragic overuse through agreed caps and enforcement exist, though pressures persist (Ostrom, 2010).

Adaptive governance: Given dynamic change, commons governance also requires multi-level social learning for participants themselves to monitor outcomes and periodically reevaluate effectiveness of inherited rules, adding or reforming policies when contexts evolve (Chaffin, Gosnell & Cosens, 2014). This adaptive orientation treats inheritance as a starting point, but privileges situated needs and agencies to tailor over time rather than immutable logics, though still anchored in core values of equity and sustainability.

In essence formal institutional designs must find balance between historical experimentation and openness to uncertainty. Beyond Ostrom's principles focused largely on local common pool resources among denser communities, newer governance thinking engages complex multi-tier regimes, digital transformations, urban encapsulation, and existential issues like climate catastrophes challenging twentieth-century environmental management. Much remains to be learned for polycentric, ecologically integrative, culturally responsive governance that sustains commons across cases and generations.

KEY THINKER: Elinor Ostrom

Elinor Ostrom (1933–2012) was an American political economist recognized for her pioneering work on economic governance and common pool resources. Awarded the 2009 Nobel Prize in Economics, Ostrom challenged the prevailing assumption that shared resources are doomed to overexploitation without state or private control.

Ostrom's research, grounded in extensive fieldwork, demonstrated that communities can sustainably manage common resources through self-devised institutions. Her findings contradicted the dominant "tragedy of the commons" theory, which held that individuals, acting in their own self-interest, would inevitably deplete shared resources. Instead, Ostrom illustrated how communities have created diverse and enduring governance systems for shared resources like pastures, fisheries, and forests—often more effective than top-down state regulation or privatization.

Initially trained in political science, Ostrom began studying groundwater management in California in the 1960s, amidst complex disputes over water rights. This experience prompted her to adopt an interdisciplinary approach combining political science, economics, law, and public policy, leading to groundbreaking research that emphasized self-organization and cooperation in managing common resources.

Her work expanded into analyzing how factors such as rules, trust, reciprocity, social capital, and culture shape commons governance. Ostrom developed a set of design principles common to successful long-standing institutions, such as clearly defined boundaries, participative rule-making, effective monitoring, accessible conflict resolution, and nested governance across multiple levels. These principles, she argued, enable communities to manage resources sustainably and avoid the free-rider problem that often undermines collective efforts.

Ostrom's research highlighted that there is no universal solution for managing shared resources—effective governance must be context-specific, adapted to local needs and conditions. This nuanced view has had a profound impact on both academic discourse and policymaking. Her work showed that local, community-based management often outperforms centralized state or market-driven models, influencing policies that prioritize decentralization and community participation.

Ostrom co-founded the International Association for the Study of the Commons (IASC), fostering a global network of researchers dedicated to advancing commons scholarship. Her ideas have influenced diverse areas such as land reform, participatory conservation, urban commons policy, and digital commons governance. Cities like Bologna, Italy, have incorporated her principles into urban policies, and her work has shaped legal frameworks protecting indigenous commons globally.

Ostrom's theoretical contributions also redefined how economists view human agency. She critiqued the rational actor model dominating economics, demonstrating that individuals are capable of cooperation based on trust, reciprocity, and long-term social interactions—contrary to the assumption that self-interest alone drives behavior.

Her insights remain relevant across many contemporary policy contexts, such as climate change, community-based renewable energy systems, and digital commons management. Ostrom's legacy, as the first woman to receive the Nobel Prize in Economics, continues to inspire researchers and policymakers seeking equitable and sustainable solutions for managing shared resources in a complex world.

Agricultural and Food Commons

Agricultural and food systems have seen a resurgence of commons-based governance approaches in recent decades to better balance farmer livelihoods, ecological sustainability, and community food security amidst pressures of agribusiness consolidation and commercialization. Various movements aim to reclaim seed, land, water, livestock breeds, and agricultural knowledge from enclosure to reestablish common pool access and participatory control against extractive market logics.

Key forms of agri-food commoning counter tendencies toward proprietary ownership and commodification of foundational resources enabling small-scale cultivation and regional food provisioning centered on collective stewardship and solidarity ethics. These emerging experiments attempt community oversight and reciprocal exchange against polarizing trends that have made agriculture both a chief driver of biodiversity loss and carbon emissions yet also economically unsustainable for many farmers caught in input-dependence and market price volatility.

The contexts and concerns vary across cases—from indigenous communities retaining customary seed sharing practices to urban residents creating gardening collectives on vacant lots. But core values around ecology, cooperation, and inclusion motivate creating and protecting communal resources for sustainable rural livelihoods and equitable food access. The various manifestations of agri-food commoning illustrate operational governance principles in practice.

Seed Commons

Indigenous seed saving: Cultivating crop diversity through saver farmer networks exchanging, breeding, and storing heirloom varieties has long historical continuity across Asia, Africa, and Latin America as communal heritage. But modern commercial seed enclosures threaten customary agrobiodiversity practices and ancestral knowledge systems through patenting and homogenization under hybrids and genetically modified organisms (GMOs) (Shiva, 2016). Yet organic farmer movements from India to Mexico retain seed commons logic and techniques like community seed banks, exchanges, and breeding cooperatives.

Open-source seed networks: Some initiatives go further seeking open-source licensing for plant germplasm by freely sharing breeding information while retaining rights for sharing resultant seeds and produce non-commercially, to keep access open against monopoly by any entity (Kloppenburg, 2014). This manifests the digital commons ethos around non-enclosed innovation transferred to the biological domain with appropriate institutional adaptation. The Open Source Seed Initiative spanning universities and farmer networks tries balancing public goods aspects of pre-competitive germplasm against needs of participatory plant breeders.

Livestock commons farm animal genetic diversity also faces threats from industrial uniformity geared to maximize conventional metrics of productivity within consolidated value chains demanding standardization across contexts (IDF, 2019). Just a few transnational breeding firms now dominate poultry, swine, and cattle worldwide, displacing locally adapted livestock diversity cultivated over centuries. However, agroecology movements try retaining heirloom working animal breeds (such as turkeys, pigs, and sheep) under community oversight through breeding clubs and cooperatives managing herdbooks, stud services, and slaughter-processing infrastructure while navigating wider commercial environments. Questions around participation, sustainability, and value distribution confront livestock commons initiatives balancing conservation, productivity, and farmer autonomy.

Farmland commons enclosure of agricultural land for real estate profits and industry has accelerated across many regions like Africa, Asia, and Eastern Europe after years of smallholder family tenure, disrupting rural livelihoods and food sovereignty (GRAIN, 2016). Speculation-fueled farmland grabbing often enjoys state support for presumed development benefits (Daniel, 2011), but communities lose control over generational resource endowments. This fuels resistance efforts.

Community land trusts secure collective legal ownership over agricultural (and housing) real estate assets to prevent market sale or development shifts. The lands are held in stewardship for conservation and sustainable cultivation benefiting producers rather than profiteers. Questions of access equity for tenants and ecological sustainability require governance attention, adapting models like forest commons. India's post-independence land reforms enshrined "ceiling limits" on individual farm property to deter concentration against small-scale family tenure. But redistributive implementation has lagged (Rawal, 2008).

Urban farm commons in neglected neighborhoods revive community gardening traditions—like 5th & Orange community garden in Philadelphia transforming abandoned lands into communal spaces for learning, recreation, and subsistence vegetables led by primarily immigrant and minority growers (Eizenberg, 2012). Such urban agricultural commons require reconciling informal occupation and variable membership with public liability issues and closure threats from land redevelopment.

Water commons community management has proven viable for small-scale irrigation systems, however, 95 percent of global food crop land relies on rainfall rather than irrigation infrastructure (WWAP, 2021). This has spurred water harvesting innovations like johads and check dams built and managed by Indian tribal farmers capturing monsoon runoff, recharging groundwater for homestead wells (Agarwal, 2001).

Farmer associations negotiate rules for pooled catchment infrastructure around rainwater and streamflow sharing as hydrological commons across communities to mitigate shortages, coordinate usage turns, and recharge natural flows (Pande & Sivapalan, 2017). Such governance blends customary norms with structured collectives for more formalized sharing protocols as complexity, conflicts, and commercialization increase pressures. Climate uncertainties add further adaptation needs.

Forest Garden Commons

Swidden cultivation shifting mosaics have operated as forest commons across South and Southeast Asia for generations under tribal norms, but face restrictions under centralized forestry bureaucracies and conservation enclosures (Scott, 1999). Some farming communities try retaining endogenous practices like integrated rotational home gardens enriched by useful trees, vines, herbs, and fungi for sustenance and cash within locally evolved governance rules on fallowing and limited commercial harvesting to balance ecology and livelihoods. This forest garden commoning straddles ambiguous boundaries between dominant property regimes and insurgent use claims driven more by household cooperation than formal legal standing. Questions around conservation and equity in distribution of benefits and responsibilities confront these commons lacking formal titles.

Knowledge and Technology Commons

Digital information networks enable unprecedented open access opportunities for farmer innovations and agroecology techniques as "open hardware" knowledge commons. Open technology equipment like low-cost drip irrigation, biofertilizer production equipment, or farm hacking devices can be locally manufactured from freely shared design specs rather than purchased expensively, aiding grassroots self-reliance. Peer learning networks likewise facilitate spread of agroecological methods on soil regeneration, intercropping systems, or botanical pest control through commons logic rather than proprietary advantage (Pimbert, 2021). However, equitable participation opportunities across gender, ethnicity, and global regions require proactive governance investments to prevent divergence in capabilities.

Alternative food distribution commons principles also inform alternative food networks aiming to build regional produce channels that sustain both farmers and consumers more equitably outside commodity chains dominated by supermarkets (Vivero-Pol, 2017). Examples include solidarity economy farming cooperatives and farmer marketplace collectives that coordinate cultivating diverse crops, aggregating supply logistics, providing technical assistance, and organizing regional provisioning channels directly to schools, hospitals, or urban neighborhoods on subsidized terms for fresh produce access, with governance input from growers, buyers, and public partners (Mount, 2012). Questions about sustaining volume, diversity, and livelihood distributions confront such counter-hegemonic food commons experiments at early stages.

In essence, diverse commoning practices attempt re-embedding ethical values of sharing, sustainability, and community accountability around foundational agrarian resources rather than leaving allocation and benefits solely to atomized market mechanisms or distant bureaucratic controls. They highlight the resurgent appeal of cooperative models that balance ecology, productivity, and economic viability for small-scale farming viability and regional food provision—illustrating pathways beyond the exhausting treadmill of agribusiness competition at odds with planetary boundaries. But realizing more equitable and sustainable alternatives depends greatly on cultivating participatory multi-stakeholder governance capabilities and preventing elite capture. Creating successful commons for inclusive rural security and urban access amidst unstable environments remains a key frontier for innovation and justice movements alike in coming years.

CASE STUDY: Open Food Network

The Open Food Network (OFN) is a multi-stakeholder cooperative working to catalyze regional food economies grounded in ecological sustainability, social justice, and food sovereignty. Emerging from Australia's food sovereignty movement, OFN provides online infrastructure connecting small-scale farmers and food enterprises directly with consumers and cooperatives. It facilitates decentralized trade in food guided by ecological values instead of global commodity logics. OFN's model indicates scalable possibilities for platform cooperatives enabling commons-based peer production and exchange alternatives.

OFN aims to transform food systems dominated by exploitative global agribusiness toward networks of socially embedded local enterprises built around ethics of ecological sustainability and solidarity economies. It provides online directories, e-commerce platforms, and logistic coordination tools connecting disparate enterprises—like small farmers, food hubs, cooperative distributors, retail co-ops, and buying groups—across decentralized regional food economies. Enterprises coordinate logistics like transport contracts and inventory management through the infrastructure.

Producers and consumers also connect through storefront profiles and food hubs on the OFN platform, enabling values-based economic exchange grounded in regional context and proximate social relationships. By facilitating links between disparate nodes, OFN helps weave an alternative food distribution tapestry aligning ethical producers and conscientious consumers. Its tools aim to bridge gaps in technical capacities and geographic distance that constrain smaller farmers and enterprises from accessing essential market channels outside exploitative global food chains.

Organizationally, OFN operates as a global peer-to-peer network and multi-stakeholder platform cooperative linking diverse contributors and users. Regional communities self-organize chapters adapting OFN's open-source software and mutually owned infrastructure to respective contexts. The global network develops shared tools, capabilities, and practices as a commons accessible by all chapters.

Governance rests on principles of platform cooperativism—where users collectively own and democratically control the digital infrastructure mediating economic activities. Working groups with members across regional communities govern areas like software development, user experience design, communications, and onboarding. Decision-making emphasizes grassroots participation and transparency through tools like Loomio, Cobudget, and Mattermost.

OFN's hybrid structure thus combines decentralized regional autonomy with global peer production of an essential resource—the software and organizational capabilities enabling ethical food economies. By mutualizing access to essential infrastructure as an ethical digital commons OFN aims to remedy the extractive design of capitalist platforms extracting rents through data and attention while imposing path dependencies. Its cooperatively governed infrastructure is designed for equitable control and gain-sharing among users facilitating regional food solutions—not outside shareholders.

In its decade-long evolution, OFN has overcome challenges in balancing decentralized community innovation with consolidating a coherent global system. Tensions between tech development priorities and diverse regional needs require constant negotiation within participative governance processes. Questions concerning scaling fast enough to meet user needs at times brush against open culture commitment to transparent deliberation.

Adapting tech architecture for low-bandwidth contexts in the Global South has also posed learning curves. OFN's mission of information and communication technology (ICT) capacity-building among food enterprises means accommodating a spectrum of technical literacies. Parts of the software ecosystem like the backend architecture have matured more slowly relative to the frontend user interfaces. Limited developer capacity earlier constrained balancing feature enhancements with technical debt inherited from successive prototyping.

Securing fiscal sustainability given grant funding uncertainties and slim financial surpluses has also been challenging for a mission-driven platform cooperative satisfying social needs, unlike profit-maximizing capitalist platforms. Experimenting with value flows, incentive alignment, and revenue streams to support maintenance and growth needs remains an evolving equation for OFN.

Despite limitations, OFN's solution indicates genuine possibilities for commons-based platforms transforming ethical production and exchange. Expanding across Europe, North America, and the Global South, OFN's tools now facilitate more than $5 million in annual trade between hundreds of producers and enterprises reaching thousands of consumers. Software development has professionalized around more stable open-source architecture supporting modular regionalization. Governance capabilities have strengthened around bottom-linked leadership and transparent contributive accounting.

OFN shows how platform cooperatives can disrupt platform capitalism by offering services like discoverability, logistics coordination, and e-commerce embedded in shared democratic control and non-extractive data governance nurturing ethical communities. Its solidarity economy tools suggest pathways for grassroots sustainability transformations rebuilding regional economic ecosystems that fulfill social needs and ecological limits beyond global commodity logics.

Energy Commons

Energy forms a vital resource shaping human prosperity and geopolitics worldwide in profoundly uneven and unsustainable ways. Polluting fossil fuel dominance threatens global climate stability while more than a billion humans lack basic electricity access amid divides separating Global North and Global South citizens. However, movements emerging around cooperativized clean energy demonstrate radical possibilities for decentralizing and democratizing energy generation and governance toward universal, resilient provision sustaining ecological and social well-being.

Conceptualizing energy infrastructure and policy as commons rather than commodities or state services fosters holistic universal access within sustainable planetary boundaries (Szeman, 2019). Commons thinking escapes capitalist profit logics degrading communities and ecologies toward collective democratic ownership enabling self-determined resilience and justice (Martinez, 2017). Exploring energy commons developments, transitions, and scalability illuminates directions for transformative sustainability that nourishes all human and ecological communities interdependently.

Modern energy regimes impose violently extractive, unequal, and unsustainable pathways for fueling contemporary civilization through pervasive market and state enclosures dispossessing commonwealth foundations for shared prosperity (Mann, 2016). Vast populations endure energy poverty without basic access, while fossil-fuel addiction drives profits over ecological stability. Renewables integration likewise remains dominated by large utilities maximizing shareholder returns rather than empowering consumers or stabilizing the climate (Baker, 2017).

Against this energy oligarchy threatening communities worldwide, commons offer a revolutionary paradigm for cooperative self-governance, decentralized sovereignty, and universal rights (Martinez, 2017). Commons thinking views foundational social goods like knowledge, water, forests, and biodiversity as shared inheritances not commodities for market profiteering or state appropriation (Ostrom, 2015). Energy likewise constitutes indispensable collective infrastructure enabling dignified, sustainable lives when organized for equitable participation.

Energy commons thus designate socio-technical systems delivering renewable, reliable power access through cooperative or public ownership models governed transparently by communities for mutual benefit beyond returns to capitalists or partisan agendas (Wolsink, 2020). Direct citizen participation in planning, investment decisions, and operations sustains focus on enabling livelihoods not maximizing financial yields stripped from place (Capaccioli, 2018). Networking energy commons fosters proliferating alternatives to concentrated grids dominated by absentee utilities and contexts.

Despite marginalization by dominant capitalist regimes, communities worldwide pioneer energy commons demonstrating radical operationalization of cooperative low-carbon resilience from grassroots innovation. For instance, civil society coalitions across German cities leverage policy openings to construct community solar platforms, wind farms, and smart microgrids governed transparently by engaged citizens as prosumption cooperatives, not profit-seeking firms (Becker et al., 2018). Seasonal exchanges of excess renewable electricity create solidarity economies empowering households as proactive infrastructure co-providers advancing climate goals.

Similarly Seoul's (South Korea) authoritarian developmentalist legacy spurred top-down smart city schemes even while civil society forged energy democracy through solar power commons cooperatives fostering participation, affordability, and decentralized capacity (Namgung, Kim & Hwang, 2022). Struggles persist against concentrated utility and construction conglomerates, but neighborhoods network piecemeal rooftop solar panel commons as cracks in the corporate energy regime. India's indigenous women likewise organize distributed microgrids for bringing village homes reliable clean electricity outpacing unreliable state development promises (Baker, 2017).

Microgrid electricity commons rural microgrid experiments in Bangladesh, Nepal, and Kenya reflect community-based solar mini-grids managed by village energy committees, operating off-grid or connecting to unreliable national grids as backup power pools through local renewable generation and battery storage (Franz et al., 2014). After covering installation and maintenance costs through connection fees and flat tariffs, surplus revenues get reinvested to extend system capacity rather than siphoned as profits. Users also gain skills around system repair. Governance arrangements balance affordability, reliability, and sustainability incentives between producers and consumers rather than merely profits for absentee owners.

Transportation fuel cooperatives farmer cooperative ownership of ethanol biorefineries and collective biodiesel processing facilities enhance livelihood security through energy production, shield members against feedstock and fuel market volatility, and embed sustainability practices from soil to fuel tanks by valuing members as stakeholders rather than purely commodity suppliers to corporations. Multi-tiered governance in Wisconsin's heralded sugar cooperative ramped farmer-led investments in integrated ethanol production driving revitalization (Mooney & Majka, 1995).

Myriad such cases reveal multidimensional value from localizing power infrastructures within inclusive community governance advancing rights, autonomy, and sustainability more than maximizing impersonal output metrics (Suonio, 2023). Even technical design processes transform through participatory engagement, for instance preferencing modular microinstallations offering flexibility over rigid centralized mega-grids (Yang, Chen & Kim, 2021). Site-specific learning also adapts provision to community preferences around dynamic pricing models, storage roles, or ancillary decarbonization offerings like e-mobility charging access or heat pumps integrating supply chains (Wolsink, 2020).

Overall energy commons initiatives balance pragmatic basic service delivery for household needs with movement-building visions for systemic transitions beyond growth obsession toward sustainability and justice through reclaimed local sovereignty over essential resources. The approach suggests scalable replication potential across villages and cities by contextual design grounded in lived community priorities rather than technocratic central regime dictates.

However, energy commons still confront steep challenges around scaling beyond isolated niches given path dependencies and dependencies locking societies into corporate-dominated unsustainable grids optimized for elite profit not collective dignity (Goldthau, 2014). Incumbent regimes actively suppress alternatives threatening fossil fuel or nuclear power shareholder interests wielding policy capture and economic coercion hampering competitor market access. Utilities likewise lobby against decentralized renewable platforms enabling self-sufficiency escaping metering fees that sustain share values (Becker et al., 2018). And decentralized provision often relies partly on brokering access into wider grids.

Nonetheless precedents across water, fisheries, forests, and knowledge commons illustrate possibilities for grassroots reclamation of essential goods provision from capitalist enclosure at ever larger scales through networking collective sovereignty and solidarity (De Angelis, 2017; Ostrom, 2015). In energy realms visionary policies like devolving grid ownership to regional cooperatives or instituting community investment quotas for all renewables development enable scaling basic access and sovereignty. And accumulating climate impacts make energy system transformation inevitable in coming decades whatever the resistance.

Energy commons potentially open pathways for post-capitalist models provisioning sustainable basic services within democratic ecological alignment beyond accumulation imperatives threatening humanity's shared climate stability inheritance. Even absent perfect system change, community solar farms or microgrids fracture monopoly regimes to build parallel resilience structures sustaining essential needs whatever the coming turbulence of energy transitions across the globe. But developing commons imaginary and education for reclaiming collective sovereignty over shared energy destinies can reinforce technical capacity building to accelerate change (Becker et al., 2018). Together deep equity and radical localization reconstruct the right to electricity as cooperative achievement through solidarity economies and politics benefiting all communities interdependently. Against violence of enclosures and externalities, energy commoning suggests the possibility of dwelling sustainably and abundantly through justice.

Digital Energy Commons

Innovative peer-to-peer solar power trading platforms using blockchain-enabled micro-contracts envision households dynamically buying and selling electricity units across distribution grids according to real-time cooperative logics beyond individual profit motives or centrally optimized efficiency algorithms. Community solar projects likewise aim at providing equitable access to subscribers who lack solar deployment options in rental apartments. However, tech-centric visions require caution in the areas of multi-stakeholder algorithm governance (Abdelmotteleb, et al., 2022), cybersecurity risks, and equity safeguards. By design, decentralized renewable energy lends itself to more democratic participation and the empowerment of communities relative to the centralized fossil fuel-based energy paradigm. . . . However, the democratizing effect that these new technologies offer is not inherent; project planners must intentionally seek inclusive, multi-stakeholder involvement (Abdelmotteleb, et al., 2022). With respect to newly networked energy commons, key procedural principles remain—access equity, transparency, platform accountability, and multi-stakeholder governance balancing diverse goals and capabilities.

In essence energy commons highlight potentials in decentralized renewable models empowering communities through cooperative structures balancing efficiency, sustainability, and resilience. But persistent gaps from pilots to mature regimes demand greater investments—in funding platforms tailored for infrastructure cooperatives retaining purpose against cooptation, participatory capabilities engaging ordinary citizens effectively, supportive state policies on common carrier obligations and decentralization, and mechanisms fostering assemblages of energy commons at regional scales across issues from reliability to debt financing. The transformative promise still requires work to elevate communities from merely "prosumers" to durable directors of systems fate.

Manufacturing Commons

The manufacturing commons refers to the shared tools, infrastructure, knowledge, software, and production capacity that enables distributed and decentralized manufacturing. Over the past decade, the manufacturing commons has seen rapid growth and development, fueled by the rise of digital fabrication, open-source hardware, and peer production models.

Digital fabrication encompasses a range of technologies like 3D printing, computer numerical control (CNC) machining, laser cutting, and other computer-controlled production methods. These technologies allow individuals to turn digital designs into physical objects on demand, on a personal desktop scale. The most widely known digital fabrication tools, 3D printers, grew from just $4.6 million in total sales in 2009 to more than

$1.6 billion in 2015 (Wohlers Report, 2016). As the costs of these tools continue to fall and more user-friendly software is developed, digital fabrication capacity is spreading.

Open-source hardware refers to physical artifacts whose design blueprints are shared under open licenses that allow modification, distribution, and production (OSHWA, 2016). The open-source approach to hardware design, popularized by projects like RepRap (self-replicating 3D printers) and Arduino (open electronics prototyping platform), enables collaborative development and free distribution of production information. Open-source hardware has helped fuel the growth of the manufacturing commons by radically expanding public access to digital product designs.

Distributed manufacturing is associated with production systems that are decentralized, flexible, on-demand, and/or local. Enabled by the tools of personal digital fabrication, distributed manufacturing shifts production control and capacity to small-scale, agile operators. Whether at the household, neighborhood, or small firm level, distributed manufacturing marks a shift away from centralized mass production. The development of open-source business models and infrastructures for distributed production birthed concepts like "makerspaces" (shared maker workshops), "fab labs" (fabrication laboratories with shared machinery), and on-demand production networks (Vickery and Wunsch-Vincent, 2016).

The manufacturing commons has grown dramatically thanks to all of these converging trends. By democratizing access to digital and physical fabrication tools, product designs, and production capacity, barriers to innovation and manufacturing are being dismantled (Vickery and Wunsch-Vincent, 2016). The open ecosystem enables faster, more agile, collaborative production while supporting localization and customization. What is more, digital fabrication technologies and distributed production models utilize production on-demand, reducing waste and inventory costs associated with mass production systems (Kohtala, 2015). The environmental promise of such sustainable production systems represents another driver in the growth of distributed manufacturing.

While still an emerging paradigm, distributed manufacturing systems are already empowering new production applications. Early examples showcase the promise of agile, digitally powered production to strengthen local economies. Field Ready, a nonprofit seeking to increase local manufacturing capacity around the world, utilizes distributed production hubs in partnership with humanitarian groups to provide appropriate technologies like 3D printed waterspouts and plastic tent pegs for disaster relief and development projects (Field Ready, 2017). By being able to digitally fabricate necessary items on-demand in the field, Field Ready avoids the waste, inflexibility, and lead times of centralized production and complex global supply chains. Such distributed production examples demonstrate the power and early adoption of distributed manufacturing to enable localized, resilient economies.

The manufacturing commons offers opportunities for wider access not just in use but in participation and leadership of production. By lowering barriers to market entry, open digital tools and platforms enable small-scale startups and community initiatives to engage in manufacturing in new ways (Jovanovic et al., 2017). What is more, the radically "open" ecosystem of editable design files and transparent documentation supports increased interoperability between software tools, machines, components, and subsystems (Vickery and Wunsch-Vincent, 2016). This interchangeable modularity speeds up distributed development and technical innovation. Emerging distributed business models are similarly advancing more participatory modes of production and consumption via concepts like crowdsourced funding, pre-orders, and micro-batch production (Vickery and Wunsch-Vincent, 2016). Together, these trends suggest opportunities to diversify participation and reimagine community-centric production ecosystems.

Not without challenges, this nascent manufacturing paradigm still relies heavily on connections to the existing global supply chain for hardware components and materials sourcing. Truly distributed production is constrained by difficulties procuring raw materials, limited selections of open-source hardware components, and reliance on proprietary software and firmware (Jovanovic et al., 2017). For distributed production and digital fabrication to progress, advances in open-source electronic components, printable electronics, organic materials, and local component production are still needed. Regulatory uncertainty also swirls around personal fabrication and decentralized production networks. Issues like protective patents, safety compliance, and material accessibility must be addressed for distributed ecosystems to mature (Laplume et al., 2016).

Nonetheless, recent years have seen an explosion of R&D investments, startups, conferences, and public fascination with digital fabrication and distributed production. More broadly, industrial production as a whole is transitioning toward networked models of mass customization and flexible batch production with the aid of automated and data-driven manufacturing concepts like the Internet of Things, "smart" production lines, and other Industry 4.0 innovations (Oesterle, 2016). Leveraging networked information flows, newer production paradigms demonstrate the competitive value of decentralized, localized production capacity to meet modern market demands. We have only begun to glimpse the innovation capacities unlocked by open access to the tools and information for designing and building manufactured goods.

The manufacturing commons, fueled by the rise of personal digital fabrication tools and peer production communities, foreshadows a more open, equitable, and sustainable production paradigm. By distributing the physical capacity to make things, the tools of production become accessible in new ways. Early examples of open-source enterprises and distributed production networks showcase the ability of localized, flexible production models to build resilience, empower communities, and drive technology innovation. The emerging ecosystem hints at revolutions in production yet to come. As the manufacturing commons continues to evolve, opportunities abound for experimentation in reimagining our material economies.

The Super-Factors Accelerating Adoption

Several key technological and social advancements fused together over the past decade to act as forcing factors rapidly maturing the manufacturing commons:

1. Ubiquitous internet access: The saturated penetration of high-speed broadband access globally has permitted remote coordination at scale never before feasible. Tens of millions scattered worldwide can now meaningfully co-design then dispatch production via a unified platform.
2. Smartphone proliferation: More than 6 billion connected handheld supercomputers in people's pockets amplify access and app-based control/monitoring over manufacturing. These portable shops interface seamlessly with digitally controlled equipment via touch/voice.
3. Sharing economy cultural shift: The popularity of platforms like Uber, Airbnb, and eBay sparked a receptiveness and trust in decentralization, peer-to-peer exchange, and crowdsourcing of economic activities along the sole domain of large centralized institutions.
4. Open-source values: The ideological drive spurring open-source movements strengthened significantly over the past decade. The modes of thinking valuing transparency, decentralization, and customization that catalyzed open-code began permeating the production of physical goods.
5. Micropayments infrastructure: Scalable digital payment systems supporting frictionless micro-transactions have arisen via platforms like Patreon, GitHub Sponsors, Stripe, and cryptocurrencies. These permit networked prosumption compensation and novel community project funding models not dependent on top-down corporate investment.

These five macro-trends will only continue intensifying into the future. Together they have cultivated the fertile substrate permitting distributed Manufacturing-as-a-Service models to take root and empower community-guided production.

Benefits to Society

Many societal benefits spring from the manufacturing commons transcending traditional mass production paradigms:

-   Lowered barriers accelerating innovation: Accessible design and maker tools plus open component libraries aid rapid prototyping of early stage concepts by small groups/startups, democratizing innovation.
-   Increased production localization: Enabling domestic manufacturing, even custom one-offs, at reasonable minimum efficient scales curtails shipping and benefits local economies over foreign offshoring.

– Production resilience: Relying on distributed fabs versus centralized factories improves supply chain robustness and redundancy when disruptions occur. Further, fabrication capacity can shift nimbly to fulfill dynamic needs.
– Circular material flows: Component reuse and recycling is simpler with localized production keeping material loops tight and traceable versus stretched across global expanses. Further, community oversight pressures sustainable practices.
– Needs-based production: The manufacturing commons permits demand-guided fabrication from user communities. This contrasts sharply with traditional "push" mass production decoupled from actual consumer needs.
– Education and skills empowerment: Participating in distributed digital fabrication builds hands-on abilities valued by Industry 4.0 while keeping skills local.

In summary, the manufacturing commons unlocks flexibility, creativity, and access largely stifled by consolidated twentieth-century style mass production. It returns production control and influence to local contexts benefiting communities.

This is not to say that mass production will disappear. Likely a hybrid landscape will emerge with open distributed fabrication filling niches. The commons offers an avenue for people globally to address local wants and needs for products the traditional system cannot, or will not provide. This filling of gaps presents the most transformative opportunity.

Challenges Hampering Mainstream Adoption

Of course some hurdles remain slowing mainstream uptake of open production models. These include both technical and social barriers:
– Hardware legality complexity: Safety, patents, business methods, and liability concerns introduce legalities less onerous for pure software. Open hardware objects operate physically in public spaces, introducing risks.
– Component traceability: Complex assemblies in open repositories often utilize anonymous donated parts lacking supply chain pedigree. This hinders certifying goods where critical traceability is essential, as in medical or aerospace contexts.
– Design tool proficiency barriers: Sophisticated open-source computer-aided design (CAD) suites and sandwiching together modular components into shareable derivative works involves non-trivial skill acquisition beyond most non-technical prosumers currently.
– Prosumer skepticism and hesitancy: Shaking consumer notions that open necessarily equates to amateur quality will take education. Additionally, concerns over the effort required for hands-on involvement may slow mainstream adoption of maker equipment in homes.

- Incumbent industry opposition: Large entrenched corporations consolidating control over mass production will enact legislation protecting revenue streams against disruptive open models threatening dominance.
- Funding ecosystem immaturity: Investor familiarity with support structures for decentralized production networks lags that for traditional mass manufacturing startups following well-worn paths to market and financing.

Over the next decade these hurdles obstructing the mainstreaming of distributed open production will erode with education, increased adoption driving familiarity, further legal codification, and funding sources tailored to the unique distributed collaborative models.

KEY THINKER: Vasilis Kostakis

Vasilis Kostakis is a prominent political economist and theorist making seminal contributions to understanding the transformations emerging from commons-based peer production. As a faculty member at Tallinn University of Technology in Estonia and founder of the P2P Lab, his interdisciplinary research focuses on new socio-economic forms enabled by networked collaboration and digital commons across multiple institutional domains.

Kostakis's pioneering scholarship builds on concepts of peer production and knowledge commons to explicate how decentralized digital networks are seeding post-capitalist modes of production, governance, and property. His theories on "commons-based peer production" explicate the interlinked political, economic, and cultural shifts catalyzed by collaborative global communities creating common pool resources like free software, open hardware designs, and open-access knowledge.

Kostakis's research centers on the deep changes unfolding from expansion of the "commons paradigm" of non-proprietary sharing and commons-based peer production (CBPP) in the information age. This frame analyzes how self-organized distributed networks are creating various open digital commons enabling new models of social value creation and economic organization beyond capitalist market logics or state control.

In seminal works like *Peer Governance and Wikipedia: Identifying and Understanding the Problems of Wikipedia's Governance* (2010) and books like *Network Society and Future Scenarios for a Collaborative Economy* (2014), Kostakis examines the emerging institutional logics and innovative forms of distributed governance regulating digital commons like free and open-source software or Wikipedia. His scholarship highlights how social sharing of knowledge as a common pool resource is transforming assumptions about production, cooperation, property, governance, and value.

Kostakis's research delineates a new CBPP paradigm interweaving shifting institutional relationships between market forms of contractual exchange and behavioral logics of social reciprocity within commons-oriented peer communities for collaborative value creation. He analyzes how customizable open design commons like 3D printing templates or hardware modules enable scalable forms of distributed manufacturing with democratization potential.

In books like *Commons Transition and P2P: A Primer* (2017), Kostakis proposes policy agendas and institutional models for transitioning toward post-capitalist futures centered on open commons pooled and stewarded by participatory communities ensuring equitable access. He advocates for polycentric governance frameworks integrating support for CBPP and digital commons across diverse institutional levels and policy domains like public service infrastructure, city planning, cooperative ownership, or basic income to catalyze a new ecological and social balance.

Kostakis's scholarship delineates core principles and institutional innovations undergirding expansive realms of commons creating collective value through open network collaboration—challenging proprietary logics dominating capitalist markets and bureaucracies. His theoretical frameworks build rigorous analytical models revealing the deep phase change in politico-economic logics and possibilities signaled by the ascent of peer governance, social sharing, and CBPP across contemporary societies.

Beyond theorization, Kostakis's engaged interdisciplinary research aims for grounded policy impacts. He has led pioneering implementations of open-source hardware for distributed manufacturing experiments and projects for the P2P Lab exploring potentials of commons-based open design. Kostakis has also helped with crafting policy proposals for integrating support and legal recognition for urban commons and CBPP in cities like Barcelona and projects for complementary cryptocurrencies enabling sustainable peer production.

His ideas have informed groundbreaking legislation in Ecuador enshrining Rights of Nature in the constitution and framing Buen Vivir policy agendas integrating indigenous conceptions of plural economies and ecological balance. Kostakis's policy models for cultivating open knowledge institutions and collaborative economic networks provide blueprints for sustainable development in both industrialized and emerging economies.

Attentive to uneven geographies in peer production, Kostakis's work pointedly tackles needs for adoption in context of the Global South. Along with other researchers (Kostakis, Latoufis & Bauwens 2018; Kostakis, Roos & Bauwens, 2016) has investigated challenges like accessibility gaps and cultural disconnects that can exclude or exploit marginalized demographic groups from CBPP benefits. Kostakis calls for conscious policy and platform designs facilitating participation of non-elite users in socially marginal regions within expanding CBPP ecosystems.

His action research engages on-ground communities across Latin America, Africa, and Asia through participative workshops and pilot projects exploring potential applications of commons-based open models in education, distributed manufacturing, service provision, food cultivation, or community-led innovation tailored for deprived populations. Kostakis seeks to narrow both the digital divide in access and epistemic divides in framing questions, data, and methods shaping next-generation infrastructure for CBPP between the industrialized and emerging worlds. His scholarship underscores ethical imperatives to nurture just transitions toward post-capitalist modes of production through global solidarities.

Health Commons

The health commons refers to shared knowledge, resources, infrastructure, and capacity aimed at democratizing healthcare and making it more accessible. It emerged as a response to restrictive patents, high drug prices, and centralized health systems that contribute to unequal access to medical knowledge and services. The health commons framework, bolstered by open-source technologies, collaborative networks, and grassroots health activism, seeks to create an equitable and justice-oriented healthcare system for all.

Open-source medicine encompasses collaborative, peer-produced medical research, open-access scholarly publications, open medical hardware and devices, open biotechnology, and open electronic health records. These initiatives challenge the privatization and commodification of medical research and medicines by promoting collective ownership and access (T1International, 2022). Projects such as the T1International Open Insulin initiative and the Open Source Malaria consortium illustrate how global partnerships can make patented medicines accessible to marginalized populations. Open-source discovery and production offer a public option to reduce costs and overcome barriers posed by proprietary pharmaceutical models.

Additionally, decentralized solidarity healthcare networks expand access through peer-to-peer aid and parallel health infrastructures grounded in community relationships and transparency. Cooperative models like the Buurtzorg home care program in the Netherlands use neighborhood-based caregiving and care coordination to universalize quality health services. Participatory community health centers, such as those pioneered by the Black Panther Party's survival programs in the 1960s, provided citizen-run healthcare and education for marginalized groups (Nelson, 2011). Women's health movements have similarly developed mutual aid networks that promote well-being and self-determination (Boston Women's Health Book Collective, 2011). Collectively, these grassroots initiatives exemplify localized, community-based approaches to health justice.

The integration of open-source medicine with decentralized health solidarity forms the basis of the emerging "health commons." This framework combines peer production and open access with mutual aid principles to build a new, equitable model for healthcare outside of mainstream institutions. The health commons ecosystem fosters collaborative, bottom-up problem-solving in public health.

For instance, medical hardware hacking spaces like the Sunshine Natural Healing Hackerspace in New York demonstrate the power of community innovation. By providing hands-on prototyping workshops to build open-source medical devices, these spaces cultivate local skills for developing affordable health technologies that are otherwise missing from the market. Similarly, patient advocacy networks like the Participatory Medicine community leverage crowdsourced knowledge sharing and open medical data to increase transparency and amplify patient voices in decision-making processes (Participatory Medicine, 2023). Community citizen science projects like the Personal Genome Project, PatientsLikeMe, and DIYgenomics connect the public as co-producers of medical research, challenging the exclusivity of conventional scientific institutions (GenetiConcept, 2022).

The health commons framework holds revolutionary potential to redistribute power and participation in medicine. It reimagines care as a collective duty and universal human right, fostering a new governance model based on shared responsibility, sustainability, and equity (Helfrich, 2012). However, challenges such as legal barriers, regulatory restrictions, and issues of transparency and accountability persist. Grassroots innovation often faces skepticism, and cooperative patient drug production or alternative treatment networks may struggle with the threat of litigation or lack of legitimacy (Kleinhout-Vliek et al., 2024). To support the health commons, creative policies and decentralized cooperation models must be developed that balance safety and flexibility for open medical research and peer-to-peer healthcare.

Health justice movements have already begun to demonstrate the potential for community agency over medicine. By utilizing open-source technologies, these movements have expanded bottom-up innovation and access, paving the way for more inclusive healthcare models. As cooperative medical communities continue to develop and share health solutions, they challenge the exclusionary nature of mainstream healthcare systems and signal opportunities for transformative change.

Vivid examples illustrate the expanding use of peer production to create a more equitable and participatory medical system. Collaborative networks like Helpful Engineering and Rapid Medical Parts, formed in response to the COVID-19 pandemic, leveraged open-source designs and digital fabrication to address urgent medical supply shortages (Rapid Medical Parts, 2022). Volunteer teams designed and produced essential supplies such as face shields and ventilators, mobilizing a distributed network of makers to meet needs neglected by centralized institutions (Beam, 2020). These efforts exemplified the power of horizontally networked design and manufacturing coordination, using open technology and a shared ethic of mutual care to achieve revolutionary outcomes.

Preceding the pandemic, initiatives like the Open Insulin project aimed to make essential medicines such as insulin accessible to those unable to afford corporate prices. Biohackers like the Four Thieves Vinegar collective seek to demystify and codify the process of small-scale insulin production to enable local manufacturing outside the pharmaceutical industry's patent-protected model (Lewis, 2020). Such biohacking initiatives prompt ethical and safety considerations while highlighting the lengths that patients will go to when denied access to life-saving drugs.

In addition to crisis response and underground medicine, cooperative clinics and health programs have shown how solidarity-based health systems can address localized needs often overlooked by formal institutions. The Black Women's Health Imperative, for example, emerged from health collectives focused on providing health education, wellness promotion, and policy advocacy for Black women marginalized by mainstream healthcare systems (BWHI, 2023). Their community-rooted approach, which centers Black women's wisdom and resilience, reshapes healthcare to address historical inequalities and empower patients to advocate for their own well-being.

Similarly, the Community Healthcare Network (CHN), founded in New York City in 1975, provides affordable, culturally competent primary care clinics and services for low-income groups failed by traditional healthcare institutions (CHN, 2023). By hiring staff from the communities they serve, CHN ensures that care is responsive to the lived realities of its patients. Such models embed health justice into the fabric of the organization, shifting control and self-determination back into disenfranchised people's hands.

These place-based clinics and peer networks sustain long-term care infrastructures rooted in mutualism and collective liberation. They demonstrate the paradigm shift promised by the health commons—healthcare centered on cooperative empowerment and community agency, rather than profit. They represent the potential for a transformed healthcare system built on mutual support, equity, and shared responsibility.

The health commons model, combining open-source medicine and decentralized health solidarity, suggests that a more equitable and participatory system is possible. As these communities continue to leverage open technologies and cooperative frameworks, they challenge the exclusionary status quo of healthcare. Their innovative approaches hint at broader societal transformations, where health justice is defined by shared abundance, dignity, and generative justice for all.

CASE STUDY: Open-Source Insulin Production

Insulin is a life-saving hormone therapy for millions globally needing to manage diabetes. However, prohibitively high costs have put insulin access out of reach for many. In the United States, more than one in four people require insulin ration or skip doses owing to an unaffordable price tag, risking serious health impacts and death. But a grassroots movement is emerging to reclaim insulin as an open access common good. Leveraging open-source biology techniques, activist-makers aim to democratize affordable insulin access for all through decentralized community production, flipping the script on big pharmaceutical corporatization.

Despite being discovered a century ago and long off-patent, insulin continues to be locked in a closed corporate production system. More than 90 percent of the global insulin market is captured by just three giant multinationals—Eli Lilly, Novo Nordisk, and Sanofi—who have systematically jacked up prices. An annual supply of insulin costing under $100 to produce is priced at more than $5000 in the United States.

Healthcare regimes granting monopolies to profit-seeking big pharma prevent availability of affordable generic biosimilars that could transform accessibility.

This artificial scarcity engineers socioeconomic rationing and avoidable misery. Globally, half of people needing insulin lack reliable access. In lower-income countries, only one in ten people gets insulin. Expert bodies have declared the insulin pricing crisis as violating universal rights to health and life.

In response, an open insulin movement to challenge the insulin cartel's enclosure of a life-saving public good is emerging. Activists are attempting to reclaim insulin as a knowledge commons, openly sharing biological production knowledge and techniques as a pathway to universal access and affordability.

Using open-source biology methods, researchers like the Open Insulin Project are developing adaptable protocols for community bio-makerspaces to produce generic insulin affordably. Their open protocols guide small-scale fermentation and purification steps biochemically synthesizing insulin using easily available starter supplies that grassroots groups can implement for local decentralized production.

Four Thieves Vinegar, a collective of anarchist biohackers, distributes an "EpiPencil" medical device delivering printable instructions for DIY insulin-making kits to empower users. Open science startup Genspace is engineering yeast strains biosynthesizing insulin for open access distribution. Non-profit Biotech Without Borders imagines community-led micro production of essential medicines through bio-labs, makerspaces, and small cooperatives everywhere utilizing open protocols—bringing power back to the people.

This open, decentralized production model for reclaiming insulin as a knowledge commons holds revolutionary possibilities for transforming healthcare affordability and accessibility. Open sourcing insulin production can overcome access barriers for millions needing affordable generics by nurturing grassroots community alternatives to capital-intensive mass manufacturing. Enabling small cooperatives, public interest entities, and maker collectives to produce insulin locally using open bio protocols promises decentralized solutions democratizing control and profits from life-saving medicines against profit-hungry big pharma gatekeepers.

Just as free software movements upended proprietary software, open insulin activism demonstrates potential for post-capitalist production anchored in sharing life-saving knowledge as a managed commons designed for universal common welfare instead of markets locking up common goods for privatized profit. The open model promises iterative toolkits for localized community production attuned for context, not one-size-fits-all. Integrating indigenous and informal expertise to solve local health needs through open knowledge could have revolutionary impacts in the Global South.

However, realizing this promise faces barriers. Biopharmaceutical production involves complex regulations around testing, licensure, and quality control, presenting policy challenges for decentralized entities and informal expertise. Scaling community production requires accessing costly materials, infrastructure, and scientific capabilities often still gatekept, though expanding community labs could bridge gaps. Sustaining unpaid open-source work also needs funding support mechanisms recognizing shared social value.

Incumbent pharma corporations fighting open models threaten the overturning of current exploitative regimes. Public investment and scientific institutions backing open biopharma research thus remain crucial for the formation of countervailing power. Political coalition-building with health rights movements is also pivotal for lobbying reformed policies that don't automatically criminalize non-proprietary medicine production by lay collectives orienting toward social needs, not profit incentives.

The open insulin movement remains a fledgling DIY effort, but its politics resonate with generations of health activism—from AIDS Coalition to Unleash Power to South Africa's Treatment Action Campaign—struggling to reclaim medicines as a common good. Its experiments reviving possibilities of decentralized community health sovereignty mirror wider currents in the platform cooperatives, open design and peer production movements reconstituting access to essential goods through open models. The swell of grassroots open biotechnology might presage transformations toward post-capitalist futures where sharing life-saving knowledge as a liberatory commons can uplift collective abundance over competitive scarcity engineered for private wealth accumulation. The open insulin movement's promise remains teaching societies to reweave an expansive tapestry of mutual care and solidarity economies anchored in the open commons ethos of "health for people, not profit for corporations."

Education Commons

The education commons encompasses shared knowledge, pedagogies, and open learning environments that facilitate more democratic and participatory education beyond traditional schooling. Rooted in the principles of openness and mutual cooperation, the education commons framework transforms where, how, and with whom education occurs. It includes open-source educational content, peer learning networks, and community-driven educational spaces.

The Open Educational Resources (OER) movement, which began in the early 2000s, played a pivotal role in advancing the education commons by promoting free and openly licensed course materials. Platforms like OER Commons and Skills Commons enable educators to access, curate, and share lesson plans, textbooks, videos, and assessments, thereby reducing barriers to educational resources and allowing for flexible reuse (Wiley, n.d.). Similarly, Massive Open Online Courses (MOOCs) provide free classes to a global audience, though they lack the reuse freedoms and collaborative spirit of OER (Veletsianos & Shepherdson, 2016). This movement toward legal and technological openness supports an abundance of shared educational resources that enhance access and participation.

Peer learning refers to cooperative, self-directed growth facilitated through knowledge exchange among equals. Enabled by digital tools, peer learning often occurs within learning networks and study groups, as learners collaboratively build understanding through dialogue and joint projects. This approach redistributes agency to learners, promoting shared discovery and co-learning. Democratic schools like Summerhill in the UK, where students self-direct their studies and self-govern the school, illustrate how alternative educational models nurture youth-driven, interest-based learning (Greenberg et al., 2003). Community learning centers, such as Freedom Schools, similarly emphasize youth leadership and empowerment by grounding education in grassroots movements and youth culture.

Hacker- and maker-spaces also embody the education commons by providing open community workshops where participants engage in hands-on building and experimentation (Halverson & Sheridan, 2014). These spaces, like medical hackerspaces or tech-based maker labs, cultivate learning through creativity and collaboration, bridging informal and formal learning environments. Together, these spaces highlight how alternative education models can serve as incubators for peer-to-peer co-learning.

A foundational element of reimagining education involves shifting away from traditional models of individualized learning toward frameworks of mutual Distributed Cognition. This concept understands learning as an interaction between people, tools, and contexts, aligning with Indigenous paradigms of learning that emphasize shared activity and community relationships (Battiste, 2022). Such relational cognition contrasts with the "banking model" of education, where knowledge is deposited into passive learners (Freire, 2014). In this context, the focus on peer learning emphasizes collective meaning-making and positions learners as active agents in constructing knowledge.

The integration of open educational content, peer-based co-learning, and community-rooted learning contexts forms the foundation of the "education commons." This ecosystem nurtures participatory pedagogies and collaborative learning, reclaiming educational public goods from restrictive privatization. For example, youth-led Participatory Action Research (PAR) programs situate learning within marginalized communities, collectively analyzing community issues and developing interventions (Stommel, 2014). Critical digital pedagogy leverages open web tools like Hypothes.is and federated social networks to facilitate collaborative analysis and debate, fostering engaged digital literacy and citizenship. Youth participatory budgeting initiatives help develop leadership and data literacy by involving students in analyzing community needs and allocating public funds, giving them hands-on experience in decision-making.

Despite its promise, the education commons faces barriers around access, inclusion, and credentialing. Online and informal learning often reflect persistent divides by race, gender, and income, which limit peer collaboration and participation (Taylor et al., 2021). Alternative programs must also address systemic inequities around disability accommodations, gender safety, and cultural responsiveness—issues that formal institutions address through policy and law. Additionally, skepticism regarding the rigor and outcomes of informal education remains, with universities and employers traditionally valuing institutional credentials over skills gained through non-formal learning (Open Knowledge Foundation, 2022). For the education commons to genuinely empower marginalized groups, these equity challenges must be actively addressed.

Impactful examples of open pedagogy and peer learning demonstrate how the education commons can reshape educational practices across contexts. During the COVID-19 pandemic, educators rapidly crowdsourced and shared open resources on social media to adapt to remote learning (Vermicelli, Cricelli & Grimaldi, 2021). Such exchanges illustrated the values of collaboration and accessibility in action, transforming classrooms into public learning spaces. The Open Textbook Library, which empowers university faculty to write and adapt open-licensed textbooks, further exemplifies the expansion of freely accessible educational materials created by and for educators (Open Textbook Library, n.d.).

Youth Participatory Action Research (YPAR) programs have also shown how youth can become community researchers and leaders in addressing local issues. In Philadelphia, Youth United for Change trains young people as community organizers and policy researchers, enabling them to design surveys, educate peers, and present data-driven recommendations to local education councils (Anyon et al., 2018). These programs empower youth to use their lived experiences and knowledge as tools for social advocacy and change.

Similarly, informal learning programs like Freedom Dreams build youth leadership through identity-driven programming that emphasizes creative expression and representation. Young people teach one another filmmaking and storytelling skills to amplify voices often marginalized by mainstream media, fostering peer talent development and self-determination (Ginwright & Cammarota, 2007). Garden-based learning collectives combine intergenerational knowledge-sharing with entrepreneurship and food justice initiatives, fortifying community resilience through youth engagement (Bendt, Barthel & Colding, 2013).

Beyond youth contexts, community-based participatory research (CBPR) models are essential in fostering equitable collaboration between researchers and marginalized communities, ensuring that health communication interventions are culturally relevant, resonate authentically with target audiences, and empower communities to influence their own health outcomes (Vilar & Johnson, 2021). Participatory design labs like the DeafSpace project co-create solutions for community needs by bridging design researchers with marginalized communities (Bauman & Murray, 2013). These initiatives reflect how situating learning within community contexts redefines expertise and empowers residents as co-producers of knowledge.

The education commons offers a transformative vision of learning centered on mutualism, solidarity, and collective leadership. Anchored by values of access, self-determination, and equity, the education commons framework has the potential to advance new models of community-based education that prioritize dignity and shared responsibility over individual success. As internet-enabled models continue to evolve, the opportunities for unlocking public agency and advancing social good through mutual uplift multiply.

Digital Commons

The digital commons signifies the expansive collections of cooperatively managed information resources, networks, and platforms that are widening access, sharing, and innovation within the online world. It encompasses the technological foundations and collaborative environments fostering more participatory, decentralized use of our digital infrastructure and understanding.

Open-source software offers freely available and reusable code for applications, algorithms, and computing systems. The open licensing model permits users rights to change, distribute, and self-host open-source platforms, fueling immense technology collaboration. Linux and Apache demonstrated the security of open source as adaptable alternatives to exclusive proprietary systems now ubiquitous worldwide (Kelty, 2008). The Android mobile operating system likewise employs shared open-source elements propelling reach. This practical and legal openness bolsters common pool technology creation that even competitors jointly advance.

Creative Commons (CC) licenses constitute the foremost legal breakthrough enabling universal access while content creators retain copyright. These open Internet Protocol (IP) licenses designed for the internet encourage sharing and adaptation without restrictive clearances. Expanding millions of CC photos, tutorials, blogs, data sets, agency documents, and academic works carry allowances for reuse unlike default copyright protections (Creative Commons, n.d.). Copyright's "all rights reserved" regime blocks flow whereas CC's "some rights reserved" eases circulation by sparing users from asking permission. This legal hack spreads voluntary allowances benefiting collaborative culture.

Decentralized peer production utilizes internet links and tools for radically transparent cooperation on complex products like software, news, videos, and encyclopedic insights. Commons-based peer production unfolds without traditional hierarchy or market price incentives, driven by intrinsic motivations like skill growth and community belonging within collaborative networks guided by social guidelines over contracts (Benkler, 2006). The paradigm shift of commons-based peer production leverages open systems for voluntary inputs toward collective purposes.

Paragon examples like Wikipedia exhibit voluntary mass collaboration on informational resources progressing public understanding. Its model utilizes open coordination without ownership enabling loosely structured collective intelligence gathering visible through the full edit history. Recent variants like media wiki ecosystem Wiki-Tribune apply collaborative news production while Creative Commons search engine

CC Search eases discovering reusable media. Peer production puts forth an alternative possibility model mobilizing collective ingenuity.

This landscape empowers the burgeoning digital commons. Digital artifacts easily become "nonrival" goods enabling shared use unlike tangible items where utilization limits others. Online abundance multiplies access potential. Therefore, enclosed artificial scarcities around copyright grow questionable (Rifkin, 2014). The digital commons paradigm counters restrictive IP assumptions by incubating shared collaborative ecosystems for generating and overseeing essential informational resources and platforms. It cultivates innovation niches tackling compromised institutional legitimacy around global trials from finance to medicine through open cooperatives and decentralized solidarity networks planting alternative infrastructures like platform coops, copyfair licensing, open access journals, blockchain currencies, and participatory eco-hacking networks.

However, barriers continue around digital access, surveillance damages, misinformation patterns, and polarization risks that can additionally isolate non-dominant technology users. Online spaces and tools still display divides by gender, race, and income that restrict peer teamwork and sharing. Centralizing platforms like Google, Facebook, and Amazon amass alarming power through panoptic data extraction controlling visibility, connections, and economic life (Nieborg & Helmond, 2019). And filter bubbles from narrow friend groups and biased algorithms distort understanding and erode shared factual knowledge endangering collective intelligence (Zuiderveen Borgesius et al., 2020). Safeguarding digital commons innovations necessitates awareness and duty across technology governance.

Despite threats, expanding public sector and civil society stewardships collaboratively create infrastructure for collective good. Cities across America utilize chief data officers applying open data practices spreading business and resident access to inform decision-making. Participatory budgeting processes employ open civic technology to amplify citizen input over spending priorities. And national open government data laws persist passing across Latin America, Africa, and Asia after pioneering Mexico, Kenya, and India mandated proactive public sector information release around budgets, transportation, education, and geographic data. This open data movement acknowledges public information as an anchor for accountable democracy and market innovation (Open Knowledge Foundation, 2020). Similarly, digital steward cooperatives like the Platform Co-op Consortium and Up & Go nourish sustainable ecosystem alternatives to extractive big tech through worker dignity, cloud computing, and cooperative structure trials. Such multi-stakeholder initiatives exemplify generative technology futures benefiting communities (Scholz & Schneider, 2017). As networked cooperation spreads, opportunities bloom for cultivating shared digital abundance.

The ascending copyfair culture, decentralized solidarity platforms and open municipalities showcase an evolving landscape reclaiming democratized governance over digital futures for pluralistic common good. The combined strength of open-source infrastructure, creative commons knowledge, and peer collaboration provide kernels of an alternative pathway to concentrate power and access within extractive regimes. Digital innovation guided by collective care over control or profit promises emancipatory openings to collaboratively advance our relationships, rights, and capabilities online designed by and for the people.

Cultural Commons

The cultural common denotes the shared resources, ideas, and creative works that are open and available to everyone within a society to use, remix, and build upon. In the contemporary context, the cultural commons has taken on new meaning and significance with the rise of digital technologies and networks that allow rapid sharing of content globally. Some key aspects of the contemporary cultural commons are:

The internet has enabled a robust digital commons where creative works, knowledge, data, and other digital cultural resources are openly shared online through various platforms and licensing schemes. Creative Commons licensing, for example, provides flexible copyright terms to allow content creators to choose sharing and remixing permissions for their works (Creative Commons, n.d., "About CC Licenses"). Platforms like Wikipedia, YouTube, Flickr, and many open access scholarly repositories rely on user contributions to build up common pools of knowledge and media. The digitization of older analogue works has also brought masses of cultural materials into the digital commons from libraries, museums, and other institutions.

However, there are tensions concerning the sustainability and governance of these digital commons, as policy battles continue around issues like net neutrality, censorship, copyright terms, and technology regulation (Benkler, 2006). Centralization of control over platforms and infrastructure threatens the openness and accessibility of the digital cultural commons. There are also concerns around privacy, surveillance, disinformation, hate speech, and other abuses that come with mass participation and anonymity online. But many advocate that the freedoms and generative nature of the net and platforms should be preserved through policy and community moderation.

The read–write nature of the digital cultural commons has unleashed incredible amounts of remixing, transforming, and user-generated content that reshapes culture (Lessig, 2008). Memes, mashups, fan edits, cover songs, and other derivative works now spread prolifically online. Amateur creators remix elements of popular and niche culture, comment and critique society, or just entertain. Platforms like YouTube and Twitch have allowed everyday users to become cultural producers and celebrities by sharing their works with global audiences. Not all derivative works are legal, but digital technologies have enabled creative expression and participation at an unprecedented scale.

However, some argue this is not the democratization of culture as promised, but rather the exploitation and free labor of users for platform capitalism (Scholz, 2017). Debates continue concerning incentive structures and fair compensation for cultural production online and appropriate licensing and regulation of remix works. But user-generated content has undoubtedly transformed cultural production and circulation online with profound impacts on media, entertainment, politics, and public discourse in the digital age.

Wikipedia exemplifies the potential of mass collaboration in building cultural works, as volunteers collectively author and edit the world's largest free encyclopedia in more than 300 languages (Lih, 2009). Open-source software communities like Linux and collaborative platforms like GitHub also allow cooperative development of complex informational resources for the common good. Crowdfunding platforms represent another form of collaborative cultural funding for all kinds of arts, media, technology, and other creative projects.

Some critics argue that only a tiny fraction of users actually create or edit most user-generated content platforms, not truly harnessing the power of the masses (Nielsen, 2006). There are also concerns around information quality, censorship, and representation on largely user-generated platforms. But online collaborative culture does enable new modes of collective action and bottom-up community governance over cultural resources. It provides alternative models of cultural production that challenge proprietary systems and expert control.

A robust public domain with freely usable cultural materials and informational resources is central to the cultural commons (Boyle, 2008). Expiring copyrights allow older creative works to continually enter the public domain over time after a period of exclusive rights. There have been efforts by corporations and governments to extend and expand copyright protections that critics argue lock up cultural materials for too long. Groups like the Electronic Frontier Foundation and Creative Commons advocate for access and reuse rights for public domain and shareable works against excessive intellectual property restrictions.

There are also calls for more taxpayer-funded and publicly accessible research and data through policies like open access mandates. Government agencies and institutions like libraries and universities can contribute to the information commons by opening up digitized collections, scientific data, government records, and scholarly publications beyond firewalls and commercial databases (Kranich, 2004). Activists argue that the results of publicly funded research and cultural heritage should not disappear behind journal paywalls and commercial data providers. Expanding public access and sharing rights serves innovation, scientific progress, and democratic culture.

In these ways, contemporary debates continue around expanding and sustaining the cultural commons as a shared resource in the public interest against restrictive IP policies and commercial or governmental control. The same debates play out across environmental, urban, and other domains around managing common-pool resources against enclosures and privatization in the neoliberal age. Shared culture remains tied to ideals of commonwealth, collective action, equal access, and democratic participation in cultural life (Hyde, 2010). Many advocate maintaining and expanding the cultural commons against economic or state monopolies.

A key critique is that the online cultural commons has mostly become dependent on centralized platforms and infrastructure owned by Big Tech companies like Google, Facebook, Amazon, and Apple. Critics argue this has allowed capital accumulation and control over data, standards, and networks that exclude others from freely participating or competing in the digital cultural arena (Lanier, 2013).

In response, many advocate building more distributed peer-to-peer networks, community owned platforms, interoperable protocols, and an empowering "social web" to regain user control and ownership of the digital commons from corporate tech giants (Benkler et al, 2015). Projects like Mastodon offer open-source, federated social networks spread across independently run servers. Cooperative platforms like Resonate promise artist-owned streaming funded via direct listener cooperatives beyond the dominant Spotify model. Groups like Creating Commons advocate reinvigorating cultural participation and connectivity through local networks and shared infrastructure in civic spaces beyond only proprietary apps and commercial online platforms. So, despite the platform dominance of Big Tech, people continue to build alternative and more participatory forms of cultivating the digital cultural commons.

The contemporary struggle to preserve inclusive access to the cultural commons connects deeply with other social movements focused on the environment, cities, software, science, and beyond. Expanding the cultural and informational commons, whether online or off, exists within larger debates concerning inequalities in resources, property rights, market capture, privatization, and governance in modern capitalist societies (Nonini, 2007). Many call for renewed focus on rights to "fair use" of cultural materials against restrictive policies that stifle expression and participation by ordinary citizens to benefit powerful industries. This intersects with many current political debates and policy developments around regulation of major tech platforms and IP-intensive industries.

There are also environmental concerns around the exploding energy demands and electronic waste from mass technology and internet infrastructure underlying today's digital cultural abundance. Groups argue for technology reforms toward sustainable and equitable models of production and consumption of electronics, given the local and global harms of cycles of disposability (Puckett et al., 2002). This connects digital cultural policies with environmental justice movements to democratize control over the material, ecological conditions we collectively depend upon alongside open access to the abundant, shared culture available online.

Urban Commons

The urban commons denotes shared urban resources that are collectively used and managed by a community. In recent years, there has been growing interest in the urban commons as a new paradigm for equitable and sustainable urban development. In the present era, rapid urbanization has put pressure on public spaces and resources, while privatization and enclosure of urban spaces have limited access and community control. Economic recession and austerity politics have also reduced public services in cities (Foster & Iaione, 2016). At the same time, more networked and engaged urban communities have emerged. This has created opportunities for collective action around shared urban resources.

Contemporary urban commons have some defining characteristics. They are urban resources that are co-created, co-governed, and co-managed by citizens and communities (Foster & Iaione, 2016). They can include public spaces, vacant or abandoned properties, maker spaces, community gardens, civic infrastructure, local knowledge and culture, among others.

An example is community land trusts, which are non-profit organizations that steward land on behalf of a community to provide long-term affordable housing or workspace using a shared ownership model (Bunce, 2016). Another example is participatory budgeting, a democratic process where community members directly decide how to spend part of a public budget. More than 1500 cities globally have implemented some form of participatory budgeting to allocate public funds or manage community projects.

Other examples include community gardens on vacant municipal land, self-governed civic spaces like the El Campo De Cebada in Madrid, citizen-managed digital infrastructure for communication sharing, and community organizing groups around cultural resources. What these cases have in common are collective community action and stewardship around urban resources for shared social and civic value.

The current urban commons movement poses alternatives to market-driven and state-controlled paradigms of urban development by enabling citizen-managed urban initiatives (Dellenbaugh et al., 2015). Urban commons provide opportunities for inclusive development and empower communities to shape their lived environments. Creative examples like collective management of urban waste streams present sustainable development opportunities in cities.

However, the urban commons movement also faces challenges. As Harvey (2012) argues, the right to collectively manage urban commons risks being co-opted by market forces without adequate regulatory protection of public interests. There are also concerns that commons-based movements may lack formal legitimacy and their benefits may not sufficiently accrue to marginalized groups. Critics argue the need to integrate urban commons frameworks with formal planning policy and resource allocation systems to create lasting transformative impact.

Institutional support and collaborative governance mechanisms are crucial in enabling the sustainable success of urban commons. Case studies point to the importance of facilitating policy environments, partnerships between citizen groups and local governments, and platforms for negotiation in creating viable urban commons (Foster & Iaione, 2016).

For example, Bologna, Italy has adopted collaborative city governance that integrates commons frameworks in municipal regulation and planning. Bologna formally recognizes urban commoning practices and uses civic collaboration in public resource management (LabGov, 2015). This example underscores the potential for policy innovation to legally empower urban commoning. Other cities around the world like Seoul, Barcelona, and New York City have also adopted progressive policies and public-common partnerships in areas like public space management, urban regeneration, and sustainable resource use.

The practice of collective urban commoning holds promise for sustainable and just cities. Scholars have proposed integrating the theory and praxis of urban commons within the New Urban Agenda global policy framework for equitable urban development adopted in 2016 (Foster & Iaione, 2018). At Habitat III, global actors acknowledged the need to view urbanization through the lens of the "right to the city" idea—where all inhabitants have shared access, use, participation, and co-production rights over the life of cities (Dellenbaugh et al., 2015). The urban commons paradigm resonates strongly with this transformative vision by placing urban communities at the center of sustainable development.

These contemporary urban contexts have sparked new forms of commons governance, demonstrating radical possibilities for inclusive and sustainable models for shared urban futures. While criticism rightfully problematizes aspects like inclusiveness and institutional legitimacy, experiments in collaborative urban commoning are rapidly evolving. As Dellenbaugh et al. (2015) note, the urban commons movement ultimately represents cultural and political processes through which urban inhabitants co-determine environments based on solidarity, cooperation, and collective action. By placing renewed focus on stewardship of shared urban resources, the promising paradigm shift toward participative and collaborative urban commoning may lead to more just, creative, democratic, and sustainable management of our cities.

CASE STUDY: LabGov

LabGov, also known as the Laboratory for the Governance of the Commons, is a pioneering research and experimentation network spearheading theory and practice on collaborative city governance and urban commons in Italy and internationally.

Founded in 2012, LabGov promotes participatory management of urban resources and public services as a commons through multi-stakeholder partnerships between citizens, public authorities, businesses, and knowledge institutions. It co-creates institutional innovations and policy frameworks, catalyzing the urban commons paradigm as sustainable models for equitable city development attuned to social and ecological needs instead of solely market logics.

Advancing the Urban Commons Concept LabGov builds on seminal commons scholarship by late economist Elinor Ostrom on self-organized collective action institutions governing shared resources through cooperation. Extending such insights to the urban context, LabGov founder and lead researcher Christian Iaione approaches the theory of "urban commons" in the 2015 article "Governing the urban commons" as shared public resources collectively used and managed by urban communities to meet social needs often hampered by market mechanisms and state structures.

This framing reimagines cities as an overarching managed commons nurturing various urban elements like public spaces, land, infrastructure, data, services, culture, or knowledge as interconnected commons pools for collective benefit instead of purely public, private, or consumer goods. LabGov develops integrated policy ecosystems and co-city governance frameworks formalizing such approaches through groundbreaking legal-economic blueprints, policy prototypes, and demonstrator projects pioneering urban commons paradigms in practice.

Notable LabGov projects experimenting with urban commons include the Co-Bologna project, which saw Bologna, Italy adopt in 2014 a collaborative public-commons city governance framework legally recognizing urban commons practices and actors with a dedicated "Commons Division" in city administration fostering citizen collaborations in public services provisioning. The subsequent Co-Mantova project implemented similar co-city models for urban regeneration in Mantua, Italy.

These projects saw LabGov formulate the Co-City Protocol—a Commons Transition Plan tailoring commons-based approaches for cities through diagnostic/design tools assessing local assets for collaborative stewardship and pegged to measurable impact metrics on economic inclusion or civic participation. The protocols codify replicable ecosystems supporting various urban commons at regulatory, financial, sociocultural, and technological levels through innovations like pooling collective resources in civic trust funds, integrative public-social partnerships, incubating grassroots pilot projects, leveraging ICT infrastructure for knowledge sharing between communities, and participative decision-making feeding into urban plans and policies.

A cornerstone of LabGov's methodology lies in pioneering legal innovations and institutional hacks re-encoding collaborative commons practices formally in law and public policy. This recognizes urban commoning initiatives as legitimate actors in formal administrative systems historically privileging just state or private sectors, helping unlock access to municipal resources and scale successes.

Notable legal tools formulated by LabGov include the Bologna Regulation for the Care and Regeneration of Urban Commons—a 2015 regulation by Bologna municipal government creating Commoning Agreements for shared stewardship of public assets like buildings, greenspaces, or civic networks between citizen groups and public agencies under accessible templates formalizing rights, duties, and monitoring mechanisms.

A modular toolkit of Commons Accords also offers customizable legal formats for partnerships and pooling assets as participatory commons trusts governed through collective stewardship mechanisms instead of overly bureaucratic controls. Such frameworks pivot public administrations from just direct rule-makers toward facilitating platforms enabling grassroots-government collaboration and peer-based governance of common goods aligned to sustainability and social priorities.

In under a decade, LabGov has significantly advanced theory and real-world implementation of the urban commons paradigm internationally through high-impact research projects, collaborations with prominent partners like UN Habitat, and advising major local governments. LabGov feeds into global sustainable development policy debates, including inputs toward the UN's New Urban Agenda signed by more than 160 countries committing to environmentally and socially regenerative cities.

With accelerating urbanization trends disproportionately impacting marginalized groups and intersecting with growing inequality, affordability crises, and climate instability, LabGov's pioneering place-based scholarship on enabling participative collective action holds increasing relevance for just urban futures. By securing legal legitimacy for cooperatively governed urban commons as vectors of empowerment and sustainability transformation challenging exclusionary private–public dichotomies, LabGov provides blueprints for radically reimagining the livability of rapidly evolving cityscapes in the 21st century.

Conclusion

The concept of the commons has roots tracing back centuries, referring to natural and cultural resources accessible to all members of a society. However, the late twentieth century and early twenty-first has witnessed a pivotal revival of commons frameworks, discourse, and action around shared management of common pool resources.

Several interconnected societal, technological, and environmental changes lie behind this resurgence of the commons. Neoliberal economics and market-fundamentalist ideologies led to enclosures and privatization of community assets (De Angelis, 2017). Growing economic inequality and disempowerment spurred a counter-movement emphasizing collective action and stewardship (Bollier & Helfrich, 2019). The information technology revolution enabled digital commons where communities create, share, and maintain knowledge resources. Environmental threats like climate change highlighted that shared natural resources face overexploitation without binding cooperation in governance (Wall, 2014).

These currents catalyzed a wave of scholarship and activism revisiting the commons concept for new socioeconomic possibilities. Crucially, Elinor Ostrom's Nobel Prize-winning work on governing the commons through collective action institutions brought academic legitimacy (Wall, 2014). A network of interdisciplinary commons research emerged (Hess, 2008). Theorizations also proliferated around the notion of "commoning" as social praxis transforming relationships between people, and between human societies and nature (Linebaugh, 2008).

Contemporary literature identifies various new types of commons and commoning practices beyond traditional natural commons like pastoral lands or irrigation systems—knowledge commons, digital commons, urban commons, infrastructure commons, food as a commons, and others. As this diversity shows, the contemporary commons sphere encompasses much broader socioeconomic realms than traditional natural resource management (Wall, 2014). Often commons can intersect across digital, urban, local, and global scales. Their conceptual breadth speaks to the influential framing power that the idea of commons activism carries today.

Scholars posit that the paradigm shift toward commons offers emancipatory political-economic promise on multiple fronts. Commons provide means for equitable access to resources especially for marginalized communities (Wall, 2014). As alternatives to capitalist market logics predicated on profit incentives and private property rights, they form pathways for sustainable prosperity within ecological limits (Bollier & Helfrich, 2019). Urban commons present avenues to participate in and co-construct cities (Stavrides, 2016). Knowledge commons support open circulation of information as a public good improving universal welfare (Frischmann, 2012).

Overall, the language of commons and commoning facilitates diverse "communities of practice" collaborating and building connections from grassroots to higher institutional levels (De Angelis, 2017). With resonances of longstanding political ideologies like anarchism, socialism, and radical democracy, commons offer frames to prefigure more cooperative, equitable, and ecologically harmonious futures inside contemporary capitalist societies (Caffentzis & Federici, 2014). If sufficiently catalyzed in coming decades, a thriving commons sphere could remake the substratum of socioeconomic systems toward post-capitalist alternatives (De Angelis, 2017).

Realizing transformative visions, however, requires tangible institutional innovations enabling commons governance. Research on common pool resources suggests that sustainable self-governed management relies on the implementation of effective rules, monitoring systems, penalties for free-riding, and mechanisms for resolving conflicts (Ostrom, 1990). Extending such findings, an assortment of innovative policies, regulations, networks, and platforms are emerging to support various contemporary commons in multiple jurisdictions.

Some examples include Italy's pioneering legislation recognizing urban commons and commons-based collaborative management in cities like Bologna (Foster & Iaione, 2016). Ecuador's constitutional recognition of the Rights of Nature for environmental policymaking and legislation in Bolivia enshrining indigenous community practices of "living well" offer models for the Global South (Bollier & Helfrich, 2019). Free/open-source software licensing developed through multi-stakeholder negotiation coordinates global digital commons (De Angelis, 2017). Participatory action research methodologies bring together communities, activists, and scholars for commons-focused knowledge co-production (Hess, 2008). Networks like the Global Tapestry of Alternatives map community alternatives across the world as incubations for cosmo-local system change (Bollier & Helfrich, 2019).

Such legal and socio-technical innovations institutionalize commons self-governance and seed opportunities for alternative post-capitalist economies. Scholars observe precedents of institutions introduced for marginal aims gradually catalyzing wider reform—like nineteenth-cnetury cooperatives preparing ideological space for subsequent welfare states (De Angelis, 2017). Through further alliances and coalitions, contemporary commons institutions could arguably pioneer systemic transformation.

Despite the promise of commons-based governance, significant challenges remain. The persistence of capitalist markets and state power can co-opt or undermine commons initiatives, limiting their transformative potential (Caffentzis & Federici, 2014). Many commons projects rely on market mechanisms for financial stability, risking alignment with capitalist interests and dilution of radical ambitions (De Angelis, 2017). Additionally, participation in commons governance can be skewed toward educated, middle-class, and digitally connected groups, potentially excluding marginalized communities (Dellenbaugh et al., 2015).

Moreover, commons discourse can oversimplify issues of solidarity and ignore deeper power imbalances within and between communities (Collard et al., 2015). Effective commons governance must address intersectional inequities related to class, gender, and ethnicity while avoiding anthropocentric views that separate humans from nature (Caffentzis & Federici, 2014). Without deliberate coalition-building across diverse groups, commons development may remain fragmented and uneven (De Angelis, 2017).

Broader structural changes like stronger public welfare institutions and progressive tax policies reducing inequality will remain vital for enabling commons participation for marginalized sections instead (Weeks, 2011). Critics thus argue possibilities of commons transition remain circumscribed within the dominant capitalist mode of power and the state apparatus looming above autonomous initiatives from below (Caffentzis & Federici, 2014). Radical reinvention of the prevailing social order may necessitate a long historical struggle.

Nevertheless, the nucleus of such radical reinvention may reside in evolving networks of contemporary commons initiatives. The limitations underscore strategic directions ahead: consolidating widening platforms of legal and policy interventions for enabling commons; mobilizing broader social movements through grassroots coalition-building between disparate groups; strengthening public service institutions to reduce inequality while limiting dependence on capitalist markets and hierarchical state bureaucracies; embedding democratic and ecological principles structurally across institutions instead of ad hoc interventions; and, fundamentally, raising consciousness toward solidarity ethics beyond individualistic incentives (De Angelis, 2017; Raworth, 2017).

Infrastructures enabling circulation of common pool resources like open access broadband also need widespread development (De Angelis, 2017). Commons transition should be seen through the holistic lens of integrated human-environmental systems transformation rather than insulated reforms. Creating generative social and institutional ecosystems nurturing sustainable commons stewardship demands long-term abandonment of Cartesian dualisms separating humans from nature, mind from matter, and means from ends (Capra & Mattei, 2015).

The essential task remains developing new systems literacy and design skills within communities for appreciating and governing complexity appropriately, not vesting overly reductionist faith in perfect blueprints or universal technocratic solutions. Thus fundamental epistemological shifts underlie seminal possibilities presented in humanity's crossroads today. The seeds may already thrive in existing commons collaborations, but conscious evolution of long-term visions rooted in fundamental values and persistent coalition-building across groups, disciplines, and worldviews is indispensable for genuine transformation. The contemporary reimagining of the commons sphere presents a significant development at this historical juncture, reflecting a pivotal counter-reaction to the social and ecological limits of capitalism. The contemporary commons movement carries immense strategic potential and symbolic power for realizing radically pluralistic, equitable, democratically participative, and sustainable economies embedded within human communities and nourishing ecological limits.

References

Abdelmotteleb, I., Fumagalli, E. & Gibescu, M. (2022). Assessing customer engagement in electricity distribution-level flexibility product provision: the Norwegian case. *Sustainable Energy, Grids and Networks*, 29, 1–14.

Acheson, J. M., & Gardner, R. J. (2004). Strategies, Conflict, and the Emergence of Territoriality: The Case of the Maine Lobster Industry. *American Anthropologist*, 106(2), 296–307.

Agarwal, B. (2001). Participatory exclusions, community forestry, and gender: An analysis for South Asia and a conceptual framework. *World Development*, 29(10), 1623–1648.

Agrawal, A. (2003). Sustainable governance of common-pool resources: Context, methods, and politics. *Annual Review of Anthropology*, 32(1), 243–262.

Agrawal, A., & Narain, S. (eds) (2001). *Dying Wisdom: Rise, Fall and Potential of India's Traditional Water Harvesting Systems*. Centre for Science and Environment.

Anderies, J. M., & Janssen, M. A. (2016). *Sustaining the Commons*. Tempe, AZ: Center for Behavior, Institutions and the Environment, Arizona State University.

Anyon, Y., Bender, K., Kennedy, H., & Dechants, J. (2018). A systematic review of Youth Participatory Action Research (YPAR) in the United States: Methodologies, youth outcomes, and future directions. *Health Education & Behavior*, 45(6), 865–878.

Aryan, V., Bertling, J., & Liedtke, C. (2021). Topology, typology, and dynamics of commons-based peer production: On platforms, actors, and innovation in the maker movement. *Creativity and Innovation Management*, 30(1), 63–79.

Ayers, P., Matthews, C., & Yates, B. (2008). *How Wikipedia Works: And How You Can be a Part of it*. San Francisco: No Starch Press.

Baker, S. H. (2017). Unlocking the energy commons: Expanding community energy generation. In Scanlan, M. K. (ed.), *Law and Policy for a New Economy* (pp. 211–234). Cheltenham and Northampton: Edward Elgar Publishing.

Bauman, H. & Murray, J. (2013). Deaf studies in the 21st century: "Deaf-gain" and the future of human diversity. In L. J. Davis (ed.), *The disability studies reader* (pp. 239–253). New York and London: Routledge.

Bauwens, M., Kostakis, V., Troncoso, S. & Utratel, A. M. (2017). *Commons Transition and P2P: A Primer*. Amsterdam: Transnational Institute.

Battiste, M. (2022). *Decolonizing Education: Nourishing the Learning Spirit*. Vancouver: UBC Press.

Beam, C. (2020). *Volunteers Produce 3D-printed Valves for Life-saving Coronavirus Treatments*. Reuters.

Becker, S., Naumann, M., & Moss, T. (2018). Between coproduction and commons: Understanding initiatives to reclaim urban energy provision in Berlin and Hamburg. In Moretto, L. and Ranzato, M. (eds.), *Coproducing Water, Energy and Waste Services* (pp. 63–85). Oxon and New York: Routledge.

Benkler, Y. (2006). *The Wealth of Networks: How Social Production Transforms Markets and Freedom*. New Haven, Conn: Yale University Press.

Benkler, Y., Shaw, A., & Hill, B. M. (2015). Peer production: A form of collective intelligence. In Malone, T. W. and Bernstein, M. S. (eds.), *Handbook of Collective Intelligence* (pp. 175–204). Cambridge, Mass: MIT Press.

Berkes, F. (1989). *Common Property Resources: Ecology and Community-based Sustainable Development*. London: Belhaven Press.

Black Women's Health Imperative (BWHI) (2023). *Who We Are*. Available at: https://bwhi.org/who-we-are/ (accessed February 15, 2024).

Bollier, D. (2014). *Think Like a Commoner: A Short Introduction to the Life of the Commons*. Gabriola: New Society Publishers.

Bollier, D. (2002). *Silent Theft: The Private Plunder of Our Common Wealth*. New York: Routledge.

Bollier, D., & Helfrich, S. (eds.) (2019). *Free, Fair and Alive: The Insurgent Power of the Commons*. Gabriola: New Society Publishers.

Boston Women's Health Book Collective (2011). *Our Bodies, Ourselves*. New York: Simon & Schuster.

Boyle, J. (2008). *The Public Domain: Enclosing the Commons of the Mind*. New Haven: Yale University Press.

Bunce, S. (2016). Pursuing urban commons: Politics and alliances in community land trust activism in East London. *Antipode, 48*(1), 134–150.

Caffentzis, G. & Federici, S. (2014). Commons against and beyond capitalism. *Community Development Journal*, 49(1), 92–105.

Capaccioli, A. (2018). *Participatory Design for Community Energy Designing the Renewable Energy Commons*. Dissertation. University of Trento.

Capra, F. & Mattei, U. (2015). *The ecology of law: Toward a legal system in tune with nature and community*. Oakland: Berret-Koehler Pubs.

Chaffin, B. C., Gosnell, H. and Cosens, B. A. (2014). A decade of adaptive governance scholarship: Synthesis and future directions. *Ecology and Society, 19*(3), 56.

Collard R. C., Dempsey J. and Sundberg, J. (2015) A manifesto for abundant futures. *Annals of the Association of American Geographers*, 105(2), 322–330.

Community Healthcare Network (CHN) (2023). *Mission and History*. Available at: www.chnnyc.org/about-us /#mission (accessed February 15, 2024).

Cook, S. (2008). The Contribution Revolution: Letting Volunteers Build Your Business. *Harvard Business Review*, 86(10), 60–69.

Cox, M. (2010). *Exploring the dynamics of social-ecological systems: the case of the Taos Valley acequias*. Dissertation. Indiana University, Bloomington, Indiana, USA.

Cox, M., Arnold, G., & Tomás, S. V. (2010). A review of design principles for community-based natural resource management. *Ecology and Society, 15*(4), 38.

Creative Commons (n.d.). *About CC Licenses*. Available at: https://creativecommons.org/about/cclicenses (accessed February 17, 2024).

Daniel, S. (2011). *The role of the international finance corporation in promoting agricultural investment and large-scale land acquisitions*. Paper presented at the International Conference on Global Land Grabbing, April 6–8, 2011, Brighton, UK.

De Angelis, M. (2017). *Omnia Sunt Communia: On the Commons and the Transformation to Postcapitalism*. London: Zed Books Ltd.

De Moor, T. (2013). *Homo cooperans: Institutions for Collective Action and the Compassionate Society*. Utrecht: Utrecht University, Faculty of Humanities.

Dellenbaugh, M., Kip, M., Bieniok, M., Müller, A. K., & Schwegmann, M. (2015). *Urban Commons: Moving beyond State and Market*. Basel: Birkhäuser.

Dietz, T., Ostrom, E., & Stern, P. C. (2003). The struggle to govern the commons. *Science, 302*(5652), 1907–1912.

Dolšak, N., & Ostrom, E. (2003). The challenges of the commons. In Dolšak, N. And Ostrom, E. (eds.), *The Commons in the New Millennium: Challenges and Adaptation* (pp. 3–34), Cambridge: MIT Press.

Eizenberg, E. (2012). The changing meaning of community space: Two models of NGO management of community gardens in New York City. *International Journal of Urban and Regional Research, 36*(1), 106–120.

Feeny, D. H. (1992). Where do we go from here? Implications for the research agenda. In: Bromley, D. W. (ed.), *Making the Commons Work: Theory, Practice, and Policy*, San Francisco: ICS press.

Field Ready (2017). *Field Ready—Humanitarian Engineering*. Available at: http://www.fieldready.org/ (accessed February 14, 2017).

Foster, S., & Iaione, C. (2016). The city as a commons. *Yale Law & Policy Review, 34*(2), 281–349.

Foster, S., & Iaione, C. (2018). Ostrom in the city: Design principles for the urban commons. In D. Cole, B. Hudson, & J. Rosenbloom (eds), *Routledge Handbook of the Study of the Commons* (pp. 235–255). New York: Routledge.

Foster, S. R. (2011). Collective action and the urban commons. *Notre Dame L. Rev., 87*, 57.

Franz, M., Peterschmidt, N., Rohrer, M., & Kondev, B. (2014). *Mini-grid Policy Toolkit: Policy and Business Frameworks for Successful Mini-grid Roll-outs*. Alliance for Rural Electrification (ARE).

Freire, P. (2014). *Pedagogy of the Oppressed: 30th Anniversary Edition*. New York: Bloomsbury Academic.

Frischmann, B. M. (2012). *Infrastructure: The Social Value of Shared Resources*. Oxford: Oxford University Press.

Frischmann, B. M., Madison, M. J., & Strandburg, K. J. (eds). (2014). *Governing Knowledge Commons*. Oxford: Oxford University Press.

GenetiConcept (2022). *Personalized Medicine 2.0: Platforms For Active Patient Participation*. Available at: https://geneticoncept.com/personalized-medicine-platforms-for-active-patient-participation/ (accessed February 15, 2024).

Ginwright, S. & Cammarota, J. (2007). Youth activism in the urban community: Learning critical civic praxis within community organizations. *International Journal of Qualitative Studies in Education*, 20(6), 693–710.

Glick, T. F. (1970). *Irrigation and Society in Medieval Valencia*. Harvard University Press.

Goldthau, A. (2014). Rethinking the governance of energy infrastructure: Scale, decentralization and polycentrism. *Energy Research & Social Science, 1*, 134–140.

GRAIN (2016). *The Global Farmland Grab in 2016: How Big, How Bad?* Available at: https://grain.org/en/article/5492-the-global-farmland-grab-in-2016-how-big-how-bad (accessed February 14, 2024).

Greenberg, D., Sadofsky, M., & Lempka, L. (2005). *The Pursuit of Happiness: The Lives of Sudbury Valley Alumni*. Framingham: Sudbury Valley School Press.

Halverson, E. R., & Sheridan, K. M. (2014). The maker movement in education. *Harvard Educational Review, 84*(4), 495–504.

Hardin, G. (1968). The tragedy of the commons. *Science, 162*(3859), 1243–1248.

Harvey, D. (2011). The future of the commons. *Radical History Review, 2011*(109), 101–107.

Harvey, D. (2012). *Rebel Cities: From the Right to the City to the Urban Revolution*. London: Verso Books.

Helfrich, S. (ed.) (2012). *The Wealth of the Commons: A World Beyond Market and State*.Amherst: Levellers Press.

Hess, C. (2008). *Mapping the New Commons* (SSRN Scholarly Paper No. ID 1356835). Social Science Research Network, Rochester, NY.

Hess, C., & Ostrom, E. (eds). (2007). *Understanding Knowledge as a Commons: From Theory to Practice.* Cambridge: MIT Press.

Hess, G. R., Moorman, C. E., Thompson, J., & Larson, C. L. (2014). Integrating wildlife conservation into urban planning. In McCleery, R. A.,Moorman, C. E. And Peterson, M. N. (eds.), *Urban Wildlife Conservation: Theory and Practice* (pp. 239–278), New York: Springer.

Homebot (2017) *Homebot—We Bring the Factory Home.* Available at: https://homebot.is/ (accessed February 14, 2024).

Hyde, L. (2010). *Common as Air: Revolution, Art, and Ownership.* Farrar, Straus and Giroux.

Iaione, C. (2015). Governing the urban commons. *Italian Journal of Public Law,* 7(1), 170–221.

IDF (International Dialogue on Food Sustainability Issues) (2019). *Livestock Biodiversity: Conserve it or Lose it Forever.* FAO.

Jovanovic, M., Rouchy, P., & Schaeffer, H. (2017). Peer to Peer and the Music Industry: The Criminalization of Sharing. London: SAGE Publications.

Kelty, C. M. (2008). *Two Bits: The Cultural Significance of Free Software.* Duke University Press.

Kleinhout-Vliek, T. H., Boon, W. P. C., Hagendijk, R. P., Hoekman, J. & Moors, E. H. M. (2024). Together for the greater goods: legitimising social innovation in the pharmaceutical field. *Innovation: The European Journal of Social Science Research,* 37(1), 60–84.

Kloppenburg, J. R. (2014). Re-purposing the master's tools: The open source seed initiative and the struggle for seed sovereignty. *The Journal of Peasant Studies,* 41(6), 1225–1246.

Kohtala, C. (2015). Addressing sustainability in research on distributed production: An integrated literature review. *Journal of Cleaner Production,* 106, 654–668.

Kostakis, V. (2010). Peer governance and Wikipedia: Identifying and understanding the problems of Wikipedia's governance. *First Monday,* 15(3).

Kostakis, V. & Bauwens M. (2014). *Network Society and Future Scenarios for a Collaborative Economy.* Basingstoke, UK: Palgrave Macmillan.

Kostakis, V., Latoufis, K., Liarokapis, M., & Bauwens, M. (2018). The convergence of digital commons with local manufacturing from a degrowth perspective: Two illustrative cases. *Journal of Cleaner Production,* 197(2), 1684–1693.

Kostakis, V., Roos, A., & Bauwens, M. (2016). Towards a political ecology of the digital economy: Socio-environmental implications of two competing value models. *Environmental Innovation and Societal Transitions,* 18, 82–100.

Kranich, N. (2004). *The Information Commons: A Public Policy Report.* Brennan Center for Justice at NYU School of Law.

LabGov (2015). *City as a Commons. Teatro Valle Occupato and Later CommuniaCommonspolis.* LabGov. Available at: http://www.labgov.it/opencity/opencity-projects/co-roma/city-as-a-commons (accessed February 14, 2024).

Lanier, J. (2013). *Who owns the Future?* New York: Simon & Schuster.

Lansing, J. S. (2006). *Perfect order: recognizing complexity in Bali.* Princeton, NJ: Princeton University Press.

Laplume, A. O., Anzalone, G. C., & Pearce, J. M. (2016). Open-source, self-replicating 3-D printer factory for small-business manufacturing. *The International Journal of Advanced Manufacturing Technology,* 85(1), 633–642.

Lessig, L. (2008). *Remix: Making Art and Commerce Thrive in the Hybrid Economy.* New York: Penguin.

Lewis, T. (2020). Biohackers are on a secret hunt for the coronavirus vaccine. *Reason Magazine.* March 13.

Lih, A. (2009). *The Wikipedia Revolution: How a Bunch of Nobodies Created the World's Greatest Encyclopedia.* New York: Hachette Books.

Linebaugh, P. (2008). *The Magna Carta Manifesto: Liberties and Commons for All.* Berkeley: University of California Press.

Lloyd, W. F. (1833). Two Lectures on Population. *Population and Development Review,* 6(3), 473–496.

Mann, P. S. (2016). On the precipice with Naomi Klein, Karl Marx and the Pope: Towards a postcapitalist energy commons and beyond. *Radical Philosophy Review*, *19*(3), 621–652.

Martinez, C. (2017). From commodification to the commons: Charting the pathway for energy democracy. In Fairchild, D and Weinrub, A. (eds.), *Energy Democracy: Advancing Equity in Clean Energy Solutions* (pp. 21–36), Washington, Covelo and London: Island Press.

Meinzen-Dick, R. (2007). Beyond panaceas in water institutions. *Proceedings of the National Academy of Sciences*, *104*(39), 15200–15205.

Meinzen-Dick, R., & Mwangi, E. (2009). Cutting the web of interests: Pitfalls of formalizing property rights. *Land Use Policy*, *26*(1), 36–43.

Mooney, P. H. & Majka, T. J. (1995). *Farmers' and Farm Workers' Movements: Social Protest in American Agriculture*. New York: Twayne.

Mount, P. (2012). Growing local food: Scale and local food systems governance. *Agriculture and Human Values*, *29*(1), 107–121.

Muradian, R., & Rival, L. (2012). Between markets and hierarchies: The challenge of governing ecosystem services. *Ecosystem Services*, *1*(1), 93–100.

Namgung, H., Kim, G., & Hwang, J. T. (2022). Putting new wine in old bottles: Merging the logic of the urban commons with Seoul's energy transition experiment. *Journal of Cleaner Production*, *336*, 130411.

Nelson, A. (2011). *Body and soul: The Black Panther Party and the fight against medical discrimination*. Minneapolis, MN: University of Minnesota Press.

Netting, R. (1981). *Balancing on an alp: ecological change and continuity in a Swiss mountain community*. Cambridge: Cambridge University Press.

Nieborg, D. B., & Helmond, A. (2019). The political economy of Facebook's platformization in the mobile ecosystem: Facebook Messenger as a platform instance. *Media, Culture & Society*, *41*(2), 196–218.

Nielsen, J. (2006). *The 90-9-1 Rule for Participation Inequality in Social Media and Online Communities*. Nielsen Norman Group. Available at: https://www.nngroup.com/articles/participation-inequality (accessed February 17, 2024).

Nightingale, A. (2019). Commoning for inclusion? Commons, exclusion, property and socio-natural becomings. *International Journal of the Commons*, *13*(1), 16–35.

Nonini, D. M. (2007). *The Global Idea of "the Commons"*. New York: Berghahn Books.

Oesterle, S. (2016) *Industrial Revolution—Industry 4.0*. Available at: http://industry40.europarl.europa.eu/ (accessed February 14, 2024).

Open Knowledge Foundation (2020). *What is Open Data?* Available at: https://opendatahandbook.org/guide/en/what-is-open-data/ (accessed February 17, 2024).

Open Knowledge Foundation (2022). *Open Jobs Report: Beyond Credentials—Getting Skills Recognised*. Available at: https://open-jobs.okfn.org/report/ (accessed February 16, 2024).

Open Source Hardware Association (2016). *Open Source Hardware (OSHWA) Statement of Principles 1.0*. Available at: http://www.oshwa.org/definition (accessed February 14, 2017).

Open Textbook Library (n.d.). *About open textbooks*. Available at: https://open.umn.edu/opentextbooks/books (accessed February 17, 2024).

Ostrom, E. (1990). *Governing the Commons: The Evolution of Institutions for Collective Action*. New York: Cambridge University Press.

Ostrom, E. (2010). Polycentric systems for coping with collective action and global environmental change. *Global Environmental Change*, *20*, 550–557.

Ostrom, E. (2015). *Governing the Commons: The Evolution of Institutions for Collective Action*. Cambridge: Cambridge University Press.

Pande, S., & Sivapalan, M. (2017). Progress in socio-hydrology: A meta-analysis of challenges and opportunities. *Wiley Interdisciplinary Reviews: Water*, *4*(4), p.e1193.

Participatory Medicine (2023). *What is Participatory Medicine?* Available at: https://participatorymedicine.org/what-is-participatory-medicine/ (accessed February 15, 2024).

Pimbert, M. P. (ed.) (2021). *Food Sovereignty, Agroecology and Biocultural Diversity: Constructing and Contesting Knowledge*. Routledge.

Ponte, S. (2012). The Marine Stewardship Council (MSC) and the making of a market for "sustainable fish". *Journal of Agrarian Change, 12*(2–3), 300–315.

Puckett, J., Byster, L., Westervelt, S., Gutierrez, R., Davis, S., Hussain, A., & Dutta, M. (2002). *Exporting Harm: The High-tech Trashing of Asia*. Basel Action Network, SVTC.

Rapid Medical Parts (2022). *Rapid Medical Parts: Our COVID-19 Response*. Available at: https://www.rapidmedicalparts.com/covid-19 (accessed February 15, 2024).

Rawal, V. (2008) Ownership holdings of land in rural India: Putting the record straight. *Economic and Political Weekly, 43*(10), 43–47.

Raworth, K. (2017). *Doughnut Economics: Seven Ways to Think Like a 21st-century Economist*. White River Junction, VE: Chelsea Green Publishing.

Reynolds, L. & Sariola, S. (2018). The ethics and politics of community engagement in global health research. *Critical Public Health, 28*(3), 257–268.

Rifkin, J. (2014). *The Zero Marginal Cost Society: The Internet of Things, the Collaborative Commons, and the Eclipse of Capitalism*. Palgrave Macmillan.

Scholz, T., & Schneider, N. (eds) (2017). *Ours to Hack and to Own: The Rise of Platform Cooperativism, a New Vision for the Future of Work and a Fairer Internet*. OR Books.

Scholz, T. (2017). *Uberworked and underpaid: How workers are disrupting the digital economy*. Cambridge: Polity Press.

Scott, J. C. (1999). *Seeing like a state: how certain schemes to improve the human condition have failed*. New Haven, CT: Yale University Press.

Scott, J. C. (2017). *Against the Grain: A Deep History of the Earliest States*. Yale University Press.

Shiva, V. (2016). *The Violence of the Green Revolution: Third World Agriculture, Ecology, and Politics*. University Press of Kentucky.

Stavrides, S. (2016). *Common Space: The City as Commons*. London: Zed Books.

Suonio, E. E. (2023). The limits of control: The smart grid as energy commons? *Knowledge Cultures, 11*(3), 101–116.

Szeman, I. (2019). *On Petrocultures: Globalization, Culture, and Energy*. Morgantown: West Virginia University Press.

Taylor, D. L., Yeung, M., & Bashet, A. Z. (2021). Personalised and Adaptive Learning. In Ryoo, J. And Winkelmann, K. (eds.), *Innovative Learning Environments in STEM Higher Education* (pp. 17–34). Springer, Cham.

T1International (2022). *The Open Insulin Project*. Available at: https://openinsulin.org (accessed February 15, 2024).

Utting, P. (2018). *Achieving the Sustainable Development Goals through Social and Solidarity Economy: Incremental versus Transformative Change*. UNRISD Think Piece Series.

Veletsianos, G., & Shepherdson, P. (2016). A systematic analysis and synthesis of the empirical MOOC literature published in 2013–2015. *International Review of Research in Open and Distributed Learning, 17*(2), 202–221.

Vermicelli, S., Cricelli, L., & Grimaldi, M. (2021). How can crowdsourcing help tackle the COVID-19 pandemic? An explorative overview of innovative collaborative practices. *R&D Management, 51*(2), 183–194.

Vickery, S. K., & Wunsch-Vincent, S. (2016). *Participative Web and User-created Content: Web 2.0, Wikis and Social Networking*. Organization for Economic Cooperation and Development (OECD).

Villar, M. E. & Johnson, P. W. (2021). Tailoring Content for Authenticity and Adoption: Community-Based Participatory Research and the Co-creation of Story-Based Health Communication for Underserved Communities. *Frontiers in Communication, 6*, 663389.

Vivero-Pol, J. L. (2017). Food as commons or commodity? Exploring the links between normative valuations and agency in food transition. *Sustainability*, *9*(3), 442.

Wall, D. (2014). *The Sustainable Economics of Elinor Ostrom: Commons, contestation and craft* (1 edition). London and New York: Routledge.

Weeks, K. (2011). *The Problem with Work: Feminism, Marxism, Antiwork Politics, and Postwork Imaginaries*. Durham and London: Duke University Press.

Welsh, R., & MacRae, R. (1998). Food citizenship and community food security: Lessons from Toronto, Canada. *Canadian Journal of Development Studies/Revue canadienne d'études du développement*, *19*(4), 237–255.

Wiley, D. (n.d.). *Defining the "Open" in Open Content and Open Educational Resources*. Available at: http://opencontent.org/definition/ (accessed February 16, 2024).

Wohlers Report (2016). *Wohlers Report 2016: 3D Printing and Additive Manufacturing State of the Industry Annual Worldwide Progress Report*. Wohlers Associates.

Wolsink, M. (2020). Distributed energy systems as common goods: Socio-political acceptance of renewables in intelligent microgrids. *Renewable and Sustainable Energy Reviews*, *127*, 109841.

WWAP (United Nations World Water Assessment Programme) (2021). *The United Nations World Water Development Report 2021: Valuing Water*. UNESCO.

Yang, S., Chen, W., & Kim, H. (2021). Building energy commons: Three mini-pv installation cases in apartment complexes in seoul. *Energies*, *14*(1), 249.

Zuiderveen Borgesius, F., Möller, J., Kruikemeier, S., Ó Fathaigh, R., Irion, K., Dobber, T., Bodo, B., & Vreese, C. (2020). Online political microtargeting: Promises and threats for democracy. *Utrecht Law Review*, *14*(1), 82–96.

Chapter 3
Cooperative Management: Organizations and Enterprises

Introduction

In this chapter, we will explore the concept of cooperatives as a unique alternative to the traditional hierarchical, competitive, and management-led organizational structures that currently dominate our economy. Cooperatives are based on the principles of mutual ownership, positive community impact, and consensual decision-making, and they represent a growing movement toward a more democratic and egalitarian approach to business.

Cooperatives have a rich history that dates back to the nineteenth century, and they have played an important role in many countries around the world. From agricultural cooperatives in the United States to worker-owned cooperatives in Europe, these organizations have provided an alternative to the capitalist model of for-profit organizations or those of traditional governments or non-governmental organizations (NGOs). Cooperatives are based on the values of democracy, equality, solidarity, and social responsibility, and they provide a space for members to work together toward common goals.

One of the key features of cooperatives is their focus on community value. They are not solely focused on generating profits for shareholders, but rather on meeting the needs of their members and the wider community. This means that they are often involved in community development projects, social welfare initiatives, and environmental sustainability efforts. By prioritizing the interests of their members and the community, cooperatives are able to create positive social and economic impacts that extend far beyond their own organization.

Cooperatives also operate on the principles of mutual ownership and democratic decision-making. Members have a say in the running of the organization, and decisions are made through a consensus-based process. This means that everyone has an equal say in the direction of the organization and can contribute their own unique skills and perspectives to the decision-making process. This democratic approach to management can lead to a more motivated and engaged workforce, as members feel invested in the success of the organization and have a sense of ownership over its outcomes.

In this chapter, we will focus on worker- and community-owned cooperatives, which are two of the most common types of cooperatives. Worker-owned cooperatives are businesses that are owned and operated by their employees. These organizations provide an alternative to the traditional capitalist model, where owners and shareholders have the final say in decision-making. By giving workers a stake in the

https://doi.org/10.1515/9783111080147-003

ownership of the organization, worker-owned cooperatives can create a more equitable and empowering workplace.

Community-owned cooperatives, on the other hand, are owned and operated by members of a local community. These organizations are often established to provide essential services to the community, such as healthcare, education, or housing. By operating on a cooperative model, these organizations are able to involve the community in decision-making and ensure that their needs are being met in a sustainable and socially responsible way.

Throughout this chapter, we will explore the guiding principles of cooperatives, the positive community impact that they can have, and the ways in which they differ across time and place. We will also examine how cooperatives are adapting to the changing economic landscape, and how they are informing new types of entrepreneurship linked to community interest companies and social enterprises. By understanding the potential of cooperatives, we can create a more inclusive, equitable, and sustainable economy that works for everyone.

The Importance of Cooperatives

Cooperatives offer an alternative vision of organizing and value creation, challenging the prevailing emphasis on private for-profit organizations that prioritize efficiency and productivity above all else. These profit-driven models, although seemingly successful, often lead to negative economic, social, and political outcomes. By contrast, cooperatives prioritize people over profits, demonstrating that by investing in individuals and their collaborative efforts, healthier and more fulfilling workplaces can be created. Furthermore, cooperatives reveal the advantages of non-hierarchical decision-making, which can lead to better strategies, goods, and services. Ultimately, cooperatives highlight the power of collaboration and cooperation, rather than competition, in driving discovery and innovation.

In the modern world, private for-profit organizations have dominated the economic landscape, promoting a management and leadership style that focuses on efficiency and productivity. The primary goal of these organizations is to maximize profits, often at the expense of other stakeholders, such as employees and the broader community. This profit-driven mentality places great emphasis on executive leadership and managerial control, fostering cultures of command and control rather than empowerment and participation. As a result, employee engagement and creativity suffer, leading to suboptimal outcomes in terms of organizational performance and overall well-being (Porter & Scully, 1987).

Cooperatives, on the other hand, challenge this paradigm by prioritizing the needs and aspirations of their members. They embody a democratic and participatory approach to decision-making, where each member has an equal say, regardless of their position or ownership stake. This non-hierarchical structure fosters a sense of empowerment and ownership among members, leading to increased engagement and motivation. By involving employees in the decision-making process, cooperatives tap into the diverse perspectives and expertise of their members, resulting in better strategies, improved goods, and enhanced services.

One of the distinguishing features of cooperatives is their commitment to the principles of cooperation, such as voluntary and open membership, democratic control, member economic participation, autonomy, education, and concern for the community (Zeuli, Cropp & Schaars, 2004). These principles reflect a broader value system that places the well-being of people and the community at the center of organizational goals. Cooperatives aim to generate sustainable economic and social development, ensuring that the benefits of their activities are distributed equitably among members and the larger community.

By prioritizing people over profits, cooperatives create healthier workplaces that foster trust, cooperation, and shared responsibility. Members have a direct stake in the success of the cooperative, promoting a sense of ownership and commitment. This ownership mindset motivates individuals to contribute their best efforts, leading to increased productivity and overall organizational performance. Additionally, cooperatives often provide fair wages and working conditions, recognizing the value of their employees' contributions and promoting a sense of dignity and well-being.

Cooperatives also challenge the notion that competition is the sole driver of progress and innovation. While competition can certainly be a powerful motivator, cooperatives demonstrate that collaboration and cooperation can lead to even greater discoveries and advancements. By pooling resources, knowledge, and expertise, cooperative members can tackle complex problems and drive innovation in a collective manner (De Peuter & Dyer-Witheford, 2010). Moreover, the cooperative model encourages the sharing of best practices and the exchange of ideas, fostering a culture of continuous learning and improvement.

The Modern History of Cooperatives

Throughout human history, cooperation and mutual exchange have played crucial roles in economic activities. While corporations may appear to have always existed, they are relatively recent phenomena, only taking their modern form in the seventeenth century with the establishment of trading companies such as the Dutch East India Company (Karakas, 2019). However, the cooperative movement, which prioritizes collaboration and fair value creation, has a much deeper and longer history, dating back centuries. This movement emerged as a response to the exploitative conditions of early industrialization and has evolved over time to become an ethical and economic alternative to traditional corporations in the twenty-first century.

The roots of cooperation can be traced back to early human societies, where mutual exchange was essential for survival. Communities relied on shared labor, resources, and knowledge to meet their needs and overcome challenges (International Cooperative Alliance, n.d.). In various parts of the world, local village cooperatives existed as organic forms of collaboration, where members worked together for the collective benefit of the community. These cooperatives emphasized reciprocity, trust, and the equitable distribution of resources, reflecting the principles that would later shape the modern cooperative movement.

The rise of corporations occurred with the emergence of trading companies during the seventeenth century. These enterprises, driven by profit motives and hierarchical structures, marked a departure from the cooperative values that had previously dominated economic interactions (Karakas, 2019). However, even in this era, cooperative practices continued to persist, particularly in regions like Russia, where communal ownership and mutual assistance were integral to local economies.

The modern cooperative movement, as we recognize it today, began to take shape in the eighteenth century. This period witnessed the formation of citizen partnerships aimed at achieving public goods and addressing common challenges (International Cooperative Alliance, n.d.). One of the most famous examples of this was Benjamin Franklin and his fellow firefighters founding a mutual fire insurance company in 1752. This cooperative initiative allowed members to pool resources and protect themselves against the risks of fire, demonstrating the power of collective action for the greater good.

By the nineteenth century, the cooperative movement gained momentum as a response to the harsh and exploitative conditions brought about by early industrialization (Stryjan, 1994). Worker cooperatives and consumer cooperatives emerged as two significant forms of cooperative organizations. Worker cooperatives sought to challenge the prevailing system of profit and wage labor by enabling workers to collectively own and manage their workplaces. This approach aimed to create fairer working conditions and more equitable distribution of rewards. Consumer cooperatives, on the other hand, aimed to provide affordable and quality goods to their members by pooling their purchasing power and eliminating middlemen. These cooperatives offered an alternative to the exploitative practices of early capitalism, empowering consumers and ensuring fairer prices.

The nineteenth century also witnessed more utopian experiments with cooperative values (International Cooperative Alliance, n.d.). Social reformer Robert Owen, for instance, founded cooperative communities both in the United Kingdom and the United States. These communities aimed to create self-sustaining societies based on cooperation, communal ownership, and shared resources. Although many of these utopian experiments faced challenges and ultimately failed, they contributed to the broader awareness and understanding of cooperative principles.

Throughout the twentieth century, the cooperative movement continued to grow and evolve, adapting to the changing social and economic landscape (Birchall, 2004). Cooperatives established footholds in a diverse range of industries, from credit unions in banking to worker-owned tech companies to agricultural collectives and cooperative housing associations. These organizations demonstrated the viability and resilience of the cooperative model in various sectors, challenging the dominance of traditional corporations.

In the twenty-first century, cooperatives have gained renewed significance as ethical and economic alternatives to corporations (Albæk & Schultz, 1998). In a world where profit maximization often comes at the expense of workers, communities, and the environment, cooperatives prioritize social and environmental sustainability alongside economic success. They promote democratic decision-making, equitable distribution of rewards, and local community development.

CASE STUDY: Rochdale Society of Equitable Pioneers

The Rochdale Society of Equitable Pioneers, established in 1844 by twenty-eight weavers and artisans in Rochdale, England, is widely regarded as the foundation of the modern cooperative movement. The Pioneers pooled their resources to open a small store selling essential items like butter and flour at lower prices than local shops. Members received dividends based on their purchases, and the store soon expanded to include additional products and services. The Rochdale model, emphasizing open membership, democratic governance, and concern for community, set a standard for future cooperatives.

The cooperative was born out of harsh conditions faced by workers during the Industrial Revolution, where low wages and long hours left many in poverty. Trapped in debt due to the use of mill-owned shops that overpriced goods, the Pioneers sought an alternative. Their cooperative store offered a path to economic autonomy, built on fair pricing and shared benefits.

The Pioneers' structure ensured that members had equal voting rights and could participate actively in decision-making, fostering a sense of ownership and empowerment. By 1848, the cooperative's success allowed it to expand its inventory and services, launching new departments and ventures, such as a Cooperative Manufacturing Society for textiles and a housing cooperative.

Rochdale's success inspired the establishment of other cooperatives across England. By the 1870s, the society had grown to more than 1400 members and began reinvesting surplus revenues into public amenities like health clinics and education centers. The Rochdale model became a beacon for equitable economic development, with its principles adopted by cooperatives globally.

The success of the Rochdale Society lay in its foundational principles—open membership, democratic control, and education—which fostered member loyalty and community engagement. These principles, later formalized as the "Rochdale Principles," guided the cooperative's operations and ensured equitable access and shared responsibility. The principles emphasized that the cooperative served not just as a store, but as a community institution prioritizing fairness and mutual support.

The International Cooperative Alliance formally adopted the Rochdale Principles in 1937, embedding them as the guiding framework for cooperatives worldwide. Today, they continue to shape the policies and operations of more than one billion cooperative members in diverse sectors, from agriculture to finance.

Although the original Rochdale Society eventually closed, its legacy lives on. The principles it established have influenced the global cooperative sector, which now generates more than $2.1 trillion in annual revenue, demonstrating the enduring power of cooperation. Cooperatives around the world continue to operate according to the model pioneered by the Rochdale Pioneers, proving that collective ownership and democratic governance can create resilient, people-centered economies.

The vision of the Rochdale Pioneers—ordinary workers building institutions grounded in mutual aid—remains a powerful testament to how cooperative principles can transform economic and social landscapes, providing a sustainable alternative to profit-driven business practices.

The Historical Evolution of Cooperatives

The history of modern cooperatives spans several centuries and is marked by distinct stages that have shaped their evolution. From the creation of utopian cooperative communities in the early 1800s to the global spread of cooperatives as an alternative developmental model in the present day, these stages highlight the growth, diversification, and impact of cooperative organizations. In broad terms, there have been six historical stages of the evolution of modern cooperatives, tracing their development from experimental communities to economically successful entities, major contributors to Western economies, providers of social justice and democratic models, providers of welfare and social care, and global alternatives to the prevailing free trade model.

Stage 1 (early 1800s): Creation of "utopian" cooperative communities and experiments: In the early nineteenth century, the cooperative movement gained momentum with the establishment of "utopian" cooperative communities. Influenced by social reformers like Robert Owen, these communities sought to create self-sustaining societies based on cooperation, communal ownership, and shared resources (Curl, 2012). Examples of such experiments include Owen's New Lanark community in Scotland and his later endeavors in New Harmony, Indiana. While many of these communities faced challenges and ultimately dissolved, they laid the groundwork for the cooperative principles and values that would shape future cooperative movements.

Stage 2 (1850–1900): Creation of viable and economically successful cooperative organizations: During the mid-nineteenth century to early twentieth, cooperative organizations shifted from experimental communities to viable and economically successful entities. This period witnessed the establishment of various types of cooperatives, including consumer cooperatives, worker cooperatives, and agricultural cooperatives (Fairbairn, 2016). Consumer cooperatives, such as the Rochdale Society of Equitable Pioneers founded in 1844, focused on providing affordable and quality goods to their members through joint purchasing power and democratic decision-making. Worker cooperatives aimed to empower workers by enabling them to collectively own and manage their workplaces. Agricultural cooperatives emerged as a response to the challenges faced by farmers, providing them with collective bargaining power, access to resources, and improved market opportunities.

Stage 3 (1917–1960): Co-operatives as major contributors to Western economies: The period from 1917 to 1960 witnessed the consolidation of cooperatives as major components of Western economies (Altman, 2009). Consumer and agricultural cooperatives played significant roles in many countries, addressing social and economic challenges brought about by the World Wars and the Great Depression. These cooperatives served as key providers of essential goods and services, stabilizing local economies and improving the livelihoods of their members. In particular, agricultural cooperatives provided farmers with access to shared resources, cooperative marketing, and fairer prices, empowering them to overcome the volatility of agricultural markets.

Stage 4 (1960s–1980s): Growth of "social justice" and democratic cooperatives: The 1960s to the 1980s marked the growth of new cooperative initiatives focused on social justice and democratic principles (Fairbairn, 2016). This period witnessed the emergence of cooperatives in various sectors, including housing, education, healthcare, and worker-owned enterprises. Housing cooperatives, for example, aimed to address housing inequality and promote affordable and community-oriented housing solutions. Democratic workplaces, through worker cooperatives, challenged traditional hierarchical models by enabling workers to participate in decision-making and share in the benefits of their labor.

Stage 5 (1980s–2000s): Cooperative sector filling the welfare and social care gap: In the late twentieth century and early twenty-first, cooperatives increasingly filled the welfare and social care gaps resulting from the reduction of the public sector's role (Altman, 2009). As governments scaled back welfare programs, cooperatives stepped in to provide essential services such as childcare, healthcare, eldercare, and community development. This demonstrated the versatility and responsiveness of cooperatives in meeting evolving community needs.

Cooperative Values

Cooperatives are distinctive organizational structures that are guided by a set of core values. Unlike traditional for-profit corporations, cooperatives prioritize the empowerment of people, foster collective and democratic decision-making, and contribute positively to the local community. These underlying values form the foundation of cooperative enterprises and guide their actions and behaviors. They are driven by essential values that amidst their differences all share a commitment to empowering individuals, promoting collective decision-making, and making meaningful contributions to the communities they serve.

Empowerment: At the heart of cooperatives is the belief in the empowerment of people. Cooperatives aim to create an environment where individuals have a sense of ownership, agency, and control over their economic activities (Ghebremichael, 2013). By allowing members to become owners and actively participate in decision-making processes, cooperatives empower individuals to shape their own destinies. This empowerment is not limited to the cooperative's members alone but extends to the broader community as well. Cooperatives strive to uplift their members and stakeholders, enabling them to improve their livelihoods, develop skills, and achieve economic self-sufficiency.

Collective decision-making: Cooperatives operate on the principle of collective decision-making. Instead of being driven by a top-down hierarchical structure, cooperatives provide equal voting rights and democratic participation to all members (Noble & Ross, 2021). This democratic approach ensures that decisions are made collectively, taking into account the diverse perspectives and interests of the members. By giving every member an equal voice, cooperatives foster inclusivity, transparency, and accountability. This collaborative decision-making process not only strengthens the cohesion and unity within the cooperative but also leads to more informed and sustainable choices that benefit the entire community.

Community contribution: Cooperatives place great importance on making positive contributions to the communities they serve. Unlike traditional corporations that prioritize profit maximization, cooperatives have a broader vision of success that extends beyond financial gains (Camargo Benavides & Ehrenhard, 2021). They actively seek to improve the social, economic, and environmental well-being of their local communities. Cooperatives invest in community development initiatives, support local businesses and suppliers, and promote fair trade practices. They prioritize the local economy by creating jobs, providing affordable goods and services, and reinvesting their profits back into the community.

Social responsibility: In addition to empowering their members and contributing to the community, cooperatives uphold the principle of social responsibility (Fernandez-Guadaño et al., 2020). They prioritize ethical business practices, transparency, and fairness. Cooperatives are guided by a strong sense of social justice, aiming to address economic inequalities and promote equitable distribution of resources. They strive to create a more just and sustainable society, focusing on long-term benefits rather than short-term gains.

KEY THINKER: William King

While the Rochdale Pioneers are credited as founders of the modern cooperative movement, Dr. William King played a key role in laying its groundwork two decades earlier. A physician and social reformer in southern England, King advocated for "communities of united interests" owned and run by working people. His early cooperative initiatives and writings inspired local experiments with cooperatively owned shops and factories that paved the way for Rochdale's success.

William King was born in 1786 in Brighton, England. After studying medicine at Guy's Hospital in London and earning his doctorate from the University of Aberdeen, he returned to Brighton in 1812 to manage a medical practice. Dr. King gained prominence for his public health work, treating diseases like cholera and typhus. His commitment to preventive care and serving all social classes made him acutely aware of the devastating impact of poverty on health. Seeing firsthand the stark inequalities between affluent and impoverished patients fueled his desire for social reform.

By the 1820s, King had developed a vision for cooperative economic models that could empower the working class. Influenced by reformers like Robert Owen, he saw mutualism as a solution to the injustices of industrial capitalism. King began spreading his ideas through pamphlets and public lectures, calling for "associations of united interests" and criticizing the concentration of wealth among elites (Mercer, 1922). His essays, like "Hints on the Necessity for and Practicability of a More General Diffusion of Education", emphasized education's role in emancipation and laid out the foundations of his cooperative philosophy (Mercer, 1922).

Determined to move beyond theory, King set up cooperative stores in his local community. In 1830, he opened the Brighton Co-operator, a small shop selling discounted goods like bread and tea. The store was run as a joint-stock company with shares affordable to working people. Although it faced financial difficulties, King's efforts sparked interest in cooperative ventures throughout Sussex, inspiring similar initiatives in neighboring towns.

Recognizing the limitations of standalone stores, King launched the Brighton Co-operative Trading Association in 1835. This wholesale operation supplied goods to regional cooperatives, allowing them to benefit from bulk purchasing and shared governance. By 1840, the association had more than twenty member societies, proving the scalability of cooperative networks. King's regional model laid the groundwork for cooperative wholesalers like the Rochdale Society.

In 1845, King expanded his cooperative vision by founding the Chartist Cooperative Land Company, aimed at providing affordable, cooperative housing for workers. More than 120 homes were built across five sites, though financial and quality issues hindered further development. Nonetheless, King's "Chartist Villages" influenced later cooperative housing models like Ebenezer Howard's Garden Cities.

Although King's early cooperative ventures were short-lived, they significantly shaped public awareness and practical understanding of cooperative principles. His work laid the conceptual and organizational foundation upon which the Rochdale Pioneers and others would build. King's legacy, though often overshadowed, remains vital in the history of cooperation, demonstrating how visionary leadership and early experiments can catalyze enduring social change.

Main Principles of Cooperatives

The cooperative movement is built upon a set of fundamental principles that guide the functioning and purpose of cooperative organizations. These principles, established by the International Co-operative Alliance (ICA), serve as a compass for cooperatives worldwide, promoting values such as voluntary membership, democratic control, economic participation, autonomy, education, cooperation among cooperatives, and concern for the community. This section explores the seven main principles of cooperatives, highlighting their significance in fostering sustainable development, democratic governance, and positive social impact.

First principle: Voluntary and open membership: The first principle emphasizes that cooperatives are voluntary organizations open to all individuals who can benefit from their services and are willing to accept the responsibilities of membership (Guzmán et al., 2020). Cooperatives reject any form of discrimination based on gender, social status, race, political affiliation, or religion. By promoting inclusivity and equal opportunity, cooperatives ensure that membership is accessible to anyone who shares their values and can actively participate in their activities.

Second principle: Democratic member control: At the core of cooperative governance is the principle of democratic member control (Meira, 2019). Cooperatives are controlled by their members, who actively participate in decision-making processes and policy formulation. This principle ensures that power is decentralized and that all members have an equal say in shaping the cooperative's direction. Elected representatives are accountable to the membership, fostering transparency, accountability, and collective responsibility.

3rd principle: Member economic participation: Member economic participation is a vital principle that highlights the equitable contribution and democratic control of capital within cooperatives (Zeuli, Cropp & Schaars, 2004). Members contribute to the capital of the cooperative, and this capital is often considered the common property of the organization. While members receive limited or no compensation on their subscribed capital, any surplus generated by the cooperative is allocated based on democratic decisions. Surpluses may be used to develop the cooperative, establish reserves, benefit members in proportion to their transactions, or support other approved activities.

Fourth principle: Autonomy and independence: Cooperatives are autonomous and self-help organizations, guided by the principle of autonomy and independence (Novković & Šimleša, 2023). They have the freedom to make decisions based on the needs and priorities of their members, ensuring democratic control and maintaining their cooperative identity. While cooperatives may enter into agreements or raise capital from external sources, these interactions are conducted on terms that safeguard the democratic control and autonomy of the cooperative.

Fifth principle: Education, training, and information: Education, training, and information form the basis of the fifth principle of cooperatives (Muñoz et al., 2020). Cooperatives are committed to providing education and training opportunities to their members, elected representatives, managers, and employees. This empowers individuals to actively contribute to the development and success of the cooperative. Additionally, cooperatives play a crucial role in informing the general public, particularly young people and opinion leaders, about the nature, benefits, and importance of cooperative enterprises. By raising awareness and promoting cooperative values, cooperatives strive to foster a cooperative culture in society.

Sixth principle: Cooperation among cooperatives: Cooperation among cooperatives lies at the heart of the sixth principle. Recognizing that collaboration strengthens the cooperative movement, cooperatives actively work together through local, national, regional, and international structures (Guzmán et al., 2020). By sharing knowledge, resources, and experiences, cooperatives enhance their capacity to serve their members effectively and promote the values and benefits of cooperation. Through collective action, cooperatives can address common challenges, advocate for supportive policies, and achieve shared goals.

Seventh principle: Concern for community: The seventh principle highlights the cooperative commitment to the sustainable development of communities (Meira, 2019). Cooperatives recognize their role in improving the social, economic, and environmental well-being of their communities. They do so by developing and implementing policies that are approved by their members and align with the interests and needs of the community. Cooperatives actively engage in initiatives that promote community development, support local initiatives, and contribute to the overall welfare of the community they serve. By prioritizing the well-being of their communities, cooperatives go beyond their primary economic objectives and become agents of positive social change.

Focus: Cooperatives and Community Impact

Cooperatives, as unique and socially responsible organizations, have the power to positively impact communities in ways that differ significantly from the traditional concept of corporate social responsibility. By prioritizing community development, local engagement, and social justice, cooperatives foster sustainable growth and collective well-being, embodying a distinct approach to business and community relationships.

One key way in which cooperatives positively impact communities is through their investments in community development projects. Cooperatives often allocate resources to initiatives that directly benefit the community, such as infrastructure improvements, educational programs, healthcare facilities, and environmental initiatives (Dobrohoczki, 2006). By directing their efforts toward these projects, cooperatives contribute to the overall advancement and sustainability of the community, enhancing the quality of life for its residents. These investments go beyond mere philanthropy; they represent a fundamental commitment to community empowerment and long-term prosperity.

Moreover, cooperatives exhibit a strong commitment to local sourcing and procurement, which sets them apart from traditional corporations. By prioritizing local businesses and suppliers, cooperatives support the local economy, create jobs, and stimulate economic growth (Ajates, 2020). This practice strengthens the community's resilience and self-reliance, fostering a sense of collective prosperity. Unlike corporations that often prioritize global supply chains and outsourcing, cooperatives demonstrate a deep-rooted connection to the local community and actively contribute to its economic vitality.

Another distinguishing feature of cooperatives is their active engagement with members and the broader community. Through regular communication channels and democratic decision-making processes, cooperatives establish a dialogue with stakeholders, seeking their input and incorporating community perspectives into their operations (Mori, 2014). This inclusive approach ensures that cooperative initiatives align with the values and priorities of the community, leading to greater social impact and community empowerment. By actively involving members and the community in decision-making, cooperatives nurture a sense of ownership and shared responsibility, fostering a stronger sense of community cohesion and resilience.

Cooperatives also play a crucial role in addressing social issues and inequalities within their communities. They are driven by a commitment to social justice, equality, and inclusion, aiming to create a more just and equitable society (Williams, 2016). Cooperatives often support initiatives that promote fair wages, worker rights, gender equality, and community development. By focusing on the well-being of their members and the community, cooperatives demonstrate a broader and more holistic understanding of social responsibility. They go beyond tokenistic gestures and integrate social sustainability and ethical business practices into their core operations.

In contrast, corporate social responsibility (CSR) initiatives often operate within a framework that primarily serves the interests of shareholders and corporate reputation. While CSR programs may involve charitable giving or environmental initiatives, they are often detached from the core business operations and decision-making processes of corporations. Moreover, CSR initiatives can be selective and driven by marketing or public relations strategies, lacking the deep-rooted commitment to community development and empowerment that cooperatives embody.

Types of Cooperatives

Cooperatives are diverse and dynamic entities that exist in various economic sectors and serve different purposes. They come in different forms and structures, each with its unique characteristics and objectives. Among the different types of cooperatives, three prominent ones are worker-owned cooperatives, consumer-owned cooperatives, and community-owned cooperatives. These types of cooperatives share the fundamental principles of cooperation, collective decision-making, and equitable distribution of benefits, while also having distinct focuses and priorities.

1. *Worker-owned cooperatives*: Worker-owned cooperatives are enterprises where the employees themselves are the owners and have an equal say in the decision-making process (Rothschild, 2009). In these cooperatives, the workers collectively manage and control the business, fostering a sense of empowerment and shared responsibility. The primary objective of worker-owned cooperatives is to create democratic workplaces that prioritize the well-being and self-determination of the workers. By providing opportunities for worker participation, these cooperatives promote a sense of ownership, job security, and fair distribution of profits among the workforce. Worker-owned cooperatives can be found in a range of sectors, including manufacturing, technology, retail, and professional services.

2. *Consumer-owned cooperatives*: Consumer-owned cooperatives, also known as retail cooperatives or co-op stores, are owned and operated by the consumers themselves (McLeod, 2006). These cooperatives are formed to fulfill the needs and aspirations of their members, who are also the customers. By pooling their purchasing power, consumers in these cooperatives can access products and services at affordable prices while ensuring high quality and ethical standards. The primary focus of consumer-owned cooperatives is to meet the specific needs and preferences of their members, whether it be food, housing, healthcare, or other essential goods and services. Consumer-owned cooperatives are prevalent in sectors such as grocery stores, housing, healthcare, and energy.

3. *Community-owned cooperatives*: Community-owned cooperatives, also known as multi-stakeholder cooperatives, bring together different stakeholders, including workers, consumers, and community members, in a cooperative structure (Dobrohoczki, 2006). These cooperatives serve broader community interests and work toward the sustainable development of the local community. The key objective of community-owned cooperatives is to ensure the social, economic, and environmental well-being of the community they operate in. By involving multiple stakeholders, these cooperatives foster collaboration, inclusivity, and a sense of shared responsibility. Community-owned cooperatives can be found in sectors such as agriculture, renewable energy, housing, and community development projects.

While the three types of cooperatives have distinct focuses, they also share common principles and values (Tainio, 1999). These include voluntary and open membership, democratic governance, equitable participation, and concern for the community. Regardless of the type, cooperatives are characterized by the active involvement of their members, democratic decision-making processes, and commitment to the well-being of their stakeholders.

Cooperatives exist in various economic sectors, showcasing their adaptability and versatility. They are not limited to specific industries but are found across different sectors, providing a cooperative alternative to traditional business models. For example, in the agriculture sector, agricultural cooperatives enable farmers to pool resources, access markets, and gain bargaining power. This allows them to enhance productivity, improve income stability, and share the risks collectively. In the financial sector, credit unions and cooperative banks provide financial services to their members, emphasizing financial inclusion, responsible lending, and community development. Cooperatives also thrive in sectors such as manufacturing, where worker-owned cooperatives create democratic workplaces and promote sustainable employment practices. In the technology sector, cooperatives are emerging as platforms for collaboration and knowledge sharing, fostering innovation and collective development.

The wide presence of cooperatives across diverse economic sectors demonstrates their adaptability and effectiveness as alternative business models. They prioritize cooperation over competition, collective decision-making over hierarchical structures, and equitable distribution of benefits over individual profit maximization. Cooperatives not only provide economic benefits to their members but also contribute positively to society as a whole. By adopting cooperative values and principles, they promote social and economic justice, sustainable development, and community empowerment.

One of the key similarities among worker-owned, consumer-owned, and community-owned cooperatives is their emphasis on democratic decision-making. In all three types, members have an equal say in the governance and operations of the cooperative. This democratic control ensures that decisions are made collectively and in the best interests of the members and the community. It empowers individuals to actively participate in shaping the direction and success of the cooperative.

Another shared characteristic is the focus on equitable distribution of benefits. Unlike traditional businesses that prioritize profit accumulation for a select few, cooperatives aim to benefit all their members. In worker-owned cooperatives, profits are shared among the workers, ensuring fair compensation and reducing income inequality. Consumer-owned cooperatives provide products and services at reasonable prices, allowing members to access quality goods and services at affordable rates. Community-owned cooperatives reinvest surplus profits into community development projects, supporting local initiatives and fostering sustainable growth. Furthermore, cooperatives exhibit a strong commitment to their communities, which sets them apart from corporations. While corporations may engage in corporate social responsibility as a means to improve their public image, cooperatives have community welfare ingrained in their very nature. Cooperatives invest in community development projects, such as infrastructure improvements, educational programs, healthcare facilities, and environmental initiatives. These investments directly contribute to the overall well-being and sustainability of the communities they serve.

Cooperatives also prioritize local sourcing and procurement, supporting other local businesses and suppliers. This practice helps stimulate the local economy, create jobs, and strengthen community resilience. By fostering economic interconnectedness within the community, cooperatives enhance its self-reliance and prosperity. In contrast to corporations, which are driven primarily by profit maximization, cooperatives prioritize the needs and aspirations of their members and the community. They are built on the foundation of cooperation, solidarity, and mutual support. This cooperative ethos allows them to address social issues and inequalities within their communities. Cooperatives often support initiatives that promote social justice, equality, and inclusion, aiming to create a more just and equitable society. By focusing on the well-being of their members and the community, cooperatives demonstrate a commitment to the broader principles of social sustainability and ethical business practices.

Worker-owned, consumer-owned, and community-owned cooperatives share the principles of cooperation, collective decision-making, and equitable distribution of benefits. They differ in their focus and priorities, with worker-owned cooperatives emphasizing democratic workplaces, consumer-owned cooperatives prioritizing the needs of members, and community-owned cooperatives serving broader community interests. Regardless of the type, cooperatives demonstrate their concern for the community through investments in community development, support for local businesses, active engagement with members and stakeholders, and a commitment to social justice. Cooperatives serve as an alternative business model that promotes social responsibility, sustainable development, and community empowerment, contributing to a more inclusive and equitable society.

Cooperative Management and Design

Cooperative management and decision-making are guided by the principles of consensus and democracy, focusing not only on increasing productivity and efficiency but also on empowering all members. Unlike traditional hierarchical management, cooperative management entails the development of formal and informal cultures of power-sharing and open discussion. Various approaches, such as sociocracy and holacracy, have emerged to facilitate effective cooperative management and decision-making.

Sociocracy is a theory of governance that aims to create psychologically safe environments and productive organizations (Eckstein, 2016). It promotes the use of consent, rather than majority voting, in discussions and decision-making among individuals who share a common goal or work process. This approach ensures that decisions are made collaboratively, considering the perspectives and expertise of all members. By fostering a culture of participation and equality, sociocracy enables cooperative members to have a meaningful voice in shaping the direction and operations of the cooperative.

Holacracy, on the other hand, is a method of decentralized management and organizational governance that distributes authority and decision-making across self-organizing teams, rather than relying on a traditional management hierarchy (Robertson, 2015). In holacratic organizations, decision-making power is dispersed, allowing teams to adapt and respond more effectively to changing circumstances. This approach promotes autonomy, accountability, and agility within the cooperative. Holacracy has gained traction in both for-profit and non-profit organizations worldwide as a means to foster transparency, effectiveness, and adaptability.

These innovative management approaches represent a broader movement within organizational design to address the complexities of modern social environments. They aim to create more inclusive and dynamic cooperative structures that encourage collaboration, creativity, and shared responsibility among members (Höhler & Kühl, 2018). By embracing these management models, cooperatives seek to enhance their ability to navigate challenges and seize opportunities in an ever-changing business landscape.

Cooperatives also vary in their structural composition based on membership. They can be classified as centralized, federated, or mixed (Cornforth, 2004).

In a centralized cooperative, individual producers comprise the membership, and the cooperative serves members within a specific geographical area. There is typically one central office, a board of directors, and a manager overseeing the entire operation. Business transactions are primarily conducted through this central office, although regional branches may exist.

A federated cooperative, on the other hand, is a cooperative of cooperatives. The members of a federated cooperative are local cooperatives, each with its own manager and staff, and a board of directors elected to represent the local associations. The local cooperatives operate as separate business entities, and the federated cooperative provides a platform for collaboration, joint initiatives, and representation at a broader level.

A mixed cooperative combines elements of both centralized and federated structures. It encompasses individual producers as well as local cooperatives, leveraging their combined resources and expertise. The mixed cooperative model allows for diverse membership and facilitates collaboration between individual producers and local cooperatives.

Creating Cooperatives

As discussed so far in this chapter, cooperatives are democratic enterprises that prioritize the collective well-being of their members and the community. They offer an alternative economic model that promotes equity, sustainability, and community empowerment. When establishing a cooperative, it is crucial to consider legal incorporation and explore financing options such as community shares. This section explores the different ways to start and maintain a cooperative, emphasizing the need for legal incorporation and highlighting the use of community shares as a form of equity investment.

Legal incorporation provides cooperatives with a recognized and protected status, ensuring compliance with applicable laws and regulations (Sutton, 2019). It also establishes a formal structure that enables the cooperative to operate efficiently and protects the rights and interests of its members.

There are four main legal types of cooperatives:

1. Community Benefit Society (CBS): A CBS is a democratic structure that serves both its members and the wider community (Zeuli & Radel, 2005). It reinvests pre-tax trading profits into the enterprise, pays interest to shareholders, or distributes funds for social or charitable purposes according to its rules. Each member has one vote, regardless of the amount invested, promoting inclusivity and empowering the community.
2. Co-operative society: A co-operative society is owned and controlled by its members and operates primarily to benefit them (Cummings, 1999). Members have equal say in decision-making and profit distribution, whether through dividends, reinvestment, or community support. Community investment and potential grant funding can contribute to the cooperative's financial stability.
3. Community Interest Company (CIC): A CIC is a company governed by its Articles of Association, written to benefit the community (Olsen, 2013). It can generate profits through trading and reinvest them in the business or make charitable donations. A CIC is subject to company law and offers limited liability to its members. While a CIC does not have share capital or shareholders, it can take out loans and potentially qualify for grant funding.
4. Company Limited by Guarantee (CLG): A CLG is a trading enterprise established to benefit the community (Dickstein, 1991). It can be limited by guarantee or shares, allowing shares to be transferable and redeemable. CLGs must adhere to company law regulations. The governance of a large membership CLG is determined by its Articles, ensuring member control and potential eligibility for grant funding.

Financing Cooperatives

Financing plays a crucial role in the establishment and growth of cooperatives, which are member-owned and member-controlled enterprises. Cooperatives employ various methods to finance their operations and expansion, including annual membership fees, member contributions, member share capital, individual member deposits, deferred payments, community shares, public and civic grants, and the retention of cooperative business surpluses. This section delves into the different financing mechanisms used by cooperatives, highlighting the importance of each and emphasizing the benefits they bring to cooperative members and the community.

1. *Membership fees*: One-time or annual membership fees are a common method of financing cooperatives (Deng, Hendrikse & Liang, 2021). These fees serve as a means for members to contribute to the cooperative's operations and growth. By paying membership fees, individuals gain access to the cooperative's services, benefits, and decision-making processes. These fees not only provide financial resources but also signify the commitment and dedication of members to the cooperative model.

2. *Member contributions:* Member contributions without individual ownership attached, such as service fees, are another way members help finance the cooperative (Cuevas & Buchenau, 2018). These contributions are typically related to patronage, where members pay for services provided by the cooperative. While these contributions may vary in amount, once given, they cannot be withdrawn. They serve as a valuable form of cooperative capital, providing stability and resources for the cooperative's functioning.

3. *Member share capital:* Member share capital represents the financial stake and commitment of individual members in the cooperative (Sexton, 1986). It signifies their ownership and provides a source of capital for the cooperative's operations. Member share capital is typically withdrawn only when a member leaves the cooperative. This form of financing ensures that members have a direct financial interest in the cooperative's success and fosters a sense of collective responsibility.

4. *Individual member deposits*: Individual member deposits with the cooperative are yet another way to finance cooperative activities (Kyazze et al., 2020). Members deposit funds with the cooperative, which can be utilized for the cooperative's business operations. These deposits serve as a form of cooperative capital, offering financial resources for various needs, such as expansion, investment, or working capital. Individual member deposits provide the cooperative with a reliable source of funds while strengthening the financial stability of the organization.

5. *Deferred payment for produce*: In some cooperatives, members receive deferred payment for part or all of the produce they deliver to the cooperative (Barton et al., 2011). This mechanism allows the cooperative to use the funds generated from the sale of the produce for its operational and investment needs. Deferred payment serves as a form of cooperative capital, ensuring a steady flow of funds while supporting member farmers and their financial stability.

6. *Cooperative business surpluses*: Funds created through the retention of cooperative business surpluses represent another vital source of cooperative capital (Boland & Barton, 2013). These surpluses, not directly allocated to members, provide long-term financial resources that contribute to the cooperative's sustainability. Unlike loans or individual member deposits, cooperatives do not have to pay interest on these retained surpluses, making them a cost-effective form of capital.

Cooperatives Internationally

Cooperatives are enterprises built on ethics, values, and principles that prioritize the well-being of people, communities, and the environment. With over 3 million cooperatives worldwide, representing more than 1 billion cooperative members, their impact on the global economy and society cannot be underestimated. This section explores the remarkable global impact of cooperatives, emphasizing their significant contributions to employment, economic growth, and sustainable development.

Cooperatives are not a marginal phenomenon but a thriving global movement. Surpassing the 12 percent mark, more than one in ten people on Earth is a cooperator, affiliated with any of the 3 million cooperatives across various sectors. These cooperatives, including the three hundred largest cooperatives or mutuals, generate a staggering turnover of 2146 billion USD, as reported by the World Cooperative Monitor. This showcases their immense economic influence and financial success.

Cooperatives play a vital role in providing jobs and work opportunities, contributing to the livelihoods of millions of people worldwide. Approximately 280 million individuals, accounting for 10 percent of the world's employed population, find employment through cooperatives. These member-owned, member-run, and member-serving businesses empower individuals to collectively realize their economic aspirations, while simultaneously fostering social and human capital development within their communities.

Cooperatives employ at least 279.4 million people globally, with 27.2 million working directly in cooperatives as employees or worker-members. The majority of employment opportunities, reaching more than 252.2 million people, are found in the agricultural sector. These cooperatives enable farmers and agricultural workers to access fair markets, secure fair prices for their produce, and enhance their overall well-being.

Cooperatives in Latin America

Cooperatives have played a significant role throughout Latin America, contributing to economic development, social inclusion, and empowerment of communities. The roots of cooperatives in the region can be traced back to pre-Columbian collectives and co-operative-like models (Bajo, 2017). However, it was the influence of participatory organizational models introduced by European colonizers and settlers that shaped the modern cooperative movement in Latin America, which began to take form in the late nineteenth century.

By the 1990s, the cooperative sector in Latin America consisted of a multitude of organizations, ranging from 30,000 to 50,000, with an estimated total membership between 17 and 23 million people, depending on the source consulted (Vásquez-León, 2010). These figures highlight the significant impact of cooperatives on the region's economies and livelihoods.

Let us explore some specific examples of the role and impact of cooperatives in Latin American countries. In Paraguay, for instance, approximately 18 percent of the population, or 783,000 people, are members of 1047 cooperatives. The direct impact of these cooperatives reaches more than 6 million people, providing them with livelihood opportunities and economic stability (Koljatic & Silva, 2011).

In Uruguay, cooperatives contribute significantly to the economy, responsible for 3 percent of the gross domestic product (GDP). They are particularly dominant in sectors such as dairy production, where they produce 90 percent of the total milk production (Cracogna, 2013). Moreover, they play a crucial role in honey production, accounting for 340 percent of the country's output, as well as contributing 30 percent of the wheat production. Notably, 60 percent of cooperative production in Uruguay is exported to more than forty countries worldwide.

In Colombia, the cooperative movement is a substantial provider of employment, creating 137,888 jobs through direct employment and an additional 559,118 jobs as worker-owners in worker cooperatives (Dias et al., 2018). This means that cooperatives contribute to 3.65 percent of all jobs in the country, promoting inclusive growth and reducing unemployment rates.

Brazil stands out as a country where cooperatives have a significant impact on both the agricultural and financial sectors. Cooperatives are responsible for 37.2 percent of the agricultural GDP and 5.4 percent of the country's overall GDP (Shapiro-Garza et al., 2020). In the healthcare sector, health cooperatives provide medical and dental services to 17.7 million people, nearly 10 percent of the population. Furthermore, financial cooperatives in El Salvador have assets exceeding $1300 million, representing 9.3 percent of the total domestic financial system.

Bolivia showcases the wide range of employment opportunities provided by cooperatives. With over 1600 cooperatives, they generate more than 32,000 direct jobs and over 128,000 indirect jobs, contributing to poverty reduction and social mobility.

The cooperative movement in Latin America is not limited to these examples. In fact, the Organization of Brazilian Cooperatives (OCB) consists of more than 6600 cooperatives with over 10 million members, providing direct employment to nearly 300,000 people. In Costa Rica, credit unions, which operate as cooperatives, own 8.5 percent of the assets of the domestic financial system. Meanwhile, the Dominican Republic has more than 1 million cooperative members, offering employment to over 40,000 people.

The success of cooperatives in Latin America can be attributed to various factors. First, cooperatives promote democratic participation, allowing members to have a say in decision-making processes and ensuring equitable distribution of benefits. This participatory nature empowers individuals and communities, fostering a sense of ownership and pride.

Cooperatives also address economic and social inequalities by providing access to financial services, markets, and resources for marginalized communities. They promote inclusive development, particularly in rural areas, by facilitating agricultural production, improving livelihoods, and enhancing food security.

Furthermore, cooperatives have proven to be resilient in times of economic downturns and crises, as they rely on collective strength, mutual support, and shared risks. This resilience contributes to the stability and sustainability of local economies, reducing dependency on external actors and fostering self-reliance.

Cooperatives have a long-standing history and a vital role in Latin America. They have evolved from pre-Columbian collectives and co-operative-like models to modern-day organizations that contribute significantly to economic development, employment generation, and social inclusion. The examples of cooperatives in countries like Paraguay, Uruguay, Colombia, Brazil, and others highlight their positive impact on livelihoods, agriculture, healthcare, and financial services. By promoting democratic participation, addressing inequalities, and demonstrating resilience, cooperatives continue to play a crucial role in shaping the socio-economic landscape of Latin America, empowering communities, and fostering sustainable development.

Cooperatives in North America

Cooperatives in North America have a rich history deeply rooted in the transformative period of the Industrial Revolution in England from 1750 to 1850. This era witnessed the disappearance of many small, home-based enterprises, which forced workers to migrate to cities and endure harsh working conditions and low wages (Pitman, 2018). In rural areas, changes in land tenure patterns and the enclosure movement pushed small farmers off their lands, compelling them to seek employment in urban centers. It was during this time that the first recognized cooperative business in the United States emerged—a mutual fire insurance company founded by Benjamin Franklin in 1752, which continues to operate today.

Early cooperative efforts in North America began with dairy and cheese cooperatives around 1810, followed by agricultural commodity cooperatives (Fulton et al., 2006). These initiatives, mostly short-lived and local, aimed to empower agricultural producers through bulk purchasing. By 1866, consumer cooperatives were spreading to major industrial towns (Pitman, 2018). The first half of the nineteenth century saw westward expansion and agricultural surpluses that led to economic challenges, such as low prices and high freight charges (Wittman et al., 2017). To address these issues, farmers formed marketing cooperatives and established the Order of the Patrons of Husbandry (Grange) after the Civil War. The Grange, which endorsed the Rochdale Principles in 1875, promoted agricultural cooperatives and cooperative stores (Fulton et al., 2006). However, the Grange declined in the 1880s due to diversification issues and low member participation.

Other organizations, such as the Farmers' Alliance and the Society of Equity, emerged with more political agendas to support cooperative development, particularly in the southern U.S. (Pitman, 2018). The Farmers' Alliance, facing racial discrimination in the South, led to the formation of the Colored Farmers' National Alliance and Cooperative Union in 1886 (Fulton et al., 2006). Despite these efforts, the discriminatory Jim Crow laws hindered further cooperative development among black farmers.

During this period, retail cooperatives also surfaced but struggled due to geographic dispersion and a lack of capital and management (Wittman et al., 2017). The Cooperative League of the United States of America (CLUSA) was formed in 1916 to promote a broad cooperative agenda (Jackall & Levin, 2021). Support came from various cooperative movements, including Finnish social democrats and agricultural purchasing associations. The first U.S. credit union law was passed in Massachusetts in 1909, spearheaded by Edward Filene and Roy F. Bergengren, who expanded credit union legislation nationwide (Fulton et al., 2006).

The Great Depression brought new federal support for cooperatives, such as the Farm Credit Act of 1933, which established Production Credit Associations and agricultural cooperative banks (Wittman et al., 2017). The Federal Credit Union Act of 1934 allowed federal credit unions in states without such statutes. The Rural Electrification Act of 1937 enabled rural communities to establish electric cooperatives, transforming rural life and boosting agricultural productivity (Pitman, 2018).

Cooperatives gained momentum in the 1930s, participating in New Deal programs and expanding in urban and agricultural sectors. They diversified into insurance, petroleum, and credit services. After World War II, agricultural cooperatives grew larger and more consolidated, engaging in value-added processing ventures (Fulton et al., 2006). This period saw a shift in CLUSA's focus toward more pragmatic business management.

Cooperatives played a pivotal role in the civil rights movement, providing support to black farmers in the South through organizations like the Federation of Southern Cooperatives (Wittman et al., 2017). The Federation advocated for independent black farmers' land retention and economic independence amid discrimination.

Consumer food cooperatives saw a resurgence in the 1960s and 1970s, driven by the demand for organic and natural foods (Jackall & Levin, 2021). Though many did not survive, those that did helped shape the organic food market.

In recent decades, agricultural cooperatives have undergone mergers and acquisitions, forming some of the largest cooperatives in the country (Pitman, 2018). These organizations operate globally, prioritizing economic considerations while influencing national agricultural policies.

Canada's cooperative movement stabilized in the late nineteenth century and early twentieth through farmers' marketing and purchasing societies (Fulton et al., 2006). Co-operative creameries and credit unions spread across rural Canada, laying the foundation for diverse cooperative sectors nationwide. Today, Canadian cooperatives remain economically significant, generating employment and providing essential services and infrastructure.

Cooperatives in Africa

The cooperative movement in Africa has experienced various stages of evolution, reflecting the continent's social, economic, and political changes over time. From the precolonial period to the post-independence era and the era of liberalization, cooperatives have played a crucial role in fostering economic development, social cohesion, and community empowerment. This essay examines the four stages of evolution of cooperatives in Africa, highlighting their historical significance, challenges faced, and potential for transformation.

Stage 1: Precolonial period—The doctrine of self-help: In the precolonial period, cooperatives in Africa were rooted in the doctrine of self-help (Okem, 2016). People recognized the interconnectedness of individuals in society and formed cooperatives as a means to achieve social and economic objectives. Examples of dominant cooperative movements during this period included savings and credit unions, collective management of farm holdings, and grazing fields (Fakude, 2016). These cooperatives enabled communities to pool resources, share risks, and support one another in various economic activities (Hamer, 1981). They aligned with traditional African philosophies of solidarity and mutual aid.

Stage 2: Colonial period—Top-down approach: During the colonial period, a top-down approach to cooperative development emerged, influenced by the colonial powers (Eckert, 2007). The British introduced a unified cooperative model that focused on agricultural production, marketing, and processing, primarily for export crops. This model resulted in powerful cooperative ventures with vertical structures, controlling significant aspects of rural economies (Wanyama, 2009). The French and Belgian colonial powers also implemented cooperative initiatives, albeit with different motivations and outcomes. The French introduced semi-public organizations to dominate rural populations and collect taxes, while the Belgian and Portuguese colonies saw limited cooperative development (Holmén, 1990). Overall, cooperatives were used as instruments of colonial control rather than democratic member empowerment.

Stage 3: Post-independence era—African socialism: After gaining independence, many African governments embraced cooperatives as a vehicle to promote African socialism and socioeconomic development (Mojo, Fischer & Degefa, 2017). State support, both financial and technical, was provided to cooperatives, granting them marketing and supply monopolies for agricultural inputs and produce. Governments entrusted cooperatives with managing strategic grain reserves and other vital functions. This period witnessed massive state intervention and control of the cooperative movement, shaping its direction and impact on rural communities. However, the top-down, state-driven approach limited member participation and accountability.

Stage 4: Era of liberalization—Facilitative role of the state: Starting in the mid-1980s, Africa underwent an era of structural adjustment, democratization, and commercialization, leading to the end of extensive government control over cooperatives (Wanyama, 2009). The state transitioned into a facilitative role, restructuring the legal framework and opening cooperative-dominated sectors to other actors. However, cooperatives faced numerous challenges during this period, including identity crises, unfavorable legal and administrative contexts, and management issues. Many cooperatives relied on subsidies, state protection, and government intervention to survive rather than member commitment and democratic participation (Wanyama, 2009).

In Kenya, the cooperative movement began in 1908 under colonial rule but took on increasing significance after independence (Wanyama, 2009). Kenya now has one of the strongest cooperative movements in Africa, with cooperatives controlling approximately 43 percent of the GDP. Savings and credit cooperatives have experienced remarkable growth, mobilizing more than 230 billion shillings in savings. Overall, Kenyan cooperatives have contributed significantly to employment, poverty alleviation, and financial inclusion.

In Ivory Coast, cooperatives play a major role in the agricultural sector, comprising more than 90 percent of cooperatives in the country (Holmén, 1990). There are more than 5000 cooperatives, mostly in coffee, cocoa, and cotton. These cooperatives have been instrumental in protecting farmer interests, improving market access, ensuring fair prices, and providing key services. They continue to contribute to rural development and agricultural growth.

In Ethiopia, while cooperative-like institutions have ancient roots, the modern cooperative movement emerged in the 1950s (Mojo, Fischer & Degefa, 2017). Cooperatives have focused on agriculture, savings and credit, consumer goods, and handicrafts. They have enabled smallholder farmers to access critical resources and services to enhance productivity and incomes. Cooperatives have also facilitated community insurance schemes and social support networks.

Cooperatives in Europe

Cooperatives in Europe have a long and rich history, with a significant presence in various sectors of the economy. In the European Union (EU) alone, there are approximately 250,000 cooperatives, collectively owned by 163 million citizens, which amounts to about one-third of the EU population (Gijselinckx & Bussels, 2014). These cooperatives employ a substantial workforce of in the region of 5.4 million people, highlighting their significant contribution to employment and economic growth.

One of the notable aspects of cooperatives in Europe is their substantial market share in various industries across countries. For instance, in the agricultural sector, cooperatives hold a significant market share in several countries (Gonzalez, 2018). In the Netherlands, cooperatives account for an impressive 83 percent of the agricultural industry. Finland follows closely with 79 percent, while Italy and France have 55 percent and 50 percent respectively. In forestry, cooperatives hold 60 percent market share in Sweden and 31 percent in Finland. In banking, France leads at 50 percent market share, followed by Cyprus, Finland, Austria, and Germany. Retail cooperatives also have a strong presence, with 36 percent market share in Finland and 20 percent in Sweden. This dominance across sectors demonstrates the pivotal role of cooperatives in ensuring fairer distribution of wealth and improving working conditions.

The cooperative movement in the United Kingdom has its roots in the Rochdale Equitable Pioneers Co-operative Society, established in 1844 during the Industrial Revolution. The founders were motivated by the need to address poverty, low wages, poor working conditions, and exploitative practices. The Rochdale Principles laid the foundation for modern cooperativism based on voluntary membership, democratic control, and service over profit. The Industrial and Provident Societies Act of 1852 provided a legal framework for English cooperatives, further facilitating their growth.

In France, the cooperative movement dates back to the mid-nineteenth century, driven by the desire to improve conditions during industrialization (Gijselinckx & Bussels, 2014). The country has a diverse history of cooperation in agriculture, finance, worker, and consumer cooperatives. The General Law on Cooperatives of 1947 established a framework for different French cooperative types. Despite challenges, the movement has contributed to employment growth surpassing the overall economy.

In Italy, there are approximately 39,600 cooperatives, employing more than 1.5 million people and boasting 12.6 million members across industries like agriculture, banking, and trade (Borzaga et al., 2014). Italian cooperatives play a crucial role in development, social inclusion, and regional cohesion.

In Spain, there are over 20,000 cooperatives with nearly 300,000 employees and more than 7 million members (Lenhoff, Niederländer & Quintana Cocolina, 2015). While Portugal's movement has been shaped by the UK, Germany's traces back to the 1840s with credit cooperatives playing a key role. Both have seen recent growth in new sectors like education, health, and information and communications technology (ICT).

Finland has over 4,000 cooperatives, with most of the population being members, and dominance in retail, banking, and insurance (Gonzalez, 2018). Poland's cooperative history predates Rochdale, with the Społem union emerging in the early 1900s, though facing challenges under Communist rule. Recently cooperatives have grown around the social economy and addressing unemployment.

Cooperatives in Asia and Pacific Region

The Asia-Pacific region has a robust presence of cooperatives and mutual enterprises (CMEs), with forty-eight CMEs featured in the Top 300 global rankings by turnover/ GDP per capita, reflecting their economic influence and purchasing power. Six of these CMEs, including Indian Farmers Fertiliser Cooperative (IFFCO) and Gujarat Co-operative Milk Marketing Federation from India, Zenkyoren, Zen-Noh, and Nippon Life from Japan, and Nonghyup (NACF) from the Republic of Korea, rank among the global top ten (Beamish, 1997; Sethumadhavan, 2020; Iyer et al., 2021).

Cooperatives in the Asia-Pacific have thrived across various sectors, making significant contributions to regional economic development. In agriculture and food industries, six of the top ten cooperatives engaged in processing and marketing agricultural goods are from the region (Rajasekhar et al., 2020). The industry and utilities sector features worker and user cooperatives in construction and infrastructure management for public services like electricity, gas, and water (Beamish, 1997). The insurance sector has four out of the top ten cooperatives, all from a single country, reflecting the strength of mutual organizations owned and democratically controlled by insured customers (Wahn, 2023). In financial services, one of the top ten global cooperatives is from this region, representing cooperative banks and credit unions that provide financial services democratically controlled by members (Iyer et al., 2021).

Cooperatives in education, health, and social work sectors are also prominent, with three out of the top ten rankings belonging to the Asia-Pacific region. These cooperatives include consumer, producer, and multistakeholder organizations that offer cost-effective community health care and social services (Rajasekhar et al., 2020).

China has a long history of cooperatives, contributing significantly to rural economies through supply and marketing cooperatives, rural credit, and e-commerce initiatives (Dongre & Paranjothi, 2020). India's cooperatives are crucial in sustaining rural livelihoods, operating in agriculture, dairy, forestry, fisheries, and more, while ensuring economic stability in rural regions (Sethumadhavan, 2020).

Pakistan has a cooperative movement focused on addressing socio-economic challenges, particularly in housing and finance (Rajasekhar et al., 2020). Iran's cooperative sector, shaped by traditional cooperation practices, was formalized after the 1979 Revolution and recognized as the third economic sector in the country's Constitutional Law, alongside public and private sectors (Rajasekhar et al., 2020).

Mongolia has seen cooperative growth since the 1990s democratic reforms, with the government promoting cooperatives to achieve Sustainable Development Goals (Rajasekhar et al., 2020). In Japan, cooperatives play a pivotal role in agriculture, forestry, and fisheries, supporting rural economies and extending into sectors like finance, insurance, and consumer services (Wahn, 2023; Beamish, 1997).

Australia's Cooperatives and Mutual Enterprises (CMEs) contribute to the national economy across financial services, agribusiness, health insurance, and housing sectors, promoting social inclusion and sustainable development (Mandigma & Badoc-Gonzales, 2022).

Cooperatives in the Asia-Pacific region are instrumental in driving economic growth, social development, and community empowerment. They operate across diverse sectors, ensuring sustainable livelihoods and lifting communities. Case studies from China, India, Pakistan, Iran, Mongolia, Japan, and Australia demonstrate the broad role and accomplishments of cooperatives in these countries (Rajasekhar et al., 2020; Dongre & Paranjothi, 2020; Mandigma & Badoc-Gonzales, 2022; Wahn, 2023; Iyer et al., 2021; Sethumadhavan, 2020; Beamish, 1997). The continued evolution and adaptation of the cooperative movement position it as a powerful tool for inclusive and sustainable development throughout the Asia-Pacific region and beyond.

Conclusion

In conclusion, cooperative ownership represents a powerful alternative to traditional business models, fostering economic democracy, and empowering communities. By putting people at the center and prioritizing their needs over profit, cooperatives create a more inclusive and sustainable economy. The principles of cooperation, such as voluntary membership, democratic governance, and equitable distribution of benefits, ensure that all stakeholders have a voice and a share in the organization's success.

Cooperative ownership has shown its potential across various sectors, including agriculture, retail, finance, energy, and technology. From farmer cooperatives improving market access for small-scale producers to platform cooperatives challenging the dominance of venture capital-funded platforms, these enterprises demonstrate that an alternative economic model is possible. They prioritize social and environmental well-being, providing fair wages, job security, and community development.

Moreover, cooperatives promote cooperation over competition, fostering solidarity and collaboration among members. They encourage the sharing of knowledge, resources, and risks, creating a supportive network that enhances the resilience and sustainability of the cooperative movement.

However, cooperative ownership also faces challenges. Access to capital, legal frameworks, and public awareness are among the key barriers that cooperatives must overcome. Supportive policies and financial institutions that understand the unique needs of cooperatives are crucial to their success and growth. Additionally, raising awareness about the benefits and values of cooperatives is essential to encourage more individuals and communities to explore this alternative form of ownership.

In conclusion, cooperative ownership offers a pathway toward a more equitable and sustainable economy. By embracing democratic governance, collective decision-making, and shared prosperity, cooperatives empower individuals, promote social cohesion, and address pressing societal challenges. As we navigate complex economic and social landscapes, it is imperative to recognize the potential of cooperative ownership and work toward creating an enabling environment for its growth. By doing so, we can build a more just and inclusive society where the principles of cooperation and solidarity guide our economic interactions.

References

Ajates, R. (2020). An integrated conceptual framework for the study of agricultural cooperatives: From repolitisation to cooperative sustainability. *Journal of Rural Studies, 78*, 467–479.

Albæk, S., & Schultz, C. (1998). On the relative advantage of cooperatives. *Economics Letters, 59*(3), 397–401.

Altman, M. (2009). History and theory of cooperatives. In H. Anheier, & S. Toepler (eds), *International Encyclopedia of Civil Society* (pp. 563–570). New York: Springer.

Bajo, C. S. (2017). Research on cooperatives in Latina America, an overview of the state of the art and contributions. *Rev. Int. Co-operation, 104*, 3–14.

Barton, D., Boland, M., Chaddad, F. & Eversull, E. (2011). Current challenges in financing agricultural cooperatives. *Choices*, 26(3), 181–184.

Beamish, P. W. (1997). *Cooperative Strategies: Asian Pacific Perspectives* (No. 3). San Francisco: Lexington Books.

Bietti, E., Etxeberria, A., Mannan, M., & Wong, J. (2021). Data cooperatives in Europe: A legal and empirical investigation. *White Paper Created as Part of The New School's Platform Cooperativism Consortium and Harvard University's Berkman Klein Center for Internet & Society Research Sprint.*

Bijman, J., Pyykkonen, P., & Ollila, P. (2014). Transnationalization of agricultural cooperatives in Europe. *DQ, 168.*

Billiet, A., Dufays, F., Friedel, S., & Staessens, M. (2021). The resilience of the cooperative model: How do cooperatives deal with the COVID-19 crisis? *Strategic Change, 30*(2), 99–108.

Birchall, J. (2004). *Cooperatives and the Millennium Development Goals.*Geneva: International Labour Organization.

Boland, M. A. & Barton, D.G. (2013). Overview of research on cooperative finance. *Journal of Cooperatives,* 27(1142-2016-92777), 1–14.

Borzaga, C., Bodini, R., Carini, C., Depedri, S., Galera, G., & Salvatori, G. (2014). *Europe in Transition: The Role of Social Cooperatives and Social Enterprises*, (Working Paper n. 69|14). Euricse Working Papers, pp. 1–17.

Camargo Benavides, A. F., & Ehrenhard, M. (2021). Rediscovering the cooperative enterprise: A systematic review of current topics and avenues for future research. *VOLUNTAS: International Journal of Voluntary and Nonprofit Organizations, 32*(5), 964–978.

Cornforth, C. (2004). The governance of cooperatives and mutual associations: A paradox perspective. *Annals of Public and Cooperative Economics, 75*(1), 11–32.

Cracogna, D. (2013). The framework law for the cooperatives in Latin America. In *International Handbook of Cooperative Law* (pp. 165–186). Berlin: Springer Berlin Heidelberg.

Cuevas, C. E. & Buchenau, J. (2018). *Financial cooperatives: Issues in regulation supervision, and institutional strengthening.* Washington, DC: World Bank.

Cummings, S. L. (1999). Developing Cooperatives as a Job Creation Strategy for Low-Income Workers. *NYU Review of Law & Social Change*, 25(2), 181–211

Curl, J. (2012). *For all the People: Uncovering the Hidden History of Cooperation, Cooperative Movements, and Communalism in America.* Oakland: PM Press.

Deng, W., Hendrikse, G. & Liang, Q. (2021). Internal social capital and the life cycle of agricultural cooperatives. *Journal of Evolutionary Economics*, 31(1), 301–323.

de Peuter, G., & Dyer-Witheford, N. (2010). Commons and cooperatives. *Affinities: A Journal of Radical Theory, Culture, and Action*, 4(1), 30–56.

Dias, M. D. O., Krein, J., Streh, E., & Vilhena, J. B. (2018). Agriculture cooperatives in Brazil: Cotribá Case. *International Journal of Management, Technology and Engineering*, 8, 2100–2110.

Dickstein, C. (1991). The Promise and Problems of Worker Cooperatives: A Survey Article. *Journal of Planning Literature*, 6(1), 16–33.

Dobrohoczki, R. (2006). Cooperatives as social policy means for creating social cohesion in communities. *Journal of Rural Cooperation*, 34(886-2016-64554), 139–159.

Dongre, Y., & Paranjothi, T. (2020). Asia Pacific cooperatives responding to Covid-19 crisis. In Rajasekhar, D., Manjula, R. & Paranjothi, T. (eds.), *Cooperatives and Social Innovation: Experiences from the Asia Pacific Region* (pp. 271–283). Singapore: Springer.

Eckert, A. (2007). Useful instruments of participation? Local government and cooperatives in Tanzania, 1940s to 1970s'. *The International Journal of African Historical Studies*, 40(1), 97–118.

Eckstein, J. (2016). Sociocracy: An organization model for large-scale agile development. In Peggy, G. and Taylor, K. (eds.), *Proceedings of the Scientific Workshop Proceedings of XP2016* (pp. 1–5). New York: Association for Computing Machinery.

Fairbairn, B. (2016). History of cooperatives. In Merrett, C. D. and Walzer, N. (eds.), *Cooperatives and Local Development* (pp. 23–51). New York: Routledge.

Fakude, G. (2016). A Review of Possible Emerging Theoretical Debates and New Interdisciplinary Perspectives on the Cooperative Movement in Africa. In Okem, A. E. (ed.), *Theoretical and Empirical Studies on Cooperatives: Lessons for Cooperatives in Africa* (pp. 15–27). Durban: Springer.

Fernandez-Guadaño, J., Lopez-Millan, M., & Sarria-Pedroza, J. (2020). Cooperative entrepreneurship model for sustainable development. *Sustainability*, 12(13), 5462.

Fulton, M., Heit, J., & Fairbairn, B. (2006). The changing landscape of cooperatives in North America. Paper presented at *XIV International Economic History Congress*, Helsinki, Finland, 21–25 August 2006.

Ghebremichael, B. (2013). The role of cooperatives in empowering women. *Journal of Business Management & Social Science Research*, 2(5), 51–54.

Gijselinckx, C., & Bussels, M. (2014). Farmers' cooperatives in Europe: Social and historical determinants of cooperative membership in agriculture. *Annals of Public and Cooperative Economics*, 85(4), 509–530.

Gonzalez, R. A. (2018). *Farmers' Cooperatives and Sustainable Food Systems in Europe*. London: Routledge.

Guinnane, T. W. (2001). Cooperatives as information machines: German rural credit cooperatives, 1883–1914. *The Journal of Economic History*, 61(2), 366–389.

Guzmán, C., Santos, F. J., & Barroso, M. D. L. O. (2020). Analysing the links between cooperative principles, entrepreneurial orientation and performance. *Small Business Economics*, 55, 1075–1089.

Hamer, J. H. (1981). Preconditions and limits in the Formation of Associations: The Self-help and Cooperative Movements in sub-Saharan Africa. *African Studies Review*, 24(1), 113–132.

Höhler, J., & Kühl, R. (2018). Dimensions of member heterogeneity in cooperatives and their impact on organization—a literature review. *Annals of Public and Cooperative Economics*, 89(4), 697–712.

Holmén, H. (1990). *State, Cooperatives and Development in Africa*. The Scandinavian Institute of African Studies, Uppsala.

Hoppe, T., & Warbroek, B. (2021). Agency of citizen collectives in sustainable transitions: The case of renewable energy cooperatives in Europe. In *Research Handbook of Sustainability Agency* (pp. 180–196). Edward Elgar Publishing Ltd.

International Cooperative Alliance (n.d.). *ICA: 125 yers, 4 voices*. Available at: https://ica.coop/sites/default/files/2021-11/125%20years%2C%204%20voices%20-%20spreads.pdf (accessed February 17, 2024).

Iyer, B., Gopal, G., Dave, M., & Singh, S. (2021). Centering cooperatives and cooperative identity within the social and solidarity economy: Views from the Asia-Pacific cooperative apexes and federations. *Journal of Co-Operative Organization and Management*, 9(2), 100145.

Jackall, R., & Levin, H. M. (eds). (2021). *Worker Cooperatives in America*. California: University of California Press.

Karakas, C. (2019). *Cooperatives: Characteristics, Activities, Status, Challenges*.

Koljatic, M., & Silva, M. (2011). Alliances in SMEs and cooperatives involved in business with low income sectors in Latin America. *Innovar*, *21*(40), 127–136.

Kyazze, L. M., Nsereko, I. & Nkote, I. (2020). Cooperative practices and non-financial performance of savings and credit cooperative societies. *International Journal of Ethics and Systems*, 36(3), 411–425.

Lehnhoff, D. J., Niederländer, K., & Quintana Cocolina, C. (2015). The power of cooperation: Cooperatives Europe key statistics 2015. Cooperatives Europe. Available at: https://coopseurope.coop/wp-content/uploads/files/The%20power%20of%20Cooperation%20-%20Cooperatives%20Europe%20key%20statistics%202015.pdf (accessed February 17, 2024).

Mandigma, M. B. S., & Badoc-Gonzales, B. P. (2022). Tax exemptions of cooperatives in the Philippines and in other countries: A comparative study. *Review of Integrative Business and Economics Research*, *11*, 144–163.

McLeod, A. (2006). *Types of Cooperatives*. NW Cooperative Development Centre. Retrieved from https://nwcdc.coop/wp-content/uploads/2012/09/CSS01-Types-of-Coops.pdf (accessed February 17, 2024).

Meira, D. (2019). The Portuguese social solidarity cooperative versus the PECOL general interest cooperative. *International Journal of Cooperative Law*, *2*, 57–71.

Mercer, T. W. (Ed.) (1922). *Dr William King and the Co-operator: 1828–1830*. Manchester: Co-operative Union Ltd. Available at: https://cooperativismodecredito.coop.br/wp-content/uploads/2021/03/William-King-The-Co-operator.pdf (accessed February 17, 2024).

Mojo, D., Fischer, C. & Degefa, T. (2017), The determinants and economic impacts of membership in coffee farmer co-operatives: recent evidence from rural Ethiopia. Journal of Rural Studies, 50, 84–94.

Mori, P. A. (2014). Community and cooperation: The evolution of cooperatives towards new models of citizens' democratic participation in public services provision. *Annals of Public and Cooperative Economics*, *85*(3), 327–352.

Muñoz, P., Kimmitt, J., & Dimov, D. (2020). Packs, troops and herds: Prosocial cooperatives and innovation in the new normal. *Journal of Management Studies*, *57*(3), 470–504.

Noble, M., & Ross, C. (2021). From principles to participation: "The statement on the cooperative identity" and higher education co-operatives. *Journal of Co-operative Organization and Management*, *9*(2), 100146.

Novković, S., & Šimleša, D. (2023). Measuring transformational impact of cooperatives. In *Humanistic Governance in Democratic Organizations: The Cooperative Difference* (pp. 423–448). Springer International Publishing.

Okem, A. E. (2016). *Theoretical and empirical studies on cooperatives: Lessons for cooperatives in South Africa*. Switzerland: Springer.

Olsen, E. K. (2013). The relative survival of worker cooperatives and barriers to their creation. In Kruse, D. (ed.), *Sharing ownership, profits, and decision-making in the 21st century* (Vol. 14, pp. 83–107). UK: Emerald Group Publishing Limited.

Pitman, L. (2018). *History of Cooperatives in the United States: An Overview*. Center for Cooperatives, University of Wisconsin. Accessible at: https://resources.uwcc.wisc.edu/History_of_Cooperatives.pdf (accessed February 17, 2024).

Porter, P. K. & Scully, G. W. (1987). Economic Efficiency in Co-operatives. *The Journal of Law and Economics*, 30(2), 489–512.

Rajasekhar, D., Manjula, R., & Paranjothi, T. (2020). *Cooperatives and Social Innovation: Experiences from the Asia Pacific Region* (pp. 1–13). Springer Singapore.

Robertson, B. J. (2015). *Holacracy: The Revolutionary Management System that Abolishes Hierarchy*. London: Penguin UK.

Rothschild, J (2009). Workers' cooperatives and social enterprise: a forgotten road to equity and democracy. *American Behavioral Scientist*, 52(7), 1023–1041.

Sethumadhavan, T. P. (2020). Successful cooperatives across Asia: ULCCS—the icon of successful cooperatives in India. In Altman et al. (eds.), *Waking the Asian Pacific Co-Operative Potential* (pp. 325–333). Academic Press.

Sexton, R. J. (1986). The Formation of Cooperatives: A Game-Theoretic Approach with Implications for Cooperative Finance, Decision Making, and Stability. *American Journal of Agricultural Economics*, 68(2), 214–225.

Shapiro-Garza, E., King, D., Rivera-Aguirre, A., Wang, S., & Finley-Lezcano, J. (2020). A participatory framework for feasibility assessments of climate change resilience strategies for smallholders: Lessons from coffee cooperatives in Latin America. *International Journal of Agricultural Sustainability*, 18(1), 21–34.

Stryjan, Y. (1994). Understanding cooperatives: The reproduction perspective. *Annals of Public and Cooperative Economics*, 65(1), 59–80.

Sutton, S. A. (2019). Cooperative cities: municipal support for worker cooperatives in the United States. *Journal of Urban Affairs*, 41(8), 1081–1102.

Tainio, R. (1999). Strategic change in the evolution of co-operatives. *The Finnish Journal of Business Economics*, 4(1999), 484–490.

Vásquez-León, M. (2010). Walking the tightrope: Latin American agricultural cooperatives and small-farmer participation in global markets. *Latin American Perspectives*, 37(6), 3–11.

Wahn, I. L. (2023). The moralities of consumption and interactions among consumer cooperatives in East Asia. *Journal of Rural Studies*, 100, 103018.

Wanyama, F. (2009). *Surviving liberalization: the cooperative movement in Kenya*, CoopAFRICA Working Paper No. 10, International Labour Organization, Dar es Salaam.

Williams, R. C. (2016). *The Cooperative Movement: Globalization from Below*. New York: Routledge.

Wittman, H., Dennis, J., & Pritchard, H. (2017). Beyond the market? New agrarianism and cooperative farmland access in North America. *Journal of Rural Studies*, 53, 303–316.

Zeuli, K. A., Cropp, R., & Schaars, M. A. (2004). *Cooperatives: Principles and Practices in the 21st Century*. Madison: Cooperative Extension Publishing.

Zeuli, K. & Radel, J. (2005). Cooperatives as a community development strategy: Linking theory and practice. *Journal of Regional Analysis and Policy*, 35(1), 43–54.

Chapter 4
Public Innovation: Technology and Change

Introduction

Across the public sector—spanning federal, state, and local governments—new technologies are emerging to fundamentally transform how public services and programs are developed, implemented, and delivered to citizens. Rapid advances in areas like cloud computing, data analytics, artificial intelligence (AI) and automation, blockchain, the Internet of Things (IoT) and more are catalyzing waves of innovation across vital areas of governance. The implications for efficiency, transparency, collaboration, and public–private partnerships are profound.

Consequently, governments now have access to state-of-the-art technology tools to enhance core objectives around public welfare, safety, sustainability, engagement, and equity. The expanded possibilities also enable pursuing innovative social economy models, with greater cooperation across government agencies, businesses, nonprofit groups, and grassroots communities. There is momentum around participatory governance, co-creation of solutions, platforms enhancing accessibility and agility, and decentralized systems empowering communities.

These technology and innovation trends have the power to redefine public benefit in the twenty-first-century digital era. Realizing this potential though requires overcoming systemic institutional barriers, funding limitations, skill gaps, and difficulties transitioning from legacy systems. Furthermore, concerns around privacy, security, inclusion, and ethics will also shape the trajectory of social impacts from public technology innovation.

While innovations are emerging across different levels of government functions, adoption is inconsistent and remains in early stages for many organizations and communities. However, investment and prioritization are accelerating rapidly. State and local governments though often face more acute budget and talent barriers relative to federal agencies. But mechanisms like the Mayor's Challenge from Bloomberg Philanthropy, or non-profit Code for America's public partnerships are spurring experimentation through funding, resources, and visibility of success cases.

One major impact area of technology adoption involves online government services and digital interactions, collectively referred to as e-government services. During the COVID-19 pandemic necessity led to the accelerated scaling of remote access and virtual delivery alternatives for public services across transportation, healthcare, education, social welfare programs, small business support, and more.

Open government data programs make non-sensitive public sector data accessible to citizens, technologists, researchers, and private sector innovators to drive more inclusive policymaking while unlocking economic opportunities. Data categories span transportation, public spending, health indicators, education metrics, and more. The impact

https://doi.org/10.1515/9783111080147-004

on civic innovation ecosystems is increased experimentation and applications development in areas like transit, public safety, environmental tracking, and access to community services. Startups and grassroots technologists are also leveraging publicly available data to build apps offering two-way community engagement and closing gaps in public provisioning.

These cutting-edge innovations bring risks and regulatory challenges. The expansion of emerging technologies raises complex questions around ethics, security, capability development, and digital divides in access and impacts from new systems. Still, the scope for decentralized citizen-centric solutions, democratized policymaking through open data flows, and harnessing market innovations for public benefit points the roadmap ahead for technology-enabled social economy models. The following sections will dive deeper into the current landscape, specific cases, and key challenges that the public sector must address to successfully leverage this new innovation paradigm.

New Trends in Public Innovation

Public sector innovation and the adoption of new technologies is rapidly transforming governments around the world. There is a "promise of digital government" to leverage these innovations to significantly enhance public sector performance, service delivery, and citizen engagement. A major priority for governments today is developing online portals and digital services to improve efficiency and better meet citizen needs. These systems allow streamlining operations, automating processes, and providing services through convenient digital channels (Drigas and Koukianakis, 2009). There has been rapid growth in e-government globally in recent years (Yang, 2017), but there remain gaps between policy ambitions and actual usage that must be addressed.

Citizen satisfaction and demand are essential drivers of successful e-government services. There is a growing preference among citizens for local governments to integrate and work across emerging online, mobile, and social media platforms (Wirtz and Kurtz, 2016a). In e-government services in Bangladesh, for instance, citizens were more satisfied when using systems that offered more completeness in services and reliability in transactions (Karim, 2015). Yet there are also growing issues of "multi-dimensional digital divide" associated with disparities in access to e-government services stemming from inequality in internet connectivity, device availability, digital literacy, trust, and more that constrain usage of digital public services (Okunola et al., 2017).

Overcoming these barriers through public access facilities and training programs is vital so that underprivileged groups are not left behind by the digital transformation. There are also often urban–rural divides to address, as Hujran et al. (2023) discuss in proposing the "SMARTGOV" extended maturity model to systematically guide governments in sustainably developing services tailored for disadvantaged communities. As the possibilities rapidly grow for public sector digital innovation, keeping the focus on inclusion and meeting all citizens where they are at will be critical for next-generation e-government success. Careful assessment of offerings and public demand along with user experience optimizations and multi-channel service delivery can help achieve ubiquitous, satisfactory access (Patergiannaki & Pollalis, 2023)

Open government data programs have likewise proliferated recently, aiming to stimulate economic activity and improve lives by freely sharing non-sensitive public sector information. In the Azores context lingering gaps remain between policymaker aims in launching initiatives and public servant readiness to implement them effectively, highlighting the need for improved change management and internal capacity building around utilizing open data (Garcia 2022). There are also ongoing debates around the impacts of open data programs, noting that while proponents tout gains for transparency, innovation, and data-driven decision making, critics argue that tangible effects remain limited thus far (Attard et al., 2015). Open data initiatives and policy must evolve to more effectively spur value creation—government agencies simply releasing more datasets will not alone guarantee usage or benefits (see Dawes et al., 2016).

An "ecosystem approach" bringing together all stakeholders, facilitating participatory design processes, and growing data literacy and analytics skills is vital to translate the promise of open data into meaningful progress. Other cutting-edge areas show promise in driving change through open data applications, from participatory planning and "open city" initiatives fostering more inclusive governance while better addressing community needs (Myros, 2023), to powerful emerging use cases in domains like agriculture (Wolfert et al., 2017), healthcare, and environmental sustainability. Ultimately, for open government data programs to achieve transformational impacts, policy evolution toward "open by default" models will be key (Sieber & Johnson, 2015). This entails normalizing practices of proactively publishing data while developing the associated technological infrastructure, administrative processes, and partnerships to unlock the value of publicly available information.

Smart cities represent an important area where innovation in sensors, real-time data, and interconnected technology allows dramatic enhancement of how urban environments function. This includes intelligent transport systems, energy efficient infrastructure, sustainable construction, and digital government service delivery (Falk et al., 2017). Barcelona's smart city model has set the pace globally, seamlessly integrating emerging technologies with legacy systems to provide better living standards while optimizing resource usage. High costs of upgrading physical infrastructure and integrating complex systems still pose barriers for many cities, however. Governance innovation through public–private partnerships can help overcome budget constraints while technical standardization and open digital platforms allow easier scaling of smart city systems.

There are also risks inherent in over-reliance on technology solutions for urban issues while losing sight of core citizen needs and well-being. Fostering truly "smart" and sustainable transformation requires factoring inclusive participatory design and equitable access into development processes (Myros, 2023). As technology continues permeating all aspects of urban life in coming years, balanced governance approaches that enable widespread resident engagement alongside expert input will be vital. Integrated cybersecurity and privacy frameworks likewise need to be implemented as information sharing expands between Internet of Things ecosystems. If the promise of data-driven urban innovation is to be fully realized, smart city development must envision metropolitan areas as diverse, internationally connected hubs that embrace technological change to elevate human welfare.

Stepping back, the exponential pace of technology change compels rapid, society-wide digital transformation in communities and institutions globally. For public sector agencies, this mandates holistic modernization initiatives rethinking processes, data practices, cyber defenses, staff capabilities, and service delivery according to visionary frameworks like the SMARTGOV model (Hujran et al., 2023). Critical foundations span high-speed, reliable digital infrastructure seamlessly accessible across devices (Wirtz & Kurtz, 2016b), to government data strategy centered on continual enhancement and creative application rather than just storage (Dawes et al., 2016). Maintaining this digital-first orientation across operations will allow public agencies to keep pace with societal technological advancement.

Transforming organizational culture is equally crucial as upgrading technology systems, ensuring staff have the mindsets and skills to constantly adapt (Garcia, 2022). Beyond upskilling administrators in core technical competencies, change management to align employee expectations and incentives with digitally powered working models is essential. If governments are to take advantage of exponential technology changes to benefit citizens, drive innovation, and elevate democratic participation, the focus must remain on inclusion and human-centric design. Technological change paired with this reimagined, equitable vision of governance's role can fulfill the promises of digital transformation in enhancing lives, economy, and democracy.

KEY THINKER: Tim O'Reilly

Tim O'Reilly is an influential author, publisher, and open-source software advocate who has helped shape the evolution of the internet and digital technology over the past few decades. Born in Ireland in 1954 but raised in California from a young age, O'Reilly studied classics at Harvard before embarking on a career combining technical writing and publishing. In the 1980s he founded O'Reilly Media, which became a leading publisher of computer manuals and books helping popularize new technologies.

A seminal moment was O'Reilly's 1993 decision to put his publishing catalog online as one of the first web portals, the Global Network Navigator. This pioneering move into digital distribution and leveraging the early internet's potential established his credentials as a forward-thinking innovator. The subsequent growing success of O'Reilly Media through the 1990s confirmed the promise of technology-focused media in the dawning digital age.

Another important contribution stems from O'Reilly's advocacy for open-source software in the late 1990s as frameworks like Linux and Apache were emerging. He tells the story of organizing a freeware summit in 1998 following Netscape's decision to release its browser code, bringing together key figures to brainstorm around more effectively propagating the open, collaborative development model. From this was born the "open source" branding, which O'Reilly promoted as a friendlier label for business and marking a major movement in software development methodology.

As he further championed decentralized, transparent, and freely reusable technology, written about in books like *Open Sources: Voices from the Open Source Revolution* (DiBona & Ockman, 1999), O'Reilly considers open source inseparable from the organic growth of the internet. He connects this back to foundational protocols like Transmission Control Protocol (TCP)/Internet Protocol (IP) and platforms like sendmail and Perl that were collaboratively built. For O'Reilly, open development or "architecture of participation" networks represent a paradigm shift from closed proprietary systems to more generative technological ecosystems unconstrained by traditional limitations.

After the dot com crash wiped out many speculative ventures built on over-hyped expectations around the 1990s internet revolution, O'Reilly sought to reignite enthusiasm by identifying the technologies and principles driving the web's ongoing evolution. In 2004 his company hosted an executive conference centered on mapping emerging usage patterns and business models leveraging user-generated content, data-driven services, and online network effects.

O'Reilly and his team focused on harnessing "collective intelligence", turning the web into an engaging participatory platform. They highlighted innovative companies like Google, Amazon, eBay, and rising social media tapping these currents and contrasted them against failed ideas from the dot com era. From this, his colleague Dale Dougherty coined the "Web 2.0" phrase, which O'Reilly then popularized as the spirit of the internet reborn post-bubble, centered on engagement not just transactions.

While initially vague, the Web 2.0 umbrella concept provided a compass for where the technology was headed and what sorts of creativity it could enable. It reframed the internet as a constantly evolving ecosystem of sites, services, and communities built on network effects and user participation. O'Reilly sees Web 2.0 as people transforming from passive consumers to "prosumers" actively co-creating value, with technology reflecting a supporting role. This ethos of democratized contribution and platforms leveraging collective intelligence has become pervasive in today's social and participatory web.

Lately O'Reilly has focused attention on how Web 2.0 principles can transform government and public services, a model he terms "government as platform." This builds on his framing of the internet as an "operating system" composed of open and freely recombinable building blocks. By adopting a platform paradigm, he envisions more effective, responsive, and inclusive governance emerging.

The core metaphor extends how the underlying infrastructures and policies of states can empower people to self-organize and collaborate toward resolving shared problems. It likewise echoes his advocacy of open data providing raw material for civic innovation. O'Reilly considers applying the collaborative lessons and accountability of open-source software to remake sclerotic bureaucracies as agile "gov 2.0" ecosystems. Citizens shift from passive clients to empowered "produsers" directly shaping public infrastructure decisions through transparency and participation.

Critics argue this overly technocratic model undermines politics by positioning complex human issues as essentially engineering challenges with optimized solutions. However, O'Reilly believes opening channels for broader input and exchange can enhance democracy's functioning. Much as how the early web decentralization unlocked innovation, carefully transforming policy processes with open data feedback and collective participation may raise collective intelligence applied toward the public good.

Looking across his influential career, Tim O'Reilly has made several major contributions cementing his reputation as a notable technology commentator and advocate shaping our digital age. His prescient business and publishing decisions, conceptual framings like Web 2.0, and championship of collaborative open-source models helped introduce the promise of emerging technologies to wider audiences. O'Reilly urges technology be designed and governed more as an enabler uplifting knowledge exchange, political participation, and the public welfare rather than primarily for commercial extraction.

As the founder and leader of O'Reilly Media, his imprint powered the explosion in skills sharing and decentralizing knowledge critical for software and internet innovation. By identifying and explaining key tech trends, his influence on developers, entrepreneurs, and policymakers propelled paradigm-shifting advances like open source and the participatory social web. Today his visions connecting open government data, collective civic problem-solving, and platform-based societal organization continue aiming to realize greater humanity-enhancing potential. Overall, O'Reilly's prolific commentary and advocacy centered on open, democratic systems hint at farther horizons for technology loosely connecting people, organizations, and ideas to maximize collaborative creation advancing the common good.

Public Sector and the Social Economy

The social economy refers to community-centered economic activities oriented toward social objectives and needs rather than profit maximization. Encompassing co-operatives, non-profit organizations, social enterprises, community projects, and ethical banking, the social economy prioritizes values of solidarity, participation, inclusion, and sustainability. It represents an "alternative economic space" to mainstream capitalist markets and traditional public sector models (Amin, Cameron & Hudson, 2003). Governments play a vital role in fostering the growth and impact of the social economy. Their policy choices and programs supporting community wealth building initiatives dramatically shape outcomes. This essay will analyze the key functions for the public sector in cultivating the social economy, from funding mechanisms to governance frameworks promoting democratized local development.

Conceptually carving out space between traditional private and public realms illustrates the unique social innovations emerging, often at local levels (Neamtan, 2005). Quebec, for instance, formally recognizes "social economy enterprises" like non-profits and co-operatives as distinct from conventional businesses, with tailored assistance. Explicit recognition—both symbolically and through dedicated institutions—affords greater visibility and understanding of values-based economic activity for community benefit (Mendell & Neamtan, 2010). Definitional clarity also allows appropriate targeting of investments, tax incentives, programs, and partnerships to bolster these organizations.

Beyond rhetorical and conceptual recognition, governments enable the social economy's growth through legislative support across areas from finance to governance. Illustrate the dramatic expansion of Spain's social economy driven by national regulatory reform, administrative capacity building, streamlined contracting processes, and easier access to capital resources (Chaves Ávila & Gallego-Bono, 2020). The EU has also begun spearheading a range of supportive policies and structures (Monzón Campos & Chaves Ávila, 2017) including public procurement frameworks favoring social enterprises.

Well-designed regulations tackle barriers facing social economy organizations while ensuring accountability. Examples include community interest company structures balancing profit distribution, bespoke legal forms for co-operatives enhancing worker participation rights, and mandated representation of stakeholder interests on directing boards. Most fundamentally, legislation protecting the non-economic social objectives and democratic process principles central to the identity of these organizations enables their sustainability (Vaillancourt, 2019).

Access to financial resources represents a perennial challenge for cash-strapped entities like non-profits or co-operatives locked out of mainstream funding channels. That's where the power of public sector purse strings comes in. Strategic investment of grants, loans, and equity-type hybrid capital offer lifelines sustaining social economy organization development, while aligning budgets with priority public policy areas (Leyden, 2016).

In the case of Quebec, where pooled public funding sources like the Chantier trust finance affordable housing initiatives, local development projects, and social enterprise startups. Meanwhile procurement policies reserving portions of public contracts for not-for-profit providers enhance revenue streams. Financial engineering arrangements also allow social purpose organizations to benefit from credit enhancement tools and flexible debt instruments tailored to their circumstances (Chaves Ávila & Gallego-Bono, 2020). Beyond direct funding, governments back creative social finance through devices like social impact bonds, ethical investment tax reliefs, community shares, or local currencies that stimulate alternative grassroots economic circuits (Amin, 2009). Manifold funding mechanisms let public sector resources reach and energize on-the-ground development aligned to democratically determined priorities.

Rather than top-down intervention, the social economy grows best through collaborative local partnerships backed by public institutions. New approaches, like community wealth building, support place-based development strategies that address needs identified directly by residents (Guinan & O'Neill, 2019). This demands an inter-linked ecosystem approach engaging governments, businesses, civil society groups, ac-ademia, and philanthropies to co-create opportunity rooted in each area's strengths and values (Theodos et al., 2021).

The public sector crucially empowers decentralized community centered plan-ning and social innovation through open data sharing, participative digital platforms, decentralized budgets, and support developing grassroots associations and networks (Lacey-Barnacle et al., 2023). For example, participatory planning initiatives in Pres-ton, UK successfully aligned procurement spending with cooperative ecological busi-ness growth and poverty reduction goals identified by marginalized area residents themselves (Webster et al., 2021). This model of networked governance and public-community collaboration around locally designed economic strategies can enhance outcomes through contextual responsiveness and shared objectives.

Beyond piecemeal community level successes, the multiplying effects of expand-ing social economies scaling up alternative models holds transformative potential. Demonstrating workability for equitable and ecologically sustainable systems meeting basic needs, they offer prototypes for wider replication (Neamtan, 2005). Sufficiently resourcing social and solidarity economy growth is key for catalyzing its upscaling and evolution—from isolated support instruments toward integrated, whole-of-government approaches targeting entire societal transitions.

Visionary public sector leadership willing to reshape roles and relationships to cede decision rights and resources into community control enables this next stage. Rather than direct state management, the platform governance ethos emerges for fa-cilitating citizen-centered development. Open data ecosystems, decentralized innova-tion funds, and permissions for autonomy over local planning and services manifest radical public empowerment (Kuziemski & Misuraca, 2020). Ultimately realigning in-stitutions around inclusive subsidiarity and democratically directing capital flows to community priorities lays foundations for system change advancing equity and sus-tainability values, as the social economy's imprint widens.

The public sector holds indispensable responsibilities for nurturing alternative economic models grounded in social benefit through recognition, funding, legislation, collaboration, and governance reforms. By embracing community wealth building ap-proaches, the state can help scale inclusive grassroots innovations demonstrating plausible pathways aligned to democratically determined goals of justice and ecologi-cal balance. Sufficient resourcing and opening institutional architectures thus pro-vides keys unlocking the social economy's latent transformative potentials. If govern-ments actively partner to support localized experiments reflecting people's values, they can contribute toward society's turn toward participation, solidarity, and sustain-ability as foundational economic pillars in place of profit-first doctrine.

Ethical "Smart Cities"

Smart cities represent urban environments enabled by pervasive sensors, data flows, and intelligent software optimizing key infrastructure and services. As this wave of networked digital transformation reshapes cities, profound questions emerge around equitable access, security, privacy, sustainability, and democratic governance. Public sector leadership grounded in ethical frameworks for technology deployment and data usage provides indispensable guidance steering smart city innovation to responsibly elevate residents' well-being.

Smart city technologies offer immense potential for problem-solving and social progress when thoughtfully implemented. Advanced connectivity and real-time monitoring facilitated by the Internet of Things allows dramatically improving how energy, transit, healthcare, and other urban systems function (Suartika & Cuthbert, 2020). Meanwhile, urban data analytics and predictive modeling can guide evidence-based policymaking, while online citizen participation platforms boost democratic involvement (König, 2021).

However, critics highlight risks of data exploitation by corporations, privacy violations, and security threats from systems hacking, not to mention widening inequality if benefits accrue narrowly (Löfgren & Webster, 2020). Beyond technical flaws, the deepest critics contend that technocratic solutionism paradigms undermine political debate over complex urban challenges by framing them as essentially technical engineering problems rather than fundamental social or environmental issues (Calvo, 2020).

These multifaceted tensions make clear smart city innovation pathways must consciously embed ethical commitments and inclusive democratic design principles (Yigitcanlar et al., 2021). Chang (2021) proposes that the core values of fairness, accountability, transparency, and privacy be foundational for urban technology deployment. Value-sensitive guidelines are needed to avoid simplistic techno-fix framings, including participation, sustainability, solidarity, and self-determination (Helbing et al., 2021).

Grounding smart city development in such ethical values frameworks helps overcome narrow technocratic assumptions. It compels asking deeper questions about long-term societal impacts and who benefits, while putting affected citizens and communities at the center of technology decision processes (Ahmad et al., 2022). Rather than deterministic technology trajectories, value-based design imagines more uplifting, empowering, and ecologically wise smart city possibilities.

Central to ethical and socially beneficial smart city innovation is tackling the "digital divide" inequities constraining who can access and leverage technologies (Kolotouchkina et al., 2022). Beyond basic connectivity infrastructure investments, this demands careful assessment of accessibility barriers and targeted support resources for marginalized groups like low-income residents or people with disabilities (Biloria, 2021). Incorporating inclusive participatory design processes where these communities help shape technology deployment and skills building programs focused on their needs is vital (Allam et al., 2022). Such human-centered approaches reaching those historically excluded avoid exacerbating inequality. They further open possibilities for smart cities not merely enhancing lives of the already privileged but activating the full spectrum of residents' capabilities and aspirations.

While technical experts retain an important role, smart cities should embrace collaborative governance empowering citizens to guide technology's use for public good. This begins by securing rights of collective data ownership, enabling people and communities authority over information about their lives and areas (König, 2021). Open data access policies and digital transparency tools allow broader scrutiny over automated decisions and algorithms.

Participatory digital platforms can significantly expand resident involvement in urban planning processes, while decentralized innovation funds support grassroots technology experiments (Löfgren & Webster, 2020). Such citizen-centric oversight and direction of smart cities' development trajectory helps ensure alignment with democratic values and accountability. Rather than imposed top-down, smart cities thereby evolve responsively from the ground up.

The massive resource footprint and emissions from expanded digital infrastructure pose sustainability concerns, especially the embodied carbon in server farms and electronic hardware (Yigitcanlar et al., 2021). This reinforces why smart city design must holistically integrate environmental stewardship principles. Energy efficient and circular economy computing architecture, renewable powered data centers, and interfacing advanced metering infrastructure with distributed clean energy resources offer technical pathways (Suartika & Cuthbert, 2020). Equally important is deploying sustainability-enhancing applications of urban informatics. Examples include intelligent transport lowering congestion and tailpipe emissions to environmental monitoring networks detecting pollution or managing ecosystems (Chang, 2021). Fusing social equity and ecological wisdom with technological innovation points toward regenerative cities nourishing human and planetary well-being.

Realizing the promise of smart cities fulfilling broad social purposes above commercial interests or technological showcases depends on public sector leadership. Core necessities include laying digital infrastructure advancing inclusion not inequality, securing rights protections around data and design processes enabling participatory citizen oversight. Embracing ethical guidelines and sustainability values for urban innovation can help technology facilitate problem-solving for shared needs rather than exacerbating divisions or environmental strains. If smart city development unfolds as a democratic, green, and solidarity-focused sociotechnical endeavor centered on advancing human capabilities in harmony with the planet, profound social progress awaits.

CASE STUDY: Code for America

The rise of civic technology, or civic tech, reflects a growing movement toward open, collaborative governance using software, data science, and design to make government services more accessible and effective. At the forefront of this movement in the United States is Code for America (CfA), a non-profit organization established in 2009 to promote technology and design solutions for the public good. CfA's initiatives span transparency, digital inclusion, social services, criminal justice reform, and civic participation.

CfA emerged from the momentum of the 2008 U.S. presidential election, when tech-savvy volunteers began supporting open government initiatives. Co-founded by Jennifer Pahlka and Andrew McLaughlin, CfA aimed to transform this civic energy into practical applications that enhance government transparency and service delivery. Initial seed funding from Omidyar Network, Google, and the John S. and James L. Knight Foundation allowed CfA to develop projects and partnerships with local governments to modernize public services. Early successes included platforms for agencies to source innovative app ideas and volunteer "brigades" of technologists donating their skills to civic causes like disaster response and infrastructure mapping.

Over the past decade, CfA has developed an extensive array of programs that address barriers to accessing and delivering public services. Some flagship initiatives include:

- GetCalFresh: An online platform simplifying enrollment for California food assistance benefits, automating manual processes, and making applications mobile-friendly.
- Clear My Record: An automated record clearance system in California using computer-vision analysis to identify and clear eligible criminal records.
- Integrated Benefits Initiative: A multi-state collaboration to streamline applications across health insurance, food assistance, and other safety net programs.
- Brigade Network: Supporting more than eighty volunteer tech communities that develop civic apps, standardize open data, and provide digital skills training.
- Markets: A suite of digital services enabling tenants to apply for rental assistance, submit maintenance requests, and access community resources. Initially launched in Houston, it now serves more than 250,000 residents across five states.
- Census tools: AI-powered text and phone-based chatbots that provided online self-response options for the 2020 U.S. Census.

These efforts have had a tangible impact on government service accessibility. For example, GetCalFresh and CfA's Census tools have connected over 350,000 Americans with essential services or political representation. CfA's work has also informed policy reforms through research on racial disparities, barriers to public systems, and the use of algorithms in public agencies.

CfA maintains collaborations with more than 150 city, county, and state partners and advises federal entities like the White House Office for Technology Policy and the General Services Administration. It supports national open data legislation, such as the 2021 Open Data Act, and leads discussions on modernizing social services and open government practices. The organization has become a central player in the civic tech ecosystem by spearheading digital transformation, developing skills, and promoting data standardization.

Despite its successes, CfA faces significant challenges in realizing systemic change. Civic tech projects can be fragmented, leading to isolated and temporary community impacts without sustained policy outcomes. Bureaucratic inertia and siloed agency collaboration often hinder service scaling and data sharing. Moreover, volunteers lack capacity for long-term product ownership, complicating project maintenance.

Governments still favor contracts with traditional vendors, restricting resources and reach for grassroots civic tech initiatives. CfA's user-centered design principles sometimes clash with entrenched institutional processes, limiting the adoption of more agile and inclusive practices. Furthermore, sustaining these efforts requires complex coordination across multiple sectors.

To address these challenges, CfA aims to cement civic tech as a permanent fixture by expanding its reach and resources. Its recently launched "Civic Graph" initiative seeks to systematically map the civic tech landscape by collecting data on global projects, funding flows, and community impacts. This evidence base can guide resources to effective solutions and accelerate civic tech adoption across jurisdictions.

Additionally, the 2021 federal infrastructure package, which allocated $100 million for data standardization and technology modernization assistance to governments, may signal greater support for civic tech. The pandemic has also accelerated digital offerings by state and local agencies, positioning them as more savvy consumers of technology in the future.

CfA's fellowship program has placed more than 100 technologists in public agencies, equipping them with human-centered design and agile development skills. This alumni network is coalescing into a seasoned civic tech workforce. CfA's consulting work and partnerships have helped diversify funding sources, reducing reliance on donors. Its venture arm scales external startups like Upsolve, which provides financial tools for low-income families.

Code for America exemplifies how community participation, design thinking, and inclusive technology can transform governance. Its initiatives support housing assistance, nutrition access, workforce entry, and criminal record relief, setting government services on course to meet constituents' evolving expectations rather than relying on outdated processes.

While civic tech's decentralized nature complicates coordination, its diversity of experiments fosters rapid learning and innovation. Open standards for data and architecture can help transfer successful models across jurisdictions. If tools, talent, and political will continue to converge, civic tech may play a crucial role in restoring public trust and modernizing government services to better serve citizens. At its core, CfA's work highlights the potential of inclusive technology and civic participation to reimagine governance for the digital age.

Innovation in Public Education

Education systems and learning processes are being transformed in the digital age through new technologies expanding access, pedagogical models adapted for remote environments, and shifting power dynamics. The "digital revolution" introduces profound questions on the future of schooling while driving experiential, personalized, and connected learning opportunities (Collins and Halverson, 2018). Realizing more equitable, empowering education featuring broader participation demands rethinking assumptions. This essay analyzes key innovations around openness, democracy, and localization that indicate directions for progressive transformation.

Significant energy focuses on harnessing technology to increase educational access and affordability, especially for disadvantaged communities. Mexico's Telesecundaria program uses broadcast television and print materials to provide middle schooling in remote areas lacking teachers or infrastructure (Craig et al., 2016). Critical during COVID-19 lockdowns were emergency remote teaching initiatives like those profiled by Huang et al. (2020) in China, demonstrating how open sharing of digital resources and public–private partnerships can enable continued learning amidst disrupted classrooms.

Meanwhile massive open online courses (MOOCs) offer free university-level classes to millions worldwide. However, as Hansen and Reich (2015) find, completion rates are low and access issues around internet connectivity, digital skills, and availability for informal learners persist, threatening to exacerbate rather than bridge educational divides. Truly democratized access will require learner-centric design and proactive outreach so innovations serve those they promise to empower.

Beyond access, digitalization compels reimagining pedagogical models themselves. Blended environments allow combining physical and virtual interactions across distributed settings (Simpson, 2018), while mobile apps spur creative engagement with real-world problems (Montiel et al., 2020). Whether through simulations, augmented reality, or embedded social networks, technology can enhance contextual, experiential, and collaborative learning happening across multiple spaces (Selwyn, 2016).

However, as caution, overly techno-optimistic assumptions risk overlooking the relational, emotional, and embodied character of education. Achieving meaningful improvements involves carefully incorporating digital capabilities to amplify (rather than replace) fundamentally human teaching and learning processes (Williamson et al., 2020). This demands participative co-design appreciating context-specific challenges and potentials.

Digital networks introduce new possibilities for decentralizing educational decision-making and governance. As Arocena et al. (2017) discuss, "developmental universities" foster participative links with marginalized communities they seek to serve through engaged scholarship and innovation. Rather than paternalistic imposition of curricula, facilitating grassroots knowledge production and peer learning networks allows more democratic determination of research and teaching agendas.

Similarly, citizen science initiatives actively involve non-specialists in scientific data collection and analysis, thereby democratizing processes for setting research priorities (Bonney et al., 2016). Educational institutions can embrace openness philosophies expanding stakeholders influencing central questions, methods, and applications around scholarly inquiry itself (Peters & Roberts, 2015). This ethos of reciprocal public collaboration hints at how digitalization may reshape rigid, hierarchical systems for more pluralistic dialogue.

However, fully empowering community-rooted education relies on local capacity building more than technology alone (Reich, 2020). As Edwards (2019) discusses, shifting perspective to concepts like social capital and participative governance is vital for sustainability. Rather than isolated technical fixes, lasting change interlinks schools, parents, public services, businesses and civil society in continually adapting learning ecosystems responsive to youth needs (Simonova et al., 2019).

Inclusive localization also enables situating education within place-based cultures and environments. Vibrant "teaching the commons" initiatives combine community self-understanding, ecological knowledge, and identity cultivation through experiential learning rooted in local natural and cultural heritage (Theobald, 2018). Such creative networking of schools with community development organizations, participatory planning processes, and indigenous knowledge systems highlights pathways for educational innovation that aligns with community priorities (Kobori et al., 2016).

Achieving more equitable, relevant, and democratic educational futures in the digital era demands complementary pedagogical, technological, and governance innovations. Expanding access through open sharing sits alongside localized empowerment and participative priority setting. Rather than panaceas, technologies like MOOCs or mobile apps enable progress when embedded in supportive ecosystems shaped by users themselves, focused on enabling self-determined and collective advancement. This future points toward education characterized by permeability, pluralism, and the public good.

Innovation in Public Health

Public health organizations are increasingly leveraging advanced technologies to enhance service delivery, expand access, improve outcomes, and reduce costs across health promotion, disease prevention, and community well-being. With global technology adoption accelerating, new possibilities emerge for using these innovations to elevate health equity and empower communities. However, careful assessment of risks around privacy, inclusion, and appropriate use remains crucial (Webster & Wyatt, 2020). This analysis explores key technology-driven trends reshaping public health alongside considerations for optimizing social impacts ethically.

One of the core opportunities from health technology adoption lies in expanding care access through improved connectivity. Innovations such as virtual mental health visits, remote monitoring devices, and online peer support groups increase convenience for patients while lowering access barriers (Hollis et al., 2015). Mobile clinics equipped with telemedicine suites now bring primary care directly to underserved areas, promoting equity for disadvantaged populations (Yu et al., 2017).

Digital platforms also enable decentralized mutual aid initiatives. For example, social media has facilitated grassroots addiction recovery communities by linking geographically dispersed individuals overcoming similar challenges (Ashford et al., 2019). During the COVID-19 pandemic, digital coordination helped swiftly organize relief efforts through grassroots emergency groups (Rendall et al., 2022). However, ensuring quality and ethical standards in these technology-driven health offerings is vital. Effective governance frameworks are needed to address risks such as misleading health information and privacy violations. Policies must also bridge the "digital divide" by enhancing accessibility, digital literacy, and user-centric design (Trencher & Karvonen, 2020).

The digitization of health records, wearables, mobile apps, and insurance claims generates unprecedented granular data on community health patterns, disease vectors, and intervention effectiveness. Advanced analytics can optimize resource allocation, predict outbreak locations, and model personalized treatment responses (Baker et al., 2017). For instance, some Chinese smart cities leverage integrated data to guide interventions like air quality improvements and proactive health screenings to contain contagions (Wu et al., 2022).

However, utilizing such data responsibly requires navigating privacy, surveillance, and consent issues. Historically excluded communities may be wary of sharing health data without trust in secure controls and ethical usage. Constructing robust data governance frameworks with inclusive citizen participation can ensure ethical management policies while minimizing biases (Burrows et al., 2019). When designed thoughtfully, such frameworks can tap health data's potential to bolster community resilience effectively.

The advent of smart city technologies also presents opportunities to promote public health by embedding sensor networks and analytical engines across urban infrastructures. Intelligent traffic coordination systems, for example, lower air pollution and accident rates, while algorithmically managed drainage systems mitigate mosquito breeding to contain diseases (Yang et al., 2022). However, these techno-solutionist approaches must be balanced with holistic planning that strengthens public health services, housing, and employment, aligning technology to human needs through democratic oversight and grounded applications.

Health agencies themselves are modernizing their technology architectures to deliver patient-centric digital services and data-driven operations. Integrated platforms now merge electronic records, virtual care delivery, remote diagnostics, and analytics to support responsive, preventive, and personalized care models. AI-powered triaging and workflow automation also enhance efficiency by freeing up personnel for tasks requiring human judgment (Su et al., 2021). Yet, over-automation risks dehumanizing care experiences if not balanced properly. Excessive automation can undermine the discretion of health professionals and weaken the interpersonal connections essential for healing. Thus, it is crucial to scope automation to enhance (rather than replace) human capabilities, grounded in participatory assessments of workplace realities (Trencher & Karvonen, 2020). Additionally, clinicians must receive training on leveraging AI effectively to maintain high-touch care, ensuring technology enhances professional purpose and compassionate patient connections.

Beyond provider modernization, technology can empower consumers by placing health knowledge and tools directly into their hands. Mobile health apps promote self-care adherence, chronic disease management, and healthy behaviors through nudges and gamification (Silva et al., 2015). Evidence of mobile health effectiveness includes areas like smoking cessation, weight loss, and mental wellness, where these tools have significantly improved risk factors and self-reported outcomes (Marcolino et al., 2018). Home diagnostic devices and wearables also provide personalized health insights, enabling timely interventions and preventive care (Baker et al., 2017).

As digital capabilities expand across service delivery channels, research, personal health tools, and monitoring infrastructure, there is immense potential for integrating data to provide holistic community health insights. Farahini et al. (2018) envision a "Fog of Things" ecosystem where environmental sensors, health wearables, and electronic records communicate seamlessly. This system would provide contextual wellness intelligence accessible across the ecosystem, facilitating early interventions and informing just-in-time policy adjustments.

Currently, however, fragmented data trapped in institutional silos constrains integration opportunities. To overcome these barriers, both technical challenges around interoperability and governance issues around trust must be addressed. Data democratization, which places collective ownership into communities' hands, is a crucial standard for establishing ethical foundations for integration (König, 2021). With collaborative data infrastructure guided by public interest, distributed health data ecosystems can reveal contextual drivers and environmental risk factors, enhancing community resilience.

While technology-enabled innovation holds significant promise for public health, realizing its full potential requires supportive policies, system reforms, and ethical data infrastructure. Thoughtful construction of these elements ensures that technology remains focused on human development rather than efficiency alone. When digital transformation is a democratically guided process that expands capabilities and minimizes risks, smarter, more empowered community health systems can emerge—ultimately enhancing public welfare and driving progress toward health equity and community well-being.

Innovation in Public Housing

Public housing plays a critical role in ensuring affordability and inclusion within urban systems. However, traditional public housing programs have often concentrated poverty and racial segregation through flawed siting decisions, and frequently fail to reflect the aspirations and lived experiences of marginalized communities. Embracing innovations in construction technologies and community-based governance offers new pathways for more equitable, sustainable, and empowering public housing models oriented toward social justice.

Rethinking design processes is a foundational step in transforming public housing. Conventional approaches imposed top-down standardized visions on residents, rather than reflecting their lived realities. Shifting to participatory models centers residents' values, enabling them to shape their own environments. Co-created affordable housing projects using human-centric methodologies attentive to social and emotional needs generate positive outcomes beyond physical dwellings (Lucchi & Delera, 2020). Such user-driven design better resonates with community identities and site-specific contexts.

Moreover, deliberative planning that prioritizes social sustainability can position public housing projects as catalysts for shared prosperity. Collaborative forums—bringing together residents, community organizations, planners, and authorities—ground interventions within participatory placemaking visions (Aernouts & Ryckewaert, 2015). These inclusive processes shift the role of public housing from paternalism to creative partnership.

On the construction front, modular building systems using prefabricated components provide multiple advantages. Standardized production under controlled factory conditions improves quality, integrates supply chains, and enables just-in-time assembly that reduces costs and environmental impact. For example, prefabricated public housing in Beijing reduced costs and carbon footprints by more than 20 percent (Shen et al., 2019). Additionally, modularity facilitates incremental development and flexibility to accommodate future societal needs (Bredenoord, 2016). Integrating networked sensors and smart appliances during manufacturing stages can also enable large-scale production of smart public housing (Shamsuddin & Srinivasan, 2021).

Reinvented housing models centered on community control and stewardship are also gaining traction. Community land trusts (CLTs), for example, provide collective land ownership through non-profit entities, balancing affordability, security, and wealth building for lower-income residents (Thompson, 2015). CLTs preserve public subsidy value for future generations while empowering cooperative management by the residents themselves.

Co-housing developments similarly support communal living through shared spaces and resident-governed associations, enhancing social well-being and inclusion (Droste, 2015). Such configurations promote intergenerational support systems, helping older residents maintain independence while fostering social interdependencies (Lang & Stoeger, 2018).

Funding remains a persistent challenge, necessitating innovative public–private investment models. Social impact bonds, for instance, allow private capital to finance transitional programs like supportive housing services, with public repayments tied to measured social outcomes (Ezema et al., 2016). Hybrid financing that combines bonds, grants, and commercial loans can better leverage resources across stakeholders to enable large-scale regeneration projects (Olojede et al., 2019).

Innovations in construction technology are also transforming public housing. Robotic arms and 3D printing enable swift, cost-effective construction of buildings with customized configurations (Hager et al., 2016). Techniques like contour crafting allow the extrusion of cement-based materials into complex forms without specialized labor, expanding possibilities for adaptive housing configurations that respond to family needs or disabilities (Aghimien et al., 2021). Using local, recycled, or renewable materials could reduce construction costs by up to 70 percent (Sakin & Kiroglu, 2017). However, ensuring these technologies translate into more empowering environments requires deliberative oversight and participatory processes that value cultural connections alongside technical outputs (Matamanda et al., 2022).

Community-embedded models are critical for creating equitable public housing policy innovations. Government agencies have started transferring public stock to cooperative ownership models, putting inhabitants in control as primary stakeholders (Crabtree et al., 2021). Rather than remotely defined service provision targets, this framework fosters participative planning that addresses local priorities like safety upgrades, disability access retrofits, or open space improvements (Blessing, 2015).

Platforms supporting grassroots housing organizations' direct access to public lands and funding are equally impactful (Aernouts & Ryckewaert, 2015). Community-based development rooted in lived realities can prevent displacement and resistance caused by imposing systems that are ill-adapted to neighborhood social fabrics. Additionally, participatory visioning supports a balance between built form and the preservation of community character (Czischke & van Bortel, 2023).

Ultimately, achieving transformative public housing innovation depends on centering social justice, ensuring that new technologies and models serve marginalized communities equitably. If developments are guided by ethical commitments to inclusion, public housing has immense latent potential to uplift marginalized city dwellers through access to secure, sustainable, and dignified environments that reflect their aspirations.

CASE STUDY: Fairbnb

Fairbnb is an ethical alternative to mainstream short-term rental platforms like Airbnb, designed to address the social, economic, and environmental impacts of the rental market. By prioritizing community welfare, sustainable tourism, and transparency, Fairbnb offers a model that benefits local communities, property owners, and travelers alike.

Fairbnb emerged in response to the negative effects of the short-term rental boom, including housing shortages, rent inflation, and neighborhood disruption. Unlike platforms that prioritize profit maximization, Fairbnb reinvests a portion of its profits into local communities. The platform partners with local entities, supports social projects, and ensures property listings adhere to ethical and sustainable guidelines.

Operating as a cooperative, Fairbnb involves community stakeholders in decision-making, with profits shared or reinvested to support local projects. It also enforces strict host guidelines to prevent the adverse effects of short-term rentals, such as limiting the number of properties per host and requiring compliance with local regulations. Environmental sustainability is another core focus—listings are encouraged to adopt eco-friendly practices, such as waste reduction and the use of renewable energy.

Fairbnb's community-centric model can significantly benefit local areas by directing profits to community infrastructure, cultural initiatives, and social services. This helps counteract negative trends like gentrification and loss of local character. By promoting responsible travel, Fairbnb encourages guests to explore local businesses, boosting economic activity and job creation.

While Fairbnb aims to balance profitability with social responsibility, it faces challenges in scaling while maintaining its ethical principles. Competing with established platforms also requires building trust and navigating complex local regulations.

Despite these hurdles, Fairbnb's focus on sustainability and ethical tourism offers a compelling alternative in the short-term rental market. As demand for responsible travel grows, Fairbnb's model could serve as a blueprint for reshaping the sharing economy to benefit all stakeholders, paving the way for a more equitable and sustainable future in tourism.

Innovation in Public Transport

Public transportation systems require constant innovation and adaptation to address evolving urban challenges around sustainability, accessibility, and rider experiences. This essay analyzes technological improvements, creative business models, and participative planning approaches reshaping transport services in cities today. From electric buses to mobilities-as-a-service, myriad advances offer tools enabling affordable, customer-centric solutions while reducing environmental footprints. However, holistic integration balancing investments, governance, and social dimensions remains vital for innovations fulfilling quality transport's public good mandates.

Various technology innovations promise cleaner, efficient public transit alternatives responding to urban sustainability pressures. Electric buses eliminate tailpipe emissions, thereby enabling cleaner air amidst traffic pollution concerns. Growing evidence shows the wide mobility and environmental gains from transitioning to non-internal combustion fleets, if supported by renewable charging infrastructure. Energy storage improvements make electric options increasingly viable across varied route terrains and range needs (Bakker & Konings, 2018). Still, the high upfront costs of upgrading vehicles and infrastructure deter adoption absent public incentives or private operator partnerships overcoming short-term profitability constraints. Governance innovations like concession tendering or coordinated fleet procurements can facilitate systemic change.

Beyond electrification, intelligent transport systems introduce sensors, real-time data and automation to enhance reliability and responsiveness. Examples range from control rooms dynamically adjusting frequencies based on rider demand to predicting failures from onboard diagnostics (Weber et al., 2014). Such smart mobility improvements allow wringing additional capacity out of existing assets. They, however, demand enabling policy environments encouraging open data access and integrated mobility management harnessing innovations advancing the public interest. Associated privacy risks equally necessitate governance guardrails upholding public trust. Still, thoughtfully employed emerging technologies promise services better aligned with rider needs.

Innovative business models offer supplementary channels improving transport accessibility, flexibility, and affordability across fragmented landscapes of mobility provision. Ride pooling services enabled by algorithms efficiently matching riders along optimized routes can provide cost-effective last mile connectivity. By aggregating latent demand, such models operate viably at lower volumes than traditional public transit. Partnerships with local providers and public agencies facilitate integration with high-capacity corridors (Shaheen & Chan, 2016).

Similarly, Mobility-as-a-Service (MaaS) platforms aggregate various public and private transport modes onto a unified interface for seamless trip planning and payments. Rather than requiring ownership, mobility is delivered as an on-demand service through subscriptions granting multimodal access. This bundling across transit, cycling, taxis and more leverages their relative strengths for door-to-door convenience. Helsinki's Whim app increased sustainable mode shares by doubling combined walking, biking, and public transport usage compared to drive-dominant baseline behaviors (Smith et al., 2020). As auto-centric ownership models decline, flexible access platforms pooling capacity promise more affordable, demand-responsive mobility.

However, transport innovations fulfilling public objectives depend on governance placing inclusive participation and social equity at the center of service planning. Research by Mehmood & Imran (2021) illustrates how community-grounded processes better identify context-specific accessibility barriers and local routing priorities. Dynamic feedback loops linking user inputs with data-driven operations enable responsive innovations directly improving underserved resident lives.

Participative decision-making likewise allows steering innovations in sustainable directions reflecting collective values. Seoul's government implemented sharing policies focused on public benefit following extensive public consultations (Yun et al., 2020). These helped develop an ethical framework addressing risks like pricing exclusions or over-privatization. Such co-creation foundations strengthen citizen investments that sustain transformative innovations delivering positive mobility futures centered on public good over profits.

Overall balancing business flexibility with social responsiveness and environmental sustainability underpins next generation mobility ecosystems driven by shared purpose. Collaboration across stakeholders avoids enclosed innovation pathways failing marginalized groups or communities. With polycentric leadership embracing public stewardship over disruptions, context-specific innovations promise transport services enabling livable, thriving, and inclusive urban futures.

Technology upgrades, business model innovations, and participative governance principles remaking urban mobility in the face of sustainability pressures and evolving usage patterns are creating new models for public transportation. Clean vehicle advancements, smart routing systems, access aggregation platforms, and grassroots planning processes illustrate renewed capacities for affordable, demand-driven, and inclusive mobility fashioned through creative responses to public needs. The analysis suggests that realizing innovations' full societal benefits relies on cooperation across industry, government, and communities guided by equity values and shared development visions. Integrated action tuning investments, regulations, and collective action offers keys unlocking sustainable transport possibilities benefiting all urban inhabitants equitably.

CASE STUDY: Seoul's "Sharing City" Initiative

In 2012, Seoul declared itself a "sharing city" and began implementing policies to support resource sharing and the development of a sustainable sharing economy. This initiative aimed to address urban challenges like overpopulation, housing shortages, and pollution by leveraging underutilized assets through peer-to-peer exchanges.

Seoul faced mounting pressures from rapid urbanization, congestion, and strained infrastructure. At the same time, the city had idle resources like vacant spaces, equipment, and skills that could be utilized more efficiently. Seoul's sharing city agenda combined social, economic, and environmental goals to: (1) unlock underemployed resources, (2) support job creation—especially for youth, and (3) foster community bonds through shared activities. This comprehensive approach presented a new model for sustainable growth centered on mutual support and optimizing existing resources.

To execute this vision, the city established the Sharing Promotion Committee, composed of representatives from public, private, and civil society sectors, to guide collaborative efforts. Seoul provided competitive seed funding, subsidies, and physical spaces to incubate sharing startups proposed by young entrepreneurs. The creation of the "Seoul Sharing Plaza" provided a dedicated venue for residents to exchange ideas and resources. Regulatory support and legal protections were put in place to encourage participation and build public trust.

The city also launched awareness programs such as the Sharing City Seoul brand and guidebook to engage the broader public. This light-touch regulatory environment and robust support system enabled grassroots sharing initiatives tailored to local needs.

A diverse range of startups and projects emerged from the initiative. For housing, platforms like Pooling Houses connected young people with seniors offering spare rooms in exchange for help around the house, while Wonderlend transformed unused spaces into dormitories. Car-sharing services like SoCar and Green Car rapidly expanded to offer shared mobility options. Other initiatives included community tool libraries, shared bookshelves, and children's clothing lending service Kiple, which facilitated the reuse of 8 million items among families.

More than fifty district-level projects earned official Sharing City Seoul certification, and, by 2016, more than 400,000 residents had engaged in sharing programs. These initiatives generated nearly $4 million in economic activity and contributed to over 30,000 tons of CO_2 reduction. Additionally, 80 percent of participants reported enhanced trust, friendships, and peer support networks, reducing social isolation.

Seoul's approach required no major new infrastructure expenditures. Instead, it focused on realigning existing assets and amending regulations to enable sharing solutions, making it a cost-effective model. The success of the Sharing City initiative demonstrates how supporting bottom-up innovation can transform urban communities by building ecosystems where creativity and collaboration thrive. Other South Korean cities have already begun adopting similar strategies.

As the initiative evolves, ensuring equitable participation and addressing fair labor conditions remain key areas of focus. With ongoing commitment, Seoul's Sharing City initiative highlights the potential of community-centered, cooperative models to create sustainable and inclusive urban futures.

Platform Cooperativism

Platform cooperativism represents an emerging economic model that offers an alternative to exploitative on-demand labor platforms within the so-called "gig economy." The concept seeks to leverage the efficiency and scale enabled by digital platforms while embodying cooperative democratic values of worker ownership and control. This essay will analyze the theory, emerging cases, and potentials of platform cooperativism as a progressive force reimagining labor in the digital age.

Platform cooperativism constitutes a critique of and challenge to dominant technology-mediated gig platforms like Uber or TaskRabbit. Under the prevailing model, for-profit companies maintain ownership over the platform mediating exchange between service providers and customers (Scholz, 2016). Workers carry the burden of asset ownership for providing services like vehicles or tools, but lack control over platform governance and rules. Profits concentrate among a small group of investors and executives, rather than accruing to workers.

Against this inequitable and disempowering status quo, platform cooperativism offers an alternative paradigm of democratized technology businesses collectively owned and governed by service-providing members (Kirsanova et al., 2020). Martinelli et al. (2019) trace conceptual roots to long-established cooperative movements emerging in nineteenth-century Europe around notions of worker solidarity, ethical exchange, and self-organization. Adapting such principles to contemporary digital platform models provides worker empowerment foundations rejected by extractive gig platforms.

These innovations are connecting emergent platform coop ideals to peer production theories where open, decentralized networks coordinate creativity toward common value creation (Pazaitis et al., 2017). When designed around principles of cooperation over competition and democratic participation, digitally mediated exchange systems can embody shared prosperity advancing public good objectives. Realizing such promise, however, depends on committed organizing and institution building attuned to members' lived realities.

Myriad organizational forms fall under the platform cooperativism umbrella, adapting its solidarity ethos across diverse sharing economy sectors. App-based driver and courier cooperatives establish collective control over crucial interaction mechanisms affecting members' livelihoods. Cloud computing platforms similarly can provide ethical alternatives to big tech centralized control, as demonstrated by data storage cooperative WeAreCloud (Martinelli et al., 2019).

In the care sector, Up & Go builds home cleaning jobs while ensuring workers—who are also members—determine policies, offerings, and fees (Scholz, 2016). Examples span sectors like short-term vacation accommodation, childcare, informal transport, and more where atomized digital work can mutually reinforce solidarity (Zygmuntowski, 2018).

Crucially, cooperatively owned tech infrastructure need not operate at global scale like dominant platforms when owned by members rooted in local contexts. For instance, Meituan is a platform cooperative operating exclusively in Kunming, China that has provided work flexibility to thousands through its app connecting service providers to customers (Mannan & Pek, 2021). Prioritizing good jobs over maximalist expansion allows focusing value creation on tangible improvements reflecting worker-owners' preferences.

However, successfully establishing genuinely democratized gig platforms still faces hurdles around competitiveness with dominant players, agreeing equitable governance models and financing startup costs (Nicoli & Paltrinieri, 2019). Self-exploitation tendencies also require guardrails as overwork may persist absent restraints (Sandoval, 2020). Thoughtful design adapting principles like platform portability and data ownership protections can better balance worker welfare (Pentzien, 2020). But realizing the liberatory promise of technology fundamentally depends on binding cooperation cementing solidarity across often isolated gig workers (Grohmann, 2023).

This underscores the irreplaceable role of dedicated organizing and movement building advocating the platform cooperative alternative (Bunders et al., 2022). Through sustained coalition efforts updating the rich histories of worker self-management for digital conditions and rallying wider public support, space can open for platform alternatives advancing dignity, voice, and equity. Just as unions aligned worker and broader social justice movements to champion rights and counter concentrated capital (Arcidia-cono & Pais, 2020), realizing platform cooperativism's potential similarly relies on integrating labor, technology, and social responsibility struggles targeting extractive gig models. In this framing the emerging practice of platform cooperativism connects visceral grievances to structural critiques while building participatory economic prototypes—laying foundations for sociotechnical transformations advancing solidarity economies at multiple scales.

In an age of exponentially advancing technology but stagnant social equity, platform cooperativism conceptually and practically fuses digitally mediated exchange efficiency with accountability to shared development visions. Instead of accepting grim inevitabilities like the disappearance of good stable jobs and the persistence of platform monopolies underpaying workers, models emerging under platform cooperativism offer existential counterpower reclaiming technology's promise. Despite formidable challenges around startup financing, governance design, and competition, the passionate experimentation with democratized platform alternatives ultimately represents aspirations for work upholding universal dignity and inclusion. Just as historical cooperatives carved out autonomy against oppressive systems, realizing platform cooperatives' radical solidarity vision relies on social movements dynamically bridging individual interests to collective advancement on human terms. But groups daring to reimagine digital futures beyond the destructive givens reopen histories where solidarity economics expanded justice—kindling hopes for emancipation against techno-capital dominion.

KEY THINKER: Trebor Scholz

The rise of companies like Uber and Airbnb has highlighted the power of digital platforms to disrupt industries and create new efficiencies. However, it has also raised concerns about monopoly control, erosion of labor standards, and wealth concentration. In response, the concept of "platform cooperativism" emerged, led by New York scholar and activist Trebor Scholz. This movement envisions a future where digital platforms are owned and governed collectively by their users, offering a more equitable and participative alternative to today's dominant tech giants.

Born in Cold War-era Germany, Scholz witnessed firsthand the daily struggles under the Iron Curtain. After moving to New York in the 1990s, he became deeply engaged in research on the impact of digital technologies on labor and democracy as an associate professor at The New School. Observing the power imbalances in platforms like YouTube and Instagram, he coined the term "platform cooperativism" in 2014, advocating for a "humane, ethical" model of online platforms that combine cooperative business structures with digital technology.

Scholz's concept quickly gained traction amid growing criticism of Big Tech's dominance. In 2015, he co-founded the Platform Cooperativism Consortium with Nathan Schneider, bringing together academics, entrepreneurs, and policymakers to explore cooperative digital models. Platform cooperatives, unlike traditional non-profits or businesses, embrace multistakeholder ownership and democratic governance. Participants—whether workers, customers, or institutions—jointly own and operate these platforms, with decisions made through open meetings and transparent rules encoded into the software itself.

Through research excavating historical precedents and contemporary experiments, Scholz animates platform cooperatives as an actionable evolution of cooperativism for current realities. Blending community organizing with technological populism, he mobilizes adherents globally to build emancipatory models that codify ethical values like transparency and accountability at the foundation.

Platform cooperatives span various sectors, from ride-hailing apps and freelance marketplaces to cloud services and 3D printing networks. Pioneering ventures like Up & Go (a house cleaning service) and Stocksy (a stock photo platform) demonstrate how platform co-ops can distribute ownership to workers, pay living wages, and prioritize equitable outcomes over profit maximization. Scholz's 2017 book *Uberworked and Underpaid* outlines these models, highlighting how technology can empower rather than exploit.

Scholz's work extends beyond scholarship. As a movement catalyst, he has helped organize over 30 international conferences, drawing more than 1000 practitioners to share ideas and launch pilot experiments in various fields. He also co-founded the Institute for the Cooperative Digital Economy to formalize advocacy efforts and support emerging platform co-ops. Scholz partners with universities, governments, and unions to offer training, funding, and policy guidance for cooperative alternatives.

Scholz believes that platform co-ops offer a structural solution to redistribute control and wealth in the digital economy. By embedding ethical principles into the very design of digital platforms, these co-ops can foster economic inclusion and rebuild community trust. Although still a niche concept, platform cooperativism has gained momentum, with funding, regulatory support, and tech infrastructure now advancing new implementations globally.

As digital technologies continue to shape society, Scholz's vision provides a pathway to reclaim user agency and ensure that platforms serve the broader public good. By promoting collective ownership and cooperation, his ideas challenge the status quo and offer a blueprint for a more equitable and sustainable digital economy.

Social Economy, Public Policy, and Regulation

Certain regulatory and policy constraints around financing, public procurement, data, and skills development often undermine the growth, innovation capacities and collaborative potentials of social economy organizations (Utting, 2018). Correcting these limitations via dedicated legal provisions, programmatic supports, and partnership frameworks hence holds substantial promise for empowering the social economy to amplify its contributions advancing equitable, sustainable futures.

This part of the chapter will explore the significance and promise of targeted policies and regulations strengthening entities across the social economy spectrum. It reviews pressing constraints requiring redress, analyzes emerging policy responses and innovations from cities leading on the agenda, and issues recommendations for multifaceted supports boosting solidarity ecosystem capacities. Insights aim to inform further legal reforms and state modernization efforts directed at community betterment. Despite the promise of collective entities filling welfare gaps and catalyzing inclusion, ambiguous legal categorizations, financial barriers, data divides, and insufficient ecosystem coordination hinder optimal success and scale of social economy organizations (OECD, 2020). Key impediments center on:

- Limited procurement rights constrain public service contracts and investment partnerships (Bauwens & Niaros, 2017). Prescriptive requirements around capitalization levels, turnover size, and organizational longevity often disadvantage cooperatives and informal collectives rightly positioned to fulfill localized needs.
- Investment gaps and uneven eligibility for loans, grants and subsidies also undermine pursuit of meso-level projects with high capital intensity like community-owned renewable energy systems and affordable housing developments.
- Digital access inequities coupled with data extraction risks impede cooperative platform development and block engagement of informal entities with essential municipal e-services around transit, licensing, and planning portals.
- Weak networking and inconsistent legal definitions across jurisdictions likewise inhibit cooperation and peer learning opportunities toward replication, harmonized reporting standards, and internationalization (OECD, 2020; Utting, 2018).

Overall, institutional uncertainty around supportive provisions for collective enterprises limits societies from fully benefiting through their multiplier effects on employment, civic participation, social cohesion, and public services innovation.

In response, pioneering governments are introducing holistic initiatives granting social economy entities enhanced legal standing, funding access, data rights and facilitative frameworks encouraging their growth and community orientation. Efforts include:

- public procurement set-asides reserving portions of municipal contracts for cooperative enterprises and social inclusion businesses focused on worker protections, local job creation and unmet social needs
- expanded eligible categories for community investment mechanisms like participatory budgeting, crowdfunding partnerships, citizens' dividends from public wealth funds, and revolving loan supports for developing community land trusts, eco-villages, social housing, and non-profit childcare centers (Avelino et al., 2019)
- open data provisions and technical assistance to improve data literacy and portal accessibility among informal entities (Nicholls & Teasdale, 2017)

–   streamlined registration channels, blockchain-enabled identifiers, tax relief, and multi-year public funding agreements that provide continuity for dynamically evolving community service organizations.

Combined adoption of such financial, legal, and informational support provides coherence enabling reciprocal partnerships between community stewards and local authorities to co-build inclusive economies.

Cities like Barcelona, Portland, New York, Seoul, and Mexico City are pioneering holistic social economy policy ecosystems granting formal recognition, financial supports, and data usage rights to securely embed alternative communal models into civic life.

Barcelona's municipal law protecting and promoting the social solidarity economy mandates public spending minimums with cooperative businesses, provides discounted rates and technical aid on government-owned manufacturing sites, offers public credit guarantees financing ecological transition projects by associations, and inhabits cooperative business development via multi-year consultative planning.

Similarly, New York City enacted worker-owner business development investments, community land trusts funding, and social enterprise procurement mandates as core tenets of economic justice (Avelino et al., 2019).

Building on the high-potential responses, further social economy supports warrant consideration:

–   Legal recognition: Codifying "public benefit" categorizations in company registers officially denoting cooperatives, associations, and social enterprises formalizes visibility and associated regulatory privileges/protections vis-à-vis conventional firms.
–   Public contracting: Earmarked funds should be allocated within infrastructure, social service, and community development requests for proposal (RFPs) explicitly for small-scale social economy bidders who can effectively link asset upgrades with local economic inclusion and climate resilience aims.
–   Investment vehicles: Tax advantaged community investment bonds and direct capital injection models like participatory budgeting processes, municipal seed funds, and crowdfunding matches stimulate complementary grassroot projects by non-profits, social enterprises, and informal community groups.
–   Data support: Open data portals should ensure complete and comprehensible publication of relevant public datasets like land use plans, vacant property registers, and small business funding eligibility criteria to assist community-based planning.
–   Network governance: Dedicated offices, advisory boards, and regular consultative processes institutionalize participation of social economy stakeholders in economic development planning while peer platforms enable vital exchange and replication.

Policy and legal provisions play a vital role in empowering collective enterprises and democratically governed entities to amplify contributions toward equitable development. By redressing constraints around investment barriers, data divides, procurement limits, and network governance, such reforms pioneer transformative configurations of market relations, welfare provisioning, and civic partnerships elevating communal well-being. Further modernization efforts directed at enabling community self-organization hence promise widespread social returns when creatively facilitated by proactive states.

Place-Based Change

The ability for communities to steer localized, participatory development grounded in social aims and ecological balance represents a pivotal pathway for building resilient, equitable futures. As the social economy consisting of cooperatives, non-profits, mutual aid networks, and socially driven enterprises offers frameworks valuing solidarity over individualism for organizing provisioning systems, public sector authorities play crucial roles mainstreaming such place-based models advancing collective well-being (Avelino et al., 2019).

Ranging from participatory policymaking to investments in shared spaces and decentralized infrastructures enabling community self-organization, facilitative public institutions provide vital scaffolds for social economic alternatives addressing pressing sustainability crises and welfare gaps. This essay analyzes high-impact roles of municipal agencies, planning authorities, and development banks in propagating place-specific solutions based on social economy principles of cooperation, mutualism, and ecological stewardship.

It reviews relevant value frameworks, discusses conduit functions around participatory planning and alternative infrastructure, and provides recommendations toward transformative systems change centered on the collective good. Insights aim to inform a refocusing of economic governance and civic partnerships around quality of life and community resilience. The social economy categorically refers to community-rooted organizations conducting activities guided by explicit social aims, ethics of solidarity and participatory self-management—in contrast to the profit maximization imperatives of the private sector (Utting, 2018; Monzón Campos & Chaves Ávila, 2012). Ranging from cooperatives and mutual societies to associations, non-profits, and socially driven enterprises, such entities develop needs-based solutions via productive deliberation and asset pooling.

Core operating principles consequently center on equitable inclusion of users, workers and community stakeholders within democratic decision-making and development planning; promotion of collaborative behaviors nurturing reciprocal support systems and regenerative processes; prioritization of social aims like affordable access, cultural renewal, and ecological harmony over financial returns across management choices; and anchoring in place-based dynamics valuing localization, self-reliance, and living heritage (Miller, 2013; Utting, 2018).

Operationalizing such frameworks for community betterment calls for public sector guidance supporting localized future-building. Municipal planning agencies play crucial but often overlooked roles intermediating between centralized visions and grassroot priorities around development strategies balancing sustainability with inclusion and social cohesion. Mainstreaming participatory planning processes offer vital pathways for bridging top-down schemes with community-led proposals grounded in social solidarity principles (Eizenberg & Jabareen, 2017; Smith & Martin, 2022).

Spatial strategies co-created via equitable engagement of civil society organizations, social movements, and marginalized locality groups in scoping needs assessments, viability deliberations and interim evaluations better resonate with people-centered aspirations than narrow technocratic exercises. Participatory planning centered on nurturing solidarity ecosystems and catalyzing community-based innovations around housing, welfare, and ecological regeneration provides conduits for public sector supports empowering social economic development (Miller, 2013).

Specialized toolbox approaches like forms of participatory budgeting allocating portions of infrastructure funds for crowdfunded neighborhood upgrades also expand civic co-building (Dias, 2018). Overall, institutionalizing collaborative development planning transfers certain decision rights and resources toward community bodies for locally attuned welfare solutions.

In tandem, public financing and construction agencies play central roles mainstreaming alternative infrastructures conducive for collective enterprises, shared services, and distributed networks enabling equitable access within ecological limits. These include investment priorities like:

- community land trusts enabling affordable eco-housing and localized mixed-use developments via anti-speculation and community asset sharing models (Miller, 2013)
- public manufacturing sites and discounted utility access preferentially allocated for cooperatives anchoring green jobs and circular material flows in neighborhoods
- open data platforms, participatory sensing networks, municipal broadband, and digital licensing easements that assist grassroot mobility innovations, care collectives, and community logistics systems
- neighborhood sharing hubs for peer-to-peer exchange and repair activities, reducing new production needs in socially bonding ways

Stewarding such human-centered built assets, shared socio-technical systems, and collective access platforms crucially assists localized transitions toward post-growth economic paradigms aligned with social aims, rather than aggregate throughput growth.

Certain high-impact measures merit adoption by development agencies seeking to nurture community self-organization and scaled social economy ecosystems:

- mainstreaming participatory planning via digital engagement platforms, citizens' assemblies, and requirement thresholds in infrastructure programs for community co-design processes (Dias, 2018)
- spatial preferential zoning for social solidarity economy entities through discounted land access and capital loans assisting the setup of cooperatives, non-profit hubs, and land trusts in areas with sufficient housing/employment density (Miller, 2013)
- municipal statutes and procurement policies formally recognizing and granting preferential treatment to cooperative enterprises and community interest companies focused on public service missions spanning social service provision, eco-innovation, and cultural renewal (Smith et al., 2022)
- knowledge exchange protocols assisting replication and adaptation efforts across towns to propagate ground-up solutions developed by informal groups and grass-root associations without deep technical expertise (Avelino et al., 2019)

Combined adoption of such supportive mechanisms promises vital transformation toward ethical economic systems centered on nurturing community resilience and living well within ecological boundaries.

Public authorities have an increasingly important role to play in propagating place-specific solutions guided by social economy values of cooperation, solidarity, and sustainability. Although further research should refine understanding of suitable hybrid configurations balancing government facilitation with community self-management, current crises facing societies warrant swift adoption of existing policy innovations to empower collective enterprises addressing interlinked welfare and ecological breakdowns through means attuned to the common good.

Conclusion

The public sector is undergoing a technology-enabled transformation in how services are delivered, programs are implemented, and citizens are engaged. Cloud computing, data analytics, artificial intelligence, blockchain, the Internet of Things, and more are driving waves of innovation across vital areas of governance like transportation, healthcare, education, housing, energy systems, and cities overall. These technologies are being applied to pursue objectives around efficiency, transparency, collaboration, and public–private partnerships, with momentum around participatory governance, co-created solutions, accessibility, and decentralized systems empowering communities.

While adoption maturity remains uneven, these innovation trends hold immense potential to redefine public benefit in the twenty-first-century digital era. However, overcoming systemic barriers around legacy systems, funding limitations, skill gaps, privacy concerns, and digital divides poses implementation challenges. Still, investment and prioritization are accelerating, indicating the trajectory toward more data-driven, platform-enabled, and collectively intelligent models of public administration.

E-government encapsulates the shift toward online portals, digital service delivery, and integrated data ecosystems, enabling convenient access and automated workflows. Open data programs publishing non-sensitive public datasets also drive transparency, accountability, and an ecosystem of civic apps harnessing newly accessible information. Cloud platforms help consolidate systems and enable on-demand scalability, with more than 90 percent of agencies expected to adopt hybrid cloud models balancing security considerations. And artificial intelligence solutions are demonstrating early promise automating administrative tasks, customer services, and augmented decision-making.

While leading jurisdictions make rapid progress, more than 3 billion global citizens still lack reliable internet connectivity posing last-mile digital divide gaps that require alternatives like Short Message Service (SMS) or voice interfaces for equitable inclusion. Risks around opaque algorithms, privacy, and security also require governance capabilities advancing alongside technology integration. But success cases prove possibilities spanning decentralized citizen services and democratized policy-making and harnessing private sector innovations for public benefit pointing the roadmap ahead.

These contemporary tools are elevating public transportation through real-time tracking apps, automation, electric fleets, integrated payments, and data-driven customization improving environmental performance, system integration, and experience quality. Shared mobility platforms like rideshares, bike rentals, and scooters also bridge innovations with cooperative business models expanding inclusive access. Overall, these developments highlight synergies between technology adoption and growth of community-oriented services guided by mobility justice and solidarity values.

Similarly, microgrids, virtual power plants, renewable exchanges, smart devices, and predictive algorithms provide means to advance distributed, decarbonized, and digitized energy systems while also linking infrastructural transformation with community sustainability initiatives through participatory planning and financing. This holds potential for just and inclusive clean energy transitions grounded in solidarity economics.

Public healthcare systems grappling with rising costs and talent shortages are turning to telemedicine, mHealth apps, and data integration to enhance access, prevention, patient monitoring, and treatment personalization efficiently to uplift community well-being. But ethical usage of data warrants emphasis. Open contracting also assists connecting system capabilities with localized service gaps through context-specific solutions.

Promising education breakthroughs leverage technologies like broadcast lessons, crowdsourced content, gamified platforms, and immersive simulations to augment teaching and expand lifelong learning preparedness. But adoption barriers around access, assessment frameworks, and procurement inhibit systemic change, requiring visionary leadership and strategic investments from governments.

Thoughtfully directed innovation in housing leveraging modular construction, sensors, geospatial analytics, fractional ownership models, and participatory design processes also illustrates potentials for upgrading infrastructure equitably while accelerating sustainable development embedded within communities.

At the intersection, smart city initiatives adopting ubiquitous connectivity, urban analytics, and civic engagement platforms provide avenues to holistically enhance social, environmental, and economic vitality of places in line with ethical digital frameworks valuing citizen well-being. Strategic integration with social economy entities via partnerships, data access policies, and monitoring thereby helps steer technological tools for common good.

Influential thought leaders like Tim O'Reilly have helped concretize "government as a platform" paradigms, reconceiving bureaucracies as enablers of secure data flows and collective participation assisting bottom-up collaborative solutions between authorities and external actors, rather than siloed centralized providers. Trebor Scholz's theory of "platform cooperativism" alternatively challenges extractive corporate intermediaries by advocating member-owned and democratically governed alternatives that structurally align governance with collective interests. Such conceptual framings provide vital philosophical grounding catalyzing impact-driven digitally enabled innovations across public systems steered responsibly toward quality of life and prosperity.

Pioneering governments are already introducing holistic legal provisions, funding channels and frameworks supporting growth of social economy entities like cooperatives and non-profits to securely embed ethical economic models focused on inclusion, solidarity, and environmental sustainability within civic life. Dedicated public contracting set-asides, preferential community investment vehicles, open data mandates granting grassroot access, streamlined registration pathways, and participative governance councils provide avenues for the public sector and communities to co-create localized solutions grounded in social aims.

Further policy support can empower communal enterprises to address modern welfare gaps and sustainability goals by fostering interdependence and prioritizing the common good. Key measures include: granting legal recognition to informal collectives, providing tailored grants for small-scale projects, establishing public-social innovation partnerships funded through matched crowdfunding, and implementing knowledge-sharing protocols to spread successful models across communities.

The intersection of participatory governance, data-driven systems, and collaborative economic paradigms offers profound opportunities rewiring social contracts to be more pluralistic, equitable, and responsive to pressing public challenges if harnessed responsibly. However, adoption complexities, uneven capabilities across jurisdictions, and risks around digital divides pose implementation hurdles requiring nuanced mitigation so technological transformation sustains human values. Still the promise of reinforcing socio-economic rights, inclusion, and ecological regeneration through purpose-driven innovation beckons continued experimentation and leadership reconceiving the role of contemporary public institutions.

References

Aernouts, N., & Ryckewaert, M. (2015). Reconceptualizing the "publicness" of public housing: The case of Brussels. *Social Inclusion, 3*(2), 17–30.

Aghimien, D., Aigbavboa, C., Aghimien, L., Thwala, W., & Ndlovu, L. (2021). 3D printing for sustainable low-income housing in South Africa: A case for the urban poor. *Journal of Green Building, 16*(2), 129–141.

Ahmad, K., Maabreh, M., Ghaly, M., Khan, K., Qadir, J., & Al-Fuqaha, A. (2022). Developing future human-centered smart cities: Critical analysis of smart city security, Data management, and ethical challenges. *Computer Science Review, 43*, 100452.

Allam, Z., Sharifi, A., Bibri, S. E., Jones, D. S., & Krogstie, J. (2022). The metaverse as a virtual form of smart cities: Opportunities and challenges for environmental, economic, and social sustainability in urban futures. *Smart Cities, 5*(3), 771–801.

Amin, A. (2009). Locating the social economy. In Amin, A. (ed.), *The Social Economy: International Perspectives on Economic Solidarity* (pp. 3–21). London: Zed Books.

Amin, A., Cameron, A., & Hudson, R. (2003). The alterity of the social economy. In Layshon, A., Lee, R & Williams, C. C. (eds.), *Alternative Economic Spaces* (pp. 27–54). Thousand Oaks, CA: SAGE Publications Ltd.

Arcidiacono, D. & Pais, I. (2020). Re-embedding the economy within digitalised foundational sectors: The case of platform cooperativism. In Barbera, F. and Jones, I. R. (eds.), *The foundational economy and citizenship: Comparative perspectives on civil repair* (pp. 27–50). Bristol: Bristol University Press.

Arocena, R., Göransson, B., & Sutz, J. (2017). *Developmental Universities in Inclusive Innovation Systems: Alternatives for Knowledge Democratization in the Global South.* Springer.

Ashford, R. D., Brown, A. M., Dorney, G., McConnell, N., Kunzelman, J., McDaniel, J., & Curtis, B. (2019). Reducing harm and promoting recovery through community-based mutual aid: Characterizing those who engage in a hybrid peer recovery community organization. *Addictive Behaviors, 98*, 106037.

Attard, J., Orlandi, F., Scerri, S., & Auer, S. (2015). A systematic review of open government data initiatives. *Government Information Quarterly, 32*(4), 399–418.

Avelino, F., Wittmayer, J. M., Pel, B., Weaver, P., Dumitru, A., Haxeltine, A., Kemp, R., Jørgensen, M. S., Bauler, T., Ruijsink, S., & O'Riordan, T. (2019). Transformative social innovation and (dis)empowerment. *Technological Forecasting and Social Change, 145*, 195–206.

Baker, S. B., Xiang, W., & Atkinson, I. (2017). Internet of things for smart healthcare: Technologies, challenges, and opportunities. *Ieee Access, 5*, 26521–26544.

Bakker, S. & Konings, R. (2018). The transition to zero-emission buses in public transport – The need for institutional innovation. *Transportation Research Part D: Transport and Environment, 64*, 204–215.

Bauwens, T., & Niaros, V. (2017). *Value in the Commons Economy: Developments in Open and Contributory Value Accounting.* Heinrich Böll Foundation.

Biloria, N. (2021). From smart to empathic cities. *Frontiers of Architectural Research, 10*(1), 3–16.

Blessing, A. (2015). Public, private, or in-between? The legitimacy of social enterprises in the housing market. *VOLUNTAS: International Journal of Voluntary and Nonprofit Organizations, 26*, 198–221.

Bonney, R., Phillips, T. B., Ballard, H. L., & Enck, J. W. (2016). Can citizen science enhance public understanding of science? *Public Understanding of Science, 25*(1), 2–16.

Bredenoord, J. (2016). Sustainable housing and building materials for low-income households. *Journal of Architectural Engineering Technology, 5*(1), 1–9.

Bunders, D. J., Arets, M., Frenken, K. & De Moor, T. (2022). The Feasibility of Platform Cooperatives in the Gig Economy. *Journal of Co-Operative Organization and Management, 10*(1), 100167.

Burrows, A., Meller, B., Craddock, I., Hyland, F., & Gooberman-Hill, R. (2019). User involvement in digital health: Working together to design smart home health technology. *Health Expectations, 22*(1), 65–73.

Calvo, P. (2020). The ethics of Smart City (EoSC): Moral implications of hyperconnectivity, algorithmization and the datafication of urban digital society. *Ethics and Information Technology, 22*(2), 141–149.

Chang, V. (2021). An ethical framework for big data and smart cities. *Technological Forecasting and Social Change, 165*, 120559.

Chaves Ávila, R., & Gallego-Bono, J. R. (2020). Transformative policies for the social and solidarity economy: The new generation of public policies fostering the social economy in order to achieve sustainable development goals. The European and Spanish cases. *Sustainability, 12*(10), 4059.

Collins, A., & Halverson, R. (2018). *Rethinking Education in the Age of Technology: The Digital Revolution and Schooling in America.* Teachers College Press.

Craig, D., Etcheverry, J., & Ferris, S. (2016). Mexico's Telesecundaria Program and equitable access to resources. *McGill Journal of Education, 51*(1), 657–666.

Crabtree, L., Perry, N., Grimstad, S., & McNeill, J. (2021). Impediments and opportunities for growing the cooperative housing sector: An Australian case study. *International Journal of Housing Policy, 21*(1), 138–152.

Czischke, D., & van Bortel, G. (2023). An exploration of concepts and polices on "affordable housing" in England, Italy, Poland and the Netherlands. *Journal of Housing and the Built Environment, 38*(1), 283–303.

Dawes, S. S., Vidiasova, L., & Parkhimovich, O. (2016). Planning and designing open government data programs: An ecosystem approach. *Government Information Quarterly, 33*(1), 15–27.

Dias, N. (ed.) (2018). *Hope for Democracy: 30 Years of Participatory Budgeting Worldwide.* Faro: Epopeia Records and Oficina.

DiBona, C. & Ockman, S. (1999). *Open Sources: Voices from the Open Source Revolution.* Sebastopol, CA: O'Reilly Media, Inc.

Drigas, A., & Koukianakis, L. (2009). *Government Online: An e-government Platform to Improve Public Administration Operations and Services Delivery to the Citizen* (pp. 523–532). Springer Berlin Heidelberg.

Droste, C. (2015). German co-housing: An opportunity for municipalities to foster socially inclusive urban development? *Urban Research & Practice, 8*(1), 79–92.

Edwards Jr, D. B. (2019). Shifting the perspective on community-based management of education: From systems theory to social capital and community empowerment. *International Journal of Educational Development, 64*, 17–26.

Eizenberg, E., & Jabareen, Y. (2017). Social sustainability: A new conceptual framework. *Sustainability, 9*(1), 68.

Ezema, I. C., Olotuah, A. O., & Fagbenle, O. I. (2016). Evaluation of energy use in public housing in Lagos, Nigeria: Prospects for renewable energy sources. *International Journal of Renewable Energy Development, 5*(1), 15–24.

Falk, S., Römmele, A., & Silverman, M. (2017). The promise of digital government. In Falk, S., Römmele, A. & Silverman, M: (eds.), *Digital Government: Leveraging Innovation to Improve Public Sector Performance and Outcomes for Citizens* (pp. 3–23). Switzerland: Springer International Publishing.

Farahani, B., Firouzi, F., Chang, V., Badaroglu, M., Constant, N., & Mankodiya, K. (2018). Towards fog-driven IoT eHealth: Promises and challenges of IoT in medicine and healthcare. *Future Generation Computer Systems, 78*, 659–676.

Feitelson, E., & Salomon, I. (2004). The political economy of transport innovations. In *Transport Developments and Innovations in an Evolving World* (pp. 11–26). Springer Berlin Heidelberg.

Garcia, L. V. (2022, October). Civil servants on open data: Perceptions of Azorean civil servants before an imminent open government data initiative. In Amaral et al. (eds), *Proceedings of the 15th International*

Conference on Theory and Practice of Electronic Governance (pp. 591–593). New York: Association for Computing Machinery.

Grohmann, R. (2023). Not just platform, nor cooperatives: Worker-owned technologies from below. *Communication, Culture & Critique, 16*(4), 274–282.

Guinan, J., & O'Neill, M. (2019). From community wealth-building to system change. *IPPR Progressive Review, 25*(4), 382–392.

Hager, I., Golonka, A., & Putanowicz, R. (2016). 3D printing of buildings and building components as the future of sustainable construction? *Procedia Engineering, 151*, 292–299.

Hansen, J. D., & Reich, J. (2015). Democratizing education? Examining access and usage patterns in massive open online courses. *Science, 350*(6265), 1245–1248.

Helbing, D., Fanitabasi, F., Giannotti, F., Hänggli, R., Hausladen, C. I., van den Hoven, J., . . . & Pournaras, E. (2021). Ethics of smart cities: Towards value-sensitive design and co-evolving city life. *Sustainability, 13*(20), 11162.

Hollis, C., Morriss, R., Martin, J., Amani, S., Cotton, R., Denis, M., & Lewis, S. (2015). Technological innovations in mental healthcare: Harnessing the digital revolution. *The British Journal of Psychiatry, 206*(4), 263–265.

Huang, R., Tlili, A., Chang, T. W., Zhang, X., Nascimbeni, F., & Burgos, D. (2020). Disrupted classes, undisrupted learning during COVID-19 outbreak in China: Application of open educational practices and resources. *Smart Learning Environments, 7*, 1–15.

Hujran, O., Alarabiat, A., Al-Adwan, A. S., & Al-Debei, M. (2023). Digitally transforming electronic governments into smart governments: SMARTGOV, an extended maturity model. *Information Development, 39*(4), 811–834.

Karim, M. R. (2015). E-government in service delivery and citizen's satisfaction: A case study on public sectors in Bangladesh. *International Journal of Managing Public Sector Information and Communication Technologies (IJMPICT), 6*(2), 49–60.

Kirsanova, E. V., Mokhirev, A. I., Sokolov, A. M., Suvorova, E. V., & Zikirova, S. S. (2020). Platform cooperativism—a new model in the knowledge economy. In Bogoviz et al. (eds.), *Frontier Information Technology and Systems Research in Cooperative Economics* (pp. 141–147). Switzerland: Springer International Publishing.

Kobori, H., Dickinson, J. L., Washitani, I., Sakurai, R., Amano, T., Komatsu, N., . . . & Miller-Rushing, A. J. (2016). Citizen science: A new approach to advance ecology, education, and conservation. *Ecological Research, 31*, 1–19.

Kolotouchkina, O., Barroso, C. L., & Sánchez, J. L. M. (2022). Smart cities, the digital divide, and people with disabilities. *Cities, 123*, 103613.

König, P. D. (2021). Citizen-centered data governance in the smart city: From ethics to accountability. *Sustainable Cities and Society, 75*, 103308.

Kuziemski, M., & Misuraca, G. (2020). AI governance in the public sector: Three tales from the frontiers of automated decision-making in democratic settings. *Telecommunications Policy, 44*(6), 101976.

Lacey-Barnacle, M., Smith, A., & Foxon, T. J. (2023). Community wealth building in an age of just transitions: Exploring civil society approaches to net zero and future research synergies. *Energy Policy, 172*, 113277.

Lang, R., & Stoeger, H. (2018). The role of the local institutional context in understanding collaborative housing models: Empirical evidence from Austria. *International Journal of Housing Policy, 18*(1), 35–54.

Leyden, D. P. (2016). Public-sector entrepreneurship and the creation of a sustainable innovative economy. *Small Business Economics, 46*, 553–564.

Löfgren, K., & Webster, C. W. R. (2020). The value of Big Data in government: The case of "smart cities". *Big Data & Society, 7*(1), 1–14.

Lucchi, E., & Delera, A. C. (2020). Enhancing the historic public social housing through a user-centered design-driven approach. *Buildings, 10*(9), 159.

Mannan, M. & Pek, S. (2021). Solidarity in the sharing economy: The role of platform cooperatives at the base of the pyramid. In I. Qureshi, B. Bhatt, & D. M. Shukla (eds.), *Sharing economy at the base of the pyramid* (pp. 249–279). Springer.

Marcolino, M. S., Oliveira, J. A. Q., D'Agostino, M., Ribeiro, A. L., Alkmim, M. B. M., & Novillo-Ortiz, D. (2018). The impact of mHealth interventions: Systematic review of systematic reviews. *JMIR mHealth and uHealth, 6*(1), e8873.

Martinelli, F., Bozzoni, S., Caroli, S., Tamascelli, F., & Guerini, G. (2019). Platform cooperativism in Italy and in Europe. CIRIEC Working Papers 1927. Liège (Belgium): CIRIEC International, Université de Liège.

Matamanda, A. R., Chirisa, I., Rammile, S., & Marais, M. (2022). Socio-cultural, Ecological and economic issues in housing and technology, and the politics. In *Housing and Technology: Special Focus on Zimbabwe* (pp. 79–93). Springer International Publishing.

Mehmood, A. & Imran, M. (2021) Digital social innovation and civic participation: toward responsible and inclusive transport planning. *European Planning Studies, 29*(10), 1870–1885.

Mendell, M., & Neamtan, N. (2010). The social economy in Quebec: Towards a new political economy. In Mook, L., Quarter, J. And Ryan, S. (eds.), *Researching the Social Economy* (pp. 63–83). Toronto: University of Toronto Press.

Miller, E. (2013). Community economy: Ontology, ethics, and politics for radically democratic economic organizing. *Rethinking Marxism, 25*(4), 518–533.

Moedas, C. (2018). *Citizen Science: Innovation in Open Science, Society and Policy*. UCL Press.

Montiel, I., Delgado-Ceballos, J., Ortiz-de-Mandojana, N. & Antolin-Lopez, R. (2020). New ways of teaching: Using technology and mobile apps to educate on societal grand challenges. *Journal of Business Ethics, 161*(2), 243–51

Monzón Campos, J. L., & Chaves Ávila, R. (2017). Recent evolutions of the social economy in the European Union. *Brussels: European Economic and Social Committee, CIRIEC. DOI, 10,* 191345.

Monzón Campos, J. L., & Chaves Ávila, R. (2012). *The Social Economy in the European Union*. European Economic and Social Committee.

Myros, K. (2023). *Open City: Applying Participatory Planning Theory to Open Data Initiatives* (Doctoral dissertation, Harvard University).

Neamtan, N. (2005). The social economy: Finding a way between the market and the state. *Policy Options, 26*(6), 71–76.

Nicholls, A., & Teasdale, S. (2017). Neoliberalism by stealth? Exploring continuity and change within the UK social enterprise policy paradigm. *Policy & Politics, 45*(3), 323–341.

Nicoli, M., & Paltrinieri, L. (2019). Platform cooperativism: Some notes on the becoming "common" of the firm. *South Atlantic Quarterly, 118*(4), 801–819.

OECD (2020). *Social Economy and the COVID-19 Crisis: Current and Future Roles*. OECD Policy Responses to Coronavirus (COVID-19). OECD Publishing.

Okunola, O. M., Rowley, J., & Johnson, F. (2017). The multi-dimensional digital divide: Perspectives from an e-government portal in Nigeria. *Government Information Quarterly, 34*(2), 329–339.

Olojede, O. A., Agbola, S. B., & Samuel, K. J. (2019). Technological innovations and acceptance in public housing and service delivery in South Africa: Implications for the Fourth Industrial Revolution. *Journal of Public Administration, 54*(2), 162–183.

Patergiannaki, Z., & Pollalis, Y. A. (2023). Bridging the gap: Assessing disparities in e-Government service offerings and citizen demand. *Transforming Government: People, Process and Policy, 17*(4), 532–551.

Pazaitis, A., Kostakis, V., & Bauwens, M. (2017). Digital economy and the rise of open cooperativism: The case of the Enspiral Network. *Transfer: European Review of Labour and Research, 23*(2), 177–192.

Pentzien, J. (2020). *The Politics of Platform Cooperativism*. Institute for Digital Cooperative Economy. https://ia801701.us.archive.org/10/items/jonas-pentziensingle-web_202012/Jonas%20Pentzien_single_web.Pdf.

Peters, M. A., & Roberts, P. (2015). *Virtues of Openness: Education, Science, and Scholarship in the Digital Age*. Routledge.

Reich, J. (2020). *Failure to Disrupt: Why Technology Alone Can't Transform Education*. Harvard University Press.

Rendall, J., Curtin, M., Roy, M. J., & Teasdale, S. (2022). Relationships between community-led mutual aid groups and the state during the COVID-19 pandemic: Complementary, supplementary, or adversarial? *Public Management Review, 26*(2), 313–333.

Sakin, M., & Kiroglu, Y. C. (2017). 3D printing of buildings: Construction of the sustainable houses of the future by BIM. *Energy Procedia, 134*, 702–711.

Sandoval, M. (2020). Entrepreneurial activism? Platform cooperativism between subversion and co-optation. *Critical Sociology, 46*(6), 801–817.

Scholz, T. (2016). *Platform cooperativism. Challenging the corporate sharing economy*. New York: Rosa Luxemburg Foundation.

Scholz, T. (2017). *Uberworked and underpaid: How workers are disrupting the digital economy*. Cambridge: Polity Press.

Selwyn, N. (2016). *Is Technology Good for Education?* John Wiley & Sons.

Shaheen, S., & Chan, N. (2016). Mobility and the sharing economy: Potential to facilitate the first-and last-mile public transit connections. *Built Environment, 42*(4), 573–588.

Shamsuddin, S., & Srinivasan, S. (2021). Just smart or just and smart cities? Assessing the literature on housing and information and communication technology. *Housing Policy Debate, 31*(1), 127–150.

Shen, K., Cheng, C., Li, X., & Zhang, Z. (2019). Environmental cost-benefit analysis of prefabricated public housing in Beijing. *Sustainability, 11*(1), 207.

Sieber, R. E., & Johnson, P. A. (2015). Civic open data at a crossroads: Dominant models and current challenges. *Government Information Quarterly, 32*(3), 308–315.

Silva, B. M., Rodrigues, J. J., de la Torre Díez, I., López-Coronado, M., & Saleem, K. (2015). Mobile-health: A review of current state in 2015. *Journal of Biomedical Informatics, 56*, 265–272.

Simonova, P., Cincera, J., Kroufek, R., Krepelkova, S., & Hadjichambis, A. (2019). Active citizens: Evaluation of a community-based education program. *Sustainability, 11*(3), 663.

Simpson, O. (2018). *Supporting Students in Online, Open and Distance Learning*. London and New York: Routledge.

Smith, A., & Martín, P. P. (2022). Going beyond the smart city? Implementing technopolitical platforms for urban democracy in Madrid and Barcelona. In Mora et al. (eds.), *Sustainable Smart City Transitions* (pp. 280–299). Oxon and New York: Routledge.

Smith, G., Sochor, J. & Sarasini, S. (2020). Problematising mobility-as-a-service: Insights from the Helsinki MaaS case. *Transp. Res. Part A Policy Pract., 141*, 300–316.

Su, Y., Hou, F., Qi, M., Li, W., & Ji, Y. (2021). A data-enabled business model for a smart healthcare information service platform in the era of digital transformation. *Journal of Healthcare Engineering, 2021*(1), 1–9.

Suartika, G. A. M., & Cuthbert, A. (2020). The sustainable imperative—smart cities, technology and development. *Sustainability, 12*(21), 8892.

Theobald, P. (2018). *Teaching the Commons: Place, Pride, and the Renewal of Community*. Routledge.

Theodos, B., Marx, R., & Nunna, T. (2021). *Community Wealth-Building Models*. Urban Institute. Available at: https://www.urban.org/sites/default/files/publication/105230/community-wealth-building-models_1.pdf (accessed February 17, 2024).

Thompson, M. (2015). Between boundaries: From commoning and guerrilla gardening to community land trust development in Liverpool. *Antipode, 47*(4), 1021–1042.

Trencher, G., & Karvonen, A. (2020). Stretching "smart": Advancing health and well-being through the smart city agenda. In *Smart and Sustainable Cities?* (pp. 54–71). Routledge.

Utting, P. (2018). *Achieving the Sustainable Development Goals through Social and Solidarity Economy: Incremental versus Transformative Change*. UNSRID.

Vaillancourt, Y. (2009). Social economy in the co-construction of public policy. *Annals of Public and Cooperative Economics*, *80*(2), 275–313.

Weber, K. M., Heller-Schuh, B., Godoe, H. & Roeste, R. (2014). ICT-enabled system innovations in public services: Experiences from intelligent transport systems. *Telecommunications Policy*, *38*(5–6), 539–557.

Webster, A., Kuznetsova, O., Ross, C., Berranger, C., Booth, M., Eseonu, T., & Golan, Y. (2021). Local regeneration and community wealth building–place making: Co-operatives as agents of change. *Journal of Place Management and Development*, *14*(4), 446–461.

Webster, A., & Wyatt, S. (2020). *Health, Technology and Society*. Springer Singapore.

Williamson, B., Eynon, R., & Potter, J. (2020). Pandemic politics, pedagogies and practices: Digital technologies and distance education during the coronavirus emergency. *Learning, Media and Technology*, *45*(2), 107–114.

Wirtz, B. W., & Kurtz, O. T. (2016a). Citizen preferences toward e-Government city portals—an empirical analysis of full online, mobile and social media services. *International Public Management Review*, *17*(1), 1–20.

Wirtz, B. W., & Kurtz, O. T. (2016b). Local e-government and user satisfaction with city portals—the citizens' service preference perspective. *International Review on Public and Nonprofit Marketing*, *13*, 265–287.

Wolfert, S., Ge, L., Verdouw, C., & Bogaardt, M. J. (2017). Big data in smart farming—a review. *Agricultural Systems*, *153*, 69–80.

Wu, W., Zhu, D., Liu, W. & Wu, C. H. (2022). Empirical research on smart city construction and public health under information and communications technology. *Socio-Economic Planning Sciences*, *80*(9), 1–40.

Yang, J., Kwon, Y. & Kim, D. (2020). Regional smart city development focus: The South Korean national strategic smart city program. *IEEE Access*, *9*, 7193–7210.

Yang, Y. (2017). Towards a new digital era: Observing local e-government services adoption in a Chinese municipality. *Future Internet*, *9*(3), 53.

Yigitcanlar, T., Mehmood, R., & Corchado, J. M. (2021). Green artificial intelligence: Towards an efficient, sustainable and equitable technology for smart cities and futures. *Sustainability*, *13*(16), 8952.

Yu, S. W. Y., Hill, C., Ricks, M. L., Bennet, J. & Oriol, N. E. (2017). The scope and impact of mobile health clinics in the United States: A literature review. *International Journal for Equity in Health*, *16*(1), 178,

Yun, J. J., Zhao, X., Wu, J., Yi, J. C., Park, K., & Jung, W. (2020). Business model, open innovation, and sustainability in car sharing industry—Comparing three economies. *Sustainability*, *12*(5), 1883.

Zygmuntowski, J. J. (2018). Commoning in the digital era: Platform cooperativism as a counter to cognitive capitalism. *Praktyka teoretyczna (Theoretical Practice)*, *27*(1), 168–192.

Chapter 5
Sustainability and the Social Economy

Introduction

Sustainability has become an increasingly important concept in recent decades as we recognize the need to preserve our planet and its resources for future generations. Sustainability refers to meeting the needs of the present without compromising the ability of future generations to meet their own needs. It requires simultaneously balancing environmental, social, and economic demands—known as the three pillars of sustainability.

Achieving sustainability is critical if we hope to address major global issues like climate change, biodiversity loss, pollution, poverty, and inequality. The way our modern societies and economies currently operate is putting unsustainable strain on planetary ecosystems and human well-being. Continuing with business-as-usual practices risks catastrophic and irreversible damage. We need deep, structural changes that transition societies onto a sustainable development pathway.

The social economy can play a key role in driving sustainability transformations. The social economy refers to community institutions, networks, collaborations, and practices that are oriented toward the common good, prioritizing social objectives over profit maximization. It includes organizations such as cooperatives, mutual societies, associations, foundations, social enterprises, credit unions, and more. Social economy organizations tend to have ethics of solidarity, participatory governance, and production that meet social needs embedded into their models.

There are several ways the social economy can foster sustainable development:

Sustainable production and consumption: The social economy enables sustainable production and consumption patterns—moving away from the linear "take–make–waste" model toward a circular system. Social enterprises can design products and business models that are regenerative by design. Platform cooperatives can leverage sharing and the collaborative economy to maximize resource efficiency. Community-supported agriculture allows for localized and ecologically conscious food production and distribution.

Community resilience: The social economy strengthens communities, enhancing their ability to cope with external shocks and stresses. It localizes economies, builds social capital, and embeds businesses structurally within communities. This is essential for community resilience in the face of accelerating climate change-related natural disasters.

Social inclusion: The social economy is more inclusive of disadvantaged groups. It provides opportunities for dignified livelihoods, skill development, participatory gover-

https://doi.org/10.1515/9783111080147-005

nance, and more. This helps tackle intersecting sustainability issues like inequality, disenfranchisement of marginalized groups, skills gaps, and unemployment.

Systems thinking: The social economy adopts a systems-thinking approach recognizing the interconnections between ecological and human systems. It shifts away from reductionist logic and short-term profits toward long-term, holistic value creation. This enables identifying root causes within systems and transformative solutions.

Grassroots innovation: The fluid, decentralized nature of the social economy fosters grassroots experimentation and innovation. Enabling conditions allow communities to develop local solutions to sustainability challenges. This process of grassroots innovation helps test and diffuse sustainable technologies and practices.

Democratic ownership: Workplace democracy advances participatory decision-making between owners, managers, and workers in the social economy. This enables incorporating sustainability considerations and stewardship at the ownership level, not just corporate social responsibility initiatives.

There is growing recognition among governments, businesses, and civil society of the vital role the social economy can play in advancing sustainability locally and globally. However, certain actions are still necessary to unleash the full potential of the social economy. These include:
–   developing better measurement tools and indicators to evaluate the sustainability impacts of social economy organizations potentially demonstrating and improving performance
–   creating more conducive legislation, policies, and incentives at multiple levels to support social enterprises and broader social innovation
–   facilitating partnerships and collaboration between stakeholders in the social economy and other sectors to increase synergies
–   setting up intermediary institutions like incubators and accelerators to provide crucial financing, capacity-building, and developmental support
–   expanding access to markets for social economy products and services through means like social public procurement
–   increasing awareness and championing local success stories to inspire replication and model sustainability solutions

The urgency and enormity of global sustainability challenges can seem daunting. However, social economy organizations provide working examples of business models advancing sustainable development on the ground. It gives agency to ordinary citizens joining together in collective action for the common good. With the right nurturing, the social economy can scale impactfully. It provides reason for hope by demonstrating possible pathways to just and sustainable futures.

Sustainability and Climate Change

Sustainability has become a pivotal concept in policy, business, and environmental discourse over the past few decades. Sustainability refers to "the ability of systems, processes, institutions, etc. to maintain themselves over long periods of time" (Scoones, 2007). The growing recognition that human economic activity threatens environmental sustainability and Earth's capacity to support human civilization has spurred increasing attention and action around ideas of sustainability (Portney, 2015).

Climate change poses one of the gravest threats to sustainability today. The release of greenhouse gasses through industrial activity and other human impacts is changing the climate in potentially catastrophic ways (Thiele, 2016). Addressing climate change is thus crucial for creating environmentally sustainable systems. However, the concept of sustainability is complex and multidimensional. Crucially, sustainability has environmental, economic, and social dimensions (Giovannoni & Fabietti, 2013). Creating truly sustainable systems requires attention to all three areas.

The history of sustainability thought provides useful context. As Caradonna (2022) explores, concepts of limits to growth and human impacts on the environment emerged starting in the late eighteenth century. However, widespread societal concern with sustainability only developed in the late twentieth century with growing evidence of issues like climate change. The 1987 Brundtland Report provided an early working definition of sustainable development that linked economic development to environmental protection (Farley & Smith, 2020). Principles and frameworks for putting sustainability into practice also began taking shape in the 1990s and 2000s through scholarship and international agreements like the 1992 Rio Summit (Dresner, 2012).

Debates continue today about how to define sustainability and operationalize it. For instance, Scoones (2016) analyzes tensions between meanings of sustainability oriented toward environmental protection versus economic development. Multiple overlapping discourses shape modern notions of sustainability. Nonetheless, a broad consensus has emerged that human society must transition toward more sustainable systems to avoid environmental catastrophe from climate change and other threats. Sustainability must become an imperative for governments, corporations, and society as a whole (Lubin & Esty, 2010).

Pursuing sustainability requires transformations across economic, social, and political institutions. Technical solutions are important but insufficient without cultural and systems change. Grassroots community initiatives offer promising models and starting points. For instance, local food systems often aim toward environmental, economic, and social sustainability goals (Connelly et al., 2011). The social and solidarity economy movement works to center ethics and sustainability across economic production and consumption (Chaves Ávila & Monzón Campos, 2012). Sharing platforms also hold potential to improve urban sustainability, though impacts remain complex (Wu & Zhi, 2016).

More broadly, frameworks integrating all three dimensions of sustainability have emerged to guide transitions. Scholars increasingly advocate for "scaling up" local alternatives like cooperatives and transition towns to drive systemic change (Markey & Roseland, 2016). Boyer et al. (2016) synthesize five key approaches to social sustainability to enable flourishing, equitable communities. Such work shows expanding recognition that incremental change is not enough; deeply transformative shifts toward sustainability are essential across all of society's systems.

Climate change makes this sustainability transition urgent. Its impacts already disproportionately harm marginalized communities and threaten to spur conflict, migration, and suffering on a massive scale if left unaddressed (Scoones, 2016). Radically reducing greenhouse gas emissions can mitigate the worst climate disruption. But adaptation is also crucial since substantial effects are already locked in due to past emissions. Building resilient, sustainable systems is vital to weather intensifying climate impacts.

Strategies to enable sustainability and climate resilience must be holistic and justice oriented. Merely technical or efficiency-based approaches will not suffice. Distributive, procedural, contextual, and social justice should infuse solutions to transform unsustainable political economies burdening people and the planet (Boyer et al., 2016). For example, sustainable development must emancipate all individuals and communities rather than further entrench inequality and power imbalances. Climate adaptation should resource vulnerable frontline communities to determine their own survival strategies rather than impose top-down policies.

In these ways, sustainability provides a broad umbrella for connecting diverse environmental, economic, and social justice efforts. As an essentially contested concept with complex discursive lineages, sustainability lacks fixed meaning but its very ambiguity can foster collaboration (Farley & Smith, 2020). Integrated social and ecological systems approaches align well with sustainability's interdisciplinary, multidimensional nature. By centering ethics, justice, and holism along with technical environmental solutions, the sustainability movement holds potential to address interconnected crises like climate change.

The coming decades are decisive for determining whether humanity can transition toward sustainability or will continue on disastrous unsustainable pathways. Climate change serves as a critical threat but also an opportunity for catalyzing systems change. Policy developments like the Paris Agreement and Sustainable Development Goals provide some governmental frameworks for progress but much more ambitious political transformation is needed. Grassroots community alternatives offer starting points along with pressure on corporations and states to support broader shifts through regulation, incentives, and public investment. No singular fixed solution exists; rather, collaborative innovation across all of society is necessary to equitably transition interconnected environment, economy, technology, culture, and politics to promote ecological sustainability, human well-being, and climate justice. The magnitude of the sustainability challenge ahead is immense but so too is the creativity, resilience, and solidarity to achieve it.

The Economics of Sustainability

The pursuit of endless economic growth sits in fundamental tension with ecological sustainability. As environmental crises like climate change intensify, the need for transformative new economic models aligned with sustainability becomes increasingly urgent. Integrating environmental costs and impacts into economic accounting represents one pathway to re-orient economics toward sustainability rather than the growth imperative.

The contemporary global economy rests on the assumption and goal of continual GDP growth. Mainstream economics long regarded the natural world as unlimited and external to economic models (Hess, 2016). However, ecological economists have demonstrated that the economy exists within and depends upon Earth's limited biophysical systems. Economic activity inevitably generates environmental costs that eventually threaten humanity's ecological life support systems, as visible through issues like climate change (Soubbotina, 2004).

Nonetheless, perpetual growth remains core to mainstream economics and policymaking. Politically and socially, growth currently serves as a key indicator of progress and prosperity, leading some to argue that abandoning GDP growth as an economic priority risks instability or losing public support (Beckerman, 2015). Growth advocates contend that environmental innovation and decoupling can potentially enable green growth aligned with sustainability (Ekins, 2002). However, critics counter that efficiency alone cannot offset the escalating resource use and emissions from perpetually rising production and consumption (Spangenberg, 2010). Fundamentally questioning growth thus emerges as essential for envisioning truly sustainable economies.

Debates continue between imagining sustainable development through evolving current capitalist systems versus requiring post-growth or degrowth transformations. Ekins (1993) provides an early analysis of these tensions between limits to growth and sustainable development discourse. Thinkers like Daly (2014) call for steady-state economics that stabilize production, consumption, and population at sustainable levels rather than pursuing endless growth. Others argue sustainable degrowth, which intentionally downscales production and consumption, is essential for just sustainability transitions (Kyrö, 2001).

Overall, the growth paradigm's dominance has stifled visionary thinking around alternative economic models. Innovations in green technology and other spaces fail to challenge the broader political economies driving unsustainability (Davies & Mullin, 2011). Resisting growth demands recognizing ecological limits while centering equity and human well-being over accumulation and throughput (Harris, 2003). Moving beyond growth opens imaginative possibilities, from circular economies to post-capitalist models grounded in care, creativity, and community rather than profit maximization (Dasgupta, 2007).

Rethinking economies requires better incorporating sustainability costs and benefits into accounting. Conventional market prices and GDP metrics distort sustainability signals and encourage unconstrained growth (Munier, 2006). For instance, depleting nonrenewable resources registers as productive economic activity. Degrading public goods like clean air and water lack dedicated price signals. Mainstream accounting frequently buries or externalizes environmental and social costs (Bartelmus & Seifert, 2018).

Green accounting helps internalize such costs and benefits to steer economies and firms toward sustainability. El Serafy (1997) offers an early vision for adjusting national income accounts based on renewable natural capital maintenance, pollution abatement costs, and more. Other approaches include corporate environmental accountability through sustainability reporting and life cycle assessments of supply chain impacts. These can shift business and consumer behavior, though have limitations in comprehensively representing environmental damage (Cho & Patten, 2013).

Implementation of green accounting practices remains uneven across contexts. Caraiani (2015) reviews initiatives to integrate environmental scorecards and metrics across accounting. Yet persisting challenges include accurately pricing "public bads" like biodiversity loss and institutionalizing sustainability indicators within managerial decisions (Caraiani, 2015). Developing countries additionally face barriers to adopting green accounting given lower awareness, technical capacity, and transparency (Farouk et al., 2012). Various efforts nonetheless display potential, from European nations' progress on environmental satellite accounts to bottom-up sustainability measurement tools (Markandya & Pavan, 2012; Maama & Appiah, 2019).

Fundamentally, green accounting requires not just new metrics but transformed economic paradigms. As currently applied, green accounting often serves to refine GDP growth rather than displace it as the predominant goal (Harris, 2003). Technocratic reforms alone risk further economizing and financializing the natural world without confronting unsustainable systems. The growth imperative itself must be challenged through new ontological framings, political contestation, and radical practice centered on livelihood well-being over capital accumulation (Davies & Mullin, 2011; Kyrö, 2001). Sustainability and green accounting must strengthen rather than circumvent economic democracy and social movements mobilizing systemic alternatives to growth-based capitalism.

In conjunction with ecological limits, rising inequality and stagnating well-being in rich countries dispels the necessity of relentless economic expansion (Spangenberg, 2010). Green accounting to guide non-growing, redistributive economies could significantly improve general prosperity. For instance, adjusting economic metrics to account for existing wealth, undercompensated labor, and free public goods exposes possibilities for work-time reduction and enhanced livelihoods even absent growth (Daly, 2014; El Serafy, 1997). Simplicity and sufficiency can orient cultural and business reinvention around prosperity for all within ecological boundaries.

Tensions nonetheless remain between just sustainability transitions, North–South equity, and varied developmental visions (Beckerman, 2015; Kyrö, 2001). Western overconsumption obliges deep cuts more than Southern countries still meeting basic needs and infrastructure. Yet planetary boundaries constrain all nations' pathways. Green accounting must navigate these complex equity dimensions amid worldwide collaboration for sustainability.

Green accounting, in this respect, offers tools to integrate sustainability signals and priorities into economic governance. Methodological refinements can help rationalize environmental policymaking and business operations. However, meaningfully confronting issues like climate change ultimately requires a cultural and civilizational shift away from prioritizing exponential economic growth above ecological limits, community well-being, and life's inherent meaning. Technological improvement and efficiency alone are insufficient to transcend growth dependence. Moving beyond growth opens imaginative possibility space for new economic forms and ways of living, perhaps grounded in care, creativity, and connection with one another and nature. Rethinking progress itself is vital for just, sustainable futures. Green accounting represents one pathway to redirect economics from its growth obsession toward supporting prosperous yet non-growing economies that thrive within our planet's ecological boundaries.

KEY THINKER: Tim Jackson

Tim Jackson is a prominent ecological economist and thought leader known for his work on sustainable prosperity and post-growth economics. As the Founding Director of the Centre for the Understanding of Sustainable Prosperity (CUSP), Jackson has shaped global debates on rethinking economic growth to promote human and ecological well-being (Jackson, 2021).

Jackson's career spans more than three decades, beginning with research on industrial ecology and clean technology before shifting to explore cultural drivers of consumption and material throughput (Jackson, 1996; Jackson, 2021). His work as the UK Sustainable Development Commissioner and his role in various international advisory bodies, including the United Nations Environment Programme (UNEP), have positioned him as a key figure in sustainability policy (Jackson, 2005; Jackson, 2021).

His 2009 book *Prosperity Without Growth* was groundbreaking, arguing that GDP growth is not essential for prosperity and calling for new economic models that prioritize well-being within ecological limits (Jackson, 2016). The book's emphasis on quality of life and systemic reforms, such as reducing working hours, resonated widely and helped legitimize post-growth thinking across mainstream politics and economics. A revised edition in 2016 deepened its proposals, responding to critics and incorporating updated data and alternative metrics for success (Jackson, 2016).

Jackson's research integrates interdisciplinary perspectives to propose alternatives to growth-centered economics. His work with ecological economist Peter Victor demonstrated viable scenarios for job creation, poverty reduction, and financial stability in zero-growth economies (Jackson & Victor, 2015). By reforming areas like money creation, investment, and inequality, their models offer a technical foundation for sustainable prosperity.

His academic contributions include his 1996 book *Material Concerns*, which pioneered concepts in industrial ecology and preventive environmental management (Jackson, 2021). He further developed these ideas through leadership of research groups like the ESRC's Research Group on Lifestyles, Values and the Environment (RESOLVE) and the Sustainable Lifestyles Research Group (SLRG), emphasizing systemic changes over individual behavior shifts (Jackson, 2021).

Jackson's latest book, *Post Growth: Life After Capitalism* (2021), provides his most radical critique of capitalism yet. It argues that equitable, sustainable futures are unattainable without transitioning beyond capitalism's growth compulsion (Jackson, 2021). He outlines community-oriented alternatives like cooperatives and commons, blending post-growth thought with anti-capitalist, eco-socialist, and ecofeminist movements.

His role as director of CUSP further amplifies his impact. The Centre convenes experts across fields to develop prosperity frameworks integrating ecology, justice, and well-being. Jackson's ability to communicate complex ideas through various mediums, including as an award-winning BBC playwright, makes his work accessible and influential across policy, academia, and cultural spaces (Jackson, 2021).

Furthermore, Jackson's extensive policy roles have included advising the UK government, serving on the Club of Rome, and advocating for civilizational shifts around growth and consumption. His work has earned him recognition, such as the 2016 Hillary Sustainability Prize, and solidified his status as a thought leader capable of inserting radical ideas into high-level discussions.

New Sustainable Economic Models

Achieving sustainable development requires holistic transformations across interconnected ecological, economic, and social dimensions. While environmental and economic sustainability dominate policy and research, social sustainability has recently gained increasing attention (Eizenberg & Jabareen, 2017). Moving beyond technocratic paradigms focused narrowly on material and economic conditions, emerging social sustainability perspectives recognize the integral importance of community resilience, justice, and well-being in realizing equitable, regenerative societal futures (Rogers et al., 2012).

However, multiple overlapping discourses and definitions characterize the contested, interdisciplinary terrain of social sustainability scholarship. Social sustainability integrates diverse theoretical lineages from development studies, urban planning, political science, and sociological theory (Littig & Griessler, 2005). Differing ideological assumptions about social relations and progress underpin debates on conceptualizing and operationalizing social sustainability. Nonetheless, several unifying principles and themes around enabling flourishing communities and social justice within ecological limits have coalesced in recent literature.

Ambiguous and multidimensional by nature, social sustainability lacks fixed universal definition. But dominant perspectives envision socially sustainable communities as those displaying resilience, justice, cohesion, and well-being within environmental constraints (Davidson, 2010; Dempsey et al., 2011). Prevalent sustainability discourses emphasize integrating equity, livelihood security, and participation in development processes (Davidson, 2009). Attention centers on strengthening social relations and institutions to equitably meet human needs while respecting ecosystems.

Critics argue such expansive, vaguely positive formulations risk conceptual incoherence and political toothlessness. Social sustainability might simply become rhetorical cover for business-as-usual unsustainability, lacking substantive parameters for evaluating or directing social change (Littig & Griessler, 2005). Indeed, policies and firms frequently employ the term rather meaninglessly to claim social responsibility without operationalizing robust criteria or questioning political-economic drivers of community impoverishment.

In response, some scholars advocate narrowing definitions of social sustainability around specific normative priorities like basic needs provision or reducing inequality (Rogers et al., 2012). However, overspecifying risks losing interconnected, contextually grounded understandings of community well-being. Ultimately social sustainability likely functions best as a broad orienting vision for socially just living conditions, with contextual judgements on appropriate indicators and policies. Rigorous evaluation frameworks tailored to varied settings offer pragmatic middle ground.

Despite definitional debates, overarching elements and dynamics of socially sustainable systems have crystallized across research fields. Emerging frameworks share focus on satisfaction of human needs, social justice, and cohesion, and democratic participation towards empowerment and self-determined development trajectories (Missimer et al., 2017). Attention centers livelihood security enabling human capabilities and dignity rather than just crude material accumulation. Psychological fulfillment and cultural meaning also feature prominently (Ajmal et al., 2018; Åhman, 2013).

Within such broad concerns, social equity and full democratic participation in decisions shaping socio-ecological futures emerge as key priorities for theory and practice (Eizenberg & Jabareen, 2017). Social sustainability occurs through inclusive, transparent processes where all community members hold power over collective conditions and rules. This centering of agency aligns with Amartya Sen's foundational capabilities approach in human development. Moreover, social sustainability requires equitable distribution of resources, capabilities, and political voice, such that no groups face marginalization (Davidson, 2010). Tackling intersectional inequalities across race, class, gender, and beyond underlies creating thriving communities.

Crucially, social sustainability interrelates deeply with environmental and economic dimensions. Socially sustainable communities minimize environmental harms from meeting needs to sustain ecological integrity (Davidson, 2010). Transitioning sectors like energy and housing toward justice and participation simultaneously enables climate change mitigation. Likewise, economic policies valorizing shared prosperity over individual accumulation reinforce social sustainability (Fernandes et al., 2021). For instance, workplace democracy and profit sharing strengthen economic security and bonds among workers.

In practice, positive feedback likely emerges within balanced pursuit of social, environmental, and economic sustainability rather than tradeoffs between them (Montabon et al., 2016). Green industries cultivating good jobs and community wealth foster simultaneous ecological regeneration, economic security, and social cohesion. Instead of positioning dimensions of sustainability in opposition, integrated approaches targeting root drivers of unsustainability across society's systems can align efforts.

While frameworks abound, practical tools and metrics to evaluate and direct social sustainability remain underdeveloped, particularly relative to quantifiable environmental and economic indicators. Nonetheless, varied emerging approaches target different scales from macro policymaking to household consumption and firm operations. At national and regional levels, social sustainability metrics integrate into policy decisions balancing economic development and ecological protection. For instance, the UN Sustainable Development Goals include targets around poverty, equality, justice, and other societal conditions. Various proprietary country benchmarking systems similarly now incorporate social inclusion, basic needs, and well-being measures (Barrier, 2017). Quantifying social objectives helps balance investments in human development rather than narrowly pursuing income growth.

Firms also operationalize social sustainability through ethical sourcing policies, disclosure rules, and production standards. Assessing supply chain impacts on community livelihoods, labor rights, and political marginalization guides ethical business models (Hutchins & Sutherland, 2008). Mandating corporate sustainability reporting and integrating site-specific social risks into management choices provides accountability mechanisms. Shared value creation principles also reconceive profitable operations by targeting social issues like nutrition or affordable housing as core business opportunities rather than peripheral externalities (Montabon et al., 2016).

At local scales, social sustainability manifests through participatory processes and grassroots initiatives cultivating community resilience and justice. Transition towns, eco-villages, and other community projects pioneer situated transition cultures and economies seeking locality-appropriate sustainability across social, ecological, and economic dimensions (Eizenberg & Jabareen, 2017). Fostering spaces for inclusive democratic deliberation, creative regeneration, and human development enables contextual grounding absent from high-level indicator frameworks.

Ultimately, qualitative and contextual understandings of dignity, justice, and well-being must inform quantitative metrics tracking macro-level societal conditions (Davidson, 2010). Raw statistical monitoring risks overlooking lived experiences of unsustainability or dignity. For instance, economic security indicators should contextualize absolute income levels with relative costs of living and psychological stress. Locally defined communal needs and aspirations provide imperative guidance for policy choices and measurement tools aiming to enact social sustainability from the ground up.

While terminology has exploded in recent decades, social sustainability perspectives remain marginalized in policy and business practice relative to prevailing economic and environmental emphases. Technocratic efficiency paradigms, overwhelmed by mathematized life cycle assessments, carbon accounting, and circular economy metrics, fail to address the growing issues of inequality and populism faced by communities. Centering social sustainability research and organizing can help repoliticize sustainability around emancipatory visions of justice, solidarity, and well-being counteracting contemporary societal fragmentation.

Social sustainability offers umbrella logic integrating varied social justice efforts from racial equity to platform cooperativism within holistic ecological visions. The fact that sustainability is an essentially contested concept fosters "discursive coalitions" between diverse change agents (Davidson, 2010). Shared discursive space facilitates building power across social movements. Moreover, foregrounding social sustainability highlights interlinkages of human and environmental crises in systemic critiques (Ajmal et al., 2018; Hutchins & Sutherland, 2008). It frames sustainability around meaningful work, thriving communities, and democratized livelihoods rather than merely cutting emissions or protecting nature devoid of people.

Within climate policy in particular, centering social sustainability injects equity and justice into transition strategies otherwise technocratically focused only on aggregate emission targets. Climate action centered on decentralization and local empowerment through renewables or public transport better supports community resilience and participation than exclusionary high-modernist decarbonization concentrated in elite hands. Joining climate justice, just transition, environmental justice, and degrowth movements, social sustainability offers radical holistic logic to reclaim sustainability politics from captured greenhouse gas bureaucracies back toward transformative democracy.

Social sustainability has gained prominence as a crucial force for equitable, regenerative futures meeting human needs within ecological limits. Despite conceptual complexity, core principles of livelihood security, social inclusion, and democratic agency broadly unite scholarship and policy frameworks. Operationalizing social sustainability requires qualitative, contextual, and participatory governance processes genuinely empowering communities toward self-determined resilience. As sustainability discourses risk deterioration into managerial greenwashing, centering social sustainability renews transformations toward justice, solidarity, and emancipation throughout ecology, economics, and society.

KEY THINKER: Kate Raworth

Kate Raworth has rapidly gained prominence as a leading economic thinker shaping twenty-first-century visions of prosperity within ecological limits. Her innovative "doughnut economics" framework offers a holistic model that integrates a social foundation and environmental ceiling to guide sustainable, just economies (Raworth, 2017).

The model envisions a "safe and just space" for humanity, where economic activity satisfies essential needs without breaching ecological boundaries.

Raworth's career began with a focus on international development, working on microenterprise projects in Zanzibar and contributing to UN Development Programme reports that highlighted globalization's uneven impacts. Her decade as a senior researcher at Oxfam exposed interconnected global challenges, deepening her resolve to rethink economic systems beyond isolated interventions (Raworth, 2017). This led to her development of the doughnut model, first introduced in her 2012 Oxfam paper "A Safe and Just Space for Humanity" (Raworth, 2012).

The doughnut framework consists of two concentric rings: an inner social foundation representing essential human needs—such as nutrition, healthcare, and education—and an outer ecological ceiling delineating planetary boundaries (e.g., climate stability, biodiversity loss) based on the work of Rockström et al. (Raworth, 2017). Economic activity should occur within this "doughnut" space, ensuring that no one falls short on life's essentials while avoiding environmental degradation.

Raworth's 2017 book *Doughnut Economics: Seven Ways to Think Like a 21st-century Economist* further develops this framework, offering practical strategies for rethinking economic priorities. By challenging the orthodox focus on GDP growth, she advocates for economies centered on human well-being and environmental health rather than perpetual accumulation (Raworth, 2017).

The doughnut model has gained traction globally, influencing academic research, civil society, and policymaking. Municipalities like Amsterdam have adopted the model to guide urban planning and sustainability policies, while cities like Portland, Melbourne, and Nanaimo are developing local doughnuts to assess progress against social and ecological goals (Raworth, 2017). The model's intuitive logic and clear visuals have made it a powerful tool for communicating complex sustainability concepts and rallying public support.

Beyond local governments, the doughnut framework has inspired national-level analyses and sector-specific transformations, from education to industry, as well as new metrics for evaluating prosperity (Page & Panfil, 2021). Raworth collaborates with diverse stakeholders, including the Wellbeing Economy Alliance and the United Nations, to translate the model into actionable policies (Raworth, 2017).

Critics caution that doughnut economics could be co-opted or reduced to a technocratic tool that overlooks systemic power imbalances (Turner & Wills, 2022). While visually compelling, simply plotting social and ecological metrics without addressing the underlying drivers of inequality and environmental harm risks depoliticizing complex issues. To maintain its transformative potential, the model must confront political-economic structures that perpetuate unsustainable practices (Wahlund & Hansen, 2022).

Despite these challenges, doughnut economics has successfully mainstreamed holistic, justice-based economic thinking. Its appeal lies in combining analytical rigor with accessibility, bridging academic research, activism, and policy innovation. Raworth's ability to communicate big ideas effectively has made her a sought-after speaker, advisor, and educator, shaping economic paradigms worldwide.

Raworth's work exemplifies the power of reimagining economics for the twenty-first century. By advocating for economies that enable everyone to thrive within the planet's limits, she has laid the groundwork for a shift from growth-driven systems to sustainable, inclusive prosperity. As more cities, institutions, and communities embrace doughnut thinking, Raworth's influence continues to grow, offering a compelling vision for navigating the intertwined social and environmental crises of our time (Raworth, 2017).

Net Zero Strategies

Achieving "net zero" greenhouse gas (GHG) emissions has become central to global climate strategies. However, the practical meaning and implementation of net zero targets remain complex and contested, lacking cohesive policy frameworks or consensus (Fankhauser et al., 2022). This essay explores definitions, strategies, and critiques around realizing net zero ambitions, highlighting technical, economic, and governance aspects required for reducing GHG emissions below levels absorbed by natural and technological carbon sinks.

Net zero broadly refers to balancing GHG emissions with equivalent removals through land, plant, or engineered sequestration (Rogelj et al., 2021). This encompasses varied strategies to reduce and remove emissions, yet definitions and timelines remain ambiguous (Allen et al., 2022). Related terms like "carbon neutrality" and "climate positivity" prioritize different approaches, complicating the landscape. Carbon neutrality often relies on offsets like renewable energy certificates or forestry schemes, without necessarily achieving absolute emissions cuts needed for planetary stability (Cole, 2015; Allen et al., 2022).

Net zero, in contrast, requires eliminating 90 percent or more of emissions through decarbonizing key sectors like energy, transportation, buildings, and industry, while neutralizing residual emissions through bioenergy carbon capture or direct air capture (Rogelj et al., 2021). This emphasizes transforming supply chains, rather than merely neutralizing unsustainable systems (Davis et al., 2018). The 2015 Paris Agreement aims to keep global warming under 2°C (preferably 1.5°C), spurring net zero pledges from more than 125 countries covering 90 percent of global emissions, along with numerous municipalities and corporations (Fankhauser et al., 2022). However, uncertainties persist on whether clean electrification, hydrogen fuels, bioenergy, or behavior changes can reshape systems quickly enough (Bistline, 2021; Pye et al., 2021).

Modeling scenarios assess various approaches, including aggressive electrification, hydrogen adoption, lifestyle changes, and large-scale carbon removal through reforestation or direct air capture (DeAngelo et al., 2021). Integrated assessments suggest that net zero requires deploying multiple solutions simultaneously, alongside profound demand reductions across diverse regions (DeAngelo et al., 2021). Rapid innovation and investment are critical to drive cost declines enabling large-scale uptake (Stern & Valero, 2021). However, overreliance on speculative negative emission technologies, rather than maximizing immediate cuts and natural solutions, remains a risk (Anderson & Peters, 2016).

Critics argue current net zero strategies often neglect equity, biodiversity, and immediate fossil fuel phaseouts. Relying on future removals while continuing fossil fuel use risks substituting deep cuts for illusory progress (McLaren et al., 2019). Robust net zero pathways must include at least 90 percent emissions cuts by 2050, prioritize fossil fuel reductions, avoid unreliable offsets, and embed social protections (Climate Action Network, 2021). Ensuring real progress requires clear sectoral phaseouts, interim targets, carbon budgets, and comprehensive roadmaps (Rogelj et al., 2021).

Policy frameworks often lack concrete pathways or accountability structures, resulting in aspirational targets detached from credible implementation. Near-term milestones, such as halving emissions by 2030, are essential to spur transitions in infrastructure, demand, and carbon removal capacity. Key sectors like buildings, transport, food, and heavy industry lack urgent plans (Climate Action Network, 2021). Transparent measurement and independent oversight are necessary to uphold accountability where goals are self-determined (Rogelj et al., 2021).

Sector-specific strategies illustrate both the possibilities and complexities of net zero transitions. For buildings, combining energy efficiency, electrification, renewable integration, and embodied carbon reductions can achieve full decarbonization with existing technologies, as seen in New York City's gas hookup bans (Rosenow & Eyre, 2022). Industry requires disruptive innovations around clean fuels, carbon capture, and energy-efficient processes. Companies like SSAB and Dow are exploring net zero operations through such innovations (Meys et al., 2021). Renewable energy scaling and transportation electrification face hurdles in storage and grid modernization but have made significant strides in systemic change (Davis et al., 2018).

Net zero futures hinge on reconfiguring entire energy, production, and consumption systems through combinations of technologies, policies, and business models (Geels et al., 2022). This necessitates coordinated governance, finance, and cultural shifts integrating supply-side and demand-side solutions (Meadowcroft & Rosenbloom, 2023).

While net zero provides a critical mid-century target, existing frameworks are plagued by overreliance on speculative fixes, neglect of equity and biodiversity, and lack of meaningful attention to governance and finance. Civil society groups advocate for binding justice-based targets with aggressive cuts rather than deferring actions to future technologies. Sophisticated governance and policy tools are essential to manage the complex interdependencies underpinning net zero ambitions (Meadowcroft & Rosenbloom, 2023).

Degrowth and Post-Growth Perspectives

Degrowth and post-growth scholarship challenges the hegemony of endless economic expansion underpinning contemporary capitalist societies. As ecological crises from climate change to biodiversity loss expose the impossibility and dysfunctionality of limitless accumulation on a finite planet, concepts of degrowth and post-growth envision alternative macrosocial arrangements centered on sufficiency, equity, and environmental sustainability rather than productivist growth imperatives.

While overlapping, post-growth and degrowth movements feature key differences in theorization and political strategies for transitions. However, both firmly reject mainstream recession fears around abandoning GDP expansion in favor of reconceptualizing prosperity, well-being, and good lives beyond growth dependence. This essay surveys defining debates within degrowth and post-growth literatures around envisioning emancipatory equitable futures no longer hitched to unsustainable expansion.

Degrowth thought arose in 1970s European left activism and scholarship concerning limits to growth, though only consolidated as an academic-activist field in the early 2000s through conferences and dedicated journals (Schmelzer et al., 2022). Degrowth is not synonymous with economic contraction or recession; rather it denotes transforming societies to reduce environmental throughput and redistribute resources regardless of—or even while shrinking—major conventional metrics like GDP (Kallis et al., 2020). As key definitions highlight, degrowth means equitably downscaling energy and material use to increase human well-being and strengthen community resilience within fair Earth system limits (Schmelzer et al., 2022).

Academic and activist circles propagate diverse degrowth visions and strategies. However, several unifying premises underpin the movement (Paulson, 2017). Conceptually, degrowth accepts the reality of biophysical limits making endless expansion impossible. Politically, degrowth argues that sustainable downscaling requires liberatory social transformations beyond technofixes or elite austerity (Kallis, 2019). Philosophically, degrowth redefines prosperity towards sufficiency and flourishing rather than wealth accumulation. A central aim entails resisting commodification of livelihoods in capitalist market systems (Pineault, 2016).

While proposed policies like work time reduction, wealth caps, commons ownership, and ecotaxes differ across degrowth advocates, common priorities include radical democratization of decisions, resources, and technology flexibly adapted to communities (D'Alisa & Kallis, 2020). Localized yet internationally solidaristic degrowth pathways enable escaping growth compulsions through changed collective imaginaries and new emancipatory institutions (Chiengkul, 2018). Researchers also analyze past societal degrowth experiences like Cuba's "special period" decline, which showed crises can spur positive transformations when communities cooperatively adapt (Prádanos, 2016).

Degrowth theory crucially foregrounds Global North overconsumption as the prime unsustainable system requiring downscaling. Calls for Southern countries to sustainably improve living standards under planetary limits highlight that degrowth signifies selective targets, not generalized austerity (Hickel, 2019). Equitably sharing the planet challenges imperial modes of living persisting through Northern income and consumption extremes built on Southern resource and labor exploitation (Healy et al., 2015). Degrowth thus connects to decolonization, climate justice, and global democratization movements by repoliticizing sustainability through moral outrage against domination and extremes in humanity's scale, distribution, and impacts (Schmelzer et al., 2022).

In recent years degrowth movement discourse bridged academic, activist, and public domains through dedicated media channels, networks like the Post-Growth Economics Network, and global conferences (Schmelzer et al., 2022; Vandeventer et al., 2019). Diverse adherents from the Global South basic income networks to European political parties to North American ecosocialists adapt frames toward respective political contexts. This diffusion of critiques and alternatives helps erode hegemonic assumptions equating prosperity with GDP growth and establish post-capitalist imaginaries within mainstream policy debates (Vandeventer et al., 2019).

Post-growth theorization closely parallels arguments from the degrowth movement in rejecting growth dependence and calling for radical sustainability transitions. However slight differences in framing and emphasis persist. Post-growth research also frequently concentrates more on meso- and micro-level transitions like organizations and business models rather than macro-societal changes favored within degrowth movements (Banerjee et al., 2021).

As key literature outlines, post-growth scholars diagnose industrial capitalist systems as locked into productivist accumulation and expansionary logic incompatible with ecological limits (Borowy & Schmelzer, 2017; Mair et al., 2020). Escape requires not just greener metrics but cultural shifts in symbolic meanings and societal goal orientation away from GDP growth maximization toward sustainment (Buch-Hansen, 2018; Pesch, 2018). This demands fundamental reforms across economic functions like finance, investment, ownership, work patterns, public infrastructure, and global trade to eradicate systemic drivers of growth obsession beyond sectors like energy or transportation (Kallis, 2017; Paech, 2017).

Post-growth research emphasizes the need for new macroeconomic models stabilized around full employment and just distribution without reliance upon relentless material expansion (Dietz & O'Neill, 2013). Steady-state visions balance births and deaths rather than pursuing endless population increases. Sharing labor and productivity gains through work time reductions provides flourishing livelihoods absent growth (Mair et al., 2020). And redefining standards for good life beyond material possessions reduces social pressures for competitive consumption (Paech, 2017).

Various post-growth proposals creatively reinvent basic economic institutions from complementary currencies to community land trusts enabling solidarity economies centered on values of sustainability, sufficiency, and justice rather than capital accumulation (Roth, 2017; Barry, 2018). Transition governance pathways develop through networks of innovations across grassroots experiments and policy regimes fostering new sustainable welfare systems and progress metrics like quality of life, time affluence, and happiness outpacing growth (Vandeventer et al., 2019).

Significant post-growth research also investigates transformations in corporate practices, business models, and organizational behavior to escape unsustainable capitalist expansion. Scholars outline scalable alternative enterprise forms from multistakeholder cooperatives to ethical banks to solidarity economy networks resisting profit maximization pressures (Banerjee et al., 2021). Models with profit caps, collaborative ownership, and sustainability-centered charters orient operations around service provision and workplace democracy rather than endless financialized asset speculation. Post-growth private sector forms emphasize commons governance, cooperative competition, and decommodification protecting ethical vocations like healthcare from capital encroachment (Peredo & McLean, 2020).

Public debate increasingly questions the feasibility of green growth rather than fundamental post-growth transitions (Borowy & Schmelzer, 2017). Climate policy circles privilege ecologically modernizing efficiency fixes, unable to significantly curb expanding production scales driving breakdowns from sinking biodiversity to disruptive global warming. However, post-growth movements steadily erode this dominant imaginary through critical research and community demonstration projects pioneering beyond-growth systems at all scales.

Despite many overlaps in concepts and proposals between post-growth and degrowth spheres, researchers identify subtle distinctions (Schmelzer et al., 2022). Degrowth emerged through more overt anti-capitalist, revolutionary politics seeking liberation from growth obsession and consumerism. Post-growth tends toward reformist transitions adapting technologies, organizations, and welfare states to stabilize production (Borowy & Schmelzer, 2017). Framings like a "prosperous way down" suggest more gradual change than degrowth demands for rapid elite consumption cuts under planetary emergency conditions.

Additionally, the post-growth clock sometimes displays greater optimism around steering capitalism evolution towards sustainability through policy reforms like eco-taxes or new indicators (Pesch, 2018). Degrowth orientations emphasize capitalism's destructive expansionary DNA necessitating post-capitalist vision as the prime catalyst and goal. This affects megacorporate governance proposals, for instance rejecting sheer corporate social responsibility pledges for community oversight and control degrowth's commons discourse favors (Banerjee et al., 2021). Additionally, post-growth policy suggestions around universal income schemes diverge somewhat from degrowth emphasis on maximizing employment through radical worktime reductions.

However, binaries overstate significant common ground and mutual influence between post-growth and degrowth spheres in diagnosing growth addiction and imagining beyond accumulation (Schmelzer et al., 2022). Most schools now accept that profound transformations rather than technical fixes alone are imperative for sustainable prosperity, given growth dependence crosses various models from welfare states to oligarchic systems. Post-growth concepts originated within earlier Marxist ecological critiques paralleling today's ecofeminist, environmental justice, and degrowth movements (Borowy & Schmelzer, 2017). And degrowth advocacy actively courts post-Keynesian economists, policy experts, and socialist ecologists toward mainstreaming proposals like public money creation and progressive taxes paying basic incomes supporting commune transitions (Vandeventer et al., 2019).

Regardless of exact political shades, both post-growth and degrowth framed interventions expand ecology discourse and economics beyond win-win delusions that marginal reforms can decouple GDP expansion from environmental breakdown. Against rampant greenwashing rhetoric, downscaling and post-growth movements inject ethical clarity around scientific necessity and social justice imperatives for deep ceilings on aggregate production amidst extreme inequity and nicely reckless Northern overconsumption. Demonstrating inspiring alternatives in everyday community projects and policy campaigns, twenty-first-century post-growth and degrowth movements represent an essential break from unsustainable growth addiction towards possible sustainable, equitable futures on our planet.

Circular and Regenerative Economy

Circular economy and regenerative economy models hold promise as sustainability pathways aligning enterprise and economic systems with natural ecologies. Both frameworks move beyond merely minimizing environmental harms to enable renewed prosperity within restored living systems. While distinct, circular and regenerative approaches overlap around cyclical production, waste elimination, renewable flows, and holistic value propositions.

As the environmental crisis intensifies, concepts of regeneration and circularity transform business practices, municipal policies and consumption lifestyles away from destructive linear take-make-waste models. Demonstrating profoundly sustainable alternatives, circular and regenerative economies expand from niche experiments toward normalized paradigms rewiring societies within ecological boundaries.

Circular economy theory and action aims moving from linear commodity production causing resource depletion and waste toward closed-loop models circulating materials continually at highest value (Walker et al., 2021). This industrial ecology perspective reimagines economic output as nutrient flows rather than end products entering waste streams. Refurbishment, recycling, cascading component reuse, and other strategies transform trash into valuable technical and biological inputs perpetually feeding subsequent enterprises (Pieroni et al., 2019).

Rather than maximizing volume sales of disposable items, circular business models monetize product access, performance, and maintenance. Firms retain ownership over high-quality durable goods rented to users through subscriptions. Products get redesigned for longevity, upgradeability, deconstruction, and recycling to retain constituent materials like metals or plastics as technical nutrients cycling perpetually without downcycling. Customers effectively purchase utility services not short-life widgets. Biological materials similarly circulate as compost and biofuels in closed regional loops maximizing ecosystem balance through regenerative agriculture (Urbinati et al., 2017).

Overall, the circular economy aims to decouple economic activity from finite resource extraction and waste dumping through smarter flows, business models and behaviors (Korhonen et al., 2018). The concept emerged from several precursors like biomimicry, ecological economics, and cradle-to-cradle design over recent decades as a more systemic alternative to incremental waste efficiency (Winans et al., 2017). Policy, corporate, and non-governmental organization (NGO) coalitions now work mainstreaming circularity across European Commission policies, Chinese five-year plans, and multinational corporate supply chains. Systemic shifts replace single-issue recycling campaigns, shaping ambitious governance and infrastructure around circular cities, processes, and lifestyles (Pieroni et al., 2019).

Implementing a circular economy at scale does face barriers around upfront financing, path dependencies, and cultural attitudes. Fledgling research analyzes required meso-level market conditions and business models fostering circular innovation and scaling. Rather than looking narrowly at firm capabilities or isolated consumer behaviors, whole value chain and institutional contexts must transform to reward and normalize circularity (Hopkinson et al., 2018; Lewandowski, 2016). This entails financial mechanisms supporting mass remanufacturing and refurbishment over new builds, redistributive last-mile aggregation platforms enabling used item circulation, and reversed logistics infrastructure making recovery cheaper than waste disposal (Pieroni et al., 2019).

Additionally, cultural shifts driving anti-consumption, sharing platforms, and sense of material stewardship rather than disposability assist normalized circularity (Walker et al., 2021). Transition governance facilitates through education, partnerships, and open knowledge platforms around modular design, reverse logistics, and industrial symbiosis. Smart policy mixes from bans on single-use plastics to landfill taxes on corporations fund renewables and infrastructure for circularity while ending perverse incentives around planned obsolescence and wasting scarce, energy-intensive materials like aluminum or concrete currently cheaper to dump than preserve (George et al., 2015).

Circular economy provides a compelling sustainability vision and transition pathway recovering post-consumer, post-industrial materials as high-quality inputs into community-rooted regional production systems mimicking nature's regeneration. Demonstrating decoupling possibilities through global examples like China's circular economy villages to Danish industrial symbiosis parks to Indian informal sector electronics remanufacturing, the concept continues diffusing from niche murmurs towards normalized policy and enterprise logic (Goyal et al., 2018).

Whereas circular economy concentrates primarily on tighter technical nutrient flows, notions of regenerative economies consider broader well-being interdependencies between human civilization and surrounding ecosystems. Regenerative systems continually support lifecycle health at all levels through holistic designed interactions honoring the whole living planet rather than maximizing isolated output metrics detached from habitats (Mang & Reed, 2020). This framework thinks beyond isolated production efficiency gains or waste elimination toward economic activities actively healing degraded social and ecological communities.

As conceptualized by regeneration scholars, achieving sustainable prosperity requires moving from dangerously exploitative extractive practices toward renewing environmental and community integrity for intergenerational well-being (Wahl, 2016). So, regeneration suggests deeper paradigmatic changes than efficiency fixes to dominant systems still oriented around maximizing monetized exchange value for shareholders rather than nourishing commonwealth shared across stakeholders benefiting mutually from lasting regional restoration (Elkington, 2020). Terms like healing, radical listening, and collective care signal profound ontological shifts in humankind's sense of belonging within—not atop—nature (Mang & Reed, 2020).

Businesses accordingly play roles as diverse as water stewards, nutrient cyclers, habitat restorers, and community Cultivators more than wealth extractors for far-away investors (Elkington, 2020). Production inputs come from surrounding regional clusters rather than global supply chains crossing ecological boundaries. Companies cooperatively develop locales, closing loops and preventing externalized damages through ethical sourcing, equitable employment, clean operations, and regenerative agriculture supporting regional restoration (Howard et al., 2019). Surrounding towns likewise democratically co-govern regional transitions through participatory processes balancing diverse community needs alongside ecosystems (Girardet, 2017).

Redesigning urban areas and settlements follows similar biomimetic principles fulfilling human needs through integrated green spaces, renewable microgrids, and nature-based solutions for water, energy, and food nourishing communities. Cradle-to-cradle material flows circulate locally alongside affordable eco-housing, clean transport, and circular procurement programs, embedding public institutions within vibrant living systems they actively heal rather than degrade (Mang & Reed, 2020). Movements like Transition Towns translate these visions into localized transitions for post-carbon, post-consumer community resilience and sovereignty.

Notions of regeneration and restorative economies signal profound paradigmatic possibilities for constructing sustainable civilizations benefiting humans and nonhumans through ethical stewardship of living systems. Accounting for multi-dimensional values beyond financial yields, regenerative models circumvent machined metaphors dominating modernity to resuscitate traditional wisdom of belonging to nature through renewed ecological ethics and encultured habits that continually nourish, rather than diminish, our commonwealth foundations for flourishing futures.

Considerable overlaps exist between circular economy and regenerative economy frameworks in orienting production and consumption patterns toward waste-free, renewing models safeguarding ecological integrity and community resilience. Both movements aim to escape unsustainability trapped in complacent efficiency narratives around doing less damage to nature imposed by careless linear take–make–waste economic logics (Morseletto, 2020). Visions of commercial and civilizational activities improving environmental and social conditions permeate circular and regenerative thought.

Nuanced distinctions characterize each approach. Circular systems concentrate tightly on material and nutrient flows—whether metals, minerals, oils, or nutrients. Exact weights get meticulously tracked given scarcity. Business cases and public policies thus fixate on closing loops, improving recycling technology, figuring reverse logistics, and maintaining highest value purity in perpetual technical cycles flowing like organisms (Korhonen et al., 2018). Critics argue environmentally conscious engineering risks technocratic overreach losing sight of human dimensions (Morseletto, 2020). And isolated material loops still ignore surrounding living habitats impacted by infrastructure enabling circulation.

Contrastingly the language of healing, listening and caring suffusing regenerative paradigms considers wider ethical and spiritual connections beyond rationalist materialism and biophysical dynamics (Mang & Reed, 2020). Rather than perfect closed loops, attention addresses community cohesion, ecosystem revitalization, collective psyche maturation and other dimensions exceeding profit-driven sustainability metrics or circular production networks. At best this holism balances technical precision and speed necessary in circular models with compassionate presence and care nurturing shared social and ecological meaning.

Ambiguities in regenerative framing also risk paralysis given overwhelming complexity or misappropriation as branding abstraction lacking substance if core principles go unelaborated. Circular economy thus offers relatively coherent decision frameworks for incrementally improving business and policy even if unable to spontaneously spark shared stakeholder purpose or transform consciousness (Howard et al., 2019). So pragmatic hybrid approaches integrating circular tools with regenerative wisdom appear necessary rather than dichotomizing movements. Collaboratively aligning human civilization within thriving living systems requires both ethical maturity and technical precision.

Circular economy and regenerative models provide inspiring sustainability pathways escaping unsustainable linear industrial systems toward ethical, renewing economies healing relationships between society and ecology. Operationalizing circularity through transformed nutrient flows, business models and incentives helps maintain prosperous production and consumption absent waste or ecological harm. Understanding broader spiritual interconnections and social responsibilities characterizing regenerative thought provides complementary awareness to sustain transitions through care, community, and justice exceeding technocratic circularity.

Together both movements energize enterprises, municipalities, and communities to move beyond damage control toward participatory regeneration benefiting all inhabitants interdependently dwelling within living systems. Our shared future livelihood depends on diffusing post-extractive models for equitable negotiated development nourishing human and ecological commonwealth. Circular economy tools and regenerative wisdom together offer holistic templates transforming civilizational habits and structures toward sustainable prosperity respectful of our descendants for generations.

CASE STUDY: REFLOW

The REFLOW project (2019–2023) aimed to catalyze circular economy transitions in six European cities by testing tools and models to reshape urban systems and promote sustainability. This collaborative initiative brought together municipalities, businesses, designers, and civil society groups to explore circular solutions for material flows like plastics, textiles, and agrifood. The project's participatory approach integrated data mapping, technological experimentation, and public engagement to advance sustainability across diverse urban contexts.

REFLOW's approach combined participatory research, co-design processes, and community engagement to identify and reconfigure linear resource flows within ecological limits. Through workshops, hackathons, and stakeholder meetings, the project developed solutions tailored to the specific needs and assets of each pilot city, promoting local resource circulation and sustainability.

Berlin Pilot

The Berlin pilot focused on harnessing waste heat, an often-overlooked renewable resource. By mapping heat emissions from buildings and industrial facilities, the project identified opportunities to recycle this heat using technologies like heat exchangers. A neighborhood hub was established to demonstrate the reuse of waste heat for powering urban agriculture and eco-enterprises, supporting community spaces, and fostering local economic development.

Milan Pilot

Milan's pilot addressed the city's unsustainable agrifood system by creating circular alternatives to meet urban nutritional needs. The project engaged farmers, food banks, chefs, and local officials to co-design food supply chains that prioritize local, regenerative farming practices. Digital platforms helped farmers visualize urban nutritional gaps and coordinate crop planning, while new distribution hubs connected urban consumers with regional produce. This pilot supported Milan's broader sustainable food policy, promoting urban–rural collaboration for a circular food economy.

Vejle Pilot

Vejle tackled plastic pollution by launching community-led circular initiatives. Seven municipal districts tested interventions to eliminate, reuse, and recycle plastic waste. Activities included public innovation camps, workshops, and design sessions where residents brainstormed new uses for plastic waste, such as creating picnic tables from recycled materials. Digital platforms tracked project impacts, identifying areas for further intervention and policy improvement.

Cluj-Napoca Pilot

The Cluj-Napoca pilot focused on inclusive governance for the city's energy transition. Through a "Transition Arena" model, policymakers, technologists, and community representatives co-developed decarbonization strategies, such as improving building insulation and integrating decentralized solar power. Open data dashboards and participatory budgeting enabled citizens to allocate funds and shape energy policies, fostering social learning and local buy-in for sustainability initiatives.

The REFLOW pilots generated valuable insights and tools for advancing urban circular economies. Each city's experience contributed to a shared knowledge base that can guide other municipalities in implementing circular economy strategies. For example, Berlin's model of reusing waste heat, Milan's localized food systems, and Vejle's plastic waste reduction efforts have been shared through the project's collaborative networks.

Overall, REFLOW emphasized the importance of participatory design and governance in achieving sustainability. By linking diverse stakeholders—citizens, policymakers, and researchers—the project demonstrated how co-creation can bridge gaps between grassroots innovation and top-down policy, enhancing community resilience and economic vitality while reducing environmental impacts. These pilots offer replicable models for other cities striving to embed circular economy principles into their urban development strategies, fostering sustainable, socially just futures across Europe and beyond.

Environmental Justice

Environmental justice refers to the fair treatment and meaningful involvement of all people regardless of race, color, national origin, or income, with respect to the development, implementation, and enforcement of environmental laws, regulations, and policies. The environmental justice movement emerged from grassroots activism and civil rights campaigns drawing attention to the disproportionate exposure of marginalized communities to environmental harms from pollution, waste dumping, resource extraction, and climate impacts.

Conceptual lineages integrate social justice, ecological sustainability and public health scholarship toward equitably valuing all communities while transforming conditions driving ecocide. Key priorities encompass procedural justice in decisions determining environmental conditions affecting lives, distributive justice in access to environmental goods and exposure to harms across populations, and corrective justice through remediation, reparations, and structural reforms healing past damages underlying present inequities. This essay surveys environmental justice theory, activism, public policy developments, and critical debates.

Scholarship on environmental inequality and ecological distribution conflicts dates from 1960s United States research on disparities in pollution burden and proximity failing to spur substantive policy reforms (Martinez-Alier et al., 2016). However, the environmental justice movement catalyzed through 1982 protests against a North Carolina landfill sited in a black community mobilizing civil rights groups alongside labor and religious networks (Cole & Foster, 2001). This grassroots coalition named interlinked discriminatory harms around waste, toxins, and industrial encroachment faced by low-income communities of color.

Seminal books and campaigns through the 1990s further developed frames and tactics against environmental racism as the movement spread nationally and internationally (Bullard, 1994). Analyses pointed to complex drivers from legacy spatial segregation patterns concentrating marginalized residents near undesired land uses to limited political-economic power and social capital in poor indigenous and immigrant neighborhoods unable to resist dumping "locally unwanted land uses" (LULUs). Mounting evidence revealed massive disparities in environmental health indicators, ranging from lead poisoning to asthma (Bullard et al., 2007).

Environmental justice paradigms integrate distributional analysis of the uneven allocation of environmental benefits and ills with procedural inquiries into the exercise of power and participation in decisions driving those outcomes (Haughton, 1999; Walker, 2012). Theorists highlight how environmental privilege and disadvantage are socially constructed along lines of race, class, and other axes of difference (Pulido, 2017). State policies and corporate actions impose toxic, polluting, and unsustainable practices onto some communities while protecting or patronizing others.

For example, market-based climate policies promising putative efficiency gains through carbon trading and offsets in practice outsource mitigation burdens Southern peasant and indigenous groups lacking climate financing resources for low-carbon transitions (Böhm et al., 2012). Similarly Northern countries disproportionately benefit from imported mass consumer goods produced through exploitative Southern supply chains generating emissions and pollution exported away from dominant constituencies (Martinez-Alier, 2014). Even well-intentioned sustainability schemes around ecotourism or wildlife conservation often appropriate traditional lands and compromise livelihoods for forest peoples (Gezon, 2014).

Such cases reveal environmental policies and transitions enacting oppression more than justice absent specific equity provisions. Truly sustainable futures demand democratizing environmental decisions, resources, and power across marginalized groups through local to global scales. Environmental justice offers vital sociological, political-economic, and moral lenses on reconstituting human–nature relationships toward mutually liberatory ends.

Environmental justice spans interconnected literatures and movements tackling varied manifestations of discrimination, exclusion, and harm propagation compounding ecosystem breakdown and human suffering. Key subfields address dimensions including:

Since inception, a central focus of environmental justice research and organizing targets disproportionate pollution burdens and denial of environmental goods across marginalized racial-ethnic and working-class communities relative to privileged whites (Pulido, 2016). Persisting racial residential segregation patterns in many US cities overlay health-damaging infrastructure like oil refineries, waste transfer stations, or diesel truck corridors onto low-income neighborhoods of color stunted from past redlining disinvestment and discrimination (Tessum et al., 2021). Similar disparities around mining, deforestation, and agricultural encroachment affect indigenous, peasant, and forest-dweller communities lacking strong land rights protections from states privileging elite or settler interests.

Ecofeminist perspectives highlight gender dynamics underlying environmental injustice issues like reproductive health harms from chemical pollution or stoves producing indoor air pollution, gender violence around contested extractive zones, and unequal burdens from climate-exacerbated household labor securing basic needs as men migrate for waged work (MacGregor, 2006). Intersectional environmental justice research grounds analysis of intersecting marginalizations of women of color and poor women facing amplified environmental health burdens and exclusion from environmental decision-making and leadership.

The vast majority of humanity lives across Africa, Asia, Latin America, and the Pacific confronting severe environmental justice challenges from colonial legacies, export-oriented extraction, weak states, and economic structural adjustment regimes elevating Northern profits over Southern people's basic needs (Martinez-Alier, 2002). Core issues span debt bondage chaining countries to resource extraction, climate finance and mitigation gaps, biodiversity loss and biopiracy, removing indigenous control over traditional plants and medicines (Bond, 2012). North–South equity thus centrally informs global climate, sustainability, and development policy debates.

Cities concentrate both sustainability potential through efficiencies yet also hazards facing impoverished residents in informal settlements lacking environmental services like water, sanitation, drainage, or green space (Haughton, 1999). As climate change accelerates, cities increasingly menace vulnerable residents through heat waves, inundation, and disasters while advanced infrastructure insulates wealthy districts. Pursuing urban environmental justice demands addressing intersecting hazards and exclusion shaping spatial inequality across metro regions.

Environmental justice activism connects multifaceted cross-issue coalitions and campaigns mobilizing against political-economic drivers of disproportionate pollution, dispossession, and vulnerability. Following early anti-toxic movement building in the United States, organizations, networks, and movements have multiplied across local to global levels (Malin, Ryder & Lyra, 2019). For instance, the Environmental Justice Atlas documents 3000 cases worldwide creating participatory mapping infrastructure around community resistance (Temper et al., 2015). Annual gatherings like the World Social Forum enable movement convergence across varied grassroots struggles opposing environmental racism, ecologically destructive development, climate injustice, and associated human rights violations by states and corporations.

In policy realms, environmental justice claims find uneven uptake within governmental reforms, where technical interventions often override principled transformation (Sze et al., 2009). For example, climate policy circles acknowledge equity but rarely embrace differentiated responsibilities and capabilities or repay ecological debts obligating historically high-emitting Northern states to stringently cut emissions while massively financing Southern climate mitigation and adaptation without onerous debt burdens (Roberts & Parks, 2009). Even domestic environmental regulation frequently fails operationalizing meaningful participation, non-discrimination, or compensatory protections that could reconcile environmental management with marginalized communities through genuine democratic process and reconciliation (Outka, 2018).

Nonetheless period efforts shine light on alternative pathways integrating justice within sustainability transitions. For instance, the European Environmental Bureau (2020) outlines four pillars for an environmentally just COVID-19 recovery addressing health equity, green job creation, democratic environmental action, and overseas sustainability financing. The US environmental justice executive order mandating non-discrimination reviews and equitable inclusion across federal agencies signals overdue embrace of core movement demands in the world's largest economy, despite uncertain implementation under business-friendly administrations (Murphy-Greene & Leip, 2002). Just transition movements call for sustainability planning that prioritizes workers and frontline communities in decarbonization, rather than upholding extractivist logics or pursuing technocratic transitions that disregard livelihood losses (Healy & Barry, 2017).

Globally, the United Nations Framework Convention on Climate Change has incorporated climate justice language and social safeguard mechanisms as touchstones activist movements successfully pressed through oppositional negotiating blocs. While implementation gaps persist, discursive victories legitimize moral *outrage* around interconnected sustainability crises threatening vulnerable communities worldwide to leverage further material reforms and restorative action benefiting those historically exploited lands and lives.

Environmental justice encompasses multifaceted scholarship and organizing, underscoring how environmental conditions, policies, and transitions reflect and reproduce social marginalization across lines of race, class, gender, and geography. Disproportionate pollution burdens concentrated through segregated residential spaces or sacrifices demanded from peasant farmers and indigenous communities to maintain overconsuming, fossil-fueled Northern lifestyles represent core issues. Within both Global North and South countries, marginalized groups face amplified environmental health hazards, exclusion from environmental amenities and decision-making while possessing fewer resources to mitigate mounting climate disruptions.

These movements target the root political, economic, and cultural drivers of such uneven ecological destruction and vulnerability. Through grassroots mobilization, research, policy advocacy, and protest, they forge North–South and cross-issue alliances between communities on environmental frontlines. Demands confront historically exclusionary, technocratic environmental governance to instead center justice, accountability, and democratic process yielding sustainability transitions improving not worsening conditions across economically and socially marginalized peoples. With climate catastrophe accelerating, centering environmental justice grows only more urgent for catalyzing trajectories of resistance, reconciliation, and radical democracy protecting all communities' safety, sovereignty, and dignity on a rapidly warming, urbanizing planet.

Multispecies Justice

Multispecies justice encompasses emergent perspectives extending moral consideration and political rights beyond anthropocentric worldviews fixated solely on human interests toward equitable, liberatory relationships with nonhuman beings, ecologies, and planetary systems. As intensifying climate change, mass extinction, and industrial animal suffering reveal violent failures of modernity's atomistic ontology and dualisms separating humanity from interdependent ecological networks of life, multi-species frameworks dignify sentience and agencies across diverse living beings.

Conceptually, multispecies justice frameworks dismantle rigid human/nature divides to recognize inextricable entanglements, vulnerabilities, and possibilities for flourishing binding all creatures (Fitz-Henry, 2022). Beyond acknowledging instrumental natural "resources" or intrinsic conservation values benefiting humankind, a multi-species ethic considers nonhuman animals, plants, ecosystems, and even landscapes as subjects with relational moral standing and legitimacy for consideration within the political community (Celermajer et al., 2022). This profound ethical and epistemological shift reorients human governance, policy, and activities toward nurturing life rather than unconstrained mastery.

In practice multispecies justice fosters peaceful, caring coexistence maximizing biodiverse resurgence enabling dignity and well-being for all earthlings. It guides interspecies and transspecies solidarity building networks of sanctuary protecting threatened beings while transforming industrial and legal apparatuses perpetrating relentless violence (Tschakert, 2022). Conceptually and concretely, multi-species perspectives cultivate reparative futures beyond modernity's fallacies.

Foundations for multispecies thinking trace across varied scholarly movements contesting dominant regimes commodifying nature as a mere instrument for human satisfaction. Radical ecology perspectives underline humanity's inextricable earthly interdependence and embeddedness within nature demolishing conceits of control or separation (Devall & Sessions, 1985). Animal rights arguments likewise contest ontological hierarchies licensing cruelty and bondage subjugating thinking, feeling creatures like livestock within totalizing regimes of mechanistic optimization (Regan, 1985). Val Plumwood's feminist philosophy explored master identity complexes othering the more-than-human world from ethical consideration (Plumwood, 1993).

Indigenous cosmologies globally sustain sensibilities of profound connectivity and reciprocal responsibilities infusing land, animals, and living systems as multidimensional kin sharing purposes beyond extractive benefit for humankind (Salmon, 2000; Todd, 2016). Decolonization scholarship adapts these relational ethics toward rebalancing violent, ecocidal formations of Western modernity and associated political-legal edifices grounded in severed society/nature dualisms (Maldonado et al., 2016). Overall, such thought pries open space for reconsidering beings inhabiting and sustaining shared ecosystems as peers rather than vassals within moral circles and political processes.

Building on those lineages, multispecies justice emerges through interdisciplinary syntheses over recent decades between previously disparate environmental philosophy, human–animal studies, anthropology, and green political theory engaging questions of community, citizenship, and governance (Celermajer et al., 2022). This cross-fertilization posits more-than-human-solidarity as vital direction for emancipatory theory and practice amidst climate emergency conditions threatening all earthly family.

Multispecies frameworks also respond to pragmatic policy and technology matters engaging nonhuman agencies, insight, and welfare. For instance, agricultural justice movements seek to liberate farm animals from systematic cruelty of factory systems toward compassionate agroecologies aligned with species' dignity (Celermajer & O'Brien, 2021). Urban wildlife conflicts highlight possibilities for cross-species coalition around co-managing ecological boundaries and services benefiting all city residents, both bioped and pixel, across zones of delighted, ethical connection beyond domains of control, extraction, or human priority (Luther, 2021; Wolch, 2002). Overall, assembling multispecies justice requires carefully renegotiating a vast diversity of relationships beyond blithe assumptions of human preeminence over aliens made other by modernity's fractured ontology.

While interpreting political specifics varies, proponents broadly coalesce around certain foundational priorities guiding multi-species governance, policy, and activism (Celermajer et al., 2022; Winter, 2022). These include:

The essential task for enabling multi-species justice entails decentering imagined human sovereignty arrogating rights to ecologically dominate, consume, and destroy other creatures and habitats (Plumwood, 2002). This demands reforming cultures and institutions embedding anthropocentrism across rights, ethics, and policy exclusively privileging a thin subset of persons and properties over multifarious forms of ecological subjecthood that together enable thriving on our living planet.

Shifting moral horizons requires embracing sentience—capacities for sensation, experience, perspective, and interest—more diffusely across species previously coded as unfeeling objects for utilization (Tschakert, 2022). Sensorial communication with domesticated companions like dogs and horses build everyday intimacy between animals and humans. Meanwhile, industrial processes ruthlessly override such sensibilities, for instance commodifying intelligent, gregarious pigs as mere bacon production units whose unceasing cries of distress signify mere inefficiencies reducing profit margins. Rendering visible and valuing sentience guides just transitions.

Beyond just limiting clearly violent harms, multi-species approaches foster balanced, mutually enriching connections where all beings offer gifts nourishing collective well-being (Celermajer & O'Brien, 2021; Todd, 2016). This entails open listening and cultivating shared worlding, co-responsibilization, and solidarity crossing difference yet respecting otherness across all creatures great and small. Human activity thereby aims perpetually renewing environmental potentials enabling flourishing futures for coming generations of untold beings.

Realizing such profound ethical renewal requires reforming industrial infrastructures like factory farming complexes and financial systems driving ecocide for accumulation that structurally exclude the more-than-human from concern (Westerlaken, 2021). Transition depends on prefiguring alternative multi-species political economies balancing diverse needs and agencies through place-based negotiation enabling situated justice and right relations given shifting assemblages forming community across blood, circuits, and ecology (Celermajer et al., 2022).

Key tensions within multi-species theorizing grapple with translating general posthumanist commitments around interrogating human/nature binaries into concrete ethical practices, legal doctrines, and governance capabilities operationalizing equitable treatment and participation rights for nonhuman members of shared ecological communities. Strategies emphasizing formal rights for prominent species like elephants, cetaceans, or primates based on apparent sentience and sapience tend toward instituting protections still centered on human analogues (Cavalieri, 2001). They risk excluding less charismatic members critical for ecological renewal like insects or microbes.

More pluralist, place-based approaches emphasize locally coevolving multispecies alliances and solidarity attuned to regional habitats and priorities (Wolch, 2002). Additionally, emphasis on sensational capacities informing who or what deserves consideration may continue commodifying nature as a pool of resources for satisfaction. Some Indigenous perspectives suggest cosmological orientations to environmental regulation and management decisions fulfilling broader reciprocal responsibilities beyond impact mitigation (Maldonado et al., 2016).

Multi-species justice remains profoundly unfinished terrain requiring iterative experimentation, negotiation, and reconciliation building a new gentler civilization no longer predicated on relentless war against the ecological kin sustaining all worlds. Though formal policies codifying nonanthropocentric priorities remain scarce, diverse social innovation efforts prefigure and prototype multi-species possibilities in varied domains engaging environmental regulation and governance. Creative projects integrate speculative design, digital interfaces, and participatory programs reconceiving human/nonhuman relations within shared spaces of community, moving beyond zero-sum logics toward interspecies equity and solidarity.

For example, researchers propose reinventing urban planning frameworks to enable wildlife flourishing as co-participants within sustainable city regions rather than externalities of development or pests breaching human infrastructure (Luther, 2021). This entails participative visioning of cohabitation priorities balancing diverse mobility, shelter, foraging, and interfacing needs for all area residents across species through zoned parks, preserved connectivity corridors, adapted transit landscapes and even political representation channels integrating nonhuman insight like migratory patterns to shape provisions enabling dignified, vibrant habitat access despite density (Sheikh et al., 2023). Such co-governance and codesigning platforms courts multispecies solidarity widening technology and built space affordances to nurture collective regional lifeworlds benefiting all families amid diversity (Heitlinger et al., 2021).

In agricultural realms, food justice efforts increasingly recognize animal rights and welfare alongside environmental sustainability and farmer livelihoods as equal pillars for transforming dominant industrial production complexes torturing billions of farmed animals annually within violent, unhealthy regimes (Celermajer & O'Brien, 2021). Creating liberatory configurations aligning human interests in nourishment within balanced, ethical participation of livestock, fish, and insects as symbiotic partners through renewed agroecological systems demands undoing entrenched speciesist power complexes and refashioning food infrastructure around nourishing just relations rather than mere productivity and convenient output traits optimized for elite palates (Moyano-Fernández, 2022). Participatory nutrition transitions reconciling health, sustainability and justice for all food community members and lifecycle stages redirects agriculture and economic policy towards incumbent rights and well-being over profits or preferences (Celermajer & O'Brien, 2021).

Across such cases, multi-species imaginaries inform structural reforms and collaborative innovations acknowledging diverse agencies co-creating contexts for mutually liberatory worlds benefiting all earthlings. They indicate profound reorientation of environmental regulation, urban development, and production networks toward posthuman ethics of care, capability, and community exceeding modernist human primacy.

Key areas for advancing multi-species justice turn on building capacities and coalitions for pluralistic environmental policymaking establishing guardrails, participative procedures, and reconciliatory initiatives nurturing right relations across all members great and small, challenging and cherished, within our shared more-than-human ecologies. Demonstrating possibilities through place-based transitions fostering situated flourishing points paths beyond violent, enclosed regime structures through laws, technologies, and normalcies entrenching relentless war against the vulnerable planet (Celermajer et al., 2022). As accumulating extinction and climate turbulence reveals costs of human chauvinism, further developing multispecies frameworks offers urgent direction for inhabiting damaged earthly neighborhoods as healing, justice-seeking families finally at home in our ecology.

CASE STUDY: Zoöp

The Zoöp model, developed in the Netherlands, is an innovative framework designed to help organizations incorporate ecological stewardship and sustainability into their core operations. Addressing the inadequacies of traditional institutions that prioritize profits while externalizing environmental and social costs, Zoöp aims to foster symbiotic relationships between organizations and the ecosystems they inhabit. It introduces a new role—"Speaker for the Living"—to represent the interests of non-human entities affected by institutional activities, creating a platform for integrating ecological values into decision-making processes.

Rooted in the philosophy of "zoönomic thought," which views human systems as deeply enmeshed in Earth's complex web of life, the Zoöp framework guides organizations to become more attuned to their environmental impacts and dependencies (Zoönomic Institute, n.d.). Instead of trying to control nature through narrow, anthropocentric goals, Zoöp promotes humility and respect for dynamic living systems. The model helps organizations transition from linear, extractive practices to circular, regenerative ones, contributing to regional ecological health and resilience.

A key element of the Zoöp model is the "Speaker for the Living" position. These representatives sit on organizational governing councils, advocating for the well-being of ecosystems, watersheds, and local species. Trained in ecological literacy and traditional ecological knowledge, Speakers lack formal decision-making power but provide essential insights into how activities like resource use or infrastructure development affect surrounding ecosystems. Through annual reviews and public reporting, they help guide organizations toward aligning operations with ecological and social sustainability principles.

Speakers are selected based on their biocultural fluency and ability to bridge human and non-human perspectives, making them uniquely equipped to address complex environmental issues. This approach helps embed ecological wisdom into organizational strategies, ensuring that decisions consider the long-term health of local ecosystems and communities.

The Zoöp model has been piloted through a network of Dutch organizations and collectives, which have developed training programs to cultivate the skills needed for the Speaker role. Curricula include deep nature connection practices, process facilitation, and systems thinking. These programs emphasize holistic understanding, allowing Speakers to effectively communicate the needs of more-than-human communities within traditionally human-centric forums.

One such pilot involves establishing a Zoöp within an organization focused on urban development. Here, the Speaker for the Living works with architects, policy-makers, and engineers to ensure that new developments respect local biodiversity and ecosystem services. This collaboration has led to the creation of green spaces that support urban wildlife, rainwater harvesting systems that nourish public gardens, and building designs that reduce energy consumption.

While the Zoöp model faces challenges in gaining mainstream adoption, particularly within traditional corporate environments, it holds significant transformative potential. Critics argue that the role of the Speaker for the Living may lack sufficient authority to enforce change. However, by bringing ecological considerations directly into organizational governance, Zoöp opens up new channels for advocacy and influence that go beyond external pressure. This internal advocacy can gradually reshape organizational priorities, moving them toward a more balanced integration of financial, social, and ecological values.

Zoöp's innovative approach positions it as a model for systemic change in governance and business practices. By formally recognizing the voices of non-human entities and incorporating ecological perspectives into strategic planning, the framework offers a pathway for reimagining how organizations can contribute to the health of the living systems they rely on. As climate crises and environmental degradation intensify, Zoöp provides a blueprint for how organizations can transform from agents of extraction to stewards of ecological and social regeneration.

Tools and Strategies for Sustainability

Sustainable development balancing economic prosperity, social equity, and environmental integrity demands profound transformations across interconnected technological, political, cultural, and economic systems (Robertson, 2021). While agreement grows on necessary wholesale paradigm changes, debate continues around strategic pathways enabling transitions reconciling human dignity for all global citizens within restored, thriving ecological habitats. This essay surveys the main classes of tools and policy approaches attempting to concretize and operationalize sustainability across governance scales from global accords to local experiments.

Tools signify defined instruments and procedures directing behaviors and evaluation to particular ends, here calibrated toward social, environmental, and economic sustainability on personal to planetary levels (Siew, 2015). Strategies structure complex change processes by selecting and coordinating appropriate tool mixes adapting general visions to situational contexts and actors. Assessment reveals varied ideological assumptions, scalar foci, solution sets, and implementation capacities distinguishing major streams. Synthesis points to complementarities more than singular best universal solutions for irreducibly contextual, contested sustainability pursuit.

High-level international agreements and national policies establish headline visions, objectives, and coordinating functions for directing sustainability efforts systemwide. Milestone UN declarations like 1987's Brundtland Report first crystallized canonical definitional frameworks integrating economic development meeting human needs with environmental protections sustaining future generations (Robertson, 2021). It inaugurated ongoing global goal setting exercises toward universal human rights, poverty alleviation, and climate change mitigation codified in accords like Agenda 2030's Sustainable Development Goals tracking socioeconomic progress while respecting planetary boundaries. Cascading into domestic planning, such direction frames tool choices balancing human security, ecosystem health, and managed growth.

Critics argue that elite global policy circles advance technocratic, depoliticized metrics detached from grounded community realities while sustaining capitalist accumulation regimes driving inequality and ecologically ruinous throughputs (Blühdorn, 2018). Nonetheless broad consensus uniting governments, corporations, and civil society continues consolidating around formal conceptual metrics and required transitions whatever precise trajectory debates. Resulting high-level roadmaps enable tools targeting economic functions, infrastructures, and behaviors requiring adaptation.

Given large footprints, private sector sustainability ranks imperative for paradigm shifts by institutionalizing restorative designs, processes, and purposes replacing extractive business models (Wheelen et al., 2018). Myriad frameworks and reporting platforms structure internal transitions and external accountability around environmental and social impacts of operations, supply chains, and product life cycles. Early corporate social responsibility efforts emphasizing reputational ethics and isolated efficiency fixes evolve toward integrated governance and enterprise strategies, making sustainability central for competitiveness across innovation and risk management (Galpin et al., 2015). Purpose-driven redesigns delivering social goods like affordable housing or resilient infrastructure flip firm roles from externality generators toward partners for public problem solving (Amui et al., 2017). Partnerships with policymakers, communities, and advocates steer sectors like finance, agriculture, and mobility towards care-centered regenerative models benefiting all stakeholders, not just shareholders.

Critics highlight that risks of cooptation and greenwashing abound through symbolic sustainability declarations rather than substantive commercial-cultural realignment (Fioramonti et al., 2022). Uneven transparency around credible goal setting and impact measurement enables misleading claims. However, emerging external disclosure standardization, internal accounting shifts, and socially minded investment pressures facilitate accountability to ethics, not just profits or regulatory compliance. Though claims should be interrogated, corporations hold enormous potential driving sustainability where governmental efforts lag (Johnson & Schaltegger, 2016).

Grassroots projects pioneering aspirational post-capitalism models also make sustainability tangible through experimental place-based transitions. These pilot localized, cooperative, commons-centric configurations of enterprise, infrastructure, and community governance that eliminate environmental externalization and distributive inequality design flaws plaguing globalized corporatism (North & Longhurst, 2013). Diverse sustainability innovations span eco-villages testing off-grid circular resource metabolism to solidarity economy networks mutualizing employment and cooperative housing assistance funds decommodifying right to public goods. Digital fab labs democratize manufacturing skills and means for customized production on demand reducing transport emissions and liberating work. Such spaces model post-growth futures meeting needs through sufficiency and sharing rather than consumerism (Nesterova, 2020).

Critics question scalability beyond small enclaves or vulnerability to cooptation and market encroachment (Smith et al., 2021). They also highlight the importance of larger political economic reforms enabling rather than restricting proliferating alternatives through supportive programs, public investments, and policy ecosystems protecting the commons. Importantly, sustainability oriented social movements increasingly unify across localist community self-help groups, degrowth advocates, and environmental justice activists to build transformative power contesting state-market complexes driving inequality and ecocide (Koch, 2022).

Transitioning complex societies requires well calibrated integration of visionary alternatives, corporate sustainability, and public governance reforms incentivizing adoption at scale. Policy significantly shapes path dependencies and selection environments, determining the destiny and viability of niche experiments against prevailing social logics (Krähmer, 2022). Regulation, planning, and programs steering investment and behaviors escaping unsustainable locks-in requires hybrid tool mixes engaging diverse societal leverage points and actors.

For instance, sustainable mobility transitions to post-carbon mass transport meld technical enhancements like electric buses and online interfaces with pricing reforms, investments in cycling infrastructure, and land use planning fostering accessibility not auto-dependence across metro regions (Panzer-Krause, 2019). Demand shifts reducing extractive overconsumption and waste depend on awareness raising but also bans on planned obsolescence, progressive consumption taxes funding basic services, and circular procurement reforms aligning infrastructure with secondary material metabolization capacity (McGreevy et al., 2022).

Careful contextual tailoring and phasing of symbiotic regulatory, fiscal, and provisioning tool combinations empowers voluntary early adoption while mandating laggard compliance (Suárez-Eiroa et al., 2019). Adaptive policy mixes critically manage trade-offs across timeline, cost, political will, and uncertainty balancing sustainability's urgency against pragmatic strategy (Kalmykova et al., 2018).

Transforming deeply embedded structures driving contemporary unsustainability requires activating diverse, context-specific mixes of visionary alternative practices, corporate transitions, and public governance reforms (Amui et al., 2017). Sustainability tools signify defined techniques proposed from global accords down to grassroots projects that concretely redirect behaviors, designs, and evaluation toward social justice, environmental regeneration, and long-term prosperity. Strategic orchestration of tailored tool portfolios and phasing leverages potential complementarities across efforts advancing on separate paths. No singular master solution suffices given irreducibly contextual and contested translating of sustainability priorities into situated decisions, infrastructures, and collective actions (Smith et al., 2021). But proliferating demonstrations through markets, states, and communities models possibilities for escaping violent status quos toward just, flourishing coexistence enriching human and ecological communities.

Sustainability and Technology

Technology shapes human progress and prosperity yet also drives escalating unsustainability degrading ecosystems and communities worldwide. However, innovations likewise offer essential tools enabling civilizational transitions toward just, sustainable futures if guided by ecological ethics rather than growth obsession (Weaver et al., 2017). As environmental crises like climate disruption and nature annihilation worsen, technological transformation becomes imperative across how societies produce and consume seeking flourishing within restored living systems.

Spanning information systems, renewable energy, circular materials, and beyond, technological innovations can slash environmental footprints and empower communities when aligned with holistic understanding of integrated social-ecological actualities exceeding siloed technical control (Wu et al., 2018). However, technological changes alone remain insufficient absent political-economic transitions redefining institutional priorities, business models, and cultural assumptions driving contemporary technosphere overshoot eroding humanity's own lifeworld foundations. As with applying tools judiciously rather than idolizing progress, advancing sustainability requires harnessing science and technology for restoring ecosystem balance benefiting all beings rather than amplifying accumulation.

Emerging and maturing technologies offer enhanced efficiencies, decentralization, and democratization potentials transforming unsustainable systems dependencies across infrastructure essential for decent living standards like energy, mobility, and shelter meeting human needs within ecological limits. For example, renewable technologies like solar photovoltaics and wind turbines now provide cheapest electricity options in most contexts, enabling affordable decarbonized energy access proliferation replacing coal and gas dominance threatening climate stability (Qazi et al., 2019). Similarly smart mobility systems optimizing demand and integrating shared autonomous electric vehicles facilitate convenient low-carbon transportation across urban and rural regions otherwise car dependent (Wadud, MacKenzie & Leiby, 2016). Digitally connected sensors, platforms, and manufacturing devices assist small-scale production on-demand that minimize waste and transport burdens relative to centralized mass industry reliant on fossil fuels and exploitation (Bai et al., 2020). Localized circular material metabolisms can provide household necessities like furniture through redesigned reuse and repair ecosystems rather than further extracting scarce minerals and forests.

Myriad social innovations similarly deploy information technologies advancing sustainability political goals. Blockchain networks enable supply chain transparency, emissions accounting, and material passports verifying ethical provenance claims to drive corporate shifts (Saberi et al., 2019). Open digital collaboration enables grassroots solutions gathering where policy efforts falter, for instance around mobilizing decentralized renewable microgrids or crisis mutual aid networks building community resilience (Klein, Klein & Luciano, 2018). Online movements can swiftly spotlight injustices and apply pressure on governments lagging on sustainability reforms from protecting biodiversity to addressing energy poverty. Information connectivity provides tools for sustainability otherwise impossible in analogue eras, though potentials remain contingent on justice-oriented application.

However, manifest risks and deficiencies burden technology alone, offering illusory fixes to fundamentally ethical and political challenges. Inequitable access to innovations across geographies and marginalized demographic groups reproduces rather than resolves sustainability class divides (Sengers et al., 2019). Technocratic infrastructure transitions risk captured green monopolization concentrating benefits among new elites rather than enabling distributed prosperity, for instance where solar plant and battery patents narrowly financially enrich shareholders not regional communities (Nicolli & Vona, 2016).

Digital optimizations also often exacerbate rebound effects as efficiencies lower costs thereby increasing net consumption and throughput, as with smart lighting inadvertently driving greater energy demand (Hueske et al., 2012). And technological systems inherit design biases privileging convenience, control, and safety for certain dominant conceptions of well-being that degrade biodiversity and traditionally sustainable lifeworlds, for example building expressways devastating forest ecologies sustaining indigenous peoples (McLaren, 2016). Modernist technical transitions alone cannot escape modernity's violent, extractive value logics. Without addressing driving forces like profit maximization imperatives and commodification of nature, tools at best modestly decelerate harm rather than fundamentally transform toward nurturing holistic balance across human communities and living habitats.

Additionally, no technology panacea singularly resolves complex sustainability predicaments from nitrogen overload to urban inequality, but rather context-tailored tool integration navigating sociotechnical interdependencies and uncertainty merits coordinated innovation ecosystems (Gielen et al., 2019). For example, heavily automative geographies require mutually reinforcing shifts in fuels, vehicles, mobility infrastructure, land uses, regulations, and cultural normalcy to establish sustainably accessible transportation systems not beholden to cars. Since breakthroughs prove largely unpredictable, transition strategy emphasizes managed experimentation and participatory evaluation adapting explorations based on sustainability indicators more than predetermined silver bullets (Sengers et al., 2019). Still avoidance of maladaptive high-risk dead-ends and responsible scaling necessitate foresight and oversight through inclusive governance.

While particular technological tools and configurations resist singular specification given contextual diversity, several key principles and perspective shifts help guide innovation trajectories toward sustainably improving universal well-being rather than pursuing myopic, unsustainable, or inequitable technological control. Core tenets include:

Holism—Adopting integrated social-ecological-technological systems perspectives understanding multifaceted interactions and values beyond efficiency maximization or risk mitigation (Weaver et al., 2017). For example, energy transitions depend on interfacing generation, distribution, storage, management, and demand innovations within transformed settlement patterns, equity guarantees, and biodiversity protections simultaneously (Gielen et al., 2019). Atomistic silo solutions fail such complex challenges.

Ethics—Recentering care, justice, and ecological alignment over profits or control as cardinal orientations guiding technology developments, application logics, and impact assessment (McLaren, 2016). This demands reforming capitalist model privileging endless accumulation driving innovation down exploitative, ecocidal pathways. Sustainability helping all beings thrive rather than serve narrow anthropocentric interests renews technology's purpose.

Agency—Fostering inclusive self-determination and capabilities enabling communities to democratically appropriate technologies on their own terms rather than impose disruptive programs undermining identity, dignity, and autonomy (Bloom, 2017). Customizability, adaptability, and participatory steering allow situating tools within diverse localized needs and biocultural lifeways while resisting standardization enforced through capitalist power structures or managerial modernization schemes.

Responsibility—Embracing accountability and reversible caution for unintended harms from uncontrolled technology diffusion given complex system emergent effects exceeding prediction, such as irreversibly eradicating disease-curing plants or diminishing insect populations vital for thriving habitats (Jonas, 1984). Recognition of inherent ignorance seeds wisdom and patience for navigating uncertain transitions rather than reckless frontier mentalities.

While core goals of meeting universal human needs within restored living systems remain clear, manifold pathways interweave technologies and wider socio-political reforms as partnered catalysts reciprocally transforming the other toward harmonized sustainable civilization. Beyond singular solutions, combinations of redistributive welfare systems, commons governance, solidary enterprise, circular material metabolisms, participatory infrastructure access, and polycentric policy deserve integrated cultivation that redefines prosperity as sustainable well-being rather than addictive accumulation (O'Neill et al., 2018).

CASE STUDY: Transition Towns Movements

The Transition Towns movement is a grassroots initiative that originated in Totnes, UK, focused on building sustainable, resilient communities as alternatives to growth-dependent consumerism. From local food sovereignty projects to decentralized energy systems, Transition Towns aim to model post-carbon economies that nurture human and environmental well-being (Hopkins, 2010). Since its inception, the network has expanded globally, demonstrating practical pathways for community-led transformations that challenge unsustainable economic systems.

Transition Towns prioritize holistic transformations across energy, economics, and culture, emphasizing community regeneration and psycho-social reorientation alongside technical sustainability upgrades (Aiken, 2012). The movement posits that achieving just transitions requires shifting collective consciousness and cultural values away from growth obsession toward stewardship, solidarity, and simplicity. Transition projects strive to "seed" new narratives and catalyze political momentum through positive visions of sustainable futures (Hopkins, 2019).

Transition initiatives vary by context but share common goals of localizing production and consumption to foster resilience. Projects include community gardens, renewable microgrids, local currencies, and cooperative businesses that support sufficiency provisioning rather than profit maximization (Connors & McDonald, 2011). These initiatives demonstrate practical applications of circular economy principles by reconfiguring food, energy, and waste systems to meet community needs while minimizing environmental impact.

For instance, energy initiatives often focus on regionalizing supply chains and reducing dependence on centralized systems through renewable installations. Similarly, local currencies and timebanks help decouple livelihoods from global markets, emphasizing non-monetized contributions like caregiving (Aiken, 2012). Waste and transport programs promote upcycling, sharing platforms, and ultra-low energy retrofits to reduce material throughput and emissions.

Transition Towns have influenced sustainability discourse and policy at various levels. Their narratives have shaped initiatives from municipal programs to national policies, such as Welsh legislation that prioritizes sustainability and well-being (Alexander & Rutherford, 2018). Cities like San Francisco, Portland, and Melbourne have integrated circular economy principles and community resilience into their planning frameworks, inspired by Transition projects (Cretney et al., 2016).

Research indicates that Transition Town participants tend to adopt more sustainable behaviors, such as meat reduction and energy efficiency upgrades, more rapidly than those in comparable areas (Alexander & Rutherford, 2018). While difficult to quantify precisely due to the movement's decentralized nature, these voluntary actions contribute to reducing local carbon footprints and promoting sustainable practices.

Despite its successes, the movement faces criticism for being overly reformist and limited in scale. Some argue that Transition Towns represent a form of "lifestyle environmentalism" that struggles to achieve broader societal transformation (Kenis & Mathijs, 2014). The movement's demographic—often older, middle-class, and highly educated—has also led to concerns about inclusivity (Aiken, 2014; Smith, 2011).

Additionally, the focus on localization has sparked debates around potential parochialism or inward-looking politics that could undermine broader cosmopolitan values and global justice (Kenis & Mathijs, 2014). Nonetheless, proponents argue that Transition Towns provide open spaces for ongoing reflection, inclusivity, and solidarity building rather than enforcing rigid ideological purity (Aiken, 2014).

Transition Towns continue to grow and evolve, offering hope against climate fatalism and demonstrating the power of small, committed groups to seed cultural shifts. Their experiments with urban food sovereignty, circular business models, and solar microgrids showcase viable alternatives to capitalist enclosure and growth-driven models. By fostering community-led solutions, Transition Towns create "Citizen Laboratories" where neighbors collaboratively shape sustainable futures rooted in shared dignity and ecological health.

Conclusion

Sustainability is a crucial priority guiding policies and business practices to preserve ecosystems and communities for future generations. While there is consensus on the need for transformative changes to ensure humanity lives within Earth's limits, debates continue around the most effective strategies that balance practicality and justice amid complex social, economic, and environmental systems.

Sustainability concepts trace back centuries, but gained mainstream prominence in the 1980s with warnings of climate change and biodiversity loss highlighting the need to respect planetary boundaries. Although definitions vary, the core focus is on maintaining human dignity within ecological limits over long timescales, emphasizing interconnected governance, technology, culture, and economics.

Climate change remains a pivotal sustainability challenge, demanding both emissions reduction and resilience-building. Strategies must integrate technical, ethical, and justice considerations, rather than merely applying efficiency fixes to unsustainable systems. Grassroots experiments offer starting points for modeling alternative futures within these limits, despite broader political inertia.

Mainstream growth economics is inherently incompatible with sustainability due to its reliance on relentless expansion and externalizing environmental and social costs. Calls are growing to stabilize production, consumption, and population at sustainable levels, emphasizing sufficiency rather than endless accumulation. However, green technology alone will not suffice without cultural shifts reorienting systemic aims away from commodification and profit. Sustainable progress requires a focus on commons governance, grassroots innovation, and just transitions that balance varied needs and capabilities within ecological limits.

Prominent leaders like Tim Jackson and Kate Raworth have gained attention for advocating post-growth and regenerative economic frameworks. Jackson critiques the destructive nature of consumerism, while Raworth's "Doughnut Economics" provides an accessible visual model that balances human needs within ecological boundaries. Her framework has inspired local and international policy experiments, pushing for an economy centered on ethics and well-being rather than growth-driven destruction.

Social sustainability has emerged as a key pillar, promoting livelihood security, inclusion, and community agency. Transitioning sectors like energy toward justice and participation not only addresses climate change but also empowers communities. Locally defined, community-driven initiatives ground sustainability transformations in values of dignity and justice.

"Net zero" emissions have become a primary climate policy target, aiming to eliminate or offset 90 percent of greenhouse gas (GHG) emissions by 2050. This requires deep cuts in emissions, a focus on equity, and avoiding reliance on speculative future fixes. Many existing net zero frameworks fall short by prioritizing abstract metrics over grounded realities, risking inadequate responses to escalating climate challenges.

Post-growth and degrowth scholarship further challenge the unsustainable nature of endless economic expansion, promoting prosperity based on sufficiency and equity rather than commodity accumulation. While these frameworks have some differences, they both reject growth as an inherent necessity, advocating instead for transformative cultural shifts away from excessive consumption and gross domestic product (GDP) fixation.

Circular and regenerative economic models envision sustainability by closing resource loops and building ethical responsibilities within human and ecological communities. Circular systems focus on keeping materials in use at their highest value, while regenerative models emphasize positive contributions to the environment and society. Both advocate for post-extractive, sustainable models that prioritize holistic well-being.

Environmental justice movements expose the disproportionate exposure of marginalized communities to environmental harms, from pollution to unsafe infrastructure. Grassroots resistance and advocacy demand systemic transformations in human–nature relationships to achieve mutual liberation, pushing for climate reparations and environmental equity programs that benefit the most impacted communities.

In conclusion, today's environmental crises require a fundamental reevaluation of dominant paradigms driving unsustainable and unjust practices. Sustainability compels political, economic, and cultural transitions grounded in cooperation, ecological healing, and a celebration of diverse human and natural systems. While no singular solution exists, interwoven experimentation and policy reforms can create resilient futures. It is imperative to urgently implement these models and dismantle the drivers of inequality and extractivism that jeopardize our planet's future. Recentering ethics of care, capabilities, and community is essential to ensuring a sustainable and just world for all life on this magnificent planet.

References

Åhman, H. (2013). Social sustainability—society at the intersection of development and maintenance. *Local Environment, 18*(10), 1153–1166.

Aiken, G. (2012). Community transitions to low carbon futures in the transition towns network (TTN). *Geography Compass, 6*(2), 89–99.

Aiken, G. (2014). *The Production, Practice and Potential of 'Community' in Edinburgh's Transition Town Network* (Doctoral dissertation, Durham University).

Ajmal, M. M., Khan, M., Hussain, M., & Helo, P. (2018). Conceptualizing and incorporating social sustainability in the business world. *International Journal of Sustainable Development & World Ecology, 25*(4), 327–339.

Alexander, S., & Rutherford, J. (2018). The "transition town" movement as a model for urban transformation. In Moore, T., de Haan, F., Horne, R. & Gleeson, B. J. (eds.), *Urban Sustainability Transitions: Australian Cases—International Perspectives* (pp. 173–189). Singapore: Springer.

Allen, M. R., Friedlingstein, P., Girardin, C. A., Jenkins, S., Malhi, Y., Mitchell-Larson, E., . . . & Rajamani, L. (2022). Net zero: Science, origins, and implications. *Annual Review of Environment and Resources, 47,* 849–887.

Amui, L. B. L., Jabbour, C. J. C., de Sousa Jabbour, A. B. L., & Kannan, D. (2017). Sustainability as a dynamic organizational capability: A systematic review and a future agenda toward a sustainable transition. *Journal of Cleaner Production, 142,* 308–322.

Anderson, K. & Peters, G. (2016). The trouble with negative emissions. *Science, 354*(3609), 182–183.

Bai, C., Dallasega, P., Orzes, G., & Sarkis, J. (2020). Industry 4.0 technologies assessment: A sustainability perspective. *International Journal of Production Economics, 229,* 107776.

Banerjee, S. B., Jermier, J. M., Peredo, A. M., Perey, R., & Reichel, A. (2021). Theoretical perspectives on organizations and organizing in a post-growth era. *Organization, 28*(3), 337–357.

Barrier, E. B. (2017). The concept of sustainable economic development. In Peezey, J. C. V. & Toman, M. A. (eds.), *The Economics of Sustainability* (pp. 87–96). London: Routledge.

Barry, J. (2018, April). Post-growth economics, sustainability and equality: Towards a green Republican political economy. Presented at ECPR 2018 Joint Sessions Workshop, *"Green Politics and Civic Republicanism: Green Republicanism as a Response to the Environmental and Political Crises of the 21st Century"*, Nicosia, Cyprus, April 10–14, 2018.

Bartelmus, P., & Seifert, E. K. (eds). (2018). *Green Accounting*. Routledge.

Beckerman, W. (2015). *A Poverty of Reason: Sustainable Development and Economic Growth*. Independent Institute.

Bistline, J. E. (2021). Roadmaps to net-zero emissions systems: Emerging insights and modeling challenges. *Joule, 5*(10), 2551–2563.

Bloom, P. (2017). Managing the self. In M. Parker, G. Cheney, V. Fournier & C. Land (Eds.), *The Routledge companion to alternative organization* (pp. 97–111). London: Routledge.

Blühdorn, I. (2018). Post-capitalism, post-growth, post-consumerism? Eco-political hopes beyond sustainability. In Foster, J. (ed.), *Post-Sustainability* (pp. 39–58). London: Routledge.

Böhm, S., Misoczky, M. C. & Moog, S. (2012). Greening capitalism? A Marxist critique of carbon markets. *Organization Studies*, *33*(11), 1617–1638.

Bond, P. (2012). *Politics of climate justice*. Pietermaritzburg: University of KwaZulu-Natal Press.

Borowy, I., & Schmelzer, M. (eds). (2017). *History of the Future of Economic Growth: Historical Roots of Current Debates on Sustainable Degrowth*. Taylor & Francis.

Boyer, R. H., Peterson, N. D., Arora, P., & Caldwell, K. (2016). Five approaches to social sustainability and an integrated way forward. *Sustainability*, *8*(9), 878.

Buch-Hansen, H. (2018). The prerequisites for a degrowth paradigm shift: Insights from critical political economy. *Ecological Economics*, *146*, 157–163.

Bullard, R. D. (1994). *Dumping in Dixie: Race, class and environmental quality*. Boulder, CO: Westview Press.

Bullard, R. D., Mohai, P., Saha, R. & Wright, B. (2007). *Toxic Wastes and Race at Twenty: 1987–2007*. Cleveland, OH: Justice and Witness Ministries.

Caradonna, J. L. (2022). *Sustainability: A History*. Oxford University Press.

Caraiani, C. (ed.). (2015). *Green Accounting Initiatives and Strategies for Sustainable Development*. IGI Global.

Cavalieri, P. (2001). *The animal question: why nonhuman animals deserve human rights*. Oxford: Oxford University Press.

Celermajer, D., & O'Brien, A. T. (2021). Alter-transitional justice; transforming unjust relations with the more-than-human. In Grear, A., Boulot, E., Vargas-Roncancio, I. D. & Sterlin, J (eds.), *Posthuman Legalities* (pp. 125–147). Glos and Massachusetts: Edward Elgar Publishing.

Celermajer, D., Schlosberg, D., Rickards, L., Stewart-Harawira, M., Thaler, M., Tschakert, P., . . . & Winter, C. (2022). Multispecies justice: Theories, challenges, and a research agenda for environmental politics. In Hayes et al. (eds.), *Trajectories in Environmental Politics* (pp. 116–137). Routledge.

Chaves Ávila, R., & Monzón Campos, J. L. (2012). Beyond the crisis: The social economy, prop of a new model of sustainable economic development. *Service Business*, *6*(1), 5–26.

Chiengkul, P. (2018). The degrowth movement: Alternative economic practices and relevance to developing countries. *Alternatives*, *43*(2), 81–95.

Cho, C. H., & Patten, D. M. (2013). Green accounting: Reflections from a CSR and environmental disclosure perspective. *Critical Perspectives on Accounting*, *24*(6), 443–447.

Climate Action Network International. (2021). *Climate Action Network annual report 2021*. Climate Action Network. Available at: https://climatenetwork.org/resource/climate-action-network-annual-report-2021 (accessed February 17, 2024).

Cole, R. J. (2015). Net-zero and net-positive design: A question of value. *Building Research & Information*, *43*(1), 1–6.

Cole, L. W. & Foster, S. R. (2001). *From the Ground up: Environmental Racism and the Rise of the Environmental Justice Movement*. New York, NY: NYU Press.

Connelly, S., Markey, S., & Roseland, M. (2011). Bridging sustainability and the social economy: Achieving community transformation through local food initiatives. *Critical Social Policy*, *31*(2), 308–324.

Connors, P., & McDonald, P. (2011). Transitioning communities: Community, participation and the Transition Town movement. *Community Development Journal*, *46*(4), 558–572.

Cretney, R. M., Thomas, A. C., & Bond, S. (2016). Maintaining grassroots activism: Transition towns in Aotearoa New Zealand. *New Zealand Geographer*, *72*(2), 81–91.

D'Alisa, G., & Kallis, G. (2020). Degrowth and the state. *Ecological Economics*, *169*, 106486.

Daly, H. E. (2014). *Beyond Growth: The Economics of Sustainable Development*. Beacon Press.

Dasgupta, P. (2007). The idea of sustainable development. *Sustainability Science*, *2*, 5–11.

Davidson, M. (2009). Social sustainability: A potential for politics? *Local Environment*, *14*(7), 607–619.

Davidson, M. (2010). Social sustainability and the city. *Geography Compass*, *4*(7), 872–880.

Davies, A. R., & Mullin, S. J. (2011). Greening the economy: Interrogating sustainability innovations beyond the mainstream. *Journal of Economic Geography*, *11*(5), 793–816.

Davis, S. J., Lewis, N. S., Shaner, M., Aggarwal, S., Arent, D., Azevedo, I. L., . . . & Caldeira, K. (2018). Net-zero emissions energy systems. *Science, 360*(6396), eaas9793.

DeAngelo, J., Azevedo, I., Bistline, J., Clarke, L., Luderer, G., Byers, E., & Davis, S. J. (2021). Energy systems in scenarios at net-zero CO_2 emissions. *Nature Communications, 12*(1), 6096.

Devall, B. & Sessions, G. (1985). *Deep Ecology: Living As If Nature Mattered*. Salt Lake City, UT: Gibbs Smith.

Dempsey, N., Bramley, G., Power, S., & Brown, C. (2011). The social dimension of sustainable development: Defining urban social sustainability. *Sustainable Development, 19*(5), 289–300.

Dicenta, M. (2020). Biocare, biosecurity, and interspecies justice: The politics of subjects as/at risk. *Sociological Research Online*. DOI:10.11156/aries.2016.AR0007740

Dietz, R. & O'Neill, D. (2013). *Enough is enough: Building a sustainable economy in a world of finite resources*. San Francisco: Berrett-Koehler Publishers.

Dresner, S. (2012). *The Principles of Sustainability*. Routledge.

Eizenberg, E., & Jabareen, Y. (2017). Social sustainability: A new conceptual framework. *Sustainability, 9*(1), 68.

Ekins, P. (1993). "Limits to growth" and "sustainable development": Grappling with ecological realities. *Ecological Economics, 8*(3), 269–288.

Ekins, P. (2002). *Economic Growth and Environmental Sustainability: The Prospects for Green Growth*. Routledge.

El Serafy, S. (1997). Green accounting and economic policy. *Ecological Economics, 21*(3), 217–229.

Elkington, J. (2020). *Green Swans: The Coming Boom in Regenerative Capitalism*. Greenleaf Book Group.

European Environmental Bureau. (2020). *Turning fear into hope: Corona crisis measures to help build a better future*. Available at: https://eeb.org/library/turning-fear-into-hope-corona-crisis-measures-to-help-build-a-better-future (accessed February 17, 2024).

Fankhauser, S., Smith, S. M., Allen, M., Axelsson, K., Hale, T., Hepburn, C., . . . & Wetzer, T. (2022). The meaning of net zero and how to get it right. *Nature Climate Change, 12*(1), 15–21.

Farley, H. M., & Smith, Z. A. (2020). *Sustainability: If it's Everything, is it Nothing?* Routledge.

Farouk, S., Cherian, J., & Jacob, J. (2012). Green accounting and management for sustainable manufacturing in developing countries. *International Journal of Business and Management, 7*(20), 36.

Fernandes, C. I., Veiga, P. M., Ferreira, J. J., & Hughes, M. (2021). Green growth versus economic growth: Do sustainable technology transfer and innovations lead to an imperfect choice? *Business Strategy and the Environment, 30*(4), 2021–2037.

Fioramonti, L., Coscieme, L., Costanza, R., Kubiszewski, I., Trebeck, K., Wallis, S., . . . & De Vogli, R. (2022). Wellbeing economy: An effective paradigm to mainstream post-growth policies? *Ecological Economics, 192*, 107261.

Fitz-Henry, E. (2022). Multi-species justice: A view from the rights of nature movement. *Environmental Politics, 31*(2), 338–359.

Galpin, T., Whitttington, J. L., & Bell, G. (2015). Is your sustainability strategy sustainable? Creating a culture of sustainability. *Corporate Governance, 15*(1), 1–17.

George, D. A., Lin, B. C. A., & Chen, Y. (2015). A circular economy model of economic growth. *Environmental Modelling & Software, 73*, 60–63.

Gezon, L. L. (2014). Who Wins and Who Loses? Unpacking the Local People Concept in Ecotourism: A Longitudinal Study of Community Equity in Ankarana, Madagascar. *Journal of Sustainable Tourism, 22*(5), 821–838.

Gielen, D., Boshell, F., Saygin, D., Bazilian, M. D., Wagner, N., & Gorini, R. (2019). The role of renewable energy in the global energy transformation. *Energy Strategy Reviews, 24*, 38–50.

Giovannoni, E., & Fabietti, G. (2013). What is sustainability? A review of the concept and its applications. In Busco, C., Frigo, M. L., Riccaboni, A. & Quattrone, P. (eds.), *Integrated Reporting: Concepts and Cases that Redefine Corporate Accountability* (pp. 21–40). Heidelberg: Springer.

Girardet, H. (2017). Regenerative Cities. In Shmelev, S. (ed,), *Green economy reader: Lectures in ecological economics and sustainability* (pp. 183–204). Springer International Publishing.

Goyal, S., Esposito, M., & Kapoor, A. (2018). Circular economy business models in developing economies: Lessons from India on reduce, recycle, and reuse paradigms. *Thunderbird International Business Review, 60*(5), 729–740.

Harris, J. M. (2003). Sustainability and sustainable development. *International Society for Ecological Economics, 1*(1), 1–12.

Haughton, G. (1999). Environmental justice and the sustainable city. In Satterthwaite, D. (ed.), *The Earthscan Reader in Sustainable Cities* (pp. 62–79). London: Routledge.

Healy, H., Martinez-Alier, J., & Kallis, G. (2015). From ecological modernization to socially sustainable economic degrowth: Lessons from ecological economics. *The International Handbook of Political Ecology, 577*(9), 1531–1546.

Healy, N. & Barry, J. (2017), Politicizing energy justice and energy system transitions: Fossil fuel divestment and a "just transition". *Energy Policy, 108*, 451–459.

Heitlinger, S., Houston, L., Taylor, A., & Catlow, R. (2021, May). Algorithmic food justice: Co-designing more-than-human blockchain futures for the food commons. In Bjørn, P., Drucker, S., Tinsman, C. & Huff, E. (eds.), *Proceedings of the 2021 CHI Conference on Human Factors in Computing Systems* (pp. 1–17). New York: Association for Computing Machinery

Hess, P. N. (2016). *Economic Growth and Sustainable Development.* Routledge.

Hickel, J. (2019). Degrowth: A theory of radical abundance. *Real-World Economics Review, 87*(19), 54–68.

Hopkins, R. (2010). *Localisation and resilience at the local level: the case of Transition Town Totnes.* Dissertation. University of Plymouth.

Hopkins, R. (2019). *From what is to what if: unleashing the power of imagination to create the future we want.* White River Junction: Chelsea Green Publishing.

Hopkinson, P., Zils, M., Hawkins, P., & Roper, S. (2018). Managing a complex global circular economy business model: Opportunities and challenges. *California Management Review, 60*(3), 71–94.

Howard, M., Hopkinson, P., & Miemczyk, J. (2019). The regenerative supply chain: A framework for developing circular economy indicators. *International Journal of Production Research, 57*(23), 7300–7318.

Hueske, F., Peters, M., Sax, M., Rheinländer, A., Bergmann, R., Krettek, A. & Tzoumas, K. (2012). Opening the black boxes in data flow optimization. *Proc VLDB Endowment, 5*(11), 1256–1267.

Hutchins, M. J., & Sutherland, J. W. (2008). An exploration of measures of social sustainability and their application to supply chain decisions. *Journal of Cleaner Production, 16*(15), 1688–1698.

Jackson, T. (1996). *Material Concerns: Pollution, Profit and Quality of Life.* London: Routledge.

Jackson, T. (2005). Live better by consuming less? Is there a 'double dividend' in sustainable consumption?. *Journal of Industrial Ecology, 9*(1–2): 19–36.

Jackson, T. (2009). *Prosperity without Growth: Economics for a Finite Planet* (1st ed.). London: Routledge.

Jackson, T. (2021). *Post Growth: Life After Capitalism.* Cambridge: Polity Press.

Jackson, T. & Victor, P. A. (2015). Does credit create a 'growth imperative'? A quasi-stationary economy with interest-bearing debt. *Ecological Economics, 120*, 32–48.

Johnson, M. P., & Schaltegger, S. (2016). Two decades of sustainability management tools for SMEs: How far have we come? *Journal of Small Business Management, 54*(2), 481–505.

Jonas, H. (1984). *The Imperative of responsibility: in search of an ethics for the technological age.* Chicago: University of Chicago Press.

Kallis, G. (2017). Economics without growth. In Castells, M. (ed.), *Another Economy is Possible: Culture and Economy in a Time of Crisis* (pp. 34–54). Cambridge: Polity Press

Kallis, G. (2019). *Limits: Why Malthus was wrong and why environmentalists should care.* Stanford: Stanford University Press.

Kallis, G., Paulson, S., D'Alisa, G., & Demaria, F. (2020). *The Case for Degrowth.* London: Polity Press.

Kalmykova, Y., Sadagopan, M., & Rosado, L. (2018). Circular economy—From review of theories and practices to development of implementation tools. *Resources, Conservation and Recycling, 135*, 190–201.

Kenis, A., & Mathijs, E. (2014). (De) politicising the local: The case of the Transition Towns movement in Flanders (Belgium). *Journal of Rural Studies, 34*, 172–183.

Klein, R. H., Klein, D. C. B. & Luciano, E. M. (2018). Open Government Data: concepts, approaches and dimensions over time. *E&G-Revista Economia e Gestão, 18*(49), 4–24.

Koch, M. (2022). Social policy without growth: moving towards sustainable welfare states. *Social Policy and Society, 21*(3), 447–459.

Korhonen, J., Honkasalo, A., & Seppälä, J. (2018). Circular economy: The concept and its limitations. *Ecological Economics, 143*, 37–46.

Krähmer, K. (2022). Degrowth and the city: Multiscalar strategies for the socio-ecological transformation of space and place. *City, 26*(2–3), 316–345.

Kyrö, P. (2001). To grow or not to grow? Entrepreneurship and sustainable development. *The International Journal of Sustainable Development & World Ecology, 8*(1), 15–28.

Lewandowski, M. (2016). Designing the business models for circular economy—Towards the conceptual framework. *Sustainability, 8*(1), 43.

Littig, B., & Griessler, E. (2005). Social sustainability: A catchword between political pragmatism and social theory. *International Journal of Sustainable Development, 8*(1–2), 65–79.

Lubin, D. A., & Esty, D. C. (2010). The sustainability imperative. *Harvard Business Review, 88*(5), 42–50.

Luther, E. E. (2021). *Multispecies Cities for the Anthropocene: Narrativizing Human-Wildlife Relations in an Urban Organizational Niche*. Dissertation. Faculty of Graduate Studies, York University.

Maama, H., & Appiah, K. O. (2019). Green accounting practices: Lesson from an emerging economy. *Qualitative Research in Financial Markets, 11*(4), 456–478.

MacGregor, S. (2006). *Beyond Mothering Earth: Ecological Citizenship and the Politics of Care*. Vancouver: University of British Columbia Press.

Mair, S., Druckman, A., & Jackson, T. (2020). A tale of two utopias: Work in a post-growth world. *Ecological Economics, 173*, 106653.

Maldonado, J., Bennett, T. M. B., Chief, K., Cochran, P., Cozzetto, K., Gough, B., Redsteer, M. H., Lynn, K., Maynard, N. & Voggesser, G. (2016). Engagement With Indigenous Peoples and Honoring Traditional Knowledge Systems. *Climatic Change, 135*(1), 111–126.

Malin, S. A., Ryder, S. & Lyra, M. G. (2019). Environmental justice and natural resource extraction: Intersections of power, equity and access. *Environmental Sociology, 5*(2), 109–116.

Mang, P., & Reed, B. (2020). Regenerative development and design. In Loftness, V. (ed.), *Sustainable Built Environments* (pp. 115–141). New York, NY: Springer.

Markandya, A., & Pavan, M. (eds). (2012). *Green Accounting in Europe—Four Case Studies* (Vol. 11). Springer Science & Business Media.

Markey, S., & Roseland, M. (2016). *Scaling Up: The Convergence of Social Economy and Sustainability*. Athabasca University Press.

Martinez-Alier, J. (2002). *The Environmentalism of the Poor: A Study of Ecological Conflicts and Valuation*. Cheltenham: Edward Elgar.

Martinez-Alier, J. (2014). The Environmentalism of the Poor. *Geoforum, 54*, 239–241.

Martinez-Alier, J., Temper, L., Del Bene, D., & Scheidel, A. (2016). Is there a global environmental justice movement? *The Journal of Peasant Studies, 43*(3), 731–755.

McLaren, D. (2016). Mitigation deterrence and the 'moral hazard' in solar radiation management. *Earth's Future, 4*(12), 596–602.

McGreevy, S. R., Rupprecht, C. D., Niles, D., Wiek, A., Carolan, M., Kallis, G., . . . & Tachikawa, M. (2022). Sustainable agrifood systems for a post-growth world. *Nature sustainability, 5*(12), 1011–1017.

McLaren, D. P., Tyfield, D. P., Willis, R., Szerszynski, B., & Markusson, N. O. (2019). Beyond "net-zero": A case for separate targets for emissions reduction and negative emissions. *Frontiers in Climate*, *1*, 4.

Meadowcroft, J., & Rosenbloom, D. (2023). Governing the net-zero transition: Strategy, policy, and politics. *Proceedings of the National Academy of Sciences*, *120*(47), e2207727120.

Meys, R., Kätelhön, A., Bachmann, M., Winter, B., Zibunas, C., Suh, S., & Bardow, A. (2021). Achieving net-zero greenhouse gas emission plastics by a circular carbon economy. *Science*, *374*(6563), 71–76.

Missimer, M., Robèrt, K. H., & Broman, G. (2017). A strategic approach to social sustainability–Part 1: exploring the social system. *Journal of Cleaner Production*, *140*, 32–41.

Montabon, F., Pagell, M., & Wu, Z. (2016). Making sustainability sustainable. *Journal of Supply Chain Management*, *52*(2), 11–27.

Morseletto, P. (2020). Restorative and regenerative: Exploring the concepts in the circular economy. *Journal of Industrial Ecology*, *24*(4), 763–773.

Moyano-Fernández, C. (2022). Rewilding identitary foodscapes: Moral challenges from a multi-species justice perspective. In *Transforming Food Systems: Ethics, Innovation and Responsibility* (pp. 152–158). Wageningen Academic Publishers.

Munier, N. (2006). Economic growth and sustainable development: Could multicriteria analysis be used to solve this dichotomy? *Environment, Development and Sustainability*, *8*, 425–443.

Murphy-Greene, C., Leip, L. A. (2002). Assessing the effectiveness of executive order 12898: Environmental justice for all?. *Public Administration Review*, *62*(6), 679–687.

Nesterova, I. (2020). Degrowth business framework: Implications for sustainable development. *Journal of Cleaner Production*, *262*, 121382.

Nicolli, F., & Vona, F. (2016). Heterogeneous policies, heterogeneous technologies: The case of renewable energy. *Energy Economics*, *56*, 190–204.

North, P. & Longhurst, N. (2013). Grassroots Localisation? The Scalar Potential of the 'Transition' Approach to Climate Change and Resource Constraint. *Urban Studies*, *50*(7), 1423–1438.

O'Neill, D. W., Fanning, A. L., Lamb, W. F. & Steinberger, J. K. (2018). A good life for all within planetary boundaries. *Nat. Sustainability*, *1*(2), 88–95.

Outka, U. (2018). Chapter 2: Fairness in the low-carbon shift: learning from environmental justice. In Salter, R., Gonzales, C. G. & Kronk Warner, E. A. (eds.), *Energy Justice* (pp. 12–40). Cheltenham: Edward Elgar Publishing.

Paech, N. (2017). Post-growth economics. In Spash, C. L. (ed.), *Routledge Handbook of Ecological Economics* (pp. 477–486). London: Routledge.

Panzer-Krause, S. (2019). Networking towards sustainable tourism: Innovations between green growth and degrowth strategies. *Regional Studies*, *53*(7), 927–938.

Peredo, A. M.,& McLean, M. (2020). Decommodification in action: Common property as countermovement. *Organization*, *27*(6), 817–839.

Pesch, U. (2018). Paradigms and paradoxes: The futures of growth and degrowth. *International Journal of Sociology and Social Policy*, *38*(11/12), 1133–1146.

Pieroni, M. P., McAloone, T. C., & Pigosso, D. C. (2019). Business model innovation for circular economy and sustainability: A review of approaches. *Journal of Cleaner Production*, *215*, 198–216.

Pineault, E. (2016). *Growth and over-accumulation in advanced capitalism: Some critical reflections on the political economy and ecological economics of degrowth*. Paper presented at the 5th Degrowth conference, Budapest, August 31, 2016.

Plumwood, V. (1993). *Feminism and the Mastery of Nature*. London: Routledge.

Plumwood, V. (2002). *Environmental Culture: The Ecological Crisis of Reason*. London: Routledge.

Portney, K. E. (2015). *Sustainability*. MIT Press.

Prádanos, L. I. (2016). Degrowth and ecological economics in twenty-first-century Spain: Toward a posthumanist economy. In Beilin, K. & Viestenz, W. (eds.), *Ethics of Life: Contemporary Iberian Debates* (pp. 143–159). Nashville, TN: Vanderbilt University Press.

Pulido, L. (2017). Geographies of race and ethnicity II: Environmental racism, racial capitalism and state-sanctioned violence. *Progress in Human Geography*, 41(4), 524–33.

Qazi, A., Hussain, F., Rahim, N. A., Hardaker, G., Alghazzawi, D., Shaban, K., & Haruna, K. (2019). Towards sustainable energy: A systematic review of renewable energy sources, technologies, and public opinions. *IEEE Access*, 7, 63837–63851.

Raworth, K. (2012). *A Safe and Just Space for Humanity: Can We Live within the Doughnut?* Oxfam.

Raworth, K. (2017). *Doughnut Economics: Seven Ways to Think Like a 21st-century Economist*. Chelsea Green Publishing.

Regan, T. (1985). The Case for Animal Rights. In Singer, P. (ed.), *In Defense of Animals* (pp. 13–26). New York: Basil Blackwell.

Roberts, J. T. & Parks, B. C. (2009). Ecologically unequal exchange, ecological debt, and climate justice. *International Journal of Comparative Sociology*, 50(3–4), 385–409.

Robertson, M. (2021). *Sustainability Principles and Practice*. Routledge.

Rogelj, J., Geden, O., Cowie, A., & Reisinger, A. (2021). Three ways to improve net-zero emissions targets. *Nature*, 591(7850), 365–368.

Rogers, D. S., Duraiappah, A. K., Antons, D. C., Munoz, P., Bai, X., Fragkias, M., & Gutscher, H. (2012). A vision for human well-being: Transition to social sustainability. *Current Opinion in Environmental Sustainability*, 4(1), 61–73.

Rosenow, J., & Eyre, N. (2022). Reinventing energy efficiency for net zero. *Energy Research & Social Science*, 90, 102602.

Roth, S. (2017). Marginal economy: Growth strategies for post-growth societies. *Journal of Economic Issues*, 51(4), 1033–1046.

Saberi, S., Kouhizadeh, M., Sarkis, J., & Shen, L. (2019). Blockchain technology and its relationships to sustainable supply chain management. *International Journal of Production Research*, 57(7), 2117–2135.

Salmon, E. (2000). Kincentric ecology: indigenous perceptions of the human–nature relationship. *Ecological Applications*, 10(5), 1327–1332.

Schmelzer, M., Vetter, A., & Vansintjan, A. (2022). *The future is degrowth: A guide to a world beyond capitalism*. London: Verso.

Scoones, I. (2007). Sustainability. *Development in Practice*, 17(4–5), 589–596.

Scoones, I. (2016). The politics of sustainability and development. *Annual Review of Environment and Resources*, 41, 293–319.

Sengers, F., Wieczorek, A. J., & Raven, R. (2019). Experimenting for sustainability transitions: A systematic literature review. *Technological Forecasting and Social Change*, 145, 153–164.

Sheikh, H., Mitchell, P., & Foth, M. (2023). Reparative futures of smart urban governance: A speculative design approach for multispecies justice. *Futures*, 154, 103266.

Siew, R. Y. (2015). A review of corporate sustainability reporting tools (SRTs). *Journal of Environmental Management*, 164, 180–195.

Smith, A. (2011). The transition town network: A review of current evolutions and renaissance. *Social Movement Studies*, 10(01), 99–105.

Smith, T. S., Baranowski, M., & Schmid, B. (2021). Intentional degrowth and its unintended consequences: Uneven journeys towards post-growth transformations. *Ecological Economics*, 190, 107215.

Soubbotina, T. P. (2004). *Beyond Economic Growth: An Introduction to Sustainable Development*. World Bank Publications.

Spangenberg, J. H. (2010). The growth discourse, growth policy and sustainable development: Two thought experiments. *Journal of Cleaner Production*, 18(6), 561–566.

Stern, N., & Valero, A. (2021). Innovation, growth and the transition to net-zero emissions. *Research Policy*, 50(9), 104293.

Suárez-Eiroa, B., Fernández, E., Méndez-Martínez, G., & Soto-Oñate, D. (2019). Operational principles of circular economy for sustainable development: Linking theory and practice. *Journal of Cleaner Production, 214*, 952–961.

Sze, J., London, J. K., Shilling, F., Gambirazzio, G., Filan, T. & Cadenasso, M. (2009). Defining and contesting environmental justice: socio-natures and the politics of scale in the Delta. *Antipode, 41*(4): 807–843.

Temper, L., Del Bene, D., & Martinez-Alier, J. (2015). Mapping the frontiers and front lines of global environmental justice: The EJAtlas. *Journal of Political Ecology, 22*(1), 255–278.

Tessum, C. W., Paolella, D. A., Chambliss, S. E., Apte, J. S., Hill, J. D. & Marshall, J. D. (2021). PM2. 5 polluters disproportionately and systemically affect people of color in the United States. *Science Advances, 7*(18), article eabf4491.

Thiele, L. P. (2016). *Sustainability*. John Wiley & Sons.

Todd, Z. (2016). An Indigenous Feminist's Take on the Ontological Turn:'Ontology' Is Just Another Word for Colonialism. *Journal of Historical Sociology, 29*(1), 4–22.

Tschakert, P. (2022). More-than-human solidarity and multispecies justice in the climate crisis. *Environmental Politics, 31*(2), 277–296.

Turner, R. A. & Wills, J. (2022). Downscaling doughnut economics for sustainability governance. *Current Opinion in Environmental Sustainability, 56*(June), 101180.

Urbinati, A., Chiaroni, D., & Chiesa, V. (2017). Towards a new taxonomy of circular economy business models. *Journal of Cleaner Production, 168*, 487–498.

Vandeventer, J. S., Cattaneo, C., & Zografos, C. (2019). A degrowth transition: Pathways for the degrowth niche to replace the capitalist-growth regime. *Ecological Economics, 156*, 272–286.

Wadud, Z., MacKenzie, D. & Leiby, P. (2016). Help or hindrance? The travel, energy and carbon impacts of highly automated vehicles. *Transportation Research Part A: Policy and Practice, 86*, 1–18.

Wahl, D. C. (2016). *Designing Regenerative Cultures*. Axminster: Triarchy Press.

Wahlund, M. & Hansen, T. (2022). Exploring alternative economic pathways: a comparison of foundational economy and Doughnut economics. *Sustainability: Science, Practice and Policy, 18*(1), 171–186.

Walker, A. M., Opferkuch, K., Lindgreen, E. R., Simboli, A., Vermeulen, W. J., & Raggi, A. (2021). Assessing the social sustainability of circular economy practices: Industry perspectives from Italy and the Netherlands. *Sustainable Production and Consumption, 27*, 831–844.

Walker, G. (2012). *Environmental Justice: Concepts, Evidence. and Politics*. London: Routledge.

Weaver, P., Jansen, L., Van Grootveld, G., Van Spiegel, E., & Vergragt, P. (2017). *Sustainable Technology Development*. Routledge.

Westerlaken, M. (2021). What is the opposite of speciesism? On relational care ethics and illustrating multi-species-isms. *International Journal of Sociology and Social Policy, 41*(3/4), 522–540.

Wheelen, T. L., Hunger, J. D., Hoffman, A. N., & Bamford, C. E. (2018). *Strategic Management and Business Policy: Globalization, Innovation, and Sustainability*. Pearson.

Winans, K., Kendall, A., & Deng, H. (2017). The history and current applications of the circular economy concept. *Renewable and Sustainable Energy Reviews, 68*, 825–833.

Winter, C. J. (2022). Introduction: What's the value of multispecies justice? *Environmental Politics, 31*(2), 251–257.

Wolch, J. (2002) Anima urbis. *Progress in Human Geography, 26*(6), 721–742.

Wu, J., Guo, S., Huang, H., Liu, W., & Xiang, Y. (2018). Information and communications technologies for sustainable development goals: State-of-the-art, needs and perspectives. *IEEE Communications Surveys & Tutorials, 20*(3), 2389–2406.

Wu, X. & Zhi, Q. (2016). Impact of Shared Economy on Urban Sustainability: From the Perspective of Social, Economic, and Environmental Sustainability. *Energy Procedia, 104*, 191–196.

Zoönomic Institute. (n.d.). *Zoönomic Annual Cycle*. Available at: https://zoop.earth/en/page/392/zo%C3% B6nomic-annual-cycle (accessed February 17, 2024).

Chapter 6
Cooperative Governance: Democracy and Consensus

Introduction

In the preceding chapters of this textbook, we have delved into the intricate dynamics of the social economy, primarily focusing on analyses at the organizational and community levels. However, the realm of economic governance and power extends far beyond these localized spheres. Understanding how economic decisions are made, and the mechanisms through which power is exercised at the macro-level, is crucial in comprehending the broader implications of the social economy. This chapter aims to shed light on how the social economy can foster greater democratic governance and cooperative decision-making within society at large.

Economic power and governance play a pivotal role in shaping relationships among various stakeholders, including employers, governments, employees, and the wider community. These powers are not detached from the prevailing values, cultural assumptions, and legal frameworks that underpin our societies. Instead, they are deeply intertwined with these factors. Recognizing the significance of economic power dynamics requires a holistic understanding of the complex interplay between different actors and the impact they have on the distribution of resources, opportunities, and influence.

Across the economic landscape, there exists a diverse array of models for economic governance. Some models prioritize the rights of individuals and firms to largely dictate their own rules, while others emphasize the role of the state in regulating and stimulating the economy. Additionally, there are models that emphasize collective bargaining and power-sharing between workers and employers, as well as traditions of community-based ownership and decision-making. It is crucial to grasp that these diverse forms of governance confer advantages upon certain stakeholders while potentially disadvantaging others. Moreover, they shape what is prioritized and valued within the economic system. As a result, the organization of the economy and the production, consumption, and evaluation of goods and services are profoundly influenced by these differing values and governance arrangements.

The social economy relies on more democratic forms of economic governance, encompassing a range of practices and structures. These include participatory budgeting, which allows individuals to engage in decision-making processes concerning resource allocation, as well as consensus-based mechanisms for determining the use of shared resources and spaces. Furthermore, the social economy embraces the principles of community ownership and management of essential resources. Over time, new technologies and social movements have emerged, providing fresh perspectives

https://doi.org/10.1515/9783111080147-006

and techniques for cooperative-based economic democracy. These advancements range from grassroots bottom-up assemblies that challenge and replace oligarchic and elitist decision-making, to digital-based community projects that leverage technology to foster democratic participation. Additionally, the collection and utilization of "commons data" for democratic planning has become an avenue for enhancing economic governance within the social economy.

Within this chapter, we will explore various theories of democratic economic management, encompassing anarchist, socialist, and emerging social economy-based perspectives. By examining these theoretical frameworks, we aim to deepen our understanding of the principles and practices that underpin democratic decision-making in the social economy. Through this exploration, we can gain insights into how these theories translate into real-world applications, informing the development of inclusive and participatory economic systems that prioritize the well-being of all members of society.

Economic Power and Governance

Economic power and governance, as we have discussed thus far, are multifaceted and have taken on different meanings throughout history. Under capitalist systems, the focus has predominantly been on the ability of individuals to freely engage in economic relationships, whether through contractual agreements or waged labor. However, in practice, economic governance is far more complex than this simplified notion. It encompasses various dimensions, including forms of state control and regulation, executive power, multilateral power-sharing arrangements among different economic actors, and collective bargaining.

Within capitalist economies, the emphasis on economic power and governance has largely revolved around striking a balance between enabling "free economic exchange" and implementing appropriate social safeguards. The ideal has been to allow market forces to function while also ensuring that certain regulations and protections are in place to safeguard the welfare of individuals and communities. However, the prevailing paradigm is increasingly being challenged due to the adverse social impacts of unfettered market freedom. There is a growing awareness that these economic relationships are inherently undemocratic and tend to favor employers and those with greater capital at the expense of workers and the broader society (Dixit, 2003).

Recognizing the limitations and imbalances inherent in existing economic power dynamics, there is a rising call for reevaluating and reshaping the governance of the economy. This entails revisiting the roles of various actors, institutions, and mechanisms that influence economic decision-making. It requires examining the power structures that shape economic relations and considering alternative approaches that prioritize democratic principles and social justice.

Efforts are underway to promote more equitable economic governance models that address the inherent power imbalances within capitalist systems. These models seek to challenge the concentration of power in the hands of a few and provide mechanisms for broader participation and decision-making. One such avenue is the exploration of new forms of democratic ownership and control, where workers, consumers, and communities have a more significant stake in the decision-making processes that impact their lives (Dixit, 2003).

Moreover, the pursuit of fairer economic governance involves reimagining the relationship between the state and the market. It calls for a reconsideration of the extent to which the state should intervene to correct market failures and promote public welfare. This includes evaluating the role of regulations, taxation policies, and social safety nets in addressing systemic inequalities and ensuring a more inclusive economic system (Eccleston, 2013).

The push for reevaluating economic power and governance is also driven by a growing recognition that market mechanisms alone are insufficient for addressing pressing social and environmental challenges. The negative consequences of unregulated economic activities, such as rising income inequality, environmental degradation, and social exclusion, have led to a reexamination of the existing economic order. Alternative models that prioritize sustainability, social responsibility, and democratic decision-making are gaining traction, offering pathways for transforming economic governance in more inclusive and participatory ways (Keohane, 2002).

Economic power and governance encompass a complex web of relationships, mechanisms, and structures that have evolved over time. Under capitalist systems, the focus has been on facilitating free economic exchange, but the realities of economic governance involve a range of dynamics, including state control, multilateral power-sharing, and collective bargaining (Eccleston, 2013, p. 105). However, there is growing discontent with the inherent undemocratic nature of these power dynamics and their tendency to favor certain actors over others (Dixit, 2003, p. 459).

To delve deeper into the multifaceted nature of economic governance, scholars have provided valuable insights. Dixit (2003) emphasizes that economic governance involves the establishment of rules for economic activities. Governance modes, according to Dixit, span from totally decentralized to fully centralized, with most real-world economies adopting mixed models that balance state, market, and civil regulation. Eccleston (2013) adds a global perspective, noting that globalization has created needs and pressures for multilateral economic governance. The dynamics of global economic governance, as highlighted by Eccleston, are shaped by power relations between states, international organizations (IOs), and non-state actors (p. 105).

Keohane (2002) contributes by asserting that governance involves establishing rules and institutions to coordinate behavior. State power, according to Keohane, is constrained by economic interdependence and non-state actors, and governance networks often involve public–private cooperation and shifting coalitions. Furthermore, Jones (2001) points out that economic governance increasingly involves partnerships between states, business, and civil society. Power dynamics between actors influence policymaking and implementation, and the rescaling of governance shapes development possibilities and outcomes.

The need for good governance is emphasized by Brautigam (1991), who argues that it requires accountability, transparency, and the rule of law. Capable public institutions are essential for implementing effective economic policies and regulations, and many developing countries need governance reforms. Fabbrini (2016) highlights the complexity of economic governance within the European Union (EU). The EU has a multi-level economic governance structure that requires balancing centralized control with member state autonomy. Institutional constraints shape policy options and effectiveness within this framework.

Corporate governance involves oversight mechanisms to direct firm behavior. Reforms in corporate governance aim for more independent boards and appropriate executive pay, with the institutional context impacting governance models and outcomes (Davis, 2005). Corporate governance also focuses on the need to balance public and investor interests (Cioffi, 2010). Regulatory politics involve power dynamics between corporations, the state, and investors, and effective governance requires balancing flexibility with accountability.

In the broader context of economic governance, neoliberalism has shifted power from states to markets (Tabb, 2004). This shift has resulted in volatility, inequalities, and the erosion of development gains, thus necessitating a renewal of public oversight over macroeconomic governance to address these issues. These changes are reflected, for instance, in the rise of the entrepreneurial city, which aims to enhance competitiveness and attract investment (Jessop, 1997). Public–private partnerships and new institutions reshape urban governance, but contradictions around democratic accountability persist.

In conclusion, the intricate tapestry of economic power and governance unfolds through various dimensions, ranging from the global stage to the corporate boardroom. The challenges posed by existing power imbalances necessitate a reconsideration of economic governance models. Scholars and practitioners alike are engaging in the discourse, offering insights and exploring alternatives that prioritize democratic principles, social justice, and sustainability. The journey toward more inclusive and participatory economic governance continues, driven by the recognition that the complexities of the economic landscape demand nuanced and innovative approaches.

KEY THINKER: Gar Alperovitz

Gar Alperovitz, a historian, political economist, author, and activist, has made significant contributions to economic theory and practice, emphasizing democratization and equity. Known for his pioneering role in the "community wealth building" movement, Alperovitz advocates for shared ownership and democratic control of resources, providing a roadmap for transforming economic systems to achieve sustainable and just outcomes. His vision of "evolutionary reconstruction" focuses on gradually building new economic relationships within the capitalist system that align with democratic principles and community well-being.

Born in Wisconsin in 1936 and shaped by the collective struggles of the Depression era, Alperovitz was influenced by the progressive, egalitarian ideals of his upbringing. His studies at the University of Cambridge under economist Joan Robinson and his examination of the post-war British Labour government's experiments with public ownership fueled his belief that alternative economic arrangements were possible. These experiences inspired his vision for a democratized economy.

Alperovitz is best known for his advocacy of community wealth building—strategies that foster community-owned and governed enterprises, such as cooperatives, municipal enterprises, and land trusts, to build local wealth and agency. He argues that concentrating corporate power and relying on private capital are inherently undemocratic and prone to crisis. In response, he envisions economic democracy achieved through decentralizing ownership and control of economic assets.

His concept of "evolutionary reconstruction" proposes that transformation will emerge through the proliferation of decentralized, democratically governed institutions, steadily replacing current capitalist structures with community-centered models. This strategy builds economic power and agency at the local level through worker and community ownership, public banking, and anchor institution procurement policies. By focusing on grassroots initiatives, Alperovitz's framework seeks to create a pluralistic, sustainable economy that empowers communities while preserving ecological integrity.

Alperovitz co-founded the Democracy Collaborative, an organization dedicated to research, advocacy, and practical implementation of community wealth strategies. A key project is the Evergreen Cooperatives in Cleveland, Ohio, a network of worker-owned businesses that harness anchor institution procurement to create living-wage jobs and build community equity. The Evergreen model demonstrates how redirecting economic flows can benefit local communities rather than enrich distant shareholders.

Such real-world applications illustrate how economic democracy can be realized through tangible projects. Alperovitz's practical work extends beyond theoretical contributions by building frameworks and piloting models that transform ownership and control dynamics, making his ideas accessible and actionable.

Alperovitz's Next System Project, which he co-chairs, provides institutional blueprints for transitioning to a new political-economic system. The project explores a range of models, from worker cooperatives to community land trusts, that align with democratic principles and can scale dynamically over time. His work has influenced the broader "solidarity economy" movement, which connects with global calls for feminist economics, degrowth, and Buen Vivir philosophies, all of which challenge the prevailing ideology of GDP growth as a measure of progress.

Despite his contributions, some critics argue that Alperovitz's approach is too reformist and may not achieve the radical transformation needed to address systemic issues. Others highlight the challenge of scaling community-based models in a globalized economy. However, Alperovitz emphasizes that these initiatives are not isolated alternatives but part of a larger process of evolutionary reconstruction that, over time, can reshape political and economic institutions based on democratic design logics.

Gar Alperovitz's work provides a compelling vision for an economy that is democratic, just, and sustainable. His contributions to community wealth building and economic democracy offer practical pathways for reclaiming economic governance in the service of human and ecological well-being. By centering historically marginalized communities and promoting collective ownership, Alperovitz's framework opens possibilities for transformative systemic change.

Theories of Power

Within the expansive realm of economic governance and power theories, a plethora of perspectives illuminates the nuanced management of economies. Capitalism, with its historical inclination toward minimizing state involvement, asserts that the free exchange of labor empowers individuals to exercise their liberties, aligning with Adam Smith's "invisible hand" concept (Smith, 1776). However, Friedrich Hayek's critique introduces the idea that full information about individual preferences is unattainable, suggesting that individuals, rather than the state, are best suited to plan their economic affairs (Hayek, 1945).

In practice, capitalist societies grapple with the inherent instability of markets, leading to cycles of boom and bust. Public regulation becomes necessary not only to address market fluctuations but also to fulfill a political imperative—ensuring societal welfare rather than solely benefiting the privileged "winners" of capitalism.

Capitalism's inclination toward monopolization necessitates government intervention to prevent unfair consolidation of economic power. Simultaneously, widespread recognition emerges that government regulations are essential to ensure the safety and well-being of workers, consumers, and communities. As capitalism evolves, varying degrees of government involvement in economic planning and publicly subsidized welfare programs emerge, reflecting a pragmatic acknowledgment of the complexities of market dynamics.

Contrasting these capitalist notions, socialism and communism propose alternatives, perceiving markets and capitalists as negative influences promoting inequality and exploitation. Advocating for increased state involvement, these ideologies envision economic systems founded on equality and shared prosperity. Anarchist and cooperative models, emphasizing self-organization and mutual assistance, offer further alternatives in the spectrum of economic organization.

The ongoing relationship between stakeholders, especially the dynamic between employees and employers in capitalist systems, remains central to economic governance. Historical struggles for workers' rights through unions, strikes, and collective bargaining illustrate the inherent conflicts in this relationship. Consumer groups and social movements join this chorus, advocating for government regulations as safeguards against capitalist malfeasance.

To deepen our understanding, various theories of power provide valuable insights. Grosz (2013) posits that power exists within complex webs of relations, challenging the notion of power as a mere possession. Gaventa (2003) introduces the multidimensional nature of power—visible, hidden, or invisible. Avelino (2021) expands on the multifaceted nature of power, identifying its coercive, structural, and institutional dimensions. Stewart (2000) contributes the idea that power is relational, contingent, and productive. Pfeffer (2013) underscores the persistence of power dynamics across different contexts. Hoffman (2013) explores the circulation of power through diffuse relations and practices, influencing truth discourses. Ortner (2006) emphasizes the need to bridge theories of power and human agency.

Adding further depth, Griffin (2012) highlights the spatial dimension of power in governance, asserting that geography conditions the exercise of power and structures relationships in political life. Stör (2017), within the context of ecological economics, stresses the crucial role of power relations in shaping decisions impacting the environment and sustainability.

Incorporating Galbraith (1983), power is not confined to the state or corporations but is widely distributed in society. Rothbard's work (2004) offers a comprehensive exploration of economic theory, stating that power, in influencing outcomes, is inherent in all actions. Nye's examination (1990) of the changing nature of global power emphasizes that, in the post-Cold War world, power involves not only military or economic aspects but also the ability to generate voluntary cooperation.

Comprehensively, these diverse perspectives on economic governance, power, and their intricate interplay create a rich tapestry of understanding. Integrating feminist perspectives (Grosz, 2013), post-Lukes theories (Gaventa, 2003), and insights into power and social change (Avelino, 2021) further enriches our comprehension. This holistic view enables the exploration of possibilities for more equitable and democratic economic systems, acknowledging the inherent tensions and dynamic interplay within various economic ideologies.

CASE STUDY: Participatory Budgeting in the Rosario Municipality, Argentina

The Argentine city of Rosario stands as a pioneer in participatory budgeting (PB), a democratic innovation that allows citizens to directly influence public spending priorities. Launched in 2002 amidst national economic turmoil, Rosario's PB model has empowered citizens and fostered state-civil society co-management, demonstrating how inclusive, bottom-up participation can democratize governance even in adverse conditions.

Argentina's 2001 financial meltdown and subsequent protests against austerity expanded space for social movements to propose alternative economic models focused on solidarity and participatory planning. Rosario, Argentina's third-largest city, became an early testing ground for these ideas. The PB process was launched under Mayor Miguel Lifschitz's administration as a way to address budget deficits and restore public confidence in governance by enabling marginalized citizens to shape policy and spending.

Rosario's PB model invites residents to participate in neighborhood assemblies where they propose projects, elect delegates to evaluate feasibility, and vote on final budget allocations. This participatory cycle spans nearly eight months each year and engages more than 50,000 residents, deciding the allocation of approximately 5 percent of Rosario's public works budget.

The PB process begins in March with nearly fifty neighborhood assemblies across Rosario's six districts. Residents identify local priorities, such as infrastructure needs, social services, and community programs, and elect representatives to further develop these proposals. District-level participatory councils, in collaboration with municipal agencies, then assess the technical and financial feasibility of proposals, refining them into actionable projects.

In October and November, all residents aged sixteen and above vote on their preferred projects, and the winning proposals are incorporated into the municipal budget. This structured cycle of neighborhood assemblies, participatory councils, and a public vote fosters citizen learning and co-management, building civic capacity and shared ownership over public resources.

Over two decades, Rosario's PB model has enabled citizen–government co-management of hundreds of public infrastructure upgrades and social programs. Approved investments include neighborhood beautification, youth centers, women's health services, public lighting, and road repairs—often addressing needs overlooked by centralized planning. Research by Lerner and Schugurensky (2007) found that participants developed skills in democratic practices, political agency, and collective action, which they transferred to other public spheres.

Additionally, Rosario's PB has strengthened state efficiency and accountability. Mandates ensure that approved projects are included in the following year's budget, and regular oversight by participants helps monitor implementation. Transparency in decision-making and resource allocation enhances public trust, while realistic goal setting aligned with municipal capacities tempers inflated expectations.

A hallmark of Rosario's PB model is its emphasis on including marginalized groups through targeted accommodations. For example, in 2013, the city launched a dedicated Youth Participatory Budget, enabling young residents to propose and vote on projects that address their specific needs. Gender balance is also promoted through quotas ensuring that a fifth of funding targets women's needs and half of council leadership roles are held by women. These measures counteract structural barriers to participation, fostering agency for groups traditionally excluded from governance.

Despite its successes, Rosario's PB model faces challenges. Critics argue that PB can become a token exercise, with recent years seeing reduced engagement and decreased citizen influence over fiscal decisions (Allegretti, 2021). Some also contend that the focus on individual projects rather than structural changes risks promoting self-advocacy over broader policy struggles, which may inadequately address underlying issues of poverty and inequality (Signorelli, 2023).

There have also been concerns regarding the introduction of new hierarchies through affirmative measures, such as gendered funding quotas, which can override organic priorities voiced by women in assemblies (Arena, 2018). These critiques highlight the need for ongoing reforms and protections to prevent PB from regressing into a symbolic process that reinforces the status quo.

Rosario's PB experience offers valuable lessons on empowering excluded publics, expanding civic stewardship, and driving community-centered investment. Affirmative accommodations—such as youth and gender quotas—showcase how equitable participation requires dismantling structural barriers beyond simply providing participatory forums. To maintain its transformative potential, PB must continuously adapt and be protected against bureaucratic capture or erosion of civil society's decision-making power.

Authoritarianism and Economic Governance

In examining the dynamics of market economies, it becomes evident that these systems frequently exhibit non-democratic and authoritarian characteristics. This analysis encompasses various dimensions, emphasizing how power imbalances, policy influences, and the endorsement of non-democratic values collectively shape social relations within market economies.

A central aspect of non-democratic market economies involves a substantial power imbalance between owners and workers. Owners, wielding control over capital and resources, exert considerable influence, as highlighted by Foa (2018). Workers often find themselves with limited agency in crucial matters such as determining wages, working conditions, and managerial decisions. This stark imbalance of power means that owners can unilaterally set the terms of employment and the distribution of gains. Workers have little input or leverage in negotiating these arrangements, which tend to disproportionately benefit owners and shareholders.

Moreover, the ability of owners to shape policies in alignment with their interests underscores the non-democratic nature of market economies. As Bruff (2016) argues, corporate interests employ tactics such as lobbying and campaign financing to influence the formulation of laws and regulations. This elite influence tends to favor policies that protect corporate profits, advance business priorities, and maintain the status quo power dynamics. Consequently, the policymaking process is skewed to serve narrow economic interests rather than the broader public good. This hinders truly democratic decision-making, as the voices and needs of ordinary citizens are drowned out by the disproportionate influence of the wealthy and corporations.

The dominance of non-democratic values, particularly efficiency and productivity, is another hallmark of market economies. As Crain (2018) notes, while these values contribute to economic growth, they can also be wielded to prioritize profits over people, often neglecting broader social considerations. The relentless pursuit of efficiency leads to the economization of all aspects of society. Democratic deliberation, worker rights, and environmental protections can all be cast as inefficiencies that impede growth. As a result, crucial debates regarding the tradeoffs inherent in economic policies are foreclosed. The unquestioned deference to metrics of productivity and efficiency elevates economic imperatives above all else.

Paradoxically, concepts like empowerment and autonomy can be co-opted to perpetuate work intensification and undermine democracy within market economies. As Somers (2022) explores, the rhetoric around empowerment places the onus entirely on individuals to succeed, masking structural barriers and inequalities. Workers are told they must develop an entrepreneurial mindset and take ownership of their careers. This ignores the constraints imposed by owners' power, instead pinning the blame for any shortcomings on workers' attitudes and efforts. Likewise, automation and digital platforms are positioned as enhancing worker autonomy, when in fact they are designed primarily to cut labor costs. This exploitative co-optation of empowerment concepts erodes worker solidarity and collective action. It also limits the ability of workers to democratically challenge management decisions that undermine their well-being.

Furthermore, market economies exhibit a tendency to infiltrate and commodify all aspects of social life. As Storm (2018) describes, marketization converts increasing domains into arenas for profit-making and transactional exchange. This undermines non-market values and ways of relating. Cooperative social relations become restructured around self-interest, competition, and maximizing personal advantage. This corrodes social cohesion and collective democratic action aimed at the public good rather than private gain. The expansion of market rationality into all areas of human existence is inherently anti-democratic.

In a similar vein, Brown (2015) argues that the application of business metrics and market principles to the public sphere erodes civic values, citizenship, and democratic decision-making. Public institutions such as schools, hospitals, prisons, and social services become driven by return on investment, cost–benefit analyses, and profitability. This supplants non-market logics focused on collective needs and the common good. Subjecting everything to a market rationality impoverishes social life and democratic participation.

Additionally, market economies tend to promote a vision of democracy reduced solely to periodic elections. As Brancati (2014) articulates, regular elections, while crucial, are an insufficient condition for meaningful democracy. True democracy requires civic engagement, worker empowerment, equitable distribution of resources, and citizens having real voice in economic decisions. Market economies disempower the majority from economic participation, concentrating power in elite hands. Periodic votes cannot compensate for this exclusion from substantial decision-making influence.

Lastly, the dominance of market imperatives engenders an instrumental view of human relations. As Ganti (2014) describes, people are valued primarily based on their economic utility and productivity. This strips away their humanity and complex subjectivity. It also pits people against one another in market competition, undermining social solidarity. Every person's worth becomes measured by their ability to buy, sell, produce, or attract profits. This instrumentalist logic profoundly degrades social bonds and mutual obligations central to a functioning democracy.

In conclusion, insights from various scholarly works, including Nasong'o (2004), Hutchful (1987), and Springer (2009), collectively unveil the non-democratic and authoritarian features embedded in market economies. These perspectives contribute to a nuanced understanding of how market reforms, political authoritarianism, and neoliberal policies intersect to undermine democratic participation, empower elites, and impose market rationality across all domains of life. Recognizing these dynamics is imperative for critically evaluating the limitations of market-based systems and advocating for alternative models that prioritize democratic governance, worker participation, and equitable power distribution.

Economic Democracy

In exploring democratic governance of the economy, there are various strategies and models that can promote a more inclusive and participatory decision-making process. One traditional approach is through collective bargaining and unionization, which can serve as catalysts for creating a more democratic framework for decision-making both within organizations and at the macro-level of economic decisions (Yates, 2006).

Collective bargaining enables workers to negotiate with employers to establish fair wages, working conditions, and benefits (Brenkert, 1992). By engaging in collective decision-making, workers have the opportunity to influence the terms of their employment and participate in shaping the policies that directly affect their lives (Dahl, 2023). This shift from a market-centric approach to a deliberative and sometimes agonistic relationship acknowledges the diverse needs and interests of individuals and fosters a more democratic and inclusive decision-making process (Johanisova & Wolf, 2012). Through collective bargaining, decisions are no longer solely driven by market forces but are guided by a deep understanding of people's needs and the promotion of their well-being.

Another avenue for democratizing the economy is through the establishment of cooperatives. Cooperatives are enterprises where decisions are made collectively by workers or community members, such as consumers or residents (Knupfer, 2013). In a cooperative, power is distributed among all participants, ensuring that decision-making is not concentrated in the hands of a small board or executive (Ellerman, 1992). Instead, a culture of consensus and consideration of people's needs guides the decision-making process. This approach prioritizes the well-being and interests of the cooperative members, fostering a democratic and participatory economic model.

The principles underlying cooperatives have also inspired anarchist experiments with complete community ownership, where resources are shared and decisions about development are made by community members (Cumbers, 2012). These experiments aim to challenge hierarchical structures and promote direct democracy in economic governance. By shifting power to the community level, decision-making becomes more participatory, allowing for collective input and shared responsibility (Archer, 1995).

In more recent times, there have been endeavors to institute participatory budgeting as a means to democratize economic decision-making (Malleson, 2014). Participatory budgeting involves giving community members the opportunity to directly vote on how public funds should be allocated. This process empowers individuals to have a say in determining priorities and allocating resources, ensuring that decisions reflect the needs and aspirations of the community (Mahaputra & Saputra, 2021). By opening up the decision-making process to broader participation, participatory budgeting promotes transparency, accountability, and the democratization of economic governance.

KEY THINKER: Jessica Gordon Nembhard

Professor Jessica Gordon Nembhard is a prominent political economist and activist-scholar who has made seminal contributions to the study and promotion of cooperatives, particularly within African American communities. Her work bridges theory and practice, emphasizing community wealth building and grassroots economic empowerment through cooperative strategies. Gordon Nembhard argues that community-based cooperatives are vital tools for advancing economic justice and addressing systemic inequalities.

In her influential book *Collective Courage: A History of African American Cooperative Economic Thought and Practice* (2015), Gordon Nembhard highlights the long but often overlooked history of African American participation in cooperative economics, which dates back to the nineteenth century. She documents early cooperative efforts such as fraternal societies and credit unions, and their growth during the Civil Rights and Black Power movements of the 1960s and 1970s. These initiatives ranged from cooperatively owned farms to community-owned supermarkets, serving as vehicles for self-determined community development and economic inclusion.

Despite the achievements, Gordon Nembhard details the persistent barriers faced by Black cooperatives, such as discriminatory policies that restricted access to credit and technical support. Internal challenges, like limited business management expertise, also hindered their long-term sustainability. She argues that the key to overcoming these challenges lies in expanded access to technical assistance, financing, and education tailored specifically to cooperative development in marginalized communities.

Gordon Nembhard's more recent scholarship shifts focus to the models and frameworks necessary for communities to establish and sustain democratic, self-managed businesses. She emphasizes that community wealth building should be seen as a core anti-poverty strategy on par with access to education, healthcare, and housing. Her article, "Community-based asset building and community wealth" (2014) in *The Review of Black Political Economy*, explores how locally rooted cooperatives and communal holdings can create wealth and assets in marginalized communities by focusing on equitable credit access, business sustainability, and ongoing skills training. She argues that wealth-building frameworks centered on anchoring jobs and providing essential goods and services locally should be a critical component of community health and resilience strategies. By promoting cooperative ownership and shared governance, communities can create systems that are less extractive and more focused on collective prosperity.

Nembhard's activism complements her scholarship. She has served on the boards of organizations like the Association of Cooperative Educators and co-founded the U.S. Federation of Worker Cooperatives. These roles have enabled her to support the cooperative movement by offering networking opportunities, training, and funding resources to underrepresented groups, including low-income women, youth, and formerly incarcerated individuals. Her efforts extend to organizations that provide loans and incubator programs for cooperative startups.

One of her notable case studies is Cooperation Jackson in Mississippi, which exemplifies grassroots economic democracy by fostering interconnected worker-owned enterprises. These initiatives provide both theoretical frameworks and practical examples of how cooperatives can be leveraged to build resilient, community-centered economies.

Gordon Nembhard maintains a rigorous perspective on the potential and limitations of cooperatives. While she champions cooperatives as microcosms of self-determined local governance and economic democracy, she also acknowledges that co-ops are not immune to the challenges faced by traditional businesses. For co-ops to succeed, they require solid business plans, sustainable funding, and mechanisms for financial transparency and governance.

She emphasizes that cooperatives must proactively address power imbalances and avoid replicating capitalist market values. Issues such as gender dynamics, race, documentation status, and labor exploitation can infiltrate cooperatives if these organizations do not prioritize equality, resource sharing, and sustainability. Her work advocates for structural accountability and careful implementation of cooperative models to ensure they truly serve marginalized communities.

A core focus of Gordon Nembhard's work is addressing racial inequities in access to resources, which she argues is essential for true economic democracy. She insists that reparative solutions—such as equitable access to capital, skills training, and policy support—are necessary for marginalized groups to establish cooperative businesses and achieve self-determined local governance. By centering historically marginalized communities, Gordon Nembhard's vision for economic democracy involves a shift toward systems that enable equitable participation and prosperity.

Gordon Nembhard's scholarship and activism have made her a leading advocate for cooperative economics as a pathway to economic justice. Her work bridges historical analysis with practical strategies, offering insights on overcoming obstacles to cooperative development and ensuring structural accountability. By highlighting the role of cooperatives in building community wealth and empowering marginalized groups, Gordon Nembhard provides a compelling framework for reimagining economic systems that prioritize justice, equity, and collective well-being.

New Models of Economic Democracy

In the pursuit of a more democratic economy, new models are emerging that aim to give people a greater voice in shaping economic development. At the heart of this endeavor is the need to democratize economic power. Policymakers today face three key challenges in achieving this objective. First, they must address the extreme concentration of economic control in the hands of a small number of corporate and financial firms, working to dismantle and rebalance this concentration (Wong, Rahman & Warren, 2020). Second, they must expand the countervailing power of both government and civil society, particularly workers, to ensure that economic decisions reflect the diverse range of interests and constituencies (Chavez & Steinfort, 2022). Finally, communities, especially those most affected, must have more direct influence in economic decision-making processes, whether within firms, on local zoning boards, or in the administration of national policymaking at the federal level (Borowiak, 2019). The principles of belonging and inclusion must guide these efforts, particularly in a multiracial America.

A recent article in the *Stanford Social Innovation Review* proposed three ways to "de-rig" the economy and make it more democratic (Wong, Rahman & Warren, 2020). First, a new policy agenda is needed to shift economic power, focusing on dismantling the concentration of corporate power and its control over the economy. This may involve stronger antitrust enforcement and the adoption of new standards of effective competition that consider the impact on workers, suppliers, and market competition more broadly, rather than focusing solely on price. By reevaluating antitrust efforts, policymakers can promote fair competition that benefits a wider range of stakeholders (Johanisova & Wolf, 2012).

Second, the countervailing power of government and civil society must be strengthened (Chavez & Steinfort, 2022). The decline of labor unions has contributed to stagnant wages and a shift in electoral returns in favor of conservatives. Furthermore, the dismantling of government regulatory regimes has further concentrated wealth and power in the corporate sector (Lee, 1986). To counter these trends, robust government intervention and regulation are crucial. This includes protecting workers' rights, ensuring fair wages, and implementing regulations that safeguard consumers and the environment (Karin, 2010). Additionally, worker organizing plays a vital role in advocating for policies that promote economic justice and fairness. Strong labor movements can counterbalance the influence of corporations and help shape economic decisions in line with workers' interests.

Lastly, institutional designs should be crafted to democratize economic governance beyond episodic moments of elections (Conaty & Ross, 2021). While elections are important, economic decision-making often occurs on a day-to-day basis within organizations and institutions. To ensure a more equitable distribution of wealth and opportunity, workers and communities most affected by economic decisions must have a voice in the governance of these economic institutions (O'Neill, 2008). New forms of worker representation, such as worker cooperatives and employee ownership models, can provide avenues for worker voice and participation. Similarly, more democratic forms of corporate governance can shift firms from acting as quasi-authoritarian "private governments" to workplaces that treat stakeholders equitably, promoting inclusive decision-making and shared prosperity.

Efforts to democratize the economy are also connected to the growing demand for greater public ownership (Chavez & Steinfort, 2022). There are increasing calls to nationalize major public goods and services, such as energy and public transportation, or to promote community ownership of these resources (Spinak, 2014). Proponents argue that public ownership ensures democratic control over essential services and enables decisions to be made in the public interest rather than solely for private profit. This resurgence in the role of the state is seen as a means to spur innovation, with the state playing an entrepreneurial role in driving economic development. Additionally, public ownership can serve as a safeguard against the concentration of power in the hands of a few corporate entities.

At a more local level, the sharing economy has gained prominence, allowing people to use digital technologies to share, borrow, and reuse common goods and services (Hofmann, 2019). This model promotes community collaboration, resource efficiency, and localized decision-making. It also facilitates crowdsourcing of decisions, enabling communities to collectively determine investment priorities and identify the most pressing needs. By leveraging technology and fostering collaborative consumption, the sharing economy empowers individuals and promotes a more participatory approach to economic decision-making.

Democratic Management

In recent decades, there has been growing interest in exploring alternatives to the dominant economic model of corporate capitalism. This has led to the emergence of new frameworks and approaches that aim to democratize economic decision-making and manage economies in ways that prioritize social and ecological well-being over profit maximization. One overarching concept that has gained significant traction is that of economic democracy, which involves giving citizens and communities greater control over economic activities that affect their lives (Durand et al., 2023). The core premise is that democratically managing and governing economic systems can lead to more just, sustainable, and resilient economies.

Various theoretical perspectives and practical initiatives have contributed to articulating the possibilities of economic democracy. For instance, Durand et al. (2023) make the case for an economic model built on the principles of degrowth and economic democracy that operates within ecological limits. They argue that democratic planning and decision-making processes, with the participation of diverse stakeholders, can help balance socio-economic needs with environmental boundaries. White (2019) links economic democracy to the framework of ecological democracy, which addresses the anti-democratic and unjust dimensions of unsustainable systems by enabling inclusive citizenship and collective control over the use of natural resources and promoting regenerative processes.

Furthermore, new municipalist movements have brought attention to the potential of democratizing governance over public services, assets, and infrastructure at the city level. As Thompson (2021) explains, practices like remunicipalization of privatized services, community ownership of municipal enterprises, and participatory budgeting can increase local democratic participation and regain public control from corporate interests to meet community needs. Analyzing the connections between environmental sustainability and democratic governance, Pickering et al. (2022) find that deliberative, inclusive decision-making processes can support sustainability transformations, provided underlying power imbalances are actively addressed.

In terms of localized economic alternatives, community wealth building has been identified as an approach to foster economic democracy and develop democratized community economies (Lizárraga, 2020). This model promotes a variety of strategies, such as developing community-owned enterprises like cooperatives and mutual institutions, democratizing capital through mechanisms like public banking, and facilitating participatory governance over investments by anchor institutions like hospitals and universities to be directed toward broad community benefit (Dubb, 2016).

By democratizing access to resources and capital, as well as decision-making power over investments, these strategies allow marginalized communities to gain greater control over their local economies. They redistribute wealth and root it locally, reducing inequality and enabling self-determined, ecologically sustainable economic development trajectories. As opposed to extractive models, community wealth building enables surpluses to recirculate locally to build community assets and capabilities.

Various institutional forms have been identified as ways to embed economic democracy. For instance, cooperatives are enterprises collectively owned and governed by members through democratic participation. As Pickering et al. (2020) highlight, cooperatives empower people through shared ownership and decision-making power. They allow people to meet economic needs, like access to food, finance, housing, and other services, in an equitable way within community structures. However, not all co-operatives equally embody ideals of justice, inclusion, and sustainability. Ecological democracy provides useful guiding principles for cooperatives to address imbalances in participation and cultivate collective capabilities for environmental stewardship and social justice (Pickering et al., 2020).

Another increasingly popular form is the community land trust, which acquires land and removes it from the speculative market to be held in stewardship for community benefit (Lizárraga, 2020). Community land trusts allow residents to have a voice in decision-making about the use of land through participatory governance structures. By taking land out of the speculative market and separating land ownership from ownership of housing, community land trusts provide affordable, democratically managed housing as an alternative to commodification. They enable communities to meet the basic need for shelter outside capitalist relations (Pickering et al., 2020).

Participatory budgeting has also emerged as an important process to democratize governance over resource allocation and public investments. As practiced in cities like Porto Alegre, Brazil, participatory budgeting allows community members to decide directly how municipal budgets will be spent through inclusive, deliberative processes (Thompson, 2021). Based on principles of social justice and shared prosperity, participatory budgeting mechanisms distribute power, especially to marginalized communities, and foster participatory democracy beyond electoral cycles (Lizárraga, 2020). They offer a model whereby people can have greater control over decisions that shape their lived economic realities.

Various networks and movements centered on solidarity economy, community economies, and new municipalism have connected these initiatives to cultivate ecosystems of economic democracy. As ecological democracy suggests, building collective capabilities and developing pluralistic economic spaces enables transformative emergence toward systems founded on sustainability, justice, and shared prosperity (Pickering et al., 2020). Despite structural constraints, economic democracy offers viable pathways to empower communities, meet needs, and redirect economies toward care, reciprocity, and ecological resilience.

However, effectively cultivating economic democracy requires actively confronting underlying power structures. Although often presented as neutral, dominant economic models encode ideological assumptions that further entrench inequalities (Pickering et al., 2022). To avoid reproducing exclusions, economic democracy initiatives must center historically marginalized voices and knowledges in decision-making, implement affirmative policies to dismantle barriers, and facilitate restorative justice (Dubb, 2016; Lizárraga, 2020). This involves building power among disenfranchised communities to meaningfully shape economic systems.

Furthermore, ecological integration and regeneration should be foundational goals across economic democracy efforts. As ecological democracy suggests, democratizing economics requires collective responsibility for long-term socio-ecological health, guided by care ethics and indigenous knowledges (Pickering et al., 2020). Economic governance must be reoriented from growth dependence toward conviviality and living well within planetary boundaries. Fostering community wealth and well-being instead of maximizing monetary wealth enables decommodified, sustainable, and socially just economies embedded within ecology and community.

In sum, economic democracy encompasses a plurality of emerging theories and initiatives that aim to transform economic systems based on principles of inclusion, participation, collective ownership, and ecological sustainability. By democratizing economic decision-making power and the distribution of resources, it offers possibilities to build community-centered economies from the ground up in ways that regenerate both social fabrics and living systems. Economic democracy provides an alternative to extractive capitalism that affirms people's capabilities to equitably and sustainably govern economies through democratic means within just limits. Despite obstacles, existing projects demonstrate that more ethical, emancipatory, and ecologically integrated economic systems are viable through processes of democratic creation.

CASE STUDY: Evergreen Cooperatives (Ohio, USA)

The Evergreen Cooperatives in Cleveland, Ohio, established in 2008, provide a compelling model of community wealth building through collective ownership, participatory governance, and sustainable practices. Initiated through a partnership involving local philanthropic organizations, public entities, and anchor institutions, Evergreen includes a network of worker-owned enterprises such as an industrial laundry facility, a large urban greenhouse, and a solar energy company. The network aims to create living wage jobs, reinvest profits back into the community, and offer marginalized groups, including formerly incarcerated individuals, pathways to economic inclusion and stability.

The roots of Evergreen's model trace back to community mobilization efforts in Cleveland during the economic upheavals of the 1960s and 1970s. Early attempts to establish worker-owned enterprises laid the groundwork for later cooperative initiatives. The vision re-emerged after the 1977 closure of Youngstown Sheet & Tube, which spurred community efforts to take over the mill democratically. Though this endeavor failed, it set the stage for new models of community-anchored, worker-owned businesses.

Evergreen's launch in 2008 was guided by The Democracy Collaborative and inspired by the Mondragón cooperative network in Spain's Basque region. With support from the Cleveland Foundation, city government, and local healthcare and educational anchor institutions, the Evergreen network was established to address the economic challenges facing Cleveland—a post-industrial city hit hard by manufacturing decline, poverty, and the 2008 financial crisis. The initiative sought to harness the purchasing power of anchor institutions like hospitals and universities to support community-owned enterprises.

Evergreen Cooperatives currently include:

- Evergreen Cooperative Laundry: Opened in 2009, the laundry facility provides environmentally sustainable services to major anchor clients like the Cleveland Clinic. The Energy Star-rated facility employs fifty workers, more than a third of whom are formerly incarcerated. Workers can become owners after a trial period, gaining equity shares and profit dividends. The laundry has been profitable and provides living wage jobs.
- Evergreen Energy Solutions (E2S): Originally launched as Ohio Cooperative Solar, E2S installs solar panels and provides weatherization and energy efficiency services. It has installed more than 5 megawatts of solar panels and plays a key role in Cleveland's renewable energy goals. It offers green jobs and training opportunities for community members, reducing energy costs for clients and carbon footprints regionally.
- Green City Growers Cooperative (GCGC): Established in 2013, GCGC operates a hydroponic greenhouse producing 5 million heads of lettuce and 300,000 pounds of basil annually. The 170,000 square foot facility supplies fresh produce to local markets and restaurants while using renewable energy and recaptured rainwater. The greenhouse employs thirty worker-owners, providing living wages and benefits.

Over a decade, Evergreen has created more than 200 jobs and generated millions of dollars in revenue and assets. Its community wealth-building model has had measurable economic, social, and environmental impacts:

- More than $4 million in salaries to local residents, with median incomes three times the poverty line.
- 50% of new hires are previously incarcerated individuals, offering second chances through stable employment.
- 500,000 pounds of local produce supplied to food-insecure neighborhoods.
- 5 megawatts of solar power installed regionally.
- Hundreds of homes weatherized, saving households $500,000 annually in energy costs.

Evergreen's model aligns anchor institutions' procurement needs with community enterprises, creating a localized economic ecosystem that fosters resilience and inclusion. This alignment has inspired replication efforts in other U.S. cities, such as Rochester, New York, and Preston, UK.

Despite its successes, Evergreen faces challenges common to social enterprises. Key issues include:

- Scaling and market diversification: As the cooperative grows, it needs to expand its customer base beyond anchor institutions to include small and medium-sized businesses. This would reduce dependency on anchor contracts and stabilize revenue streams.

- Capital access and financing: Evergreen's thin operating margins limit internal financing for expansion. Securing growth capital without compromising its mission is crucial.
- Workforce development: Recruiting and training employees from marginalized communities, and offering supportive services like child care and transportation, are vital for sustainable growth.
- Policy engagement: Participation in policy activism to support cooperative-friendly regulations and public financing options could strengthen Evergreen's broader impact.

Evergreen's community wealth building model has gained national and international recognition as a viable alternative to traditional economic development approaches. By giving marginalized groups shared ownership and governance, Evergreen manifests restorative economic justice and collective empowerment. Its "solidarity economy" framework, which emphasizes cooperation and ethical consumption, aligns with global efforts to promote sustainable, inclusive economic systems.

Its success demonstrates that worker-owned cooperatives can compete effectively in the market while delivering triple-bottom-line benefits—economic, social, and environmental. This model offers a blueprint for transforming local economies through shared prosperity and sustainable practices. Its example has inspired cities across the U.S. to explore adopting similar strategies, fostering a movement for place-based economies that keep wealth circulating locally rather than being extracted by absentee corporate ownership.

Managing the Social Economy

Innovative approaches to democratic management have emerged that empower communities to actively participate in economic decision-making and foster local resilience. These contemporary examples illustrate the potential for inclusive, participatory economies aligned with community needs and values.

Participatory Budgeting

Participatory budgeting has gained traction globally as a process that enables citizens to directly decide how public funds are allocated. Through a series of meetings, deliberations, and voting, residents have the opportunity to propose, discuss, and prioritize projects that address local needs (Sintomer et al., 2008; Aziz & Shah, 2021). More than 3000 cities have implemented participatory budgeting, with demonstrated impact on reducing poverty and improving services in disadvantaged areas (Cabannes, 2004; Wampler, 2012). As noted by Cabannes (2004), "Participatory budgeting has significantly contributed to participatory democracy by including citizens in defining the distribution of public financial resources" (p. 27). In Porto Alegre, Brazil, participatory budgeting catalyzed "substantial democratization in state-civil society relations," redistributing power and resources to poorer communities (de Sousa Santos, 1998, p. 461). By promoting transparency, inclusivity, and accountability, participatory budgeting enables citizens to shape their urban environments and public spending priorities based on local needs.

Crowdfunding

Crowdfunding has emerged as a powerful tool for democratic economic management, leveraging collective contributions to fund community-driven endeavors. Bypassing traditional financing gatekeepers, crowdfunding allows "distributed non-professionals" and community members to decide which initiatives receive backing (Hui et al., 2014; Josefy et al., 2017). Research shows that community support and engagement play a key role in crowdfunding success, enabling grassroots projects aligned with local values (Josefy et al., 2017; Gooch et al., 2020). Crowdfunding serves as a "community-based resource mobilization mechanism" that empowers communities to shape their local economies (Murray et al., 2020, p. 960). It has funded diverse initiatives including local businesses, community gardens, social enterprises, and cultural projects that may lack access to mainstream capital (Lam & Law, 2016; Duncan & Pascucci, 2017).

Skills Matching and Sharing

Online platforms have emerged to match community members possessing specific skills and expertise with others needing those skills. By creating networks for collaboration and mutual exchange, these platforms allow community members to support one another through mentoring, training, and problem-solving (Bader & Hirst, 2012). Skills matching and sharing enables individuals to contribute their unique talents to community projects, promoting economic resilience and social cohesion by valuing diverse abilities (Haus & Sweeting, 2006). This form of collaborative community action fosters empowerment and makes full use of skills already existing within communities.

Network of Democratic Enterprises

Some communities have established networks of cooperatives, community gardens, makerspaces and other democratically governed organizations catering to local needs (Anheier & Themudo, 2002). With decision-making power distributed among members, these entities enable community control over economic activity aligned with shared values (Bijman et al., 2011). For instance, a democratically managed network may include community gardens providing local produce, cooperatives meeting manufacturing needs with 3D printers, and social enterprises addressing community challenges (Duncan & Pascucci, 2017). By decentralizing economic power and promoting grassroots entrepreneurship, such networks foster economic democracy and resilience (Bader & Hirst, 2012).

These emergent practices illuminate possibilities for more democratic and participatory economies where community members wield decision-making power. Participatory budgeting enables citizens to shape public spending priorities based on local needs and values. Crowdfunding allows communities to fund desired projects by circumventing traditional gatekeepers. Skills sharing platforms facilitate mutual exchange and collaborative problem-solving within communities. Networks of democratic enterprises encourage grassroots entrepreneurship aligned with community interests.

Such innovations in economic governance highlight the transformative potential of participatory democracy. By embracing inclusive decision-making processes, communities can build robust, equitable, and resilient economies where resources are allocated and enterprises are managed to benefit all members. This future vision is one of economic systems designed to empower individuals, foster social cohesion, and effectively address community challenges.

Conclusion

This chapter has shown how the concept of economic democracy holds immense significance in shaping the future of our societies. It is an approach that seeks to dismantle the concentration of economic power, expand the countervailing power of government and civil society, and provide communities with a direct influence on economic decision-making. By addressing these challenges, we can foster a more inclusive and equitable economy that benefits all members of society.

One of the fundamental principles underlying economic democracy is the notion of democratizing economic power. This involves rebalancing economic control by breaking up the extreme concentration of power held by a small number of corporate and financial firms. By promoting effective competition and considering the broader interests of workers, suppliers, and market competition, we can ensure a fairer distribution of wealth and influence.

Furthermore, economic democracy emphasizes the need to strengthen the countervailing power of both government and civil society. This requires revitalizing labor unions and defending workers' rights, as well as restoring government regulatory regimes to prevent the unchecked concentration of wealth and power in the corporate sector. By fostering a robust and inclusive economy, we can create an environment that prioritizes the well-being and interests of all citizens.

At the heart of economic democracy is the principle of community empowerment. Communities, especially those most affected, should have a direct say in economic decision-making processes. This can be achieved through various means, such as creating spaces for participatory budgeting, utilizing crowdfunding platforms to support community initiatives, implementing skills matching and sharing systems, and fostering networks of democratically run organizations that cater to local needs.

Examples of contemporary democratic management models further illustrate the transformative potential of economic democracy. Participatory budgeting allows community members to directly participate in the allocation of public resources, giving them a voice in determining local priorities. Crowdfunding platforms enable individuals to collectively fund projects and initiatives that align with their values and aspirations, bypassing traditional sources of capital and empowering communities to shape their economic landscape.

Additionally, the use of skills matching and sharing platforms connects individuals with complementary skills and resources, fostering collaboration and empowering communities to address their own needs. By creating networks of democratically run organizations, ranging from community gardens to 3D printer manufacturing, communities can take control of their economic destiny, promoting local resilience and ensuring that economic decisions are made in the best interest of the community.

In summary, economic democracy is crucial for building a more just and inclusive society. By dismantling concentrated economic power, expanding countervailing power, and empowering communities, we can create an economy that serves the interests of all. It is an approach that seeks to redistribute economic control, promote equity and inclusion, and foster a sense of ownership and agency among individuals and communities. By embracing economic democracy, we can strive toward a future where economic decision-making reflects the diverse needs and aspirations of our society, leading to a more equitable and sustainable world for all.

References

Allegretti, G. (2021). Common patterns in coping with under-representation in participatory processes: evidence from a mutual learning space for Portuguese local authorities (Las). *Innovation: The European Journal of Social Science Research*, 34(5), pp. 729–765.

Anheier, H., & Themudo, N. (2002). Organisational forms of global civil society: Implications of going global. *Global Civil Society*, 2(1), 42–47.

Archer, R. (1995). *Economic Democracy: The Politics of Feasible Socialism*. New York: Clarendon Press.

Arena, E. (2018). Participatory budgeting in Argentina (2002-2018): Advances and setbacks in the construction of a participatory agenda. In Dias, N. (ed.), Hope for Democracy: 30 Years of Participatory Budgeting Worldwide (pp. 123–133). Epopeia Records.

Avelino, F. (2021). Theories of power and social change. Power contestations and their implications for research on social change and innovation. *Journal of Political Power*, 14(3), 425–448.

Aziz, H., & Shah, N. (2021). Participatory budgeting: Models and approaches. In Rudas, T. & Péli, G. (Eds.), *Pathways Between Social Science and Computational Social Science: Theories, Methods, and Interpretations* (pp. 215–236). Cham, Switzerland: Springer.

Bader, V., & Hirst, P. (2012). *Associative Democracy: The Real Third Way*. Routledge.

Bijman, J., Muradian, R., & Cechin, A. (2011). Agricultural cooperatives and value chain coordination. In Helmsing, A. H. J. & Vellema, S. (Eds.), *Value Chains, Social Inclusion and Economic Development: Contrasting Theories and Realities* (pp. 82–101). London and New York: Routledge.

Borowiak, C. (2019). Poverty in transit: Uber, taxi coops, and the struggle over Philadelphia's transportation economy. *Antipode, 51*(4), 1079–1100.

Brancati, D. (2014). Democratic authoritarianism: Origins and effects. *Annual Review of Political Science, 17*(1), 313–326.

Brautigam, D. (1991). *Governance and Economy: A Review.* Policy Research Working Paper Series 815. Washington, DC: The World Bank.

Brenkert, G. G. (1992). Freedom, participation and corporations: The issue of corporate (economic) democracy. *Business Ethics Quarterly, 2*(3), 251–269.

Brown, W. (2015). *Undoing the Demos: Neoliberalism's Stealth Revolution.* New York: Zone Books.

Bruff, I. (2016). Neoliberalism and authoritarianism. In *Handbook of Neoliberalism* (pp. 106–117). Routledge.

Cabannes, Y. (2004). Participatory budgeting: A significant contribution to participatory democracy. *Environment and Urbanization, 16*(1), 27–46.

Chavez, D., & Steinfort, L. (2022). The future is public! The global reclaiming and democratization of public ownership beyond the market. *Development, 65*(2–4), 207–216.

Cioffi, J. W. (2010). *Public Law and Private Power: Corporate Governance Reform in the Age of Finance Capitalism.* Cornell University Press.

Conaty, P., & Ross, P. (2021). Worker co-operatives and economic democracy. In Tam, H. (Ed.), *Tomorrow's Communities* (pp. 71–90). Bristol: Policy Press.

Crain, C. (2018). Is capitalism a threat to democracy?. *The New Yorker.* May 6, 2018. Retrieved from https://www.newyorker.com/magazine/2018/05/14/is-capitalism-a-threat-to-democracy (accessed February 17, 2024).

Cumbers, A. (2012). *Reclaiming Public Ownership: Making Space for Economic Democracy.* Bloomsbury Publishing.

Dahl, R. A. (2023). *A Preface to Economic Democracy* (Vol. 28). University of California Press.

Davis, G. F. (2005). New directions in corporate governance. *Annu. Rev. Sociol., 31*, 143–162.

de Sousa Santos, B. (1998). Participatory budgeting in Porto Alegre: Toward a redistributive democracy. *Politics & Society, 26*(4), 461–510.

Dixit, A. (2003). On modes of economic governance. *Econometrica, 71*(2), 449–481.

Dubb, S. (2016). Community wealth building forms: What they are and how to use them at the local level. *Academy of Management Perspectives, 30*(2), 141–152.

Duncan, J., & Pascucci, S. (2017). Mapping the organisational forms of networks of alternative food networks: Implications for transition. *Sociologia Ruralis, 57*(3), 316–339.

Durand, C., Hofferberth, E., & Schmelzer, M. (2023). Planning beyond Growth. The Case for Economic Democracy within Limits. *Journal of Cleaner Production, 437*, 140351.

Eccleston, R. (2013). *The Dynamics of Global Economic Governance: The Financial Crisis, the OECD, and the Politics of International Tax Cooperation.* Cheltenham, UK: Edward Elgar.

Ellerman, D. P. (1992). *Property and Contract in Economics: The Case for Economic Democracy.* Cambridge, MA: Basil Blackwell.

Fabbrini, F. (2016). *Economic Governance in Europe: Comparative Paradoxes and Constitutional Challenges.* Oxford: Oxford University Press.

Foa, R. S. (2018). Modernization and authoritarianism. *Journal of Democracy, 29*(3), 129–140.

Fotopoulos, T. (1999). Welfare state or economic democracy. *Democracy & Nature: The International Journal of Inclusive Democracy, 5*(3), 433–468.

Galbraith, J. K. (1983). The anatomy of power. *Challenge, 26*(3), 26–33.

Ganti, T. (2014). Neoliberalism. *Annual Review of Anthropology, 43*(1), 89–104.

Gaventa, J. (2003). *Power after Lukes: An Overview of Theories of Power since Lukes and their Application to Development*. Participation Group, Institute of Development Studies.

Gooch, D., Kelly, R. M., Stiver, A., van der Linden, J., Petre, M., Richards, M., . . . & Walton, C. (2020). The benefits and challenges of using crowdfunding to facilitate community-led projects in the context of digital civics. *International Journal of Human-Computer Studies, 134*, 33–43.

Gordon Nembhard, J. (2006). Principles and strategies for reconstruction: Models of African American community-based cooperative economic development. *Harvard Journal of African American Public Policy, 12*(Summer), 39–55.

Gordon Nembhard, J. (2015). *Collective Courage: A History of African American Cooperative Economic Thought and Practice*. Penn State University Press.

Griffin, L. (2012). Where is power in governance? Why geography matters in the theory of governance. *Political Studies Review, 10*(2), 208–220.

Grosz, E. (2013). Contemporary theories of power and subjectivity. In *Feminist Knowledge: Critique and Construct* (pp. 59–120). London: Routledge.

Haus, M., & Sweeting, D. (2006). Local democracy and political leadership: Drawing a map. *Political Studies, 54*(2), 267–288.

Hayek, F. (1945). The Use of Knowledge in Society. *The American Economic Review, 35*, 519–530.

Hoffman, M. (2013). *Foucault and Power: The Influence of Political Engagement on Theories of Power*. Bloomsbury Publishing USA.

Hofmann, J. (2019). Mediated democracy—Linking digital technology to political agency. *Internet Policy Review, 8*(2). DOI: 10.14763/2019.2.1416.

Hui, J. S., Greenberg, M. D., & Gerber, E. M. (2014, February). Understanding the role of community in crowdfunding work. In Fussel, S. & Lutters, W. (Eds.), *Proceedings of the 17th ACM Conference on Computer Supported Cooperative Work & Social Computing* (pp. 62–74). New York: Association for Computing Machinery.

Hutchful, E. (1987). The crisis of the new international division of labour, authoritarianism and the transition to free-market economies in Africa. *Africa Development/Afrique et Développement, 12*(2), 35–55.

Jessop, B. (1997). The entrepreneurial city: Re-imaging localities, redesigning economic governance, or restructuring capital. *Transforming Cities: Contested Governance and New Spatial Divisions, 46*, 28–41.

Johanisova, N., & Wolf, S. (2012). Economic democracy: A path for the future? *Futures, 44*(6), 562–570.

Jones, M. (2001). The rise of the regional state in economic governance: "Partnerships for prosperity" or new scales of state power? *Environment and Planning A, 33*(7), 1185–1211.

Josefy, M., Dean, T. J., Albert, L. S., & Fitza, M. A. (2017). The role of community in crowdfunding success: Evidence on cultural attributes in funding campaigns to "save the local theater". *Entrepreneurship Theory and Practice, 41*(2), 161–182.

Karin, B. (ed.). (2010). *Environmental Politics and Deliberative Democracy: Examining the Promise of New Modes of Governance*. Edward Elgar Publishing.

Keohane, R. O. (2002). *Power and Governance in a Partially Globalized World*. Psychology Press.

Knupfer, A. M. (2013). *Food Co-ops in America: Communities, Consumption, and Economic Democracy*. Cornell University Press.

Lam, P. T., & Law, A. O. (2016). Crowdfunding for renewable and sustainable energy projects: An exploratory case study approach. *Renewable and Sustainable Energy Reviews, 60*, 11–20.

Lee, R. (1986). The new populist campaign for economic democracy: A rhetorical exploration. *Quarterly Journal of Speech, 72*(3), 274–289.

Lerner, J., & Schugurensky, D. (2007). Who learns what in participatory democracy?: Participatory budgeting in Rosario, Argentina. In van der Veen, R., Wildemeersch, D., Youngblood, J. & Marsick, V. (Eds.), *Democratic Practices as Learning Opportunities* (pp. 85–100). Rotterdam: Sense Pulishers.

Lizárraga, F. A. (2020). The case for community wealth building. *Polis (Santiago)*, *19*(56), 95–112.

Mahaputra, M. R., & Saputra, F. (2021). Application of business ethics and business law on economic democracy that impacts business sustainability. *Journal of Law, Politic and Humanities*, *1*(3), 115–125.

Malleson, T. (2014). *After Occupy: Economic Democracy for the 21st Century*. Oxford University Press.

Murray, A., Kotha, S., & Fisher, G. (2020). Community-based resource mobilization: How entrepreneurs acquire resources from distributed non-professionals via crowdfunding. *Organization Science*, *31*(4), 960–979.

Nasong'o, S. W. (2004). From political dictatorship to authoritarian economism: Plural politics and free market reforms in Africa. *Journal of Third World Studies*, *21*(2), 107–125.

Nye Jr, J. S. (1990). The changing nature of world power. *Political Science Quarterly*, *105*(2), 177–192.

O'Neill, M. (2008). *Three Rawlsian Routes towards Economic Democracy*.

Ortner, S. B. (2006). *Anthropology and Social Theory: Culture, Power, and the Acting Subject*. Duke University Press.

Pfeffer, J. (2013). You're still the same: Why theories of power hold over time and across contexts. *Academy of Management Perspectives*, *27*(4), 269–280.

Pickering, J., Bäckstrand, K., & Schlosberg, D. (2020). Between environmental and ecological democracy: Theory and practice at the democracy-environment nexus. *Journal of Environmental Policy & Planning*, *22*(1), 1–15.

Pickering, J., Hickmann, T., Bäckstrand, K., Kalfagianni, A., Bloomfield, M., Mert, A., . . . & Lo, A. Y. (2022). Democratising sustainability transformations: Assessing the transformative potential of democratic practices in environmental governance. *Earth System Governance*, *11*, 100131.

Rothbard, M. N. (2004). *Man, Economy, and State: A Treatise on Economic Principles with Power and Market*. Auburn, Alabama: Ludwig von Mises Institute.

Signorelli, G. (2023). From the instituting to the managerial model. The participatory budget cycle in Rosario, Argentina (2002–2022). *Local Development & Society*, 1–18.

Sintomer, Y., Herzberg, C., & Röcke, A. (2008). Participatory budgeting in Europe: Potentials and challenges. *International Journal of Urban and Regional Research*, *32*(1), 164–178.

Smith, A. (1776). *The Wealth of Nations*. Hoboken: John Wiley and Sons, Ltd.

Somers, M. R. (2022). Dedemocratizing citizenship: How neoliberalism used market justice to move from welfare queening to authoritarianism in 25 short years. *Citizenship Studies*, *26*(4–5), 661–674.

Spinak, A. A. E. (2014). *Infrastructure and Agency: Rural Electric Cooperatives and the Fight for Economic Democracy in the United States* (Doctoral dissertation, Massachusetts Institute of Technology).

Springer, S. (2009). Renewed authoritarianism in Southeast Asia: Undermining democracy through neoliberal reform. *Asia Pacific Viewpoint*, *50*(3), 271–276.

Stewart, A. (2000). *Theories of power and domination: The politics of empowerment in late modernity*. London: Sage.

Stör, L. (2017). Theories of power. In Spash, C. L. (Ed.), *Routledge Handbook of Ecological Economics* (pp. 141–151). London: Routledge.

Storm, S. (2018). Financialization and economic development: a debate on the social efficiency of modern finance. *Development and Change*, *49*(2), 302–329.

Tabb, W. K. (2004). *Economic Governance in the Age of Globalization*. Columbia University Press.

Thompson, M. (2021). What's so new about new municipalism? *Progress in Human Geography*, *45*(2), 317–342.

Wampler, B. (2012). Participatory budgeting: Core principles and key impacts. *Journal of Public Deliberation*, *8*(2), 1–13.

White, D. F. (2019). Ecological democracy, just transitions and a political ecology of design. *Environmental Values*, *28*(1), 31–53.

Wong, F., Rahman, K. S. & Warren, D. (2020) Democratizing economic power to break the cycle of American inequality. *The Stanford Social Innovation Review*. Available at: https://ssir.org/articles/entry/democratizing_economic_power_to_break_the_cycle_of_american_inequality (accessed February 27, 2024).

Yates, J. (2006). Unions and employee ownership: A road to economic democracy? *Industrial Relations: A Journal of Economy and Society*, *45*(4), 709–733.

Chapter 7
Social Marketing: Cooperative Knowledge and Communications

Introduction

Marketing strategies and techniques have traditionally been associated with the buying and selling of capitalist products. However, their significance extends beyond commercial transactions. Marketing plays a crucial role in understanding people's needs and effectively promoting solutions that align with their understanding and desires. In the context of the social economy, marketing becomes a powerful tool for knowledge exchange, promotion, and fostering the adoption of social economy principles at various levels.

At its core, marketing in the social economy aims to enhance economic democracy by creating awareness, generating interest, and fostering engagement with alternative economic models. This chapter explores how marketing can be harnessed and adapted to promote the social economy in diverse geographic and social contexts, ranging from public policy initiatives to organizational advertising and individual consumption choices. By leveraging marketing strategies, the social economy can thrive and contribute to a more equitable and participatory economic system.

Governments have long employed marketing techniques to promote public campaigns aimed at addressing social issues and driving behavior change. Similarly, cooperative organizations utilize marketing to raise awareness about their existence and highlight the benefits of participation and engagement in worker and community-owned cooperatives. By strategically employing marketing tactics, these entities can reach wider audiences and empower individuals to make informed choices aligned with their values.

Marketing initiatives within the social economy can operate at various levels, each serving a specific purpose. At the macro level, public policy campaigns can employ marketing to advocate for legislative changes, support the growth of social enterprises, and foster a supportive environment for the social economy to flourish. By effectively communicating the societal benefits and economic impact of the social economy, policymakers can garner public support and create an enabling environment for alternative economic models.

On the meso level, organizational marketing plays a crucial role in raising awareness about specific social enterprises, cooperatives, and other community-driven initiatives. Through branding, advertising, and other marketing strategies, these entities can establish their presence, communicate their mission, and attract both customers and potential members. Effective marketing allows social economy organizations to differentiate themselves from traditional profit-driven businesses and highlight their

https://doi.org/10.1515/9783111080147-007

unique value propositions, such as community engagement, environmental sustainability, and equitable wealth distribution.

At the micro level, marketing enables individuals to make informed consumption choices aligned with their values and contribute to the social economy. By promoting products and services offered by social enterprises, consumers can actively support organizations that prioritize social impact over pure profit. Marketing strategies such as storytelling, influencer marketing, and social media campaigns can help individuals connect with the social economy on a personal level, fostering a sense of belonging and shared purpose.

Adapting marketing techniques for the social economy requires sensitivity to the diverse contexts in which it operates. Different geographic and social contexts may require tailored approaches to effectively engage with target audiences. Cultivating an understanding of local cultures, values, and communication preferences is essential for crafting messages that resonate with the target population. Furthermore, marketing strategies should prioritize inclusivity, ensuring that the voices of marginalized communities are heard and their needs addressed.

Marketing, thus, plays a vital role in promoting and advancing the social economy. By harnessing marketing strategies and techniques, the social economy can increase its visibility, engage with wider audiences, and contribute to the overall goal of economic democracy. Whether through public policy campaigns, organizational advertising, or individual consumption choices, marketing can effectively communicate the benefits of the social economy and inspire individuals to actively participate and support alternative economic models. By embracing marketing as a tool for knowledge exchange and promotion, the social economy can pave the way for a more inclusive, equitable, and participatory economic future.

Social Marketing

Marketing has evolved significantly over the years, adapting to changes in technology, consumer behavior, and societal values. In recent years, the concept of social marketing has gained prominence as organizations increasingly recognize the importance of addressing social issues and promoting positive behavior change. Social marketing is an approach that applies traditional marketing principles and techniques to influence behaviors that benefit individuals and communities for the greater social good (Kotler & Lee, 2008). It emerged as a distinct discipline in the 1970s, with the recognition that marketing could be used to promote social causes and address societal challenges (Andreasen, 2006). An overview of the approach and effects of social marketing highlights its potential to promote healthy behaviors, prevent injuries, and support environmental sustainability (Smith, 2006). Social marketing is most effective when it is based on a deep understanding of the target audience and their needs, motivations, and barriers to change (Smith, 2006).

Developing effective social marketing strategies requires a systematic approach that takes into account the unique characteristics of the social issues being addressed, the target audience, and the broader social and cultural context (Wymer, 2011). Social marketing should be grounded in theoretical and practical perspectives, drawing on insights from psychology, sociology, and other social sciences (Goldberg et al., 2018). One key strategy for effective social marketing is the use of segmentation and targeting. By identifying distinct subgroups within the target audience and tailoring messages and interventions to their specific needs and preferences, social marketers can increase the relevance and impact of their campaigns (Andreasen, 2006). Another important strategy is the use of partnerships and collaborations. Social marketing often requires the involvement of multiple stakeholders, including government agencies, non-profit organizations, and private sector partners (Kotler & Lee, 2008). By working together, these partners can leverage their respective strengths and resources to achieve greater impact and scale.

Cooperatives are organizations that are owned and controlled by their members, who are also their customers or suppliers. The potential for cooperatives to engage in sustained brand marketing is explored, arguing that their unique structure and values can be a source of competitive advantage (Beverland, 2007). Cooperatives often have a strong social mission and are well-positioned to engage in social marketing activities that align with their values and objectives. For example, agricultural cooperatives may promote sustainable farming practices or support local food systems, while financial cooperatives may promote financial literacy and inclusion. However, cooperatives face unique challenges in brand marketing, such as the need to balance the interests of multiple stakeholders and maintain democratic decision-making processes (Beverland, 2007). Successful cooperative branding requires a deep understanding of the cooperative's values and culture, as well as the needs and preferences of its members and customers.

The sharing economy refers to the peer-to-peer exchange of goods and services, often facilitated by digital platforms. The implications of the sharing economy for marketing are explored, arguing that it presents both opportunities and challenges for marketers (Eckhardt et al., 2019). On the one hand, the sharing economy enables new forms of value creation and exchange, such as the ability for individuals to monetize their underutilized assets or skills. This can create new markets and customer segments for marketers to target. On the other hand, the sharing economy also disrupts traditional business models and marketing strategies, requiring marketers to adapt to new forms of competition and consumer behavior. Several key marketing strategies for success in the sharing economy are identified, including the use of trust-building mechanisms, the creation of brand communities, and the development of personalized and customized offerings (Eckhardt et al., 2019). The importance of data analytics and platform design in facilitating successful sharing economy transactions is also highlighted.

As societal challenges continue to evolve and new technologies emerge, the field of social marketing is likely to continue to grow and innovate. Social marketing in the twenty-first century will need to be more strategic, evidence-based, and inclusive, engaging a wider range of stakeholders and leveraging new forms of media and communication (Andreasen, 2006). The future of social marketing will be shaped by advances in behavioral science, digital technologies, and data analytics (Goldberg et al., 2018). Social marketers will need to be skilled in using these tools to develop more targeted and personalized interventions, as well as to measure and optimize campaign effectiveness. At the same time, social marketers will need to be attuned to the ethical implications of their work, particularly in areas such as data privacy, cultural sensitivity, and unintended consequences. Social marketing has the potential to be a powerful force for positive social change, but it also carries risks and responsibilities that must be carefully managed (Wymer, 2011).

Marketing and strategy play a crucial role in the social economy, enabling organizations to effectively promote social causes, influence behavior change, and create value for stakeholders. Social marketing has emerged as a key approach for addressing societal challenges, drawing on insights from traditional marketing and the social sciences to develop targeted and evidence-based interventions. Cooperatives and the sharing economy present unique opportunities and challenges for social marketers, requiring new strategies and approaches to branding, partnerships, and value creation. As the field continues to evolve, social marketers will need to be skilled in leveraging new technologies and data analytics, while also being attuned to the ethical implications of their work. Ultimately, the success of social marketing will depend on its ability to create meaningful and sustained behavior change, improving the lives of individuals and communities while also contributing to broader social and environmental goals. By drawing on the insights and strategies discussed, social marketers can continue to push the boundaries of what is possible in the social economy, driving positive social change and creating value for all stakeholders.

KEY THINKER: Alan R. Andreasen

Alan R. Andreasen is a renowned figure in the field of marketing, particularly known for his groundbreaking contributions in social marketing, non-profit marketing, and marketing research. As a professor of marketing and former dean for faculty affairs at Georgetown University's School of Business, Andreasen's influence extends from academia to real-world applications, impacting a diverse array of organizations and causes.

Andreasen is best known for advancing social marketing, which adapts traditional marketing principles to promote behaviors benefiting individuals and communities. He has been a staunch advocate for using social marketing to address complex social issues like public health, environmental conservation, and poverty alleviation. His expertise has been applied in collaborations with organizations such as the National Cancer Institute, where he contributed to campaigns promoting healthy behaviors like smoking cessation and increased cancer screening.

His research and practical work with non-profit organizations have focused on the distinct challenges they face, such as limited resources and the need to build trust and credibility. Andreasen has emphasized developing clear value propositions, understanding target audience motivations, and leveraging branding and communication to enhance non-profit effectiveness. His efforts have helped organizations better reach their audiences and achieve greater impact.

Andreasen's work includes several influential books, such as *Cheap But Good Marketing Research* (1991) and *Strategic Marketing for Nonprofit Organizations* (4th ed., 1991), coauthored with Philip Kotler. The former offers guidance on conducting high-quality research on a limited budget, covering topics like survey design and data analysis, making it a go-to resource for organizations seeking actionable insights without extensive funding. The latter provides a cornerstone in non-profit marketing literature, covering essential topics such as market segmentation, branding, and customer relationship management. The book has been instrumental in guiding non-profit organizations to adopt customer-centric approaches, ultimately helping them to better understand their target audiences and communicate the value they provide.

In these and other works, Andreasen has argued that understanding and addressing the specific needs of non-profit stakeholders are crucial to organizational success. He also emphasizes the need for non-profits to adopt a strategic approach to marketing that positions them competitively in their sectors, even when resources are constrained.

Andreasen's contributions have been particularly influential in public health. He has worked extensively to integrate marketing strategies into public health campaigns, using social marketing to promote physical activity, encourage healthy eating, and reduce health disparities. By applying marketing techniques to public health, Andreasen has helped organizations develop more effective strategies to change health behaviors and improve public outcomes.

Another key area of Andreasen's work is marketing research, particularly his focus on ethical considerations when working with vulnerable populations. His "cheap but good" research framework advocates for the use of affordable methods like focus groups and secondary data analysis to gain a deep understanding of target markets. Andreasen emphasizes the importance of ethical research practices, such as informed consent and protecting participant confidentiality, ensuring that research findings genuinely benefit the communities being studied.

Beyond his academic and consulting contributions, Andreasen has been a leader in professional organizations and non-profit boards. He chaired the Social Marketing Institute and served on the boards of the American Marketing Association and the Association for Consumer Research. His leadership and advocacy have solidified his standing as a pioneer in bringing marketing expertise to social and non-profit sectors. His impact on the field of marketing has been recognized through numerous awards, including the Lifetime Achievement Award from the American Marketing Association's Nonprofit Marketing Conference and the Distinguished Marketing Educator Award from the Academy of Marketing Science.

Andreasen's legacy is defined by his commitment to using marketing principles to create positive social change. He has shown how marketing can be a force for good, helping organizations and communities to communicate, engage, and build trust effectively. His emphasis on ethical research practices, strategic marketing for nonprofits, and leveraging social marketing for public benefit continues to influence how marketers approach their roles and responsibilities in society.

Cooperative Marketing

Cooperative marketing strategies have been a topic of interest for researchers and practitioners for nearly a century. As early as 1922, the potential of cooperative marketing was recognized in a seminal work published in the *Iowa Law Review* (Sapiro, 1922). Since then, numerous studies have explored the antecedents, implementation, and effectiveness of cooperative marketing strategies across various sectors and contexts (Dickinson & Ramaseshan, 2004; Karantininis et al., 2007; Palmer, 2002).

One of the key aspects of cooperative marketing is the structure of the cooperatives themselves. The structure of marketing cooperatives has been examined from a members' perspective, highlighting the importance of understanding the needs and expectations of cooperative members in developing effective marketing strategies (Karantininis et al., 2007). Similarly, the role of worker-owned cooperatives in fostering social capital has been explored, suggesting that the cooperative model can contribute to building strong communities and networks that support marketing efforts (Majee & Hoyt, 2014).

The implementation of cooperative marketing strategies often involves a comprehensive approach that leverages various channels and tactics. For example, the launch of a comprehensive SNAP-Ed social marketing campaign utilizing the cooperative extension model has been described, which involved a multi-faceted approach to reach and engage target audiences (Walker et al., 2016). This highlights the importance of considering the unique strengths and resources of cooperatives in developing marketing strategies that are tailored to their specific contexts and goals.

The effectiveness of cooperative marketing strategies has been a subject of much research. The causes of effectiveness in cooperative marketing associations have been investigated, identifying factors such as clear objectives, strong leadership, and member commitment as key drivers of success (Palmer, 2002). Similarly, the marketing and performance of fruit and vegetable cooperatives have been examined, highlighting the importance of market orientation and innovation in driving success (Arcas & Ruiz, 2003).

In the context of small firms, cooperative marketing strategies can be particularly valuable. Case studies from Australian and French cooperatives have been presented, demonstrating how cooperatives can serve as strategic networks for small firms, enabling them to access resources, knowledge, and markets that would be difficult to achieve independently (Mazzarol et al., 2013). This suggests that cooperative marketing can be a powerful tool for small businesses looking to compete in an increasingly competitive and globalized marketplace.

Consumer cooperatives, which are owned and controlled by their members, present unique challenges and opportunities for marketing. How consumer cooperatives compete in the marketplace has been explored, highlighting the importance of staying true to their mission and values while also adapting to changing consumer needs and preferences (Jussila et al., 2008). This suggests that cooperative marketing strategies for consumer cooperatives may need to balance the dual goals of member satisfaction and market competitiveness.

The role of cooperatives in sustainable development has also been a topic of interest in recent years. The potential of rural cooperatives to contribute to sustainable development has been examined, highlighting the importance of community engagement, environmental stewardship, and social responsibility in cooperative marketing strategies (Gertler, 2001). Similarly, the common ground between values, marketing, and cooperation has been explored, suggesting that cooperatives have a unique opportunity to promote ethical and sustainable business practices through their marketing efforts (Ferguson, 1997).

Despite the many benefits of cooperative marketing strategies, there are also challenges and limitations to consider. One of the key challenges is the need for effective coordination and collaboration among cooperative members. The antecedents to cooperative marketing strategy implementation have been investigated, identifying factors such as trust, commitment, and communication as critical to success (Dickinson & Ramaseshan, 2004). This suggests that cooperatives need to invest in building strong relationships and communication channels among members in order to effectively implement marketing strategies.

Another challenge is the need to adapt to changing market conditions and consumer preferences. As noted in the context of cooperative marketing in India, cooperatives need to be responsive to the evolving needs and expectations of their customers to remain competitive (Singh, 2000). This may require ongoing market research, innovation, and the development of new products and services that meet the changing demands of the marketplace.

Despite these challenges, cooperative marketing strategies remain a valuable tool for businesses and organizations looking to achieve their goals in a collaborative and socially responsible manner. By leveraging the strengths of the cooperative model, such as shared resources, knowledge, and values, cooperatives can develop marketing strategies that are both effective and aligned with their mission and values.

Moreover, cooperative marketing strategies can contribute to broader social and economic goals, such as community development, environmental sustainability, and social justice. By promoting ethical and responsible business practices, cooperatives can serve as a model for other organizations and contribute to the creation of a more equitable and sustainable economy.

In conclusion, cooperative marketing strategies have been a topic of interest for researchers and practitioners for nearly a century, and for good reasons. The cooperative model offers unique opportunities for businesses and organizations to collaborate, share resources, and achieve common goals in a socially responsible manner. While there are challenges and limitations to consider, such as the need for effective coordination and adaptation to changing market conditions, the benefits of cooperative marketing strategies are clear.

By leveraging the strengths of the cooperative model, such as shared values, knowledge, and resources, cooperatives can develop marketing strategies that are both effective and aligned with their mission and values. Moreover, cooperative marketing strategies can contribute to broader social and economic goals, such as community development, environmental sustainability, and social justice.

As the world continues to face complex social, economic, and environmental challenges, the importance of cooperative marketing strategies is likely to only grow. By working together in a spirit of collaboration and shared purpose, cooperatives can not only achieve their own goals but also contribute to the creation of a more equitable, sustainable, and prosperous future for all.

Community Marketing

Community-based marketing has emerged as a powerful approach to promote sustainable behaviors, foster responsible communities, and drive social change. This approach combines the principles of social marketing with community engagement strategies to create targeted interventions that address specific social and environmental challenges (McKenzie-Mohr, 2011). By involving community members in the planning, implementation, and evaluation of marketing campaigns, community-based marketing aims to create lasting impact and empower individuals to act toward a common goal (Carrigan et al., 2011).

One of the key elements of community-based marketing is the identification of critical success factors that enable effective community engagement and behavior change. These factors include a deep understanding of the target audience, the development of trust and credibility, the use of tailored messaging and communication channels, and the creation of supportive environments that facilitate the adoption of new behaviors (Kim et al., 2009). By addressing these factors, community-based marketing initiatives can overcome barriers to change and create sustainable solutions to complex social and environmental problems (Kennedy, 2010).

Community-based marketing also emphasizes the importance of building relationships and fostering a sense of community among participants. This approach recognizes that individuals are more likely to adopt new behaviors when they feel connected to a larger social network and supported by their peers (Juárez, 2011). By creating opportunities for community members to interact, share experiences, and support one another, community-based marketing can create a sense of belonging and motivation that drives long-term behavior change (Bryant et al., 2007).

Another key aspect of community-based marketing is the integration of various marketing and communication strategies to reach and engage diverse audiences. This includes the use of social marketing techniques, such as segmentation, targeting, and positioning, as well as community readiness assessment and media advocacy (Slater et al., 2000). By combining these strategies, community-based marketing initiatives can create a comprehensive and coordinated approach that addresses the unique needs and preferences of different community segments (Flaherty et al., 2020).

Community-based marketing has been applied to a wide range of social and environmental issues, from promoting recycling and energy conservation to improving public health and reducing poverty. For example, a community-based social marketing program in Canada aimed to increase recycling rates by identifying barriers to behavior change and developing targeted interventions, such as providing feedback on recycling performance and creating social norms around recycling (Haldeman & Turner, 2009). Similarly, a community-based marketing campaign in Australia focused on reducing household energy consumption by providing personalized energy-saving tips and creating a sense of community around energy conservation (Dahl et al., 2015).

The success of community-based marketing initiatives depends on the ability to create meaningful and lasting impact that goes beyond individual behavior change. This requires a systemic approach that addresses the root causes of social and environmental problems and creates enabling environments for sustainable change (Hamby et al., 2017). By engaging community members in the co-creation of solutions and building capacity for ongoing action, community-based marketing can contribute to the development of resilient and empowered communities (Lefebvre, 2012).

However, community-based marketing also faces several challenges and limitations that need to be addressed. One of the main challenges is the need for long-term commitment and investment in community engagement and capacity building (Saunders et al., 2015). This requires a shift from short-term, project-based approaches to more sustainable and collaborative models that involve community members as equal partners in the marketing process (Domegan et al., 2013).

Another challenge is the need to balance the goals of social marketing with the needs and priorities of diverse community stakeholders. This requires a participatory and inclusive approach that values the knowledge, skills, and experiences of community members and incorporates their perspectives into the design and implementation of marketing initiatives (Lefebvre, 2013). By creating a sense of shared ownership and responsibility for the outcomes of community-based marketing, practitioners can build trust, credibility, and support for their initiatives (Chandy et al., 2021).

Community-based marketing also needs to adapt to the changing landscape of consumer behavior and the emerging trends in the sharing economy. This includes the use of peer-to-peer platforms, collaborative consumption, and social innovation to create new forms of value exchange and community engagement (Lim, 2020). By leveraging these trends, community-based marketing can create more inclusive, equitable, and sustainable models of social and economic development that benefit all members of the community.

In conclusion, community-based marketing offers a promising approach to promote sustainable behaviors, foster responsible communities, and drive social change. By combining the principles of social marketing with community engagement strategies, this approach can create targeted interventions that address specific social and environmental challenges and empower individuals to act toward a common goal. However, the success of community-based marketing initiatives depends on the ability to create meaningful and lasting impact that goes beyond individual behavior change and addresses the root causes of social and environmental problems.

To achieve this, community-based marketing needs to adopt a systemic and collaborative approach that values the knowledge, skills, and experiences of community members and incorporates their perspectives into the design and implementation of marketing initiatives. This requires a long-term commitment to community engagement and capacity building, as well as a willingness to adapt to the changing landscape of consumer behavior and the emerging trends in the sharing economy.

By creating a sense of shared ownership and responsibility for the outcomes of community-based marketing, practitioners can build trust, credibility, and support for their initiatives and contribute to the development of resilient and empowered communities. Ultimately, the goal of community-based marketing is to create a more inclusive, equitable, and sustainable society that benefits all members of the community and promotes the common good.

Ethical Consumption

Ethical consumption has emerged as a significant topic of academic and public discourse in recent years, reflecting growing concerns about the social and environmental impacts of consumer behavior. At its core, ethical consumption involves making purchasing decisions based on moral and ethical considerations, such as the treatment of workers, the protection of the environment, and the promotion of social justice (Barnett et al., 2005). This approach to consumption challenges the dominant narrative of consumer sovereignty and individualism, and instead emphasizes the collective responsibility of consumers to promote positive social and environmental change (Adams & Raisborough, 2010).

However, despite the growing popularity of ethical consumption, there remains a significant gap between consumers' stated ethical values and their actual purchasing behavior (Carrington et al., 2016). This "ethical consumption gap" has been attributed to a range of factors, including the availability and affordability of ethical products, the complexity of ethical decision-making, and the influence of social and cultural norms (Lewis & Potter, 2013). As a result, many consumers struggle to translate their ethical concerns into consistent and meaningful changes in their consumption practices (Starr, 2009).

To address this challenge, researchers have sought to develop a more nuanced understanding of the motivations and barriers to ethical consumption. One key insight is that ethical consumption is not a monolithic or uniform phenomenon, but rather a complex and diverse set of practices that are shaped by different cultural, social, and economic contexts (Barnett et al., 2010). For example, studies have shown that ethical consumption can take different forms in different countries and regions, reflecting variations in consumer values, market structures, and regulatory frameworks (Carrier & Luetchford, 2022).

Another important factor is the role of social and community networks in shaping ethical consumption practices. Research has shown that consumers are more likely to engage in ethical consumption when they are part of a community of like-minded individuals who share their values and support their actions (Long & Murray, 2013). This suggests that ethical consumption is not just an individual choice, but a collective and collaborative process that requires the development of shared norms, practices, and institutions (Carrigan et al., 2004).

At the same time, ethical consumption is not without its critics, who argue that it can be a form of "consumer citizenship" that privileges individual choice over systemic change (Carrier, 2008). From this perspective, ethical consumption can be seen as a way of depoliticizing social and environmental issues, by suggesting that they can be addressed through individual purchasing decisions rather than collective action and political mobilization (Cabrera & Williams, 2014). This critique highlights the need for a more holistic and transformative approach to ethical consumption, one that goes beyond individual behavior change to challenge the underlying structures and power relations that shape consumer culture (Kosnik, 2018).

To achieve this, some scholars have argued for a more radical and politicized vision of ethical consumption, one that is grounded in a critique of the dominant paradigm of economic growth and consumerism (Soper, 2016). This approach emphasizes the need for a fundamental reorientation of the economy and society toward more sustainable and equitable forms of production and consumption, based on values such as sufficiency, simplicity, and solidarity (Pecoraro & Uusitalo, 2014). This vision of ethical consumption as a form of cultural and political transformation challenges the idea that consumer behavior can be reduced to a set of individual choices, and instead emphasizes the need for collective action and systemic change (Holt, 2012).

However, achieving this vision of ethical consumption is not without its challenges, given the complex and contested nature of consumer culture and the entrenched power of corporate interests. One key challenge is the need to develop alternative systems of production and consumption that are more socially and environmentally sustainable, such as cooperative and community-based enterprises, sharing economies, and circular economies (Long & Murray, 2013). These alternative systems require not only changes in consumer behavior, but also changes in public policies, market structures, and cultural norms, which can be difficult to achieve in the face of powerful vested interests (Barnett et al., 2010).

Another challenge is the need to engage and empower consumers as active agents of change, rather than passive recipients of ethical products and services. This requires a shift from a top-down, paternalistic approach to ethical consumption, toward a more participatory and democratic model that recognizes the agency and creativity of consumers (Carrigan et al., 2004). This approach emphasizes the importance of consumer education, empowerment, and mobilization, through initiatives such as consumer cooperatives, community-based marketing, and participatory certification schemes (Carrier & Luetchford, 2022).

There is a need for more research and reflection on the ethical and political dimensions of consumption, and how they intersect with broader questions of social justice, environmental sustainability, and human well-being. This requires a more interdisciplinary and critical approach to the study of consumption, one that draws on insights from fields such as philosophy, sociology, anthropology, and political economy (Barnett et al., 2005). By interrogating the underlying assumptions and values that shape consumer behavior, and by exploring alternative visions of the good life and the common good, researchers can contribute to a more robust and transformative understanding of ethical consumption (Soper, 2016).

Ethical consumption represents a significant and growing challenge to the dominant paradigm of consumer culture, one that seeks to promote more socially and environmentally sustainable forms of production and consumption. While there are many barriers and challenges to achieving this vision, there are also many opportunities for innovation, collaboration, and transformation, through initiatives such as alternative economies, participatory governance, and critical reflection. By engaging with these opportunities and challenges, researchers, practitioners, and consumers can contribute to a more just and sustainable future, one that recognizes the inherent interdependence of people and planet, and the urgent need for a more ethical and responsible approach to consumption.

CASE STUDY: Fairtrade International

As a global multi-stakeholder organization, Fairtrade International focuses on improving the lives of farmers and workers through fair trade initiatives. Its mission is to ensure that producers earn a living income and agricultural workers receive fair wages. By promoting the Fairtrade Certification Mark for more than 300 commodities, the organization emphasizes sustainability and fairness in key sectors such as coffee, cocoa, bananas, flowers, tea, and sugar.

Founded in 1997, the organization was established to set private standards on labor conditions and cooperative organization practices. It later divided into two entities in 2004: Fairtrade International and FLOCERT. While Fairtrade International develops standards, supports producer certification, and enhances market access, FLOCERT acts as an independent certifier ensuring compliance and monitoring how Fairtrade benefits are reinvested in communities.

With a diverse membership, Fairtrade International includes three producer networks and nineteen national fairtrade organizations spread across Latin America, Africa, and Asia, as well as in Europe, North America, and other regions. Each member entity plays a role in marketing and upholding the integrity of the Fairtrade Mark, fostering collaborative development initiatives across multiple countries.

To manage its operations, the organization is structured into six units focused on areas such as standard setting, finance, commodity management, and brand licensing. Fairtrade standards define minimum and progress requirements. For instance, small farmers' organizations must meet criteria for democratic decision-making and effective investment of the Fairtrade premium, while hired labor standards ensure decent wages and labor rights on certified plantations.

Over the years, the organization has made a significant impact by channeling the Fairtrade premium—a sum paid on top of the minimum price—to fund community projects such as schools and health clinics. The rigorous standards, regularly reviewed by the Fairtrade Standards and Policy Committee, have helped thousands of producers improve their livelihoods, emphasizing gender equity, environmental protection, and community development.

Despite these achievements, the organization has faced scrutiny. For instance, a 2020 report from the Institute for Multi-Stakeholder Initiative Integrity (MSI Integrity) critiqued its use of private standards, leading Fairtrade International to defend its policies on labor rights and sustainable practices. Ensuring transparency and accountability remains central to its mission.

The organization's effectiveness has been called into question by some critics, who argue that its standards are not stringent enough and do not fully address the root causes of poverty. Concerns about child labor and the impacts of climate change on certified farms have highlighted ongoing challenges. Additionally, the Fairtrade model, while providing short-term benefits, may not always lead to long-term systemic change in global supply chains.

Looking ahead, Fairtrade International has outlined several key priorities: expanding the reach of the Fairtrade Mark, strengthening producer organizations, and increasing transparency in supply chains. Climate change adaptation is also a major focus, as farmers in developing countries are disproportionately affected by environmental changes. By continuing to innovate and engage with producers, traders, and consumers, the organization hopes to create a more just and sustainable global economy.

Digital Marketing and Ethical Consumption

Digital technologies have revolutionized the way people consume and engage with ethical and sustainable products and services. The rise of social media platforms, mobile applications, and e-commerce websites has created new opportunities for promoting ethical consumption and driving social change (Blair, 2017). These digital tools have enabled consumers to access information, share experiences, and make informed decisions about their purchases, while also providing a platform for businesses and organizations to communicate their values and engage with their stakeholders (Salido-Andres, 2018; Ali et al., 2023).

One of the key benefits of digital technologies for ethical consumption is their ability to increase transparency and accountability in supply chains. Through the use of blockchain, radio-frequency identification (RFID) tags, and other traceability technologies, consumers can now access detailed information about the origin, production, and environmental impact of the products they buy (Graham & Haarstad, 2014). This increased transparency has put pressure on companies to adopt more sustainable and ethical practices, while also empowering consumers to make more informed choices (Lekakis, 2014).

Social media platforms have also played a crucial role in promoting ethical consumption by providing a space for consumers to connect, share information, and mobilize around social and environmental issues (Mahoney & Tang, 2024). These platforms have enabled the creation of online communities and social movements that advocate for ethical consumption and hold businesses accountable for their actions (Dokhanchi et al., 2019). For example, the #FashionRevolution campaign, which emerged in response to the Rana Plaza disaster in Bangladesh, has used social media to raise awareness about the human and environmental costs of fast fashion and promote more sustainable alternatives (Freeman et al., 2015).

Digital marketing strategies have also been used to promote ethical consumption by targeting consumers with personalized and engaging content that resonates with their values and interests (Saura et al., 2020). Through the use of data analytics, machine learning, and artificial intelligence, businesses can now identify and segment their target audience based on their ethical and sustainable preferences, and deliver tailored messages and offers that encourage them to make more responsible choices (Nayyar, 2023). For example, the app Good On You uses data from more than 500 sources to rate the ethical and environmental performance of fashion brands and provide personalized recommendations to users based on their values and style preferences (Hoelscher & Chatzidakis, 2021).

However, the use of digital technologies for ethical consumption also raises important ethical and social concerns. One of the main challenges is the digital divide, which refers to the unequal access to digital technologies and skills among different segments of the population (Reed, 2018). This divide can limit the ability of marginalized and disadvantaged groups to participate in online conversations and movements around ethical consumption, and can exacerbate existing social and economic in-equalities (Humphery & Jordan, 2018).

Another challenge is the issue of data privacy and security, as the collection and use of personal data by businesses and platforms can lead to concerns about surveil-lance, manipulation, and exploitation (Hanlon, 2020). The use of algorithms and artifi-cial intelligence in digital marketing can also perpetuate biases and discrimination, as they may reflect the values and assumptions of their creators and reinforce existing power structures (Polanco-Diges & Debasa, 2020).

To address these challenges, it is important to develop ethical and responsible ap-proaches to the use of digital technologies for promoting ethical consumption. This includes ensuring that digital platforms and tools are accessible, inclusive, and trans-parent, and that they respect the privacy and autonomy of users (Romprasert & Triv-edi, 2021). It also requires collaboration and partnerships between businesses, civil so-ciety organizations, and policymakers to create a supportive ecosystem for ethical consumption and social change (Freeman et al., 2015).

One promising approach is the use of participatory and collaborative design methods that involve consumers and stakeholders in the development and implemen-tation of digital technologies for ethical consumption (Hoelscher & Chatzidakis, 2021). This can help to ensure that these technologies are aligned with the needs and values of different communities, and that they promote empowerment and agency rather than manipulation and control (Lekakis, 2014).

Another important strategy is the use of digital storytelling and narrative techni-ques to communicate the human and environmental impacts of consumption and pro-duction, and to inspire empathy and action among consumers (Mahoney & Tang, 2024). By using multimedia content such as videos, images, and testimonials, busi-nesses and organizations can create compelling and authentic stories that connect with the emotions and experiences of their audience, and that motivate them to make more ethical and sustainable choices (Freeman et al., 2015).

Finally, it is crucial to foster digital literacy and critical thinking skills among con-sumers, so that they can navigate the complex and often contradictory information that they encounter online, and make informed and reflective decisions about their consumption practices (Humphery & Jordan, 2018). This requires investing in educa-tion and awareness-raising programs that help consumers to understand the social and environmental impacts of their choices, and to develop the skills and confidence to advocate for change (Reed, 2018).

Digital technologies, thus, offer significant opportunities for promoting ethical consumption and driving social change, by increasing transparency, accountability, and engagement in supply chains and consumption practices. However, they also raise important ethical and social concerns, such as the digital divide, data privacy, and algorithmic bias, which need to be addressed through responsible and participa-tory approaches. By developing inclusive, transparent, and empowering digital tech-nologies, and by fostering digital literacy and critical thinking skills among consumers, we can harness the power of digital platforms and tools to create a more sustainable and equitable future for all.

CASE STUDY: Shareable

Shareable is a non-profit organization that has played a key role in the sharing economy movement since its founding in 2009. Emerging from a collaboration between the SHIFT Foundation and Free Range Graphics and inspired by Annie Leonard's *The Story of Stuff*, Shareable was created to foster a society centered on sustainability, equity, and cooperation through shared resources. Over the past decade, it has become a major hub for knowledge, news, and guidance on how sharing-based solutions can create connected and resilient communities.

At its core, Shareable advocates for cooperative and sustainable solutions that empower communities to address social and ecological challenges. The organization recognizes that many communities lack the resources and infrastructure needed for grassroots solutions and believes that collaborative action is crucial for building a just and regenerative economy. Shareable's values include solidarity, abundance, curiosity, liberation, and celebration—principles that guide its mission to foster connected, generous, and resilient communities.

Since its inception, Shareable has launched numerous projects and publications that support the sharing economy. In 2013, it initiated the Sharing Cities Network to build community resilience through local organizing. This network facilitated over 50 ShareFests, 100 MapJams (community mapping of sharing resources), and 40 Seed Grants, helping numerous communities develop grassroots sharing projects.

In 2018, Shareable released *Sharing Cities: Activating the Urban Commons*, a comprehensive publication with 137 case studies and model policies from around the globe. This book, co-authored with fifteen fellows in nine countries, featured a global book tour and helped establish partnerships that continue to shape Shareable's programs today. The initiative strengthened the sharing movement's global reach, connecting activists, policymakers, and researchers working on community-led economic models.

Some of Shareable's most impactful partnerships include *The Response* film and podcast series, which explore how communities build resilience in the face of disasters, and the Cities@Tufts Colloquium, an open-lecture series that uplifts diverse voices in urban planning. Additionally, the Rural Power Coalition supports the just transition to renewable energy for the 42 million member-owners of the United States' Rural Electric Cooperatives.

Recognizing a need to move from inspiration to action, Shareable recently launched SolidarityWorks, a learning lab that mobilizes grassroots organizers to build new social infrastructure. This program provides training, resources, and support to community organizers, strengthening their capacity to develop impactful projects. Alongside this shift, Shareable has transitioned to a worker self-directed organizational structure, empowering staff to play a larger role in decision-making and governance.

In advancing these initiatives, Shareable acknowledges that the sharing economy must be thoughtfully constructed to avoid perpetuating existing inequities. The organization prioritizes inclusivity and equity, ensuring that its principles and practices allow all people to thrive as their full, authentic selves. Addressing complex challenges such as climate change, entrenched systems of oppression, and economic instability requires a multi-pronged approach that centers on democratic participation and community-led solutions.

Throughout its history, Shareable has cultivated a strong network of change-makers and shared valuable knowledge with the public. It has become a trusted source of information and inspiration for community organizers, social entrepreneurs, and policymakers. As a storyteller, convener, and advocate, Shareable has contributed significantly to the narrative around sharing as a pathway to a more equitable and sustainable world.

Looking ahead, Shareable seeks to deepen its impact by empowering communities to govern themselves and build economies that serve everyone. Its ultimate vision is a world where people have access to the resources, knowledge, and power they need to thrive—creating a more resilient, equitable, and joyful society through the power of sharing and cooperation.

Online Activism

In the digital age, online activism has emerged as a powerful force for driving social change and challenging the status quo. With the rise of social media platforms and digital communication technologies, individuals and organizations now have unprecedented opportunities to raise awareness, mobilize support, and influence public opinion on a wide range of issues (Wymer, 2010). The phenomenon of online activism, also known as digital activism or cyberactivism, involves the use of digital tools and platforms to advocate for social, political, or environmental causes. The advent of the internet and social media has transformed the landscape of activism, enabling individuals and groups to connect, organize, and take action on a global scale. As noted by Moorman (2020), the rise of online activism has blurred the boundaries between marketing and activism, challenging traditional notions of corporate social responsibility and brand engagement.

One of the key advantages of online activism is its ability to amplify marginalized voices and bring attention to issues that might otherwise be overlooked by mainstream media (Hill, 2020). Through social media campaigns, online petitions, and viral content, activists can quickly mobilize large numbers of supporters and generate significant public pressure on decision-makers. This has led to a democratization of activism, empowering individuals and grassroots movements to challenge powerful interests and advocate for change (Corcoran et al., 2016).

Online activists employ a wide range of strategies and tactics to achieve their goals, from raising awareness and educating the public to pressuring corporations and governments to act. One of the most common strategies is the use of social media campaigns, which involve creating and sharing content across various platforms to generate buzz and engagement around a particular issue (Key et al., 2021). These campaigns often rely on hashtags, memes, and other forms of viral content to spread their message and mobilize supporters.

Another key tactic of online activism is the use of online petitions and letter-writing campaigns (Pimentel & Didonet, 2021). By leveraging the power of digital platforms, activists can quickly gather signatures and testimonials from supporters around the world, putting pressure on decision-makers to take action. This has been particularly effective in cases where traditional forms of activism, such as protests and demonstrations, are difficult or impossible due to geographic or logistical constraints.

Online activists also rely heavily on storytelling and personal narratives to build empathy and inspire action (Key et al., 2021). By sharing the stories of individuals and communities affected by social and environmental issues, activists can humanize complex problems and make them more relatable to a wider audience. This has been particularly effective in cases where activists are seeking to challenge dominant narratives or counter misinformation spread by powerful interests.

The impact of online activism has been significant and far-reaching, with numerous examples of successful campaigns that have led to tangible policy changes and social reforms. For example, the #MeToo movement, which began as a hashtag on social media, has led to a global reckoning with sexual harassment and assault, resulting in the downfall of numerous high-profile figures and significant changes in workplace policies and practices (Rao, 2008).

Similarly, the Black Lives Matter movement, which gained momentum through online activism following the murder of George Floyd in 2020, has led to widespread protests and calls for police reform and racial justice (Richardson, 1995). The movement has also had a significant impact on the business world, with numerous companies pledging to address systemic racism and support Black-owned businesses and communities.

Online activism has also been effective in holding corporations accountable for their social and environmental impacts. For example, the #DeleteUber campaign, which emerged in response to the company's perceived support for President Trump's travel ban, led to a significant drop in the company's market value and forced it to make changes to its leadership and policies (Sibai et al., 2021). Similarly, the #BoycottNRA campaign, which emerged in the wake of the Parkland school shooting, led to numerous companies cutting ties with the National Rifle Association and supporting gun control measures (Spar & La Mure, 2003).

The rise of online activism has significant implications for marketing and consumer behavior, as brands increasingly find themselves caught in the crosshairs of social and political debates. As noted by Corcoran et al. (2016), consumers are increasingly expecting brands to take a stand on social and environmental issues, and are willing to reward or punish companies based on their perceived values and actions.

This has led to the emergence of "brand activism," where companies actively engage in social and political issues as a way to build brand loyalty and differentiate themselves from competitors (Pimentel & Didonet, 2021). However, as noted by Key et al. (2021), brand activism can also be a double-edged sword, as companies risk alienating certain segments of their customer base or being perceived as inauthentic or opportunistic.

To navigate this complex landscape, marketers need to develop a deep understanding of the issues and values that matter most to their customers, and develop authentic and meaningful ways to engage with them (Sibai et al., 2021). This may involve partnering with activist organizations, supporting grassroots campaigns, or developing their own initiatives that align with their brand values and purpose.

Marketers also need to be prepared to respond quickly and effectively to online activism that targets their brand or industry. This may involve developing crisis communication plans, monitoring social media sentiment, and engaging in dialogue with activists and stakeholders to address concerns and find common ground (Peattie & Samuel, 2018).

As digital technologies continue to evolve and become more ubiquitous, the future of online activism looks bright. With the rise of artificial intelligence, virtual and augmented reality, and other emerging technologies, activists will have even more powerful tools at their disposal to raise awareness, mobilize support, and drive change.

However, the future of online activism also poses significant challenges and risks. As noted by Wymer (2010), the proliferation of fake news, misinformation, and propaganda on social media platforms can undermine the credibility and effectiveness of activist campaigns. There is also a risk that online activism could become co-opted or commercialized by powerful interests, diluting its impact and authenticity.

To address these challenges, activists and marketers alike will need to develop new strategies and approaches that prioritize transparency, accountability, and authentic engagement with stakeholders. This may involve developing new metrics and frameworks for measuring the impact and effectiveness of online activism, as well as building stronger partnerships and collaborations across sectors and industries.

Online activism has emerged as a powerful force for driving social change and challenging the status quo in the digital age. Through a wide range of strategies and tactics, from social media campaigns to online petitions and storytelling, activists have been able to raise awareness, mobilize support, and influence public opinion on a global scale.

The impact of online activism has been significant and far-reaching, from holding corporations accountable for their social and environmental impacts to driving policy changes and social reforms. For marketers and brands, the rise of online activism poses both challenges and opportunities, as consumers increasingly expect companies to take a stand on social and political issues.

To navigate this complex landscape, marketers need to develop authentic and meaningful ways to engage with customers and stakeholders, while also being prepared to respond quickly and effectively to online activism that targets their brand or industry. As digital technologies continue to evolve, the future of online activism looks bright, but also poses significant challenges and risks that will require new strategies and approaches to address.

KEY THINKER: Naomi Klein—"No Logo"

Naomi Klein, a Canadian author, social activist, and filmmaker, has made substantial contributions to political analysis, ecofeminism, and organized labor movements. Born in Montreal in 1970, Klein grew up in a family of peace activists who fled the United States during the Vietnam War. Influenced by her parents' dedication to social justice and equality, Klein initially rejected politics in favor of consumerism, but two transformative events—the 1989 École Polytechnique massacre and her mother's stroke—propelled her toward activism and social engagement.

Klein's rise to prominence began with the publication of her first book, *No Logo* (1999), which quickly became a manifesto for the anti-globalization movement. Released shortly after the Seattle World Trade Organization (WTO) protests, the book critiques the practices of large corporations and their exploitative effects on workers in developing countries. It examines how branding extends beyond products into cultural and social spheres, reshaping identities and limiting consumer choice.

No Logo is divided into four sections: "No Space," which critiques the shift in branding from product-focused to lifestyle-oriented strategies; "No Choice," which examines how corporate consolidation reduces competition and limits consumer options; "No Jobs," which addresses the displacement of local jobs due to the relocation of production to countries with lax labor laws; and "No Logo," which explores emerging resistance movements like Adbusters and Reclaim the Streets. Klein's call for a shift from consumerism to active citizenship resonated widely, making *No Logo* a foundational text in the alter-globalization movement.

Following the success of *No Logo*, Klein continued her incisive critique of neoliberalism with *The Shock Doctrine* (2007), where she argues that crises are systematically exploited to impose neoliberal policies that would otherwise face resistance. The book became influential in understanding how economic and political elites capitalize on societal shocks to advance controversial reforms. In *This Changes Everything: Capitalism vs. the Climate* (2014), Klein connects capitalism's structural imperatives with environmental destruction, arguing for systemic change to address the climate crisis effectively.

Klein's works extend beyond theoretical critique—she is also an activist and advocate for change. Her engagement with the climate justice group 350.org and her support for ecofeminist and leftist movements exemplify her dedication to merging scholarship with activism. In recognition of her contributions, she was awarded the Sydney Peace Prize in 2016 for her work on climate justice.

Klein's influence is evident in her numerous accolades and frequent appearances on global lists of top thinkers. Her work is known for blending scholarly rigor with accessible language, enabling her to engage a broad audience in discussions on corporate power, worker exploitation, and environmental justice. Klein's appointment as a professor of climate justice at the University of British Columbia in 2021 further cemented her role as an advocate for addressing the intersecting crises of capitalism and climate change.

While *No Logo* established her reputation, her subsequent works have reinforced Klein's status as a thought leader in the struggle against neoliberalism and climate injustice. Her work challenges readers to question entrenched systems of power and to envision alternatives rooted in justice and sustainability.

Gamification and Social Change

Gamification, the application of game design elements and principles in non-game contexts, is an increasingly powerful tool for driving social change and promoting sustainable behaviors. By leveraging the motivational and engaging aspects of games, gamification can encourage individuals to adopt new habits, take action on social and environmental issues, and contribute to the transformation of society and organizations (Marin et al., 2021). This essay explores the potential of gamification for social change, examining its theoretical foundations, practical applications, and future directions.

At its core, gamification is based on the idea that games are inherently motivating and engaging, and that by incorporating game-like elements into non-game contexts, it is possible to increase participation, engagement, and motivation (Mitchell et al., 2017). This is achieved through the use of game mechanics such as points, badges, leaderboards, and challenges, which provide feedback, rewards, and social recognition to users, and encourage them to continue engaging with the gamified system (Spanellis & Harviainen, 2021). By tapping into the psychological needs for competence, autonomy, and relatedness, gamification can create a sense of agency, mastery, and social connection that drives behavior change and fosters intrinsic motivation (Maan, 2013).

One of the key areas where gamification has been applied for social change is in the domain of sustainability and climate change. As Mazur-Stommen and Farley (2016) argue, games have the potential to engage and educate individuals about the complex and often abstract issues related to sustainability, and to motivate them to act in their daily lives. For example, the game "Save the Park" by Schell Games uses gamification to encourage users to reduce their energy consumption and adopt sustainable behaviors, while also raising awareness about the impacts of climate change. Similarly, the "Greenify" app by Columbia University's Games Research lab uses gamification to foster sustainable communities by encouraging users to take eco-friendly actions and compete with others to reduce their environmental footprint (Lee et al., 2013).

However, the effectiveness of gamification for sustainable consumption is limited by the inherent limitations of persuasive technologies, which often fail to address the underlying structural and systemic barriers to behavior change (Huber & Hilty, 2015). To overcome these limitations, they argue for a more holistic and participatory approach to gamification, one that engages users as active co-creators of the gamified system, and that takes into account the broader social, cultural, and political contexts in which consumption occurs. This requires a shift from a top-down, one-size-fits-all approach to gamification, toward a more context-specific and user-centered approach that recognizes the diversity and complexity of human behavior (Mitchell, 2020).

Another important application of gamification for social change is in the domain of education and engagement. Gamification can be an impactful tool for promoting pro-environmental behaviors and raising awareness about sustainability issues, particularly among younger generations (Ouariachi et al., 2020). By incorporating game-based learning and engagement strategies into educational curricula and outreach programs, it is possible to create more interactive, immersive, and memorable learning experiences that foster critical thinking, problem-solving, and action-oriented skills (Hassan & Leigh, 2021). This approach has been successfully applied in a range of contexts, from climate change education in schools to citizen science projects that engage the public in environmental monitoring and data collection (Fernández Galeote et al., 2021).

However, the effectiveness of gamification for social change also depends on the broader institutional and cultural contexts in which it is implemented (Padilla-Zea et al., 2019). In the case of social economy entrepreneurship, for example, gamification can be used to promote collaboration, innovation, and social impact, but only if it is integrated into a broader ecosystem of support and resources that enable entrepreneurs to thrive. This requires a more systemic and holistic approach to gamification, one that takes into account the complex interplay of individual, organizational, and societal factors that shape behavior and social change (Popan et al., 2023).

Looking to the future, there are many exciting possibilities for the application of gamification for social change. One emerging area is the use of gamification in the sharing economy, where it can be used to promote trust, cooperation, and social responsibility among users and providers (White & Marchet, 2021). By incorporating game-based incentives and feedback mechanisms into sharing platforms, it is possible to encourage more sustainable and equitable forms of consumption and production, while also fostering a sense of community and shared purpose (Alibakhshi et al., 2024). Similarly, gamification can be used to promote sustainable tourism, by encouraging travelers to adopt more responsible and eco-friendly behaviors, and by supporting local communities and conservation efforts (Negruşa et al., 2015).

However, the success of gamification for social change also depends on the active participation and engagement of stakeholders, including users, organizations, and policymakers (Adornes and Muniz, 2019). This requires a more collaborative and inclusive approach to gamification design and implementation, one that considers the diverse needs, interests, and perspectives of different stakeholders, and that fosters a sense of ownership and agency among participants. By creating more participatory and empowering forms of gamification, it is possible to unleash the full potential of this powerful tool for driving social change and creating a more sustainable and equitable future.

Gamification represents a promising and innovative approach to promoting social change and sustainable behaviors. By leveraging the motivational and engaging aspects of games, gamification can encourage individuals and organizations to adopt new habits, act on social and environmental issues, and contribute to the transformation of society. However, the effectiveness of gamification for social change depends on a range of factors, including the design and implementation of the gamified system, the broader institutional and cultural contexts in which it is applied, and the active participation and engagement of stakeholders.

To fully realize the potential of gamification for social change, it is necessary to adopt a more holistic, participatory, and context-specific approach that takes into account the complexity and diversity of human behavior and social systems. This requires a shift from a top-down, one-size-fits-all approach to gamification, toward a more collaborative, inclusive, and empowering approach that engages users and stakeholders as active co-creators of the gamified system. By embracing this more systemic and participatory approach, it is possible to create more effective, equitable, and sustainable forms of gamification that drive positive social change and contribute to a better future for all.

CASE STUDY: The Video Game *Common'Hood*

Common'hood is a unique video game that explores themes of homelessness, community-building, and sustainable living within a post-economic collapse scenario. Developed by a socially conscious team, the game challenges players to build a new society in an abandoned factory by using creativity, resourcefulness, and collaboration. It pushes beyond traditional survival gameplay by emphasizing collective problem-solving and community empowerment.

Set in a world grappling with economic collapse, *Common'hood* invites players to craft shelter, scavenge for resources, and grow food, while managing a workshop and building machines from open-source blueprints. The aim is to create a thriving, self-sustaining community. Players must ensure the well-being of their crew by providing shelter, food, and water in exchange for contributions, while balancing individual needs and skills to optimize community development.

One of the game's distinctive features is its strong focus on collaboration and social responsibility. As players encounter new characters with unique stories and abilities, they must incorporate them into the community by fostering cooperation. The game emphasizes teamwork over individual success, positioning the player as a steward of a shared social economy.

Inspired by the Maker Movement and DIY culture, *Common'hood* enables players to design and customize structures like Tiny Homes, farming rigs, and modular furniture. The Blueprint system allows players to automate construction or delegate tasks to community members, enabling larger-scale projects. This innovative approach encourages players to experiment and share their designs in the game's online marketplace, enhancing interaction and idea exchange among a global player base.

The online marketplace is another standout feature, where creations can be shared in a "creative commons" format or sold for resources. This fosters a sense of community beyond the in-game world, encouraging collaboration and skill-sharing. Players gain reputation and attract skilled characters, further expanding their community's capabilities.

Dynamic characters and events bring additional complexity. Players must address the diverse needs and conflicts within their community, adding layers of social simulation. As they engage with characters, they must navigate interpersonal dynamics, making the game as much about managing relationships as it is about survival.

Automation also plays a key role, enabling players to streamline production processes and create self-sustaining systems for food and energy. By researching and developing technologies, players can build an automated ecosystem that addresses basic needs, freeing up resources to focus on innovation and expansion.

Beyond gameplay mechanics, *Common'hood* conveys a deeper social message. It invites players to rethink traditional economic models and envision alternative systems rooted in cooperation, sustainability, and community. By promoting eco-friendly practices like renewable energy and sustainable agriculture, the game echoes real-world imperatives to address climate change and environmental degradation.

In addressing poverty and homelessness, *Common'hood* exposes players to the systemic issues that lead to these crises. Characters' stories and the harsh realities they face are interwoven into the gameplay, prompting reflection on the root causes of inequality. The game serves as a commentary on how communities can rebuild and support one another when conventional economic systems fail.

Ultimately, *Common'hood* functions as both a game and a social experiment. It challenges players to imagine a world where community resilience and social justice take precedence over profit. The game provides a hopeful vision of a future where collective action can overcome adversity and establish a society built on principles of equity and sustainability. As the game evolves, it has the potential to become a platform for real-world social innovation, inspiring players to translate in-game lessons into tangible actions.

Cooperative Knowledge Sharing

Cooperative marketing transcends individual consumer outreach, extending its purview to encompass engagement with other cooperatives, businesses, and organizations. While business-to-consumer (B2C) marketing is pivotal for customer attraction, the significance of business-to-business (B2B) marketing cannot be overstated, especially in the context of building relationships and fostering collaboration within the cooperative ecosystem (Yee & Yazdanifard, 2015).

As integral components of the social economy, cooperatives are compelled to promote themselves not solely to consumers but also to extant businesses, community members, and fellow cooperative entities. This necessitates the formulation of marketing strategies harmonious with cooperative principles, resonating with potential partners. For instance, cooperatives can articulate their value proposition to third-sector non-profit organizations founded on shared values, such as social impact, sustainability, and community empowerment. This approach accentuates the cooperative nature of these organizations, facilitating the establishment of symbiotic relationships (Gordon et al., 2022).

However, cooperative marketing goes beyond mere profit-driven motives or the establishment of competitive advantages. It serves as a conduit for constructing cooperative networks and nurturing collaboration among organizations. In lieu of merely vending products or services, cooperatives endeavor to forge relationships grounded in the exchange of knowledge, skills, and resources (Gordon, 2013). These cooperative networks furnish avenues for knowledge dissemination, capacity augmentation, and joint initiatives that fortify the social economy holistically.

Through cooperative marketing initiatives, organizations engage in meaningful interconnections, sharing best practices, and leveraging collective strengths. This collaborative ethos empowers cooperatives to surmount challenges, penetrate new markets, and amplify their impact (Duong, 2017). For example, a cooperative concentrating on sustainable agriculture might synergize with a counterpart specializing in food processing to architect a comprehensive farm-to-table value chain. Through collaborative efforts, production processes can be streamlined, costs mitigated, and consumers provided with a holistic and sustainable food experience.

The engagement of cooperative marketing with other cooperatives and businesses extends beyond conventional advertising or branding endeavors. It necessitates an exhaustive comprehension of the target audience's needs, interests, and values (Gordon et al., 2018). Market research becomes imperative to identify potential partners, evaluate their understanding of cooperatives, and dispel any misconceptions (Nzili, 2003). Tailoring marketing messages and materials to suit the B2B audience enables cooperatives to effectively communicate the advantages and value inherent in collaborative ventures.

In addition to promoting cooperative principles and the societal impact of their offerings, cooperatives must underscore their capacity to deliver high-quality products and services ethically. By showcasing their commitment to fair trade, sustainability, and democratic decision-making, cooperatives distinguish themselves from traditional for-profit enterprises. This distinction becomes a competitive advantage, particularly among consumers who prioritize ethical consumption and support socially responsible initiatives (Gopaldas, 2015).

Furthermore, cooperative marketing serves as a conduit for educating businesses and organizations about the cooperative model itself. By presenting successful cooperative case studies, offering resources, and providing training opportunities, cooperatives can inspire and facilitate the formation of new cooperatives. This proactive engagement contributes to the expansion of the cooperative movement, furthering the growth of the social economy (Viardot, 2013).

Cooperative marketing extends beyond the scope of individual consumer engagement to encompass other cooperatives, businesses, and organizations. Its essence lies in the development of marketing strategies aligned with cooperative principles, fostering collaboration and mutual exchange (Bob, 2001). By elucidating the benefits of cooperation and accentuating their societal impact, cooperatives can attract like-minded partners and cultivate cooperative networks conducive to knowledge sharing, skills development, and collaborative initiatives. Through cooperative marketing endeavors, these entities fortify their presence in the marketplace, cultivate enduring relationships, and contribute substantively to the advancement of the social economy at large.

In tandem with business-to-business (B2B) marketing, cooperative marketing encompasses what can be termed as C2C marketing, signifying "cooperative-to-cooperative marketing" and "community-to-community marketing." These facets of marketing pivot around the collaborative and mutually advantageous interactions between cooperatives and communities, underscoring the preeminence of cooperation vis-à-vis competition.

Cooperative-to-cooperative marketing revolves around the capability of cooperatives to promote themselves to other cooperatives in a spirit of collaboration and solidarity (Burksiene et al., 2019). Eschewing a competitive lens, cooperatives acknowledge the value inherent in consolidating their resources, sharing expertise, and embarking on joint ventures. This mode of marketing fosters robust relationships, broadens networks, and collectively addresses challenges that might be insurmountable in isolation. It enables cooperatives to leverage their collective strengths and expertise, benefiting not only the participating entities but also their members and the broader community.

Similarly, community-to-community marketing centers on the individual and collective marketing efforts of community members directed toward one another. This approach recognizes the inherent diversity within communities, comprising individuals with distinct skills, knowledge, and resources. Cooperative marketing within communities transpires as community members share expertise, extend support, and collaborate on community-centric projects. Rooted in the principles of cooperation and reciprocity, this form of marketing sees community members contributing their skills and knowledge for the collective betterment.

Community-to-community marketing aspires to enhance the overall capacity and capabilities of community members and the community itself. By nurturing a culture of cooperation over competition, individuals and groups within the community converge to address shared needs and challenges. This cooperative interaction empowers community members to leverage one another's strengths, pool shared resources, and devise innovative solutions. Through such cooperative endeavors, communities bolster their resilience, fortify social cohesion, and pave the way for sustainable development.

Both cooperative-to-cooperative marketing and community-to-community marketing underscore the transformative potential of cooperation and collaboration. These approaches create arenas for shared learning, reciprocal support, and the exchange of ideas, skills, and resources (Mabry & Mackert, 2014). By embracing cooperation as opposed to competition, both cooperatives and communities can collectively confront social, economic, and environmental challenges, fostering a sense of ownership, belonging, and empowerment among their members.

In conclusion, cooperative marketing encompasses not solely business-to-business marketing but also cooperative-to-cooperative marketing and community-to-community marketing. These forms of marketing accentuate the significance of collaboration, mutual support, and shared resources. By championing cooperation between cooperatives and fostering collaboration among community members, these approaches fortify the cooperative movement, enhance community resilience, and contribute meaningfully to the overarching development and well-being of individuals and communities alike.

Cooperative Branding

In the modern economic landscape, marketing plays a crucial role in the success of any organization, including cooperatives. While marketing is commonly associated with for-profit enterprises, cooperatives also need to effectively market themselves to their communities. Cooperative marketing involves not only promoting specific goods and services but also educating potential users about the cooperative model and its benefits. Additionally, cooperatives have the unique challenge of conveying their social impact and democratic principles to differentiate themselves from traditional for-profit organizations. This section explores the significance of cooperative marketing, highlighting the need for branding, market research, and promoting the cooperative values and social impact within the community.

One of the primary challenges faced by cooperatives is helping potential users grasp the concept of what a cooperative is and how it can better serve their needs (Beverland, 2007). Cooperative marketing aims to bridge this knowledge gap and create awareness about the cooperative model. This can be achieved through various channels, including traditional marketing strategies like print, radio, and TV advertising as well as increasingly important digital marketing efforts through websites, social media, and targeted online ads. Cooperatives must communicate their structure, democratic decision-making processes, and shared ownership to potential members and customers (Youn & Lee, 2019). By clearly explaining how cooperatives function and the role of members, they can highlight the benefits of cooperatives, such as fair pricing, active member engagement, and shared profits.

Cooperatives must develop a branding strategy that promotes both the cooperative movement in general and their own specific cooperative (Giorgos et al., 2012). This involves identifying the cooperative's unique attributes and values, creating a visual identity through logos and packaging, using consistent messaging across platforms, and finding opportunities to tell the cooperative's story. To effectively market themselves, cooperatives also need to conduct market research to understand the knowledge and preconceived assumptions about cooperatives within their potential user base (Nilsson et al., 2007). This research helps identify the target audience's needs, preferences, and misconceptions about cooperatives, enabling tailored marketing messages.

By emphasizing the cooperative principles of equality, participation, and community impact, cooperatives can differentiate themselves from traditional for-profit firms (White, 2015). Marketing content should highlight how the cooperative model gives members a voice, allows coordination of efforts for mutual benefit, and aims to serve community needs. This provides a point of difference from corporations focused on maximizing profits for a small group of shareholders.

The cooperative advantage lies in its ability to demonstrate its positive social impact and ethical practices. Members often join cooperatives because they value the social mission and view cooperatives as upholding ethical business standards (Challita et al., 2019). Cooperatives are driven by a commitment to social responsibility and the well-being of their members and communities. Marketing efforts should focus on highlighting the social and environmental benefits that cooperatives bring, such as job creation, local economic development, sustainable practices, and community programs. By showcasing the cooperative's contributions to the community, they can attract socially conscious consumers who prioritize ethical consumption.

Cooperatives can position themselves as viable alternatives to traditional for-profit organizations by emphasizing their ability to deliver high-quality goods and services while upholding ethical values (Hardesty, 2005). By investing in quality control, innovation, and professional management, cooperatives can demonstrate that they are on par with or even surpass their for-profit counterparts in product excellence and customer service. Cooperative marketing should emphasize this value proposition of ethical consumption, where customers can contribute to positive social change while enjoying high-quality offerings comparable or superior to private corporations.

Messaging should highlight product or service attributes most valued by consumers, as determined through market research. For example, agricultural cooperatives may emphasize sustainable farming practices, farmer empowerment, and transparency around ingredients and production methods to appeal to educated middle-class shoppers. Marketing should leverage the cooperative's reputation and community ties while also appealing to self-interest by touting product quality, competitive pricing, and member rewards programs.

Cooperative marketing extends beyond individual cooperatives. Cooperatives can collaborate and form networks to collectively promote the cooperative movement as a whole on a regional, national, or international scale (Beverland, 2010). By working together, cooperatives can pool resources for wider research and marketing efforts, amplify their message, and create a stronger presence in the market. Cooperative federations and associations, such as the International Cooperative Alliance, play a crucial role in coordinating marketing and education campaigns to build awareness of cooperatives globally.

In regions where the cooperative model is not widely known, broader marketing efforts are needed to educate the public and policymakers about cooperatives, their principles and benefits. Improved legal frameworks and government support can bolster development of new cooperatives. Once the model gains wider acceptance, individual cooperatives can then focus on more targeted marketing highlighting their specific offerings and community role. This collective action is vital for enabling cooperatives to compete with large multinational corporations that already benefit from established brand recognition and economies of scale in advertising.

In the social economy, effective marketing is essential for the success of cooperatives and for raising awareness of cooperative enterprise as an alternative economic model. Cooperative marketing goes beyond the promotion of goods and services; it involves educating potential users about the cooperative structure, conducting market research into perceptions and needs, developing strong cooperative branding, and highlighting the social impact and ethical principles of cooperatives. By undertaking these key strategies, cooperatives can counter misconceptions, attract committed members and customers, and position themselves as competitive alternatives to traditional for-profit organizations. Through collaborative marketing efforts, the cooperative movement can gain greater visibility and make significant contributions to building a more sustainable, equitable, and democratic economy.

Conclusion

Marketing plays a crucial role in advancing the social economy by promoting knowledge exchange, increasing visibility, and fostering the adoption of social economy principles (Blair, 2017; Salido-Andres, 2018; Ali et al., 2023). It operates at three levels: macro, advocating for legislative support; meso, raising awareness of social enterprises and cooperatives; and micro, enabling individuals to make consumption choices aligned with their values (Mahoney & Tang, 2024; Saura et al., 2020).

Social marketing, which applies marketing principles to drive positive behavior change, has gained prominence as organizations increasingly address social issues and promote community welfare (Kotler & Lee, 2008; Andreasen, 2006; Smith, 2006). Effective social marketing strategies include audience segmentation, partnerships, and collaboration with cooperatives that have strong social missions (Beverland, 2007; Eckhardt et al., 2019). These strategies must consider the social and cultural context to be effective (Wymer, 2011; Goldberg et al., 2018).

Cooperative marketing has a long history, focusing on strategies that support small firms by providing access to resources, knowledge, and markets, often through shared channels and tactics (Sapiro, 1922; Karantininis et al., 2007; Majee & Hoyt, 2014; Walker et al., 2016; Palmer, 2002). The role of cooperatives in sustainable development and ethical business practices has also been highlighted (Gertler, 2001; Ferguson, 1997).

Community-based marketing combines social marketing with community engagement to create targeted interventions for social and environmental issues, such as recycling and public health (McKenzie-Mohr, 2011; Carrigan et al., 2011). Successful community-based marketing initiatives depend on building relationships and fostering a sense of community among participants (Kim et al., 2009; Kennedy, 2010; Juárez, 2011). The success of these initiatives depends on addressing root causes of social problems and creating lasting impact (Hamby et al., 2017; Lefebvre, 2012).

Ethical consumption, which involves making purchases based on moral and ethical considerations, has become a significant topic but faces challenges such as the "ethical consumption gap" between values and behavior (Carrington et al., 2016; Lewis & Potter, 2013). Studies suggest that ethical consumption is influenced by social and community networks, making it a collective process rather than an individual choice (Long & Murray, 2013; Carrigan et al., 2004). Critics argue that focusing on individual choice limits systemic change, underscoring the need to challenge structures that shape consumer culture (Carrier, 2008; Cabrera & Williams, 2014; Kosnik, 2018; Soper, 2016).

Digital technologies have revolutionized engagement with ethical products, increasing transparency and providing platforms for activism and consumer mobilization (Blair, 2017; Salido-Andres, 2018; Ali et al., 2023). However, they also pose challenges such as privacy concerns, the digital divide, and algorithmic biases (Reed, 2018; Humphery & Jordan, 2018; Hanlon, 2020; Polanco-Diges & Debasa, 2020). Addressing these challenges requires developing ethical and responsible digital marketing approaches (Romprasert & Trivedi, 2021; Freeman et al., 2015; Hoelscher & Chatzidakis, 2021).

Online activism has emerged as a powerful tool for social change, amplifying marginalized voices and mobilizing public support through strategies like social media campaigns and petitions (Wymer, 2010; Moorman, 2020; Hill, 2020). This has led to "brand activism," where companies are expected to take stands on social and political issues (Corcoran et al., 2016; Pimentel & Didonet, 2021; Key et al., 2021). Marketers must authentically engage with issues that matter to their customers while preparing to respond to activism targeting their brand (Sibai et al., 2021; Peattie & Samuel, 2018).

Gamification, the use of game design elements in non-game contexts, has proven effective in driving sustainable behaviors and promoting social change (Marin et al., 2021; Mitchell et al., 2017; Spanellis & Harviainen, 2021). It has been used in areas such as sustainability, climate change, and the sharing economy (Lee et al., 2013; Ouariachi et al., 2020). However, its effectiveness depends on design, implementation, and stakeholder engagement (Mitchell, 2020; Padilla-Zea et al., 2019).

Cooperative marketing extends beyond consumer outreach to include business-to-business (B2B) and cooperative-to-cooperative (C2C) interactions (Yee & Yazdani-fard, 2015; Gordon et al., 2022). C2C marketing focuses on collaboration among cooperatives through shared resources and joint ventures (Burksiene et al., 2019; Mabry & Mackert, 2014). This helps build a supportive network that strengthens the cooperative movement and promotes social economy growth (Viardot, 2013; Duong, 2017).

References

Adams, M., & Raisborough, J. (2010). Making a difference: Ethical consumption and the everyday. *The British Journal of Sociology, 61*(2), 256–274.

Adornes, G. S., & Muniz, R. J. (2019). Collaborative technology and motivations: Utilization, value and gamification. *Innovation & Management Review, 16*(3), 280–294.

Ali, I., Balta, M., & Papadopoulos, T. (2023). Social media platforms and social enterprise: Bibliometric analysis and systematic review. *International Journal of Information Management, 69*, 102510.

Alibakhshi, S., Seyyedamiri, N., Nazarian, A., & Atkinson, P. (2024). A win-win situation: Enhancing sharing economy platform brand equity by engaging business owners in CSR using gamification. *International Journal of Hospitality Management, 117*, 103636.

Andreasen, A. R. (1991). *Cheap but good marketing research*. Hinsdale, IL: Irwin Professional.

Andreasen, A. R. (Ed.). (2006). *Social Marketing in the 21st Century*. Sage.

Arcas, N., & Ruiz, S. (2003). Marketing and performance of fruit and vegetable co-operatives. *Journal of Co-operative Studies, 36*(1), 22–44.

Barnett, C., Cafaro, P., & Newholm, T. (2005). Philosophy and Ethical Consumption.In Harrison, R., ewholm, T. & Shaw, D. (Eds.), *The Ethical Consumer* (pp. 11–24). Sage Publications Ltd.

Barnett, C., Cloke, P., Clarke, N., & Malpass, A. (2010). *Globalizing Responsibility: The Political Rationalities of Ethical Consumption*. John Wiley & Sons.

Beverland, M. (2007). Can cooperatives brand? Exploring the interplay between cooperative structure and sustained brand marketing success. *Food Policy, 32*(4), 480–495.

Beverland, M. B. (2010). Can cooperatives build and sustain brands? In Lindgree, A., Hingley, M. & Custance, P. (Eds.), *Market Orientation: Transforming Food and Agribusiness around the Customer* (pp. 137–152). New York: Routledge.

Blair, M. K. (2017). Using digital and social media platforms for social marketing. In French, J., Blair-Stevens, C., McVey, D. & Merrit, R. (Eds.), *Social Marketing and Public Health: Theory and Practice* (pp. 201–216). Oxford: Oxford University Press.

Bob, C. (2001). Marketing rebellion: Insurgent groups, international media, and NGO support. *International Politics, 38*, 311–334.

Bryant, C. A., McCormack Brown, K. R., McDermott, R. J., Forthofer, M. S., Bumpus, E. C., Calkins, S. A., & Zapata, L. B. (2007). Community-based prevention marketing: Organizing a community for health behavior intervention. *Health Promotion Practice, 8*(2), 154–163.

Burksiene, V., Dvorak, J., & Duda, M. (2019). Upstream social marketing for implementing mobile government. *Societies, 9*(3), 54.

Cabrera, S. A., & Williams, C. L. (2014). Consuming for the social good: Marketing, consumer citizenship, and the possibilities of ethical consumption. *Critical Sociology, 40*(3), 349–367.

Carrier, J. G. (2008). Think locally, act globally: The political economy of ethical consumption. In De Neve, G., Peter, L., Pratt, J. & Wood, D. C. (Eds.), *Hidden Hands in the Market: Ethnographies of Fair Trade,*

Ethical Consumption, and Corporate Social Responsibility (pp. 31–51). Leeds: Emerald Group Publishing Limited.

Carrier, J. G., & Luetchford, P. G. (eds). (2022). *Ethical Consumption: Social Value and Economic Practice*. Berghahn Books.

Carrigan, M., Moraes, C., & Leek, S. (2011). Fostering responsible communities: A community social marketing approach to sustainable living. *Journal of Business Ethics, 100*, 515–534.

Carrigan, M., Szmigin, I., & Wright, J. (2004). Shopping for a better world? An interpretive study of the potential for ethical consumption within the older market. *Journal of Consumer Marketing, 21*(6), 401–417.

Carrington, M. J., Zwick, D., & Neville, B. (2016). The ideology of the ethical consumption gap. *Marketing Theory, 16*(1), 21–38.

Challita, S., Aurier, P., & Sentis, P. (2019). Linking branding strategy to ownership structure, financial performance and stability: Case of French wine cooperatives. *International Journal of Entrepreneurship and Small Business, 36*(3), 292–307.

Chandy, R. K., Johar, G. V., Moorman, C., & Roberts, J. H. (2021). Better marketing for a better world. *Journal of Marketing, 85*(3), 1–9.

Corcoran, M., Newman, K., & Devasagayam, P. R. (2016). Consumer perception of corporate activism: Strategic implication for marketing. *International Journal of Academic Research in Business and Social Sciences, 6*(10), 52–61.

Dahl, S., Eagle, L., & Low, D. (2015). Integrated marketing communications and social marketing: Together for the common good? *Journal of Social Marketing, 5*(3), 226–240.

Dickinson, S., & Ramaseshan, B. (2004). An investigation of the antecedents to cooperative marketing strategy implementation. *Journal of Strategic Marketing, 12*(2), 71–95.

Dokhanchi, A., Manian, A., Amiri, M., & Hassanzadeh, A. (2019). Social campaigns on online platforms as a new form of public sphere in digital era: A critical review. *Journal of Information Technology Management, 11*(3), 81–95.

Domegan, C., Collins, K., Stead, M., McHugh, P., & Hughes, T. (2013). Value co-creation in social marketing: Functional or fanciful? *Journal of Social Marketing, 3*(3), 239–256.

Duong, H. T. (2017). Fourth generation NGOs: Communication strategies in social campaigning and resource mobilization. *Journal of Nonprofit & Public Sector Marketing, 29*(2), 119–147.

Eckhardt, G. M., Houston, M. B., Jiang, B., Lamberton, C., Rindfleisch, A., & Zervas, G. (2019). Marketing in the sharing economy. *Journal of Marketing, 83*(5), 5–27.

Ferguson, A. (1997). Values, marketing, and cooperation: Where's our common ground? In *Marketing our co-operative advantage: Creativity, innovation, success*. MOCA Conference, 14–16 November 1996, Marlboro, MA. Greenfield, MA, and Antigonish, NS. Co-operative Development Institute, St. Francis Xavier University Extension Department.

Fernández Galeote, D., Rajanen, M., Rajanen, D., Legaki, N. Z., Langley, D. J., & Hamari, J. (2021). Gamification for climate change engagement: Review of corpus and future agenda. *Environmental Research Letters, 16*(6), 063004.

Flaherty, T., Domegan, C., Duane, S., Brychkov, D., & Anand, M. (2020). Systems social marketing and macro-social marketing: A systematic review. *Social Marketing Quarterly, 26*(2), 146–166.

Freeman, B., Potente, S., Rock, V., & McIver, J. (2015). Social media campaigns that make a difference: What can public health learn from the corporate sector and other social change marketers. *Public Health Res Pract, 25*(2), e2521517.

Gertler, M. E. (2001). *Rural Co-operatives and Sustainable Development* (No. 1754-2016-141539).

Giorgos, T., Eleni, T., Theodossia, L., Stelios, K., & George, R. (2012). The dynamics of branding in a small agricultural cooperative. *MIBES TRANSACTIONS International Journal, 6*, 78–89.

Goldberg, M. E., Fishbein, M., & Middlestadt, S. E. (eds). (2018). *Social Marketing: Theoretical and Practical Perspectives*. Psychology Press.

Gopaldas, A. (2015). Creating firm, customer, and societal value: Toward a theory of positive marketing. *Journal of Business Research*, *68*(12), 2446–2451.

Gordon, R. (2013). Unlocking the potential of upstream social marketing. *European Journal of Marketing*, *47*(9), 1525–1547.

Gordon, R., Dibb, S., Magee, C., Cooper, P., & Waitt, G. (2018). Empirically testing the concept of value-in-behavior and its relevance for social marketing. *Journal of Business Research*, *82*, 56–67.

Gordon, R., Spotswood, F., & Dibb, S. (2022). Critical social marketing: Towards emancipation? *Journal of Marketing Management*, *38*(11–12), 1043–1071.

Graham, M., & Haarstad, H. (2014). Transparency and Development: Ethical Consumption through Web 2.0 and the Internet of Things.*Open Development: Networked Innovations in International Development, 7*, 1–18.

Haldeman, T., & Turner, J. W. (2009). Implementing a community-based social marketing program to increase recycling. *Social Marketing Quarterly*, *15*(3), 114–127.

Hamby, A., Pierce, M., & Brinberg, D. (2017). Solving complex problems: Enduring solutions through social entrepreneurship, community action, and social marketing. *Journal of Macromarketing*, *37*(4), 369–380.

Hanlon, A. (2020). Digital marketing and social media. In Eagle, L., Dahl, S., De Pelsmacker, P. & Taylor, C. R. (Eds.), *The SAGE Handbook of Marketing Ethics* (pp. 424–443). London: Sage Publications.

Hardesty, S. D. (2005). Cooperatives as marketers of branded products. *Journal of Food Distribution Research*, *36*(856-2016-57476), 237–242.

Hassan, L., & Leigh, E. (2021). Do you have a moment to increase world awesome? Game-based engagement with social change. In Spanellis, A. & Harviainen, J. T. (Eds.), *Transforming Society and Organizations through Gamification: From the Sustainable Development Goals to Inclusive Workplaces* (pp. 49–65). Cham: Springer International Publishing.

Hill, S. (2020). Politics and corporate content: Situating corporate strategic communication between marketing and activism. *International Journal of Strategic Communication*, *14*(5), 317–329.

Hoelscher, V., & Chatzidakis, A. (2021). Ethical consumption communities across physical and digital spaces: An exploration of their complementary and synergistic affordances. *Journal of Business Ethics*, *172*, 291–306.

Holt, D. B. (2012). Constructing sustainable consumption: From ethical values to the cultural transformation of unsustainable markets. *The ANNALS of the American Academy of Political and Social Science*, *644*(1), 236–255.

Huber, M. Z., & Hilty, L. M. (2015). Gamification and sustainable consumption: Overcoming the limitations of persuasive technologies. In Hilty, L. M. & Aebischer, B. (Eds.), *ICT Innovations for Sustainability* (pp. 367–385). Basel: Springer International Publishing.

Humphery, K., & Jordan, T. (2018). Mobile moralities: Ethical consumption in the digital realm. *Journal of Consumer Culture*, *18*(4), 520–538.

Juárez, F. (2011). A critical review of relationship marketing: Strategies to include community into marketing in development contexts. *African Journal of Business Management*, *5*(35), 13404–13409.

Jussila, I., Tuominen, P., & Saksa, J. M. (2008). Following a different mission: Where and how do consumer co-operatives compete? *Journal of Co-operative Studies*, *41*(3), 28–39.

Karantininis, K., Nilsson, J., Kalogeras, N., Pennings, J. M., Dijk, G. V., & van der Lans, I. A. (2007). The structure of marketing cooperatives: A members' perspective. In Karantininis, K. & Nilsson, J. (Eds.), *Vertical Markets and Cooperative Hierarchies: The Role of Cooperatives in the Agri-Food Industry* (pp. 73–92). Dordrecht: Springer.

Kennedy, A. L. (2010). Using community-based social marketing techniques to enhance environmental regulation. *Sustainability*, *2*(4), 1138–1160.

Key, T. M., Keel, A. L., Czaplewski, A. J., & Olson, E. M. (2021). Brand activism change agents: Strategic storytelling for impact and authenticity. *Journal of Strategic Marketing*, *31*(7), 1–17.

Kim, S. H., Yang, K. H., & Kim, J. K. (2009). Finding critical success factors for virtual community marketing. *Service Business, 3*, 149–171.

Klein N. (1999). *No Logo: Taking Aim at the Brand Bullies*. New York: Picador.

Klein, N. (2007). *The Shock Doctrine: The Rise of Disaster Capitalism*. New York: Metropolitan Books.

Klein, N. (2014). *This Changes Everything: Capitalism vs. The Climate*. New York: Simon & Schuster.

Kosnik, E. (2018). Production for consumption: Prosumer, citizen-consumer, and ethical consumption in a postgrowth context. *Economic Anthropology, 5*(1), 123–134.

Kotler, P., & Andreasen, A. R. (1991). *Strategic Marketing for Nonprofit Organizations* (4th edition). Englewood Cliffs, NJ: Prentice Hall.

Kotler, P., & Lee, N. (2008). *Social Marketing: Influencing Behaviors for Good*. Sage.

Lee, J. J., Matamoros, E., Kern, R., Marks, J., de Luna, C., & Jordan-Cooley, W. (2013). Greenify: Fostering sustainable communities via gamification. In Mackay, W. E. (Ed.), *CHI'13 Extended Abstracts on Human Factors in Computing Systems* (pp. 1497–1502). New York: Association for Computing Machinery.

Lefebvre, R. C. (2012). Transformative social marketing: Co-creating the social marketing discipline and brand. *Journal of Social Marketing, 2*(2), 118–129.

Lefebvre, R. C. (2013). *Social Marketing and Social Change: Strategies and Tools for Improving Health, Well-being, and the Environment*. John Wiley & Sons.

Lekakis, E. J. (2014). ICTs and ethical consumption: The political and market futures of fair trade. *Futures, 62*, 164–172.

Lewis, T., & Potter, E. (2013). *Ethical Consumption: A Critical Introduction*. Routledge.

Lim, W. M. (2020). The sharing economy: A marketing perspective. *Australasian Marketing Journal, 28*(3), 4–13.

Long, M. A., & Murray, D. L. (2013). Ethical consumption, values convergence/divergence and community development. *Journal of Agricultural and Environmental Ethics, 26*, 351–375.

Maan, J. (2013). Social business transformation through gamification. *International Journal of Managing Information Technology, 5*(3), 9–16.

Mabry, A. & Mackert, M. (2014). Advancing use of norms for social marketing: extending the theory of normative social behavior. *International Review on Public and Nonprofit Marketing, 11*(2), 129–143.

Mahoney, L. M., & Tang, T. (2024). *Strategic Social Media: From Marketing to Social Change*. John Wiley & Sons.

Majee, W., & Hoyt, A. (2014). Are worker-owned cooperatives the brewing pots for social capital? In Gonzales, V. & Phillips, R. (Eds.), *Cooperatives and Community Development* (pp. 111–124). London and New York: Routledge.

Marin, S., Lee, V., & Landers, R. N. (2021). Gamified active learning and its potential for social change. In *Transforming Society and Organizations through Gamification: From the Sustainable Development Goals to Inclusive Workplaces* (pp. 205–223). Springer International Publishing.

Mazur-Stommen, S., & Farley, K. (2016). *Games for grownups: The role of gamification in climate change and sustainability*. Washington, DC: Indicia Consulting LLC.

Mazzarol, T., Limnios, E. M., & Reboud, S. (2013). Co-operatives as a strategic network of small firms: Case studies from Australian and French co-operatives. *Journal of Co-operative Organization and Management, 1*(1), 27–40.

McKenzie-Mohr, D. (2011). *Fostering Sustainable Behavior: An Introduction to Community-based Social Marketing*. New Society Publishers.

Mitchell, R. (2020). *Gamification and Behaviour Change: Understanding the Mechanism and its Implications for Social Marketing* (Doctoral dissertation, Queensland University of Technology).

Mitchell, R., Schuster, L., & Drennan, J. (2017). Understanding how gamification influences behaviour in social marketing. *Australasian Marketing Journal, 25*(1), 12–19.

Moorman, C. (2020). Commentary: Brand activism in a political world. *Journal of Public Policy & Marketing, 39*(4), 388–392.

Nayyar, V. (2023). The role of marketing analytics in the ethical consumption of online consumers. *Total Quality Management & Business Excellence, 34*(7–8), 1015–1031.

Negruşa, A. L., Toader, V., Sofică, A., Tutunea, M. F., & Rus, R. V. (2015). Exploring gamification techniques and applications for sustainable tourism. *Sustainability, 7*(8), 11160–11189.

Nilsson, J., Ruffio, P., & Gouin, S. (2007). Do consumers care about cooperatives? In Karantininis, K. & Nilsson, J. (Eds.), *Vertical Markets and Cooperative Hierarchies* (pp. 225–243). Dordrecht: Springer.

Nzili, J. M. (2003). *Strategic Marketing and Performance of NGOs in Kenya: The Case of Development Non-Government Organisations* (Doctoral dissertation, University of Nairobi).

Ouariachi, T., Li, C. Y., & Elving, W. J. (2020). Gamification approaches for education and engagement on pro-environmental behaviors: Searching for best practices. *Sustainability, 12*(11), 4565.

Padilla-Zea, N., Aceto, S., & Burgos, D. (2019). Social seducement: Empowering social economy entrepreneurship. The training approach. *International Journal of Interactive Multimedia & Artificial Intelligence, 5*(7), 135–150.

Palmer, A. (2002). Cooperative marketing associations: An investigation into the causes of effectiveness. *Journal of Strategic Marketing, 10*(2), 135–156.

Peattie, K., & Samuel, A. (2018). Fairtrade towns as unconventional networks of ethical activism. *Journal of Business Ethics, 153*, 265–282.

Pecoraro, M. G., & Uusitalo, O. (2014). Conflicting values of ethical consumption in diverse worlds—A cultural approach. *Journal of Consumer Culture, 14*(1), 45–65.

Pimentel, P. C., & Didonet, S. R. (2021). Brand activism as a marketing strategy: Proposing a typology. Presented online at *IX Encontro De Marketing Da Anpad-EMA 2021 (9th ANPAD—EMA Marketing Meeting)*. Retrieved from https://anpad.com.br/uploads/articles/110/approved/05049e90fa4f5039a8cad c6acbb4b2cc.pdf (accessed February 17, 2024).

Polanco-Diges, L., & Debasa, F. (2020). The use of digital marketing strategies in the sharing economy: A literature review. *Journal of Spatial and Organizational Dynamics, 8*(3), 217–229.

Popan, C., Perez, D., & Woodcock, J. (2023). Cards against gamification: Using a role-playing game to tell alternative futures in the gig economy. *The Sociological Review, 71*(5), 1058–1074.

Rao, H. (2008). *Market Rebels: How Activists Make or Break Radical Innovations.* Princeton University Press.

Reed, T. V. (2018). *Digitized Lives: Culture, Power and Social Change in the Internet Era.* Routledge.

Richardson, J. (1995). The market for political activism: Interest groups as a challenge to political parties. *West European Politics, 18*(1), 116–139.

Romprasert, S., & Trivedi, A. (2021). Sustainable economy on community enterprise and digital marketing. *ABAC Journal, 41*(1), 62–80.

Salido-Andres, N. (2018). *Social Marketing and Digital Platforms: Donation-based Crowdfunding Campaigns.* Dissertation. University of Coruña.

Sapiro, A. (1922). Cooperative marketing. *Iowa L. Rev., 8*, 193.

Saunders, S. G., Barrington, D. J., & Sridharan, S. (2015). Redefining social marketing: Beyond behavioural change. *Journal of Social Marketing, 5*(2), 160–168.

Saura, J. R., Palos-Sanchez, P., & Rodríguez Herráez, B. (2020). Digital marketing for sustainable growth: Business models and online campaigns using sustainable strategies. *Sustainability, 12*(3), 1003.

Shareable (Ed.) (2018). *Sharing Cities: Activating the Urban Commons.* Shareable. Available at: https://www. shareable.net/sharing-cities (accessed February 17, 2024).

Sibai, O., Mimoun, L., & Boukis, A. (2021). Authenticating brand activism: Negotiating the boundaries of free speech to make a change. *Psychology & Marketing, 38*(10), 1651–1669.

Singh, L. P. (2000). *Cooperative marketing in India and abroad.* Mumbai: Himalaya Publishing House.

Slater, M. D., Kelly, K., & Edwards, R. (2000). Integrating social marketing, community readiness and media advocacy in community-based prevention efforts. *Social Marketing Quarterly, 6*(3), 124–137.

Smith, W. A. (2006). Social marketing: An overview of approach and effects. *Injury Prevention, 12*(suppl 1), i38–i43.

Soper, K. (2016). Towards a sustainable flourishing: Ethical consumption and the politics of prosperity. In Shaw, D., Carrington, M. & Chatzidakis, A. (Eds.), *Ethics and Morality in Consumption* (pp. 43–59). New York and London: Routledge.

Spanellis, A., & Harviainen, J. T. (2021). An introduction to societal transformation through gamification. In *Transforming Society and Organizations through Gamification: From the Sustainable Development Goals to Inclusive Workplaces* (pp. 3–9). Springer International Publishing.

Spar, D. L., & La Mure, L. T. (2003). The power of activism: Assessing the impact of NGOs on global business. *California Management Review, 45*(3), 78–101.

Starr, M. A. (2009). The social economics of ethical consumption: Theoretical considerations and empirical evidence. *The Journal of Socio-Economics, 38*(6), 916–925.

Viardot, E. (2013). The role of cooperatives in overcoming the barriers to adoption of renewable energy. *Energy Policy, 63*, 756–764.

Walker, B., Wolford, B., Sasser, D., Verbois, C., & Bell, L. (2016). Launching a comprehensive SNAP-Ed social marketing campaign utilizing the cooperative extension model. *Journal of Nutrition Education and Behavior, 48*(7), S84.

White, T. (2015). The branding of community supported agriculture: Collective myths and opportunities. *Journal of Agriculture, Food Systems, and Community Development, 5*(3), 45–62.

White, T., & Marchet, F. (2021). Digital social markets: Exploring the opportunities and impacts of gamification and reward mechanisms in citizen engagement and smart city services. In Aldinhas Ferreira, M. I. (Ed.), *How Smart Is Your City? Technological Innovation, Ethics and Inclusiveness* (pp. 103–125). Cham: Springer.

Wymer, W. (2010). Rethinking the boundaries of social marketing: Activism or advertising? *Journal of Business Research, 63*(2), 99–103.

Wymer, W. (2011). Developing more effective social marketing strategies. *Journal of Social Marketing, 1*(1), 17–31.

Yee, F. M., & Yazdanifard, R. (2015). The comparison between NGO marketing and conventional marketing practices from SWOT analysis, marketing mix, and performance evaluation perspectives. *International Journal of Management, Accounting & Economics, 2*(9), 1075–1087.

Youn, S., & Lee, S. (2019). Consumer cooperative brand identity. In Jang, S. (Ed.), *The Management of Consumer Co-Operatives in Korea: Identity, Participation and Sustainability* (p. 81). London: Routledge.

Chapter 8
Cooperative Strategy: Social Value Creation

Introduction

The social economy refers to economic activities and organizations that prioritize social goals and reinvesting profits for community benefit over private gain. This includes cooperatives, mutual societies, associations, foundations, social enterprises, and other entities that operate based on principles of cooperation, equality, democracy, and valuing people over profit. Realizing the potential of the social economy requires thoughtful strategy and planning to effectively translate its core values into concrete models of value creation that improve goods, services and community well-being.

Strategy is crucial because there is no singular blueprint or "one size fits all" approach for building a thriving social economy. Rather, for it to successfully take root, strategies must be innovative, contextualized and tailored to the diverse needs, challenges, and aspirations of different communities. At its core, effective social economy strategy requires clearly understanding the relationships between its guiding principles and values, and how to design economic structures, processes, and incentives that bring these values to life.

Fundamentally, the social economy aims to foster cooperation rather than competition, embracing collaborative business models such as cooperatives where workers or consumers collectively own and govern enterprises. Strategies should consider how to cultivate meaningful cooperation across organizations, sectors, and even regions. This could involve creating social economy clusters or networks for peer learning and joint initiatives. It entails building connections along value chains, from production to consumption, that are underpinned by solidarity and reciprocity versus profit maximization by single entities.

Further, the social economy seeks to advance equality, which has implications for strategy to genuinely shift power dynamics. Leadership and decision-making authority must be distributed across stakeholders, not concentrated at the top. Strategies should enable democratic governance and participation within organizations. There is also a broader question of how the social economy can reduce wealth inequality and improve economic outcomes for marginalized groups through community wealth building approaches.

In terms of enacting the value of democracy, this points to the need for participatory strategic planning processes that engage all those impacted to define shared goals and the strategies to attain them. This can be assisted by facilitative leadership that supports collective strategic thinking versus hierarchical management practices. Strategies should also foster local self-organization and self-management versus centralized control, enabling context-specific solutions tailored to community needs and priorities.

https://doi.org/10.1515/9783111080147-008

At a nuts-and-bolts level, social economy strategies must grapple with the design of appropriate ownership models, governance structures, finance and funding mechanisms, and value chains that embed principles of cooperation and mutualism into core economic activities. For instance, introducing shared platforms and commons approaches for collaborative production and consumption. Or configuring value chains that directly link ethically driven producers with community members. Strategies should seek to combine the strengths of alternative models like cooperatives and social enterprises to create hybrid approaches when helpful to reconcile both economic and social imperatives.

Given the diversity of community contexts, social economy strategies should have flexibility for local adaptation rather than monolithic solutions. This calls for ongoing social innovation to respond to emerging realities on the ground. Strategic skill is required to leverage existing assets and regional strengths, while addressing gaps and introducing new models tailored to support disadvantaged populations. A key question is how to plan for financially self-sustaining social economy organizations and activities that can operate effectively over the long-term without dependence on charitable funding.

In essence, advancing the social economy requires reimagining economic strategies from the ground up, starting from principles rather than just pursuing profit. This entails understanding value creation not narrowly in terms of money but more broadly, advancing human dignity, social justice, ecological sustainability, cooperative community, and democratic self-governance. With thoughtful, context-driven strategies guided by its underlying values, the social economy offers a powerful pathway to build economies that work for all people and the planet.

Critical Strategy

Strategy is crucial for realizing the potential of the social economy, which refers to economic activities prioritizing social goals like cooperation and community benefit (Husted et al., 2015). Strategy provides a plan of actions that fit together to reach a destination (Johnson et al., 2020). There are traditionally three levels of strategy relevant to the social economy.

Corporate strategy defines the overall direction and vision for advancing the social economy on a societal level. This involves setting broad goals, like growing the ecosystem of social economy organizations, mainstreaming social procurement policies, and assessing the macro conditions needed for the model to thrive (Porter, 1991). Corporate strategy also entails movement-building to unite diverse stakeholders under a shared vision of an economy centered on meeting human needs versus profit maximization (Frynas, 2015).

Business strategy exists under the corporate strategy to outline how specific social economy entities like cooperatives, social enterprises, and associations can achieve impact on the ground (Bowman & Ambrosini, 2000). This includes designing sustainable business models, securing financing, identifying target beneficiaries, and developing products/services tailored to their needs (Dobni, 2010). Business strategy is where the rubber meets the road in terms of translating the ideals of the social economy into concrete organizational activities and impact (Haksever et al., 2004).

Functional strategy describes how individuals within social economy organizations make decisions aligned with broader strategic aims. This refers to the day-to-day choices of managers, employees, and volunteers that should reflect the entities' social mission and values (Freedman, 2015). Functional strategy is thus the micro-level of aligning processes and individual actions with the meso-level of organizational strategy and macro-level societal vision.

Importantly, while traditional businesses often have strategy flowing top-down, the social economy requires integrating strategy across levels (Johnson et al., 2020). Participatory planning engages stakeholders at all levels to define collaborative strategies reflecting joint priorities. There is also significant feedback between levels, with lessons from on-the-ground activities informing adaptation of organizational and movement-wide approaches (Porter, 1991).

A reference point is the European Union's Social Economy Action Plan, which identifies strategies needed at the EU level to create an enabling environment for the model to grow (Dobni, 2010). This includes assessing legal frameworks, access to finance, capacity building, and raising awareness. The plan serves as a macro-level strategy identifying supportive conditions for the social economy ecosystem.

National governments also play a key strategic role through policies like preferential procurement from social enterprises or tax incentives for non-profit reinvestment of surplus (Bowman & Ambrosini, 2000). These macro-level public policies create fertile ground for meso-level organizations by shaping the broader environment.

Meanwhile, civil society networks pursue movement-building strategies to unite stakeholders under a shared vision for transforming economies to center mutualism over individualism (Frynas, 2015). They promote narratives and cultural mindset shifts to mainstream the social economy's values.

On the meso-level, individual social economy entities engage in organizational strategy and planning to translate principles into practice (Haksever et al., 2004). This means designing business models, target beneficiaries, performance metrics, marketing approaches, and funding models that enact values of cooperation, community benefit, and sustainability.

At the micro-level, social economy managers, employees, and volunteers make tactical choices reflecting the organization's social mission. This day-to-day integration of strategic principles operationalizes strategy on the frontlines. Workers in a social cooperative govern themselves and share profits based on strategic commitments to equality and participation (Freedman, 2015). Non-profit association staff choose programs responding to community needs identified through inclusive strategic planning.

In essence, an aligned social economy strategy requires coordination across societal, organizational and individual levels (Johnson et al., 2020). This ensures a unified ecosystem supporting the propagation of economic activities for the common good.

KEY THINKER: J. K. Gibson-Graham

J.K. Gibson-Graham, the pen name shared by feminist economic geographers Julie Graham and Katherine Gibson, has made groundbreaking contributions to rethinking economic systems and exploring diverse economies beyond capitalism. Their work challenges conventional views that see capitalism as the dominant or only viable economic structure and illuminates the varied economic practices that coexist globally. Through their influential books, collaborative research networks, and community-based projects, they've paved the way for new possibilities to envision more equitable and sustainable economies.

The intellectual partnership between Julie Graham and Katherine Gibson began in the 1990s, driven by a shared interest in critiquing capitalism and uncovering alternative economic forms. Under the joint pen name J. K. Gibson-Graham, they published their seminal book *The End of Capitalism (As We Knew It)* in 1996, which redefined understandings of capitalism's place in the global economy. The book argued that mainstream economic thinking imposes a "capitalocentric" perspective—one that frames all economic activities as part of, in opposition to, or dependent on capitalism. This narrow view obscures the diversity of economic practices such as cooperatives, gift exchanges, and subsistence activities that don't fit neatly into capitalist categories.

Their work introduced a language of economic diversity that emphasizes the variety of transactions, labor forms, enterprise types, and ecological relationships. By exposing these multiple economic identities, they sought to dismantle the notion that capitalism is the only framework through which economies can be understood. This has opened up space for recognizing, valuing, and nurturing non-capitalist economic practices.

Building on these theoretical interventions, Gibson-Graham's later work focuses on constructing community economies in practice. They have argued that critiques of capitalism need to be complemented by concrete, localized efforts to build economic systems rooted in community values, environmental sustainability, and social well-being. Their involvement in the Community Economies Research Network (CERN) and the Community Economies Collective (CEC) has connected researchers and activists worldwide to collaboratively develop community-centered economic projects.

A key feature of their approach is local action research, which involves engaging closely with communities to co-create initiatives based on local strengths and needs. This participatory research method aims to foster the development of community-based enterprises, cooperative structures, and solidarity economies that prioritize human and ecological well-being over profit maximization. By supporting communities in identifying their own assets and aspirations, Gibson-Graham emphasizes that economic transformation should emerge from the collective actions of communities rather than from top-down directives.

Gibson-Graham's work also critiques the dominant narrative of economic development that equates progress with GDP growth. They advocate for alternative narratives that measure success through social and ecological well-being, community resilience, and economic justice. This includes elevating the value of unpaid and non-market work, such as caregiving and subsistence production, as well as non-monetary forms of exchange like gift-giving and sharing.

Their concept of "economic subjectivity" emphasizes the role of individuals as active agents in creating their economic futures. By shifting mindsets from passive recipients to empowered participants, their work aims to cultivate capacities for democratic participation and local economic governance.

While their contributions have inspired a generation of scholars and activists, some critics argue that Gibson-Graham's focus on local, community-based approaches risks underestimating the structural constraints and power relations that influence broader economic outcomes. Others question whether such initiatives alone can address systemic global challenges like inequality and ecological crisis.

Despite these critiques, Gibson-Graham's emphasis on economic diversity and their commitment to rethinking economic possibilities beyond capitalism remain highly influential. Their work continues to offer valuable strategies for constructing more diverse, democratic, and sustainable economies. Through local action, collaborative research, and ongoing advocacy, their contributions shape efforts to build inclusive and resilient communities that prioritize social and ecological well-being over economic growth.

Values and Value Creation

Values deeply shape what is considered "valuable" and the aims of value creation initiatives. Different ideologies and economic models hold distinct core values, which translate into divergent approaches to improving processes, goods, and services (Husted et al., 2015).

In the private sphere, value creation typically focuses on maximizing profitability, efficiency, and satisfying consumer demand (Low, 2000). The main actors are private corporations and businesses driven by the values of self-interest, competition, and capital accumulation (Haksever et al., 2004). Strategies for value creation revolve around increasing revenues, reducing costs, capturing market share, developing new revenue streams and raising shareholder returns (Prahalad & Ramaswamy, 2004). Financial worth is the primary metric of value (Grönroos & Voima, 2013).

The public sphere emphasizes universal access, welfare, and benefits for the population at large (Tantalo & Priem, 2016). Main actors include government agencies and public institutions guided by values of equity, collective well-being, and social rights (Schiuma et al., 2012). Value creation centers on the availability and quality of public goods like healthcare, education, infrastructure, and environmental health that market forces alone cannot provide (Foster, 2007). The key measure of value is social impact (Chui et al., 2012).

The social economy and commons-based approaches stress cooperation, solidarity, and grassroots self-governance (Laukkanen & Tura, 2020). Key actors are cooperatives, non-profit associations, mutual societies, and local community groups (Matei & Dorobantu, 2015). Value creation focuses on improving community conditions and supporting disadvantaged groups through collaborative methods (Potts & Hartley, 2015). Democratic participation in decision-making is a core process value. The generation of mutual value rather than only individual gain is the hallmark.

A private corporation motivated by shareholder returns might pursue value creation by cutting labor costs, externalizing social/environmental costs, and lobbying for tax breaks and regulatory exemptions (Low, 2000). Public interest is secondary. In contrast, a public hospital aims to enhance healthcare availability and quality for all as a primary value, though fiscal sustainability remains important (Haksever et al., 2004).

A cooperative agricultural enterprise could pursue value creation through fair trade supply chains benefiting small farmers, organic production methods, and humane livestock practices reflecting the environmental and social values of members (Prahalad & Ramaswamy, 2004). Surpluses could fund community programs versus private profits. This mutual value approach diverges from conventional agribusiness models maximizing investor returns (Grönroos & Voima, 2013).

Often these spheres interact and overlap in practice. Public–private partnerships between governments and businesses aim to develop infrastructure and services by blending public and private interests (Tantalo & Priem, 2016). Efficacy depends on how well values are aligned for the partnership purpose. Social enterprises also bridge sectors, pursuing community benefits through commercial activities in contrast to profit-maximizing firms (Schiuma et al., 2012).

Likewise, governments support cooperatives and social economy organizations through procurement contracts, funding, and capacity building to catalyze alternative approaches to value creation (Foster, 2007). Some local authorities have shifted from procuring services from large corporations toward contracting local social enterprises and non-profits, better aligning with public values of community benefit (Chui et al., 2012).

Multi-stakeholder partnerships between communities, government, businesses, and non-profits allow aligning diverse values to co-create initiatives serving each constituency (Laukkanen & Tura, 2020). For instance, an economic development project with joint design bringing skills and finance from businesses, facilities and land from government, and grassroots networks and labor from communities (Matei & Dorobantu, 2015).

In essence, value creation is inextricable from underlying values and worldviews about what constitutes improvement and progress (Potts & Hartley, 2015). Private, public, and social/mutual conceptions of value can either be oppositional or can forge thoughtful syntheses depending on the initiative (Low, 2000). Strategy involves articulating how value creation in a given context aligns with core values and advances a version of social, environmental, and economic progress (Haksever et al., 2004). What might enhance financial returns for some, may undermine collective well-being for others (Prahalad & Ramaswamy, 2004). Clarifying these relationships is key (Grönroos & Voima, 2013).

Businesses guided by shareholder primacy often subscribe to values of individualism, self-interest, and unfettered markets as producing optimal social outcomes (Tantalo & Priem, 2016). Value creation focuses on maximizing share price, revenues, profits, market share, and satisfying customer demand through efficiency and competitive advantage (Schiuma et al., 2012). Financial worth is the key metric. Negative externalities on workers, communities or environment may be discounted if they don't directly impact the bottom line (Foster, 2007).

In contrast, the public sector is mission-driven to serve broad citizen interests and provide essential goods unmet by markets (Chui et al., 2012). Key values are equity, collective well-being, fairness, and social rights. Value creation prioritizes availability and quality of social services, infrastructure, environmental protection, and economic stability for all (Laukkanen & Tura, 2020). The measure is social impact. Fiscal prudence remains important, but subordinated to public benefit (Matei & Dorobantu, 2015).

The social/solidarity economy stresses cooperation, ethics, democracy, sustainability, and grassroots self-governance as core values (Potts & Hartley, 2015). It seeks to generate mutual value, benefiting disadvantaged populations through organizations like co-ops, associations, social enterprises, and community land trusts (Low, 2000). Strategies involve equitable trade, organic agriculture, platform cooperatives, and peer-to-peer collaborative production guided by social and ecological values rather than only profit motives (Haksever et al., 2004).

In practice, blurred boundaries exist across spheres. Public–private partnerships can align government oversight and private sector efficiency to build infrastructure and deliver services (Prahalad & Ramaswamy, 2004). The balance of values shapes outcomes. Social enterprises blend commercial means with social missions, creatively navigating tensions between earning income and community benefit (Grönroos & Voima, 2013).

Governments increasingly contract social economy entities for services, recognizing their local ties and social values. Multi-stakeholder collaboratives allow diverse partners to negotiate shared values and co-design initiatives advancing mutual interests (Tantalo & Priem, 2016). A community land trust can integrate public financing, private investment, non-profit stewardship, and resident control to develop affordable housing and communal assets.

Ultimately, surfacing the connection between underlying values, visions of progress, and approaches to value creation across economic spheres provides clarity (Schiuma et al., 2012). Private, public, and social logics should thoughtfully synthesize, not assume inherent conflict (Foster, 2007). Hybrid approaches blending market, state, and community can forge inclusive, sustainable models of value creation (Chui et al., 2012). But this requires unpacking assumptions, bridging worldviews, and negotiating shared values to expand considerations of what is truly "valuable" for society (Laukkanen & Tura, 2020).

CASE STUDY: Banca Etica—A Pioneering Model of Cooperative Ethical Finance

Founded in 1999, Banca Etica in Italy represents a unique model of cooperative finance dedicated entirely to ethical banking. Its core mission is rooted in a vision of finance that prioritizes societal well-being, environmental stewardship, and social justice over profit. This case study examines how Banca Etica translates these values into a successful banking model, offering an alternative to conventional finance through a focus on community, sustainability, and transparency.

Banca Etica operates on the belief that financial institutions should serve the interests of society as a whole, guided by the principle that "the highest interest is that of everyone." Its mission is based on principles of justice, reciprocity, and equal dignity for all. The bank promotes a model of development that prioritizes both individual and community needs, viewing wealth as more than just monetary gain. Banca Etica's definition of wealth includes knowledge, diversity, social bonds, and ecological capital. By promoting sustainable development, supporting marginalized communities, and advancing social inclusion, the bank positions itself as an active player in fostering collective growth.

The bank's cooperative approach involves collaboration between public institutions, businesses, and civil society organizations to reinforce local welfare systems. Banca Etica sees its role as not merely financial but as a partner in civil and economic growth. It champions volunteering, encourages stakeholder engagement, and supports bottom-up co-planning processes, all while working alongside public entities to uphold citizenship rights and ensure access to essential services.

Banca Etica's financial model directs its activities toward the real economy, supporting initiatives that create social, cultural, and environmental value. This commitment is reflected in its investment strategy, which prioritizes projects and organizations that adhere to sustainability and social justice principles. Examples of Banca Etica's ethical finance in action include:

– Social and cooperative projects: The bank provides loans to social cooperatives and non-profits working with marginalized groups, such as people with disabilities, refugees, and those in poverty. These loans help these organizations expand their services and achieve greater social impact.
– Environmental sustainability: Banca Etica finances renewable energy projects, organic agriculture, and other eco-friendly enterprises. Its support for green projects aligns with its broader goal of promoting sustainability and environmental responsibility.

- Microcredit and local economic development: The bank offers microcredit and other financial services aimed at small entrepreneurs and local businesses, fostering economic growth and social inclusion in local communities.
- Shareholder activism and corporate responsibility: Banca Etica engages in shareholder activism, advocating for corporate social responsibility and promoting divestment from industries that cause harm, such as fossil fuels and arms manufacturing.

A core component of Banca Etica's model is transparency. The bank is committed to providing detailed information on how depositors' funds are used and involves customers in decision-making processes about which projects to finance. This openness has built a high level of trust and loyalty among its stakeholders.

Despite its successes, Banca Etica faces challenges in maintaining its financial sustainability while adhering to strict ethical criteria, particularly in a competitive market dominated by larger banks. Balancing ethical commitments with economic viability can be difficult, especially during economic downturns. However, Banca Etica's resilience during crises, such as the 2008 financial collapse, highlighted the strength of its model. While other banks reduced lending, Banca Etica continued to support the real economy, demonstrating the robustness and reliability of ethical finance.

Banca Etica's pioneering approach has had a tangible impact on communities and the broader banking sector. By financing projects that generate social, environmental, and cultural value, the bank showcases how finance can be a tool for positive change. Its practices have supported the development of cooperative businesses, advanced sustainability initiatives, and promoted social inclusion. The bank's emphasis on stakeholder engagement and transparency has also set new standards for accountability in the finance industry.

While small compared to other Italian banks, Banca Etica's unique value proposition and loyal customer base have enabled it to weather market fluctuations. Its continued growth and positive social impact serve as a testament to the viability of a cooperative, ethically driven banking model.

Commons Value Chains

Value creation is fundamentally shaped by underlying principles and motivations, whether competition and self-interest or cooperation and mutual benefit (Antràs & Chor, 2022). Cooperation provides an alternative pathway for value creation based on collaborative advantage versus competitive advantage (Johnson, 2018). This is embodied in cooperative value chains.

Value chains encompass the full lifecycle of goods and services, from material sourcing through production, distribution, consumption, and disposal/recycling (Kano et al., 2020). Traditional corporate value chains maximize efficiency and profitability for the focal company (Feller et al., 2006). In contrast, cooperative value chains optimize value creation for multiple stakeholders through cooperation (Barber, 2008).

Cooperatives are member-owned enterprises run democratically to meet shared economic, social, and cultural needs (Cattaneo et al., 2010). Core principles are self-help, self-responsibility, democracy, equality, equity, and solidarity (Liverpool-Tasie et al., 2020). Profits are reinvested or shared equitably among members.

By organizing collectively, cooperatives can achieve efficiencies and compete in markets dominated by large corporations (Nemarundwe et al., 2008). Shared facilities, joint marketing, and bulk purchasing offer economies of scale unavailable to individuals. Democratic governance gives members voice and control.

Beyond economic benefits, cooperatives create social value (Chopra et al., 2021). They build community wealth, generate local employment, and empower marginalized groups. Environmental principles can also be embedded into production and distribution processes (Handfield et al., 2020).

Cooperative value chains directly connect production and consumption in an integrated system of mutuality and shared benefit (Miller, 2022). Farming cooperatives enable small-scale producers to access markets. Consumer cooperatives source directly from local producers, eliminating intermediaries. Workers' cooperatives collaborate in socially responsible manufacturing. Purchasing cooperatives create markets for ethically produced goods. Credit unions finance initiation of new cooperatives (Giovannetti et al., 2021).

Shared platforms allow cooperatives to jointly develop products, services, and innovations (Cadilhon et al., 2005). Alliance building multiplies cooperative influence on value chains. Peak bodies facilitate trans-regional trade between cooperatives. Rather than passively accepting terms set by conventional businesses, cooperatives can proactively shape value chains based on solidarity (Azadi et al., 2023).

By circumventing profit-driven intermediaries, cooperative value chains ensure that a greater share of end value stays with producers (Antràs & Chor, 2022). Surpluses are reinvested to support members and communities versus accruing to external shareholders. More equitable distribution of gains increases capabilities and livelihoods of disadvantaged groups (Johnson, 2018).

In essence, cooperative value chains restructure market relationships around shared interests versus polarized roles of capital and labor (Kano et al., 2020). Mutual service provision replaces one-sided exploitation of suppliers and workers. Democratic structures increase transparency and accountability (Feller et al., 2006).

The cooperative model provides a strategy to transform value chains based on inclusive participation, ethical production, and economic justice (Barber, 2008). It embeds cooperation structurally into the DNA of value-generating enterprises and their interconnections. This in turn enhances human dignity, environmental sustainability, and community benefit (Cattaneo et al., 2010).

Cooperatives counterbalance the dominance of investor-driven corporations in value chains by empowering people to meet common needs through mutual self-help

(Liverpool-Tasie et al., 2020). As member-owned and democratically governed businesses, cooperatives work to benefit their members rather than maximize returns to outside shareholders (Nemarundwe et al., 2008).

By leveraging collective resources, capabilities, and bargaining power, cooperatives can achieve competitive advantage based on cooperation versus polarization (Chopra et al., 2021). Shared facilities, collaborative innovation, and joint marketing create cooperative advantage in value chains (Handfield et al., 2020).

Cooperative farms, retailers, and manufacturers directly link together in supplying goods and services, cutting out exploitative intermediaries (Miller, 2022). Platform cooperatives leverage shared digital infrastructure to challenge extractive sharing economy monopolies (Giovannetti et al., 2021).

Financial cooperatives like credit unions and mutual insurers reinvest member deposits into supporting local economic development (Cadilhon et al., 2005). Housing cooperatives provide affordable resident-controlled housing. Purchasing cooperatives create markets for independent producers (Azadi et al., 2023).

Cooperative alliances and peak associations facilitate trade between cooperatives across entire value chains. Rather than passively accept terms set by big business, cooperatives can proactively structure ethical value chains centered on community benefit over profit maximization (Antràs & Chor, 2022).

Surpluses generated are redistributed back to members or reinvested to support further cooperative development (Johnson, 2018). More equitable distribution of value added increases capabilities and incomes of marginalized groups like small farmers and informal workers (Kano et al., 2020).

Shared ownership and democratic control provide transparency and accountability within cooperative value chains (Feller et al., 2006). Members steward resources and make decisions balancing financial, social, and environmental considerations (Barber, 2008).

By embedding cooperation and mutuality into the core structure of value-generating enterprises, cooperatives transform value chain relationships around shared interests and ethical principles (Cattaneo et al., 2010). This models an alternative paradigm of value creation grounded in equity, sustainability, and solidarity (Liverpool-Tasie et al., 2020).

Cooperative Value Creation

Cooperation provides an alternative pathway for value creation based on collaborative advantage versus competitive advantage (Olk & West, 2020). By working together with a shared purpose, cooperatives and social enterprises can often produce goods and services in a more efficient, accessible, and impactful manner (Borzaga et al., 2014).

In conventional competitive markets, firms seek to maximize their own profits and market share at the expense of others (Dagnino, 2009). Relationships are transactional means to an end. Cooperatives and social enterprises take a collaborative approach that generates mutual benefits for multiple stakeholders (Farabi & Bouazza, 2022).

Cooperatives are member-owned enterprises run democratically to meet common economic, social, and cultural needs (Camarinha-Matos & Afsarmanesh, 2006). Core principles are self-help, self-responsibility, democracy, equality, equity, and solidarity (Esposito et al., 2021). Surpluses are reinvested or shared equitably among members.

Social enterprises pursue social missions through entrepreneurial activities (Wieland, 2014). They aim to have a positive societal impact while operating sustainably. Profits are principally reinvested to further their social purpose (Vieta & Lionais, 2015).

By working together, cooperatives and social enterprises gain collaborative advantage unavailable to individual entities (Huemer, 2014). Shared facilities, joint purchasing, and collaborative marketing provide economies of scale. Knowledge sharing facilitates innovation. Democratic structures give members voice and control over decisions (Lei et al., 1997).

Cooperatives strengthen the position of small-scale producers in markets (Birchall, 2003). Farmers cooperatives enable coordinated sales and access to inputs and services. Purchasing cooperatives create markets for independent artisans. Worker cooperatives allow collaboration in manufacturing and service provision (Gertler, 2004).

Social enterprises often deliver critical goods and services that governments and for-profits do not sufficiently provide (Westermann-Behaylo et al., 2016). Affordable housing associations, healthcare clinics, and clean energy projects are examples. Social enterprises reinvest surpluses to increase their social impact (Basterretxea, 2011).

Strategic partnerships and alliances amplify reach and influence (Olk & West, 2020). Fair trade networks connect ethical producers to global markets. Cross-sector partnerships like social enterprises contracting with cooperatives leverage complementary capabilities (Borzaga et al., 2014).

By collectively organizing and democratically governing operations, cooperatives and social enterprises empower disadvantaged groups (Dagnino, 2009). Resources and opportunities are shared rather than concentrated in a few hands. Local employment, community wealth building, and environmental sustainability can be prioritized over profit maximization (Farabi & Bouazza, 2022).

In essence, the collaborative approaches of cooperatives and social enterprises enable pursuing shared goals more effectively than working alone (Camarinha-Matos & Afsarmanesh, 2006). Mutual interest and participatory decision-making replace zero-sum competition and hierarchical control. Embracing cooperation as a guiding principle allows orienting collaborative activities toward the common good (Esposito et al., 2021).

Cooperatives counterbalance the dominance of investor-driven corporations by empowering people to collectively meet common needs (Wieland, 2014). As member-owned and democratically governed businesses, cooperatives work to benefit their members rather than outside shareholders (Vieta & Lionais, 2015).

By leveraging pooled resources and capabilities, cooperatives gain efficiencies and influence beyond what individuals can achieve alone (Huemer, 2014). Shared facilities, joint purchasing of inputs, and collaborative innovation strengthen cooperative advantage (Lei et al., 1997).

Farmer cooperatives coordinate sales and access agricultural services and inputs. Purchasing cooperatives aggregate demand enabling independent producers to access markets. Worker cooperatives provide employment opportunities and facilitate collaboration (Birchall, 2003).

Credit unions and cooperative banks increase access of marginalized groups to affordable finance. Housing cooperatives enable resident control over housing provision. Cooperatives democratize access to resources that would otherwise be controlled by elites (Gertler, 2004).

Alliances between cooperatives multiply scale and scope. Participation in cross-regional federations and peak bodies facilitates trade flows between cooperatives across entire value chains (Westermann-Behaylo et al., 2016). Rather than passively accept terms set by big business, cooperatives can proactively structure ethical value chains centered on community benefit over profit maximization (Basterretxea, 2011).

Social enterprises apply commercial strategies to achieve positive social impacts (Olk & West, 2020). By reinvesting surpluses into their social mission rather than maximizing profits for shareholders, social enterprises can sustainably deliver critical goods and services underserved by governments and for-profits (Borzaga et al., 2014).

Affordable housing associations, healthcare clinics, clean energy projects, and sustainable agriculture are some domains where social enterprises create substantial community value (Dagnino, 2009). Strategic partnerships with cooperatives and non-profits can further amplify social impacts through collaboration (Farabi & Bouazza, 2022).

Through embracing cooperation and stakeholder participation, cooperatives and social enterprises pave pathways to create holistic value across social, economic, and environmental dimensions (Camarinha-Matos & Afsarmanesh, 2006). The collaborative approaches of these organizations provide models of an economy oriented around mutual benefit and the common good rather than zero-sum competition (Esposito et al., 2021).

CASE STUDY: Seikatsu Club Consumers' Co-operative Union (Japan)

The Seikatsu Club Consumers' Co-operative Union (SCCCU) is a renowned example of sustainable consumer cooperation in Japan. Established in 1965 by a small group of women in Tokyo, the SCCCU has grown into a federation of 33 consumer cooperatives operating across 21 prefectures, with more than 307,000 members—predominantly women. Known for its innovative approach to consumer cooperation, the SCCCU promotes democratic participation, food safety, and environmental sustainability, earning international acclaim, including the Right Livelihood Award in 1989.

The SCCCU began as a voluntary association under the name Seikatsu Club with the aim of improving members' lives, communities, and society. In 1968, it was formally incorporated as a consumer co-operative, establishing democratic management to further its objectives. Driven by the motto of "autonomous control of our lives," the co-op expanded its focus beyond food to encompass production, distribution, environmental protection, social services, and even political engagement. Independent Seikatsu Clubs spread throughout Japan, each developing unique activities tailored to their local contexts, all while sharing a commitment to self-governance and member-led operations.

A cornerstone of the SCCCU's success is its pre-order collective purchase system, introduced to secure "safe food at reasonable prices." The co-op collaborates closely with producers to establish specifications for products—including materials, production methods, and environmental factors—ensuring quality and safety. Members place their orders in advance, allowing for planned production and distribution, which benefits both consumers and producers by reducing costs, waste, and environmental impact.

This system enables the SCCCU to negotiate better terms for its members and helps producers plan their operations more effectively. By collectively determining what to purchase and how it's produced, members exert significant influence over the food system, reinforcing their rights as consumers and promoting sustainable agricultural practices.

The SCCCU's cooperative model relies heavily on active member participation in investment, purchasing, and operation. Each local co-op is an independent entity responsible for managing its own activities, yet all are united under the SCCCU federation. The federation provides central services like collective purchasing, new product development, and IT infrastructure, benefiting from economies of scale. It also facilitates coordination and shared decision-making through a general assembly and board of directors that include representatives from each local co-op.

To accommodate varying needs, the SCCCU employs several models for collective purchasing:

- Han groups: Small member groups order and purchase goods collectively, fostering community and mutual aid.
- Individual delivery system: Members can order independently, yet often engage in group activities, preserving the cooperative spirit.
- Depot model: Depots are managed and operated by members and workers' collectives, serving as hubs for activities like food education and events with producers.

The SCCCU prioritizes organic food and avoids products derived from genetically modified organisms (GMOs). This reflects the members' concerns about health and environmental risks associated with conventional agriculture. In addition to purchasing, the SCCCU engages directly in production activities, such as producing its own milk and biodegradable soap to meet stringent quality and environmental standards.

Beyond its internal practices, the SCCCU advocates for eco-friendly behavior among its members and communities. Initiatives include promoting waste reduction, recycling, and the use of sustainable products. The co-op's commitment to sustainability has made it a leader in advancing responsible production and consumption practices in Japan.

Recognizing the need for political action to complement consumer activism, the SCCCU began fielding candidates for political office through the Tokyo Seikatsusha Network in 1979. More than 100 members have been elected to local councils, enabling the co-op to advocate for policies that align with its vision of sustainable, health-conscious, and community-oriented development. This political engagement underscores the SCCCU's belief that systemic change requires direct involvement in governance.

The SCCCU's activities extend beyond consumer cooperation into mutual aid and community support services. Local co-ops operate businesses that provide childcare, eldercare, and community-based healthcare. A federation-wide mutual aid program also allows members across different local co-ops to support one another during hardships, creating a robust safety net and fostering a sense of solidarity and shared responsibility.

The SCCCU's success has inspired cooperative initiatives worldwide, particularly in Europe, North America, and other parts of Asia. Its approach to consumer cooperation has been recognized as a "sustainable model of production and consumption" by the Right Livelihood Award. Through its commitment to ethical, safe, and sustainable practices, the SCCCU has established itself as a model for integrating social, environmental, and economic goals.

Despite its successes, the SCCCU faces challenges typical of cooperative models. Balancing economic sustainability with strict ethical standards, navigating political complexities, and ensuring continued member engagement are ongoing concerns. However, its strong governance framework, loyal membership, and adaptability have helped it overcome these challenges and remain resilient.

The SCCCU continues to serve as a beacon for consumer-driven change, demonstrating that it is possible to build a cooperative economy rooted in fairness, sustainability, and shared prosperity. Through continued innovation and engagement, the SCCCU seeks to strengthen its model and inspire broader social and economic transformation in Japan and beyond.

Managing Abundance

Mainstream economics is premised on the notion of scarcity (Chase, 1934). Resources are assumed to be finite and insufficient to meet everyone's needs and desires (Peach & Dugger, 2006). This manufactured scarcity is maintained through institutions and policies that restrict access and artificially boost demand. An economy of abundance offers an alternative model for shared prosperity within ecological limits (Auty, 2001). This requires participatory decision-making and distributed leadership to collectively manage abundance in a socially equitable and environmentally regenerative manner (Dugger & Peach, 2015).

Automated manufacturing technologies can potentially produce most goods in abundance given adequate renewable inputs (Hoeschele, 2016). Solar energy alone exceeds global energy usage by orders of magnitude. Yet scarcity persists due to institutions that concentrate wealth and power. Reform is needed to expand access to abundant resources and goods for all (Daoud, 2011).

Cooperatives and social enterprises can help create an economy of abundance through cooperative value chains and commons governance (Goertzel et al., 2017). Cooperatives are member-owned enterprises that operate democratically to meet shared needs. Social enterprises conduct commercial activities to generate social and environmental impact (Sheehan, 2009).

By working together, cooperatives and social enterprises gain efficiencies unavailable individually (Gary et al., 2020). Shared facilities, joint purchasing, and collaborative innovation provide economies of scale. Knowledge and resources are pooled as a common good. Democratic member control replaces autocratic decisions by faraway executives (Selloni & Selloni, 2017).

Abundant renewable energy can be generated and distributed through energy cooperatives (Bauwens, 2010). Smart grids allow locally produced renewable electricity to be shared efficiently at scale. Purchasing cooperatives for conservation equipment boost adoption in households and businesses (Brescia, 2016).

Automated production based on open-source designs enables low-cost, democratically governed manufacturing (Cohen & Sundararajan, 2015). Workers' cooperatives can operate advanced factories under shared ownership. Products can be designed for durability, recyclability, and disassembly to recover materials (Celata et al., 2017).

In farming, agroecology cooperatives can spread regenerative practices that work with natural cycles to restore biodiversity and soil health (Schneiders et al., 2022). Produce can be distributed through food cooperatives and community-supported agriculture programs, providing nutritious food while minimizing waste (Hielscher & Smith, 2014).

Platform cooperatives utilize shared open-source platforms for connecting providers to consumers while cutting out extractive middlemen (West & Greul, 2016). Transportation, delivery, and home services can be provided this way to increase worker autonomy and access for users (Cutcher-Gershenfeld et al., 2018).

Affordable housing cooperatives expand resident control over housing development and management (Smith et al., 2013). Community land trusts keep housing permanently affordable by separating ownership of land and buildings. Mutual housing associations pool resources for collaborative construction and maintenance (Corsini et al., 2019).

Transitioning to an economy of abundance requires reforming traditional corporations too (Iivari et al., 2016). Shared prosperity and ecological sustainability must define business success, not just profits. Workplace democracy can engage employees in decision-making and make jobs more meaningful (Kostakis & Papachristou, 2014).

True abundance transcends material consumption (Chase, 1934). An economy oriented to human development focuses on providing healthcare, education, social services, and arts/culture that allow all people to flourish (Peach & Dugger, 2006). Nonprofit cooperatives and social enterprises can play a greater role in these areas (Auty, 2001).

In essence, an economy of abundance centered on collective welfare and environmental regeneration is possible with thoughtful strategy and reimagined institutions (Dugger & Peach, 2015). Transition involves reforming both market structures and cultural values. It will not arise automatically from technological progress alone without democratically governed models like cooperatives and commons (Hoeschele, 2016). Participatory decision-making and distributed leadership that empower communities are key enablers (Daoud, 2011).

Under the prevailing economic system, scarcity persists despite potential material abundance (Goertzel et al., 2017). Concentrated ownership of resources and technology limits broad access. Cooperative, commons-based models offer pathways to manage abundance for shared prosperity (Sheehan, 2009).

Automation makes possible advanced yet localized production of a wide range of goods in small batches (Gary et al., 2020). Open-source designs and digital fabrication tools like 3D printing greatly lower barriers for local manufacturing (Selloni & Selloni, 2017). Shared maker spaces empower communities.

Energy cooperatives enable distributed renewable energy generation and democratic management of the grid as a common good (Bauwens, 2010). Smart metering balances supply and demand while minimizing waste (Brescia, 2016). Conservation cooperatives spur adoption of renewable heating/cooling and efficient appliances (Cohen & Sundararajan, 2015).

Farming cooperatives can increase adoption of agroecology, permaculture, and regenerative methods that restore ecosystems (Celata et al., 2017). Food cooperatives and community supported agriculture allow direct consumer access to sustainably grown, local produce (Schneiders et al., 2022).

Platform cooperatives use shared platforms to connect users to providers of services like transportation, delivery, and home services (Hielscher & Smith, 2014). They increase worker autonomy and maintain affordability by eliminating intermediary exploitation (West & Greul, 2016).

Housing cooperatives give residents democratic control over housing provision (Cutcher-Gershenfeld et al., 2018). Mutual housing pools member resources for construction and maintenance. Community land trusts keep housing affordable over the long term by separating land and building ownership (Smith et al., 2013).

Realizing an economy of abundance requires steering technology and markets toward collective prosperity through democratic, participatory models (Corsini et al., 2019). It ultimately needs cultural transformation beyond just material plenty (Iivari et al., 2016). An economy oriented around developing human capabilities and social well-being could focus less on endless consumption (Kostakis & Papachristou, 2014).

Glocal Strategies

Globalization has interconnected the world economically and culturally, yet often concentrates power and wealth (Patel, 2020). "Glocalization" offers a model to link local communities across borders in mutually enriching networks of exchange and solidarity (Bressi, 2003). Glocal cooperative value chains can connect localized production to global peers and markets, sharing knowledge and technology while building community resilience.

Glocalization blends global connectivity and local autonomy (Eriksen, 2005). It means adapting global resources to empower local communities while sharing locally generated innovations globally (Manca et al., 2021). This fosters equitable two-way exchange and horizontal learning versus vertical dependence.

The sharing economy also facilitates glocal collaboration (Swyngedouw et al., 2003). Underutilized assets from spaces to tools to skills can be shared for mutual benefit. Cooperatives are member-owned platforms that democratize the sharing economy. Platform cooperatives replace extractive sharing corporations by putting communities in control (Tufte, 2011).

One sharing approach is distributed manufacturing (Carasik, 2008). Peer production commons design modular, open-source products for local, small-batch manufacturing. Smart tools like computer numerical control mills, 3D printers, and laser cutters allow customization. Skills sharing spreads production knowledge (Haller et al., 2019).

Farming knowledge can be exchanged through global cooperatives. Agroecology techniques that regenerate local soils and biodiversity are shared. Food artisans connect to markets through fair trade cooperatives that provide equitable incomes. Surpluses fund community programs (Alcadipani & Rosa, 2011).

Energy cooperatives share renewable energy innovations across regions (Fasenfest, 2010). Locally owned wind, solar, and biogas generators provide distributed power. Smart grids manage cooperative energy pools. Household consumption data aids forecasting. Excess power is sold to the grid to boost local incomes (Barton & Román, 2012).

Healthcare cooperatives enable glocal telemedicine (Munck et al., 2012). Rural clinics access global expertise. Preventative information is tailored locally. Public health researchers share antimicrobial resistance data and mitigation strategies globally. Gene banks preserve biodiverse medicinal plants (De Leeuw, 2001).

Arts and culture are shared cooperatively too (Patel, 2020). Local artists gain global exposure via creative commons while retaining rights. Works reflect unique regional styles and perspectives. Global inspiration remixes with deep local roots. Surpluses fund traditional craft revitalization and cultural sustainability initiatives (Bressi, 2003).

Housing cooperatives address local needs through global cooperation (Eriksen, 2005). Eco city designs are locally adapted. Construction knowledge empowers community builders. Affordable housing models aid displacement resistance. Community land trusts protect local tenure. Cooperative recyclable modular buildings are customized (Manca et al., 2021).

Informal community counseling groups share psychosocial recovery knowledge (Hemer & Tufte, 2005). Local support circles enable overflowing care resources to assist wider needs globally. Wisdom of trauma healing traditions is preserved digitally. Recovery is supported holistically through social cooperatives providing healthcare, housing, and work.

Cooperative transitional cities can model glocal regeneration (Swyngedouw et al., 2003). Local circular economies minimize waste while sharing surplus. Green spaces are commons fostering ecological health and social mixing. Walkable neighborhoods cluster housing, agriculture, and community facilities. Transition movements link sites globally as sustainability learning labs (Tufte, 2011).

Essentially, glocal cooperative networks enable blending global knowledge exchange, technology transfer, and skill sharing with deep localization of production, consumption, and governance (Carasik, 2008). This balances global connections with community autonomy. It fosters solidarity economies that spread inclusive innovations while respecting local cultures (Haller et al., 2019). Cooperation is emphasized over competition to navigate interdependence in a complex world.

Digital networks empower glocal cooperation through global connectivity and local creativity (Alcadipani & Rosa, 2011). Open licensing and peer sharing of knowledge, designs, and code enhance access. Customization to local contexts is enabled. Platform cooperatives replace extractive sharing corporations by democratizing exchange (Fasenfest, 2010).

Distributed manufacturing facilitates small-scale, localized production of open-source designs (Barton & Román, 2012). Smart digital tools like 3D printers allow custom making. Skills are shared cooperatively. Products can meet unique local needs sustainably and equitably (Munck et al., 2012).

Agroecology and permaculture farming techniques regenerate soils and ecosystems. Knowledge spreads through cooperatives along with technologies like drip irrigation. Farmers access fair trade markets and obtain fair prices to fund community programs (De Leeuw, 2001).

Energy cooperatives pool locally owned renewable resources. Innovations transfer between regions. Smart grids balance supply and demand. Surplus clean power boosts incomes. Healthcare cooperatives share telemedicine and knowledge to improve access (Patel, 2020).

Arts cooperatives preserve traditional knowledge while fostering contemporary cultural expression. Unique local creations access global audiences. Funds are reinvested to support cultural sustainability and revitalization initiatives (Bressi, 2003).

Eco-city designs are localized to site conditions. Construction skills empower community builders. Housing cooperatives model inclusive development and anti-displacement. Transition towns link in regenerative glocal networks (Eriksen, 2005).

Glocal cooperative networks, thus, synergistically blend global exchange of ideas, technology, and resources with deep community roots and participation (Manca et al., 2021). This approach fosters equitable development, sharing innovations without homogenization or dependence. It provides a model of ethical globalization centered on mutual aid and solidarity (Hemer & Tufte, 2005).

Empowering Change

Radical concepts hold inherent potential for transformation, yet turning ideals into reality requires thoughtful strategy (Blühdorn, 2017). Two key interrelated components enable radical visions to take form. First, innovative ideas must be rooted locally through concrete prefigurative experiments that demonstrate feasibility (Alexander, 2020). Second, expanding from isolated niches necessitates coordinating efforts to build systemic alternatives across dispersed grassroots initiatives (Dermody et al., 2021).

Prefigurative politics involves creating and cultivating in the present the social relations and practices of the desired future society rather than deferring change to a distant end goal (Powell, 2002). As exemplified by cases like the self-managed factory Vio.Me and Metropolitan Community Clinic at Helliniko, participatory projects can embody radical ideals of cooperation and mutual aid within their operations and communities (Dinerstein & Pitts, 2018). Though limited in scale, such grassroots endeavors model alternative approaches to production and service provision grounded in principles of direct democracy and equal participation. Tangibly manifesting radical concepts allows moving past abstract theories to demonstrate concrete feasibility (Schismenos et al., 2020).

However, isolated local experiments alone cannot catalyze broad societal transformation (Archibugi, 2000). Constructing effective systemic alternatives fundamentally relies on linkages between diverse grassroots projects to build wider movements. Contemporary horizontalist activism rejects hierarchical vanguardist leadership in favor of autonomous decentralized networks and direct democratic participation (Jossa, 2016). Yet horizontalist movements recognize that while resistance to current structures remains essential, opposition alone is an insufficient basis for change. Activists must also proactively generate creative alternative models across spheres of life to construct another world. Building connections between multifaceted efforts oriented toward system change from different angles is vital (Jones, 2019).

Horizontalist perspectives argue that realizing systemic goals necessitates synthesizing both resistance and social creation (Davies, 2017). Resistance mounts pressure against dominant institutions through protest and campaigns. Social creation involves actively building new economic or political alternatives behind the opposition. The strength of mobilizations like Occupy in 2011 was combining protests with constructing alternative institutions for mutual aid in healthcare, food, and education (Anderson et al., 2023).

Grassroots relief networks formed in response to disasters demonstrate this as well (Celata & Stabrowski, 2022). Occupy Sandy rapidly mobilized after Hurricane Sandy to provide aid when established institutions failed, fostering lasting solidarity. Such organizing shows potential to meet needs directly through horizontal cooperation, prefiguring autonomous alternatives (Dey et al., 2016).

Territorial organizing to construct autonomous spaces remains vital within our current context of globalized capitalism and authoritarian governance (Dinerstein & Pitts, 2022). Mutual aid projects cultivate popular power and self-governance capacities. However, localized spaces alone cannot achieve systemic change. Realizing radical visions requires strategic connections between dispersed mutual aid projects to form wider social movements (Pellizzoni, 2021).

Integrated movement-building synthesizes political education, alternative institutions, mobilization, and electoral efforts (Monticelli, 2018). Without ongoing education, programs, and mobilization, even progressive politicians lack the social base to institute change. Transformation relies on alternative values and structures materializing locally first. But projects and campaigns can interlink translocally into decentralized webs of mutual aid and self-governance, with elections as just one prong (Blühdorn, 2017).

Critically, connecting local alternatives translocally relies on a glocal strategy that blends global connectivity and localized autonomy (Alexander, 2020). Radical visions are adapted to local contexts while sharing innovations across grassroots networks worldwide. This allows discovering universal principles and tools for empowerment while respecting diverse needs (Dermody et al., 2021). Digital media facilitates global knowledge sharing and solidarity. Cities can then function as hubs integrating global ideals with grassroots organizing (Powell, 2002).

In synthesis, localized grassroots action remains essential for demonstrating alternative modes of social organization and mutual aid (Dinerstein & Pitts, 2018). Yet realizing the potential of radical concepts ultimately requires coordinated efforts between autonomous spaces. Continually developing participatory democratic forms of "living otherwise" remains critical for resisting co-optation and maintaining liberatory horizons (Schismenos et al., 2020). Connecting diverse self-managed projects creates wider movements and networks with transformative potential. In this manner, radical visions take root through decentralized community organizing and small-scale experiments, while coordinating horizontally through glocal connections to construct viable systemic alternatives that make radical ideas empowering realities (Archibugi, 2000).

Prefigurative projects cultivate in the present radically different social relations of cooperation, solidarity, and mutual aid (Jossa, 2016). Though limited in scale, they demonstrate potential for collective self-management and horizontal organization as living alternatives to hierarchy (Jones, 2019). However, connections between diverse grassroots experiments are vital to catalyze broad transformation (Davies, 2017).

Contemporary horizontalist movements reject vanguardism for autonomous decentralization and direct democracy (Anderson et al., 2023). Developing creative alternative models across all spheres of life is as crucial as resistance to dominant institutions. Strategic linkages between multifaceted localized projects oriented to system change can construct viable systemic alternatives (Celata & Stabrowski, 2022).

Mutual aid initiatives formed in disasters demonstrate radical ideals in action by meeting urgent needs directly through cooperation. However, lasting change requires going beyond isolated projects (Dey et al., 2016). Building wider movements necessitates thoughtful organizing that synthesizes political education, alternative institutions, mobilization, and elections as interconnected components (Dinerstein & Pitts, 2022).

Realizing radical visions relies on networks between diverse grassroots experiments. A glocal strategy blends global connectivity for sharing innovations while respecting local autonomy (Pellizzoni, 2021). Digital media enables global solidarity and knowledge exchange. Cities integrate global ideals into localized organizing. In essence, radical concepts take root through community projects demonstrating feasibility, while coordinating translocally constructs systemic alternatives (Monticelli, 2018).

KEY THINKER: Camila Piñeiro Harnecker

Camila Piñeiro Harnecker is a prominent Cuban economist and researcher known for her work on cooperatives, workplace democracy, and the social and solidarity economy. Her interdisciplinary academic background includes a PhD in Economics and an MBA from the University of Havana, and a master's degree in Sustainable Development from the University of California at Berkeley. This diverse educational foundation has enabled Harnecker to integrate economic theory with social justice and environmental sustainability in her research and advocacy.

Harnecker's academic career includes serving as a professor, researcher, and consultant at the Center for the Study of the Cuban Economy at the University of Havana from 2009 to 2017. During this period, she focused on understanding how cooperatives and other alternative economic models can contribute to building a more equitable and inclusive society, especially within Cuba's unique political and economic context.

Her 2012 edited volume, *Cooperatives and Socialism: A View from Cuba*, is a seminal work that explores the role of cooperatives in the Cuban economy and their potential to advance socialism. Bringing together insights from Cuban scholars and practitioners, the book examines both the opportunities and challenges faced by cooperatives within a socialist framework.

In her 2009 article, "Workplace Democracy and Social Consciousness: A Study of Venezuelan Cooperatives," published in *Science & Society*, Harnecker investigates how workplace democracy influences the development of social consciousness among cooperative members in Venezuela. The study illustrates how cooperatives' participatory and egalitarian nature can foster collective identity, solidarity, and awareness of broader social and political issues, thereby encouraging civic engagement and social transformation.

Harnecker's commitment to translating research into actionable strategies is evident in her role as the Practice Area Director for Strengthening Cooperatives and Producer Organizations at NCBA CLUSA (National Cooperative Business Association, CLUSA International). Previously, she served as a Cooperative Development Consultant at the Keystone Development Center, providing technical support to cooperatives. Harnecker has also held research fellowships at institutions like the Center for Latin American and Latino Studies at American University and the University of California, Riverside.

Her engagement with cooperatives extends beyond academia. By providing technical assistance, policy advice, and practical support, Harnecker ensures that her research is grounded in the lived experiences of cooperative members and addresses real-world challenges. This integration of theory and practice has positioned her as an influential figure in cooperative movements in Cuba, Latin America, and globally.

Central to Harnecker's work is the conviction that cooperatives can play a transformative role in building a more just, democratic, and sustainable world. She argues that cooperatives, by prioritizing workers and community needs over profit, can address issues like income inequality, worker exploitation, environmental degradation, and community disempowerment. By giving workers a stake in decision-making and control over their work, cooperatives foster a sense of ownership, responsibility, and collective identity.

Harnecker sees cooperatives as integral to the broader social and solidarity economy—a movement that subordinates economic activities to social and environmental goals. In her view, cooperatives are more than just business enterprises; they are part of a transformative economic system rooted in principles of mutual aid, concern for the community, and equitable distribution of resources.

Harnecker's work challenges conventional economic models by proposing cooperatives as viable alternatives to capitalism. Her advocacy emphasizes that cooperatives can create a fairer distribution of wealth and power by fostering democratic participation, social responsibility, and sustainable economic practices. Her contributions have had a profound impact on the study and promotion of cooperatives, inspiring a new generation of scholars and activists to envision and enact alternative economic models that prioritize people and the planet over profit.

Conclusion

This chapter explored strategies for the social economy to create value cooperatively as an alternative to extractive capitalist models. Realizing this transformation requires implementing radical ideas through creative organizing at multiple scales.

Prefigurative local projects demonstrate cooperative values. Initiatives like self-managed factories and mutual aid clinics embody direct democracy and equal participation in production and services. Though limited in scope, these grassroots models prove the concrete viability of social economy principles.

Yet isolated efforts alone cannot catalyze systemic change. Diverse local projects must interlink to construct cooperative alternatives. Horizontalist perspectives recognize that resistance requires proactively building new systems. Occupy demonstrated this by combining protests with organizing mutual aid networks as working alternatives.

Horizontalist movements fuse opposition with constructing functioning cooperative models. Territorial organizing develops autonomous spaces for participatory self-governance and solidarity economics. However, system change needs connecting localized efforts into decentralized mutual aid networks, social movements, and governance structures.

Integrated strategies interweave education, grassroots institutions, mobilization, and policy campaigns. Without ongoing groundwork, political victories will falter. Transformation relies on cooperative models first taking local form, then scaling up through horizontal coordination.

A glocal approach blends global connectivity and local autonomy. Digital tools enable global sharing of knowledge, innovations, and solidarity, localized and adapted through grassroots organizing. Cities integrate global cooperative visions with local alternatives as network hubs.

In conclusion, realizing the social economy's radical potential requires rooting cooperative values in community organizing and small-scale ventures. Through incrementally cultivating living alternatives, mobilizing movements, and building translocal alliances, the social economy can create post-capitalist systems centered on democracy and sustainability. The path forward entails constructing new models from the ground up, connecting diverse efforts locally and globally to make cooperative commonwealths possible.

This chapter has illuminated how creative grassroots strategy, fusing global cooperative ideals with grounded local action, can turn the social economy's radical vision into an empowering force that fundamentally transforms extractive capitalism into systems of shared prosperity centered on the commons.

References

Alcadipani, R., & Rosa, A. R. (2011). From global management to glocal management: Latin American perspectives as a counter-dominant management epistemology. *Canadian Journal of Administrative Sciences/Revue Canadienne des Sciences de l'Administration, 28*(4), 453–466.

Alexander, S. (2020). Post-capitalism by design not disaster. *The Ecological Citizen, 3*(Suppl B), 13–21.

Anderson, G. L., Desai, D., Heras, A. I., & Spreen, C. A. (2023). *Creating Third Spaces of Learning for Post-Capitalism: Lessons from Educators, Artists, and Activists.* Taylor & Francis.

Antràs, P., & Chor, D. (2022). Global value chains. *Handbook of International Economics*, 5, 297–376.

Archibugi, F. (2000). *The Associative Economy: Insights Beyond the Welfare State and into Post-capitalism*. Springer.

Auty, R. M. (ed.). (2001). *Resource Abundance and Economic Development*. Oxford University Press.

Azadi, E., Moghaddas, Z., Saen, R. F., Mardani, A., & Azadi, M. (2023). Green supply chains and performance evaluation: A multiplier network analytics model with common set of weights. *Journal of Cleaner Production*, *411*, 137377.

Barber, E. (2008). How to measure the "value" in value chains. *International Journal of Physical Distribution & Logistics Management*, *38*(9), 685–698.

Barton, J. R., & Román, Á. (2012). Social movement strategies for articulating claims for socio-ecological justice: Glocal asymmetries in the Chilean forestry sector. *Globalizations*, *9*(6), 869–885.

Bauwens, M. (2010). Toward a P2P economy. In Araya, D. & Peters, M. A. (Eds.), *Education in the Creative Economy: Knowledge and Learning in the Age of Innovation* (pp. 305–330). New York: Peter Lang.

Birchall, J. (2003). *Rediscovering the Cooperative Advantage: Poverty Reduction through Self-help*. International Labour Organization (ILO).

Blühdorn, I. (2017). Post-capitalism, post-growth, post-consumerism? Eco-political hopes beyond sustainability. *Global Discourse*, *7*(1), 42–61.

Borzaga, C., Bodini, R., Carini, C., Depedri, S., Galera, G., & Salvatori, G. (2014). *Europe in Transition: The Role of Social Cooperatives and Social Enterprises*, (Working Paper n. 69|14). Euricse Working Papers, pp. 1–17.

Bowman, C. & Ambrosini, V. (2000). Value creation versus value capture: Towards a coherent definition of value in strategy. *British Journal of Management*, *11*(1), 1–15.

Brescia, R. H. (2016). Regulating the sharing economy: New and old insights into an oversight regime for the peer-to-peer economy. *Neb. L. Rev.*, *95*, 87.

Bressi, G. (2003). The impact of globalization: Opportunities and challenges for glocal development in Europe, Latin America and the Caribbean. Presented in the seminar *Global and Local: Confronting the Challenges of Regional Development in Latin America and the Caribbean*, Milan. University of Turin. Unpublished.

Cadilhon, J. J., Fearne, A. P., Thi Giac Tam, P., Moustier, P., & Poole, N. D. (2005). Collaborative commerce or just common sense? Insights from vegetable supply chains in Ho Chi Minh City. *Supply Chain Management: An International Journal*, *10*(3), 147–149.

Camarinha-Matos, L. M., & Afsarmanesh, H. (2006, June). Collaborative networks: Value creation in a knowledge society. In *International Conference on Programming Languages for Manufacturing* (pp. 26–40). Springer US.

Carasik, L. (2008). Think glocal, act glocal: The praxis of social justice lawyering in the global era. *Clinical L. Rev.*, *15*, 55.

Cattaneo, O., Gereffi, G., & Staritz, C. (eds). (2010). *Global Value Chains in a Postcrisis World: A Development Perspective*. World Bank Publications.

Celata, F., Hendrickson, C. Y., & Sanna, V. S. (2017). The sharing economy as community marketplace? Trust, reciprocity and belonging in peer-to-peer accommodation platforms. *Cambridge Journal of Regions, Economy and Society*, *10*(2), 349–363.

Celata, F., & Stabrowski, F. (2022). Crowds, communities, (post) capitalism and the sharing economy. *City*, *26*(1), 119–127.

Chase, S. (1934). *The Economy of Abundance*. New York: Macmillan.

Chopra, S., Sodhi, M., & Lücker, F. (2021). Achieving supply chain efficiency and resilience by using multi-level commons. *Decision Sciences*, *52*(4), 817–832.

Chui, M., Manyika, J., Bughin, J., Dobbs, R., Roxburgh, C., Sarrazin, H., Sands, G. & Westergren, M. (2012). *The Social Economy: Unlocking value and productivity through social technologies*. London: McKinsey Global Institute.

Cohen, M., & Sundararajan, A. (2015). Self-regulation and innovation in the peer-to-peer sharing economy. *U. Chi. L. Rev. Dialogue*, *82*, 116.

Corsini, L., Aranda-Jan, C. B., & Moultrie, J. (2019). Using digital fabrication tools to provide humanitarian and development aid in low-resource settings. *Technology in Society*, *58*, 101117.

Cutcher-Gershenfeld, J., Gershenfeld, A., & Gershenfeld, N. (2018). Digital fabrication and the future of work. *Perspectives on work, labor and employment relations*, *22*, 8–13.

Dagnino, G. B. (2009). Coopetition strategy: A new kind of interfirm dynamics for value creation. In Dagnino, G. B. & Rocco, E. (Eds.), *Coopetition Strategy: Theory, experiments and cases* (pp. 45–63). London: Routledge.

Daoud, A. (2011). *Scarcity, Abundance and Sufficiency: Contributions to Social and Economic Theory* (Doctoral dissertation, University of Gothenburg).

Davies, S. (2017). Basic income, labour, and the idea of post-capitalism. *Economic Affairs*, *37*(3), 442–458.

De Leeuw, E. (2001). Global and local (glocal) health: The WHO healthy cities programme. *Global Change and Human Health*, *2*(1), 34–45.

Dermody, J., Koenig-Lewis, N., Zhao, A. L., & Hanmer-Lloyd, S. (2021). Critiquing a utopian idea of sustainable consumption: A post-capitalism perspective. *Journal of Macromarketing*, *41*(4), 626–645.

Dey, P., Marti, L., Teasdale, S., & Seanor, P. (2016). Alternative enterprises, rhythms and (post) capitalism: Mapping spatio-temporal practices of reproduction, escape and intervention.Paper submitted to *32nd EGOS Colloquium*, Naples 2016. Available at: https://www.alexandria.unisg.ch/entities/publication/402fd4b4-3909-4904-a347-7cc1e9846353 (accessed February 17, 2024).

Dinerstein, A. C., & Pitts, F. H. (2018). From post-work to post-capitalism? Discussing the basic income and struggles for alternative forms of social reproduction. *Journal of Labor and Society*, *21*(4), 471–491.

Dinerstein, A. C., & Pitts, F. H. (2022). Prefiguration and the futures of work. In Monticelli, L. (Ed.), *The Future is Now: An Introduction to Prefigurative Politics* (pp. 93–105). Bristol: Bristol University Press.

Dobni, C. B. (2010). Achieving Synergy Between Strategy and Innovation: The Key to Value Creation. *International Journal of Business Science and Applied Management*, *5*(1), 48–58.

Dugger, W. M., & Peach, J. T. (2015). *Economic Abundance: An Introduction*. London: Routledge.

Eriksen, T. H. (2005). *Media and Glocal Change: Rethinking Communication for Development*. Buenos Aires: CLACSO.

Esposito, P., Brescia, V., Fantauzzi, C., & Frondizi, R. (2021). Understanding social impact and value creation in hybrid organizations: The case of Italian civil service. *Sustainability*, *13*(7), 4058.

Farabi, Z., & Bouazza, A. (2022). Specificities of the governance mechanisms of social organizations and their contribution to value creation: Case of Moroccan cooperatives. *Governance*, *15*, 16.

Fasenfest, D. (2010). The glocal crisis and the politics of change. *Critical Sociology*, *36*(3), 363–368.

Feller, A., Shunk, D., & Callarman, T. (2006). Value chains versus supply chains. *BP Trends*, *1*, 1–7.

Foster, R. J. (2007). The work of the new economy: Consumers, brands, and value creation. *Cultural Anthropology*, *22*(4), 707–731.

Freedman, L. (2015). *Strategy: A History*. Oxford University Press.

Frynas, J. G. (2015). Strategic CSR, value creation and competitive advantage. In Lawton, T. C. & Rajwani, T. S. (Eds.), *The Routledge Companion to Non-market Strategy* (pp. 245–262). Abingdon: Routledge.

Gary, R. F., Fink, M., Belousova, O., Marinakis, Y., Tierney, R., & Walsh, S. T. (2020). An introduction to the field of abundant economic thought. *Technological Forecasting and Social Change*, *155*, 119796.

Gertler, M. E. (2004). Synergy and strategic advantage: Cooperatives and sustainable development. *Journal of Cooperatives*, *18*(1142-2016-92700), 32–46.

Gibson-Graham, J. K. (1996). *The End of Capitalism (As We Knew It): A Feminist Critique of Political Economy*. Oxford and Cambridge: Blackwell Publishers.

Giovannetti, E., Bertolini, P., & Russo, M. (2021). Rights, commons, and social capital: The role of cooperation in an Italian agri-food supply chain. *Sustainability*, *13*(21), 12161.

Goertzel, B., Goertzel, T., & Goertzel, Z. (2017). The global brain and the emerging economy of abundance: Mutualism, open collaboration, exchange networks and the automated commons. *Technological Forecasting and Social Change*, *114*, 65–73.

Grönroos, C., & Voima, P. (2013). Critical service logic: Making sense of value creation and co-creation. *Journal of the Academy of Marketing Science*, *41*, 133–150.

Haksever, C., Chaganti, R., & Cook, R. G. (2004). A model of value creation: Strategic view. *Journal of Business Ethics*, *49*(2), 295–307.

Haller, T., Breu, T., De Moor, T., Rohr, C., & Znoj, H. (eds). (2019). *The Commons in a Glocal World: Global Connections and Local Responses*. Routledge.

Handfield, R., Finkenstadt, D. J., Schneller, E. S., Godfrey, A. B., & Guinto, P. (2020). A commons for a supply chain in the post-COVID-19 era: The case for a reformed strategic national stockpile. *The Milbank Quarterly*, *98*(4), 1058–1090.

Harnecker, C. P. (2012). *Cooperatives and Socialism: A View from Cuba*. New York: Palgrave Macmillan.

Hemer, O., & Tufte, T. (2005). The challenge of the glocal. *Glocal Times*, (1)., p. 71

Hielscher, S., & Smith, A. (2014). Community-based digital fabrication workshops: A review of the research literature. SSRN Scholarly Paper No. ID 2742121, Social Science Research Network, Rochester, NY.

Hoeschele, W. (2016). *The Economics of Abundance: A Political Economy of Freedom, Equity, and Sustainability*. CRC Press.

Huemer, L. (2014). Creating cooperative advantage: The roles of identification, trust, and time. *Industrial Marketing Management*, *43*(4), 564–572.

Husted, B. W., Allen, D. B., & Kock, N. (2015). Value creation through social strategy. *Business & Society*, *54*(2), 147–186.

Iivari, N., Molin-Juustila, T., & Kinnula, M. (2016). The future digital innovators: Empowering the young generation with digital fabrication and making. In Barendregt, W. & Bødker, S. (Eds.), *NordiCHI '16: Proceedings of the 9th Nordic Conference on Human–Computer Interaction* (pp. 1–16). New York: Association for Computing Machinery.

Johnson, J., Whittington, R., Regnér, P., Angwin, D., Johnson, G., & Scholes, K. (2020). *Exploring Strategy*. Pearson UK.

Johnson, R. C. (2018). Measuring global value chains. *Annual Review of Economics*, *10*, 207–236.

Jones, E. (2019). Feminist technologies and post-capitalism: Defining and reflecting upon xenofeminism. *Feminist Review*, *123*(1), 126–134.

Jossa, B. (2016). *Labour Managed Firms and Post-capitalism* (Vol. 8). Taylor & Francis.

Kano, L., Tsang, E. W., & Yeung, H. W. C. (2020). Global value chains: A review of the multi-disciplinary literature. *Journal of International Business Studies*, *51*, 577–622.

Kostakis, V., & Papachristou, M. (2014). Commons-based peer production and digital fabrication: The case of a RepRap-based, Lego-built 3D printing-milling machine. *Telematics and Informatics*, *31*(3), 434–443.

Laukkanen, M., & Tura, N. (2020). The potential of sharing economy business models for sustainable value creation. *Journal of Cleaner Production*, *253*, 120004.

Lei, D., Slocum Jr, J. W., & Pitts, R. A. (1997). Building cooperative advantage: Managing strategic alliances to promote organizational learning. *Journal of World Business*, *32*(3), 203–223.

Liverpool-Tasie, L. S. O., Wineman, A., Young, S., Tambo, J., Vargas, C., Reardon, T., . . . & Celestin, A. (2020). A scoping review of market links between value chain actors and small-scale producers in developing regions. *Nature Sustainability*, *3*(10), 799–808.

Low, J. (2000). The value creation index. *Journal of Intellectual Capital*, *1*(3), 252–262.

Manca, S., Bocconi, S., & Gleason, B. (2021). "Think globally, act locally": A glocal approach to the development of social media literacy. *Computers & Education*, *160*, 104025.

Basterretxea, I. M. (2011). Sources of competitive advantage in the Mondragon Cooperative Group. In Bakaikoa, B. & Albizu, E. (Eds.), *Basque Cooperativism* (pp. 131–151). Reno: Center for Basque Studies, University of Nevada in conjunction with University of the Basque Country UPV/EHU.

Matei, A., & Dorobantu, A. D. (2015). Social economy—added value for local development and social cohesion. *Procedia Economics and Finance, 26*, 490–494.

Miller, M. A. (2022). Market-based commons: Social agroforestry, fire mitigation strategies, and green supply chains in Indonesia's peatlands. *Transactions of the Institute of British Geographers, 47*(1), 77–91.

Monticelli, L. (2018). Embodying alternatives to capitalism in the 21st century. TripleC: Communication, Capitalism & Critique. *Open Access Journal for a Global Sustainable Information Society, 16*(2), 501–517.

Munck, R., McQuillan, H., & Ozarowska, J. (2012). Civic engagement in a cold climate: A glocal perspective. In McIlrath, L., Lyons, A. & Munch, R. (Eds.), *Higher Education and Civic Engagement: Comparative Perspectives* (pp. 15–29). New York: Palgrave Macmillan US.

Nemarundwe, N., Ngorima, G., & Welford, L. (2008, July). *Cash from the Commons: Improving Natural Product Value Chains for Poverty Alleviation*. 12th Biennial Conference of the International Association for the Study of Commons (IASC). Available at: http://iasc2008.glos.ac.uk/conference%20papers/pa pers/N/Nemarundwe_219401.pdf (accessed April 19, 2011).

Olk, P., & West, J. (2020). The relationship of industry structure to open innovation: Cooperative value creation in pharmaceutical consortia. *R&D Management, 50*(1), 116–135.

Patel, F. (2020). Glocal development for sustainable social change. In Servaes, J. (Ed.), *Handbook of Communication for Development and Social Change* (pp. 501–517). Singapore: Springer.

Peach, J., & Dugger, W. M. (2006). An intellectual history of abundance putting abundance in context. *Journal of Economic Issues, 40*(3), 693–706.

Pellizzoni, L. (2021). Prefiguration, subtraction and emancipation. *Social Movement Studies, 20*(3), 364–379.

Porter, M. E. (1991). Towards a dynamic theory of strategy. *Strategic Management Journal, 12*(S2), 95–117.

Potts, J., & Hartley, J. (2015). How the social economy produces innovation. *Review of Social Economy, 73*(3), 263–282.

Powell, J. (2002). Petty capitalism, perfecting capitalism or post-capitalism? Lessons from the Argentinean barter experiments. *Review of International Political Economy, 9*(4), 619–649.

Prahalad, C. K., & Ramaswamy, V. (2004). Co-creation experiences: The next practice in value creation. *Journal of Interactive Marketing, 18*(3), 5–14.

Schismenos, A., Niaros, V., & Lemos, L. (2020). Cosmolocalism: Understanding the transitional dynamics towards post-capitalism. *tripleC: Communication, Capitalism & Critique, 18*(2), 670–684.

Schiuma, G., Carlucci, D., & Lerro, A. (2012). Managing knowledge processes for value creation. *Vine, 42*(1), 4–14.

Schneiders, A., Fell, M. J., & Nolden, C. (2022). Peer-to-peer electricity trading and the sharing economy: Social, markets and regulatory perspectives. *Energy Sources, Part B: Economics, Planning, and Policy, 17*(1), 2050849.

Selloni, D., & Selloni, D. (2017). New forms of economies: Sharing economy, collaborative consumption, peer-to-peer economy. In Selloni, D. (Ed.), *CoDesign for Public-Interest Services* (pp. 15–26). Cham: Springer International Publishing.

Sheehan, B. (2009). An introduction to the economics of abundance. *Heterodox Economics Newsletter, 1*, 76.

Smith, A., Hielscher, S., Dickel, S., Soderberg, J., & van Oost, E. (2013). Grassroots digital fabrication and makerspaces: Reconfiguring, relocating and recalibrating innovation? University of Sussex, SPRU Working Paper SWPS, 2.

Tantalo, C. & Priem, R. L. (2016). Value creation through stakeholder synergy. *Strategic Management Journal, 37*(2), 314–329.

Tufte, T. (2011). Mediapolis, Human (In) Security and Citizenship: Communication and Glocal Development Challenges in the Digital Era. In Christensen, M., Jansson, A. & Christensen, C. (Eds.), *Online Territories: Globalization, mediated practice and social space* (pp. 113–131). New York: Peter Lang Publishers.

Vieta, M. & Lionais, D. (2015). *Editorial: The Cooperative Advantage for Community Development*. SSRN Scholarly Paper ID 2639138. Rochester, NY: Social Science Research Network.

West, J. & Greul, A. (2016). Atoms matter: The role of local "makerspaces" in the coming digital economy. In Xavier Olleros, F. & Zhegu, M. (Eds.), *Research handbook on digital transformations* (pp. 182–202). Bingley, UK: Edward Elgar Publishing.

Westermann-Behaylo, M. K., Van Buren, H. J. & Berman, S. L. (2016). Stakeholder capability enhancement as a path to promote human dignity and cooperative advantage. *Business Ethics Quarterly*, 26(4), 529–555.

Wieland, J. (2014). *Governance ethics: Global value creation, economic organization and normativity*. Cham: Springer International Publishing.

Chapter 9
Conclusion: Commons and Cooperative Futures

Introduction

This textbook has aimed to elucidate theories and practices for constructing alternative systems to extractive capitalism built on values of democratic participation, cooperative organization, and shared ownership. Turning these values into concrete realities requires not just envisioning alternative models, but learning how to implement, manage, and continuously enhance them. This concluding chapter will summarize key concepts about value creation strategies from the social and solidarity economy, then explore pathways for putting such alternatives into practice.

Previous chapters illuminated models where common resources are collectively governed, workplaces are cooperatively owned, and economic governance involves robust grassroots participation. Case studies ranged from self-managed factories in Argentina to agroecology farming in India to community land trusts in the United States. Each demonstrates principles of production, consumption, and exchange oriented around democracy, cooperation and sustainability rather than capital accumulation.

Yet inspiring examples alone are insufficient; actualizing systemic change requires skillful strategy and organizing. How can cooperative values move from abstract ideals to empowering realities improving people's lives? This chapter will synthesize learnings about applying social economy approaches, from initiating small-scale projects to influencing wider institutions.

We will discuss hybrid models blending cooperative practices with social enterprises and mission-driven businesses. Legislative and regulatory policies that incentivize regenerative approaches will be explored, alongside public procurement and decentralized participatory budgeting. The merits of open participation through contributory democracy versus representational forms will be weighed. Progressive municipalism movements transforming city governance provide instructive models.

Tactics that leverage anchor institutions, land trusts, and participatory investment will be considered for greater community control of resources. Horizontalist networking of autonomous local efforts into global knowledge commons and social movements will be highlighted as a scaling strategy. The ecosystem of support organizations needed to nourish social innovation will be outlined. Worker and consumer cooperatives will be examined as strategies for democratizing ownership and supply chains (Gibson-Graham, 2006; Wright, 2010).

Throughout, the focus will be on frameworks, policies, and institutions that make cooperation the default and embed commons-based models into everyday practice. How can solidaristic alternatives penetrate all facets of life, from childcare to elder care, agriculture to industry, housing to credit systems? How can post-capitalist logics become common sense?

https://doi.org/10.1515/9783111080147-009

This chapter will synthesize the diverse cases and concepts presented throughout the book into integrative recommendations for action. Building mass movements, electing progressive municipal coalitions, and training social entrepreneurs are important tactics. But the core emphasis will be placed on how citizens can create vibrant commons and cooperate at the grassroots, empowering communities with concrete capacities to meet their needs equitably and sustainably.

Through this people-centered approach, we will explore how to turn local alternatives into building blocks of new systems. By linking efforts translocally and globally into facilitated networks, seeds of change can take root and blossom in fertile soil. Rather than waiting for system reforms, ordinary citizens can cultivate the communities and livelihoods they wish to inhabit right now.

This concluding chapter surveys pathways for implementing models that make cooperation the norm, democracy the process, and shared well-being the goal. The social and solidarity economy offers living examples of embedding care, reciprocity, and stewardship into our structures. As the textbook has demonstrated, transformative ideas must be grounded in grassroots realities to succeed. Our ultimate focus will be equipping readers with conceptual resources and strategic knowledge to bring these revolutionary visions to life.

Cooperative Futures

The last few decades have seen the emergence of exciting new socio-economic perspectives that present alternatives to our current capitalist economy. Neoliberal ideology espouses the notion that "there is no alternative" to free market capitalism. However, recurring crises like climate change, financial crashes, and public health pandemics reveal the urgent need to imagine and implement alternative systems that prioritize collective well-being over profits. This has catalyzed innovative economic thinking centered on shared prosperity, sustainability, and social justice.

The "social economy" conceptualizes organizations founded on principles of cooperation, solidarity, ethics, and democratic self-management that aspire to benefit communities, not just accumulate profits. This includes cooperatives, mutual societies, associations, foundations, social enterprises, and charities (Amin, 2009). These organizations address pressing economic and social needs like healthcare, social housing, education, and employment training. The social economy democratizes ownership and governance so that people have greater control over economic resources and their livelihoods. It employs entrepreneurial strategies for social rather than personal gain (Nyssens, 2007). Mainstreamed across Europe, Quebec, and Canada, the social economy illustrates potentials for pluralistic markets with room for enterprises that enhance social welfare alongside shared prosperity.

Community wealth building is a systems approach to developing place-based economies grounded in justice, sustainability, and democratic control. This framework was pioneered by The Democracy Collaborative as an alternative to extractive capitalism that concentrates wealth in the hands of a few at the expense of communities (The Democracy Collaborative, n.d.). It aims to create an inclusive economy where control and benefits are broadly shared rather than flowing out of communities. Strategies include developing cooperatives and worker-owned businesses, building community land trusts for affordable housing, expanding local purchasing by anchor institutions, and establishing publicly or community-owned utilities and banks. Community wealth building constructs community economies on a democratic basis and from the bottom up. Successful examples like the Evergreen Cooperatives in Cleveland, Ohio demonstrate potential for building generative forms of community ownership.

Post-growth economics contends that endless economic growth dependent on extractive capitalism and consumerism is incompatible with ecological sustainability. It calls for delinking human progress from GDP growth and developing economic models focused on adequate standards of living, human flourishing, and environmental regeneration (Dietz & O'Neill, 2013). This requires transitioning to steady-state or degrowth models that consume less energy and natural resources. It necessitates redistributing existing resources and income rather than growing production and consumption indefinitely. Post-growth economists like Giorgos Kallis outline policies like resource caps, carbon taxation, shorter working weeks, and universal basic services that could facilitate this transition (Kallis, 2018). The degrowth movement provides vital critiques of the limits of growth while advocating for ecological economics centered on sufficiency rather than accumulation.

Visions of a post-work society imagine a future where technological automation and provision of a universal basic income reduce the centrality of wage labor for survival. This liberates human energies toward more creative, meaningful, and socially useful activities (Srnicek & Williams, 2015). While recognizing potential for disruption, post-work theorists like André Gorz and Kathi Weeks advocate seizing the possibilities for autonomy, community building, self-actualization, and care work offered by reducing time dominated by paid work. However, realizing post-work futures requires contesting the neoliberal logic of jobs at any cost and instituting policies like a shortened work week and universal basic income to decouple livelihoods from labor (Weeks, 2011). Post-work imaginaries remind us that human flourishing should determine economic possibilities rather than economic demands dictating human lives.

The solidarity economy, community wealth building, post-growth economics, and post-work proposals offer transformative visions for an economy founded on cooperation, justice, sustainability, and liberatory potentials. However, making systemic change requires policy levers capable of fundamentally restructuring capitalism toward these ends. Social housing and just transition policies that shift economic control and resources toward marginalized communities provide examples. Democratizing ownership in sectors like energy could support bottom-up, community-governed systems. Worker cooperatives that distribute power internally and anchor jobs locally exemplify generative enterprises. Participatory budgeting gives citizens shared budget decision-making power while universal basic services supply housing, food, healthcare, and education as rights.

Diverse economic innovations are emerging that suggest alternative futures beyond capitalism are possible. However, realizing systemic change also necessitates cultural shifts toward values of solidarity, sustainability, cooperation, and democratic participation. This calls for new narratives and political education that spur mass mobilization toward post-capitalist possibilities. As Milton Friedman recognized, when thinkers unite around new paradigms for political economy, the seemingly impossible can rather quickly become inevitable. The need and opportunities have never been greater for progressives to energize around inspirational visions for an economy built on justice and liberation.

Commons Value Creation

Dominant perspectives on value creation tend to view it either through the lens of profit maximization by private firms or as a public good overseen by the state. However, commons-based approaches offer a vital third pathway for value creation grounded in shared benefits, mutual aid, and grassroots democracy. The commons provides an alternative model to rethink how we produce goods, deliver services, and improve processes in ways that foster sustainability, equity, and human flourishing (Bollier & Helfrich, 2014).

Historically, commons were perceived as natural resources collectively stewarded by communities, such as fisheries, forests, and water systems. But the logic of the commons has much wider relevance for reimagining value creation today. It counters the privatized, individualistic ethos of modern capitalism with an ethic of cooperation, solidarity, and shared responsibility. Rather than an abstract ideal, putting commons principles into practice requires translating them into new kinds of enterprises and value chains.

Cooperatives are member-owned, democratically governed businesses that embody commons values (Ostrom, 1990). In contrast to corporations seeking to maximize profits for shareholders, cooperatives are designed to meet members' economic, social, and cultural needs holistically. Core principles are self-help, self-responsibility, democracy, equality, equity, and solidarity. Surpluses generated are reinvested or shared equitably among members.

By organizing collectively, cooperatives gain efficiencies of scale and capabilities to compete in markets dominated by large corporations. Shared facilities, joint purchasing, and collaborative marketing confer advantages unavailable to individuals acting alone. Democratic governance empowers members with voice and control over decisions that impact them.

Beyond economic benefits, cooperatives also create social value and community empowerment. They build local wealth, generate employment, and provide new opportunities particularly for marginalized groups. Cooperatives can also embed environmental principles into production, distribution, and governance processes.

The cooperative model catalyzes new types of value chains based on mutuality and shared interests rather than one-sided exploitation. Producer cooperatives enable small farmers or artisans to access markets. Consumer cooperatives source directly from local producers, cutting out corporate intermediaries. Workers' cooperatives allow collaborative, ethical manufacturing and services. Purchasing cooperatives aggregate demand for sustainable products. Credit unions provide accessible financing to launch new cooperatives.

By linking different forms, the cooperative model creates integrated value chains rooted in common needs and horizontal relationships. Farming cooperatives, food processing cooperatives, retail food cooperatives, and credit unions can collaborate to construct sustainable local food systems controlled by communities. Shared platforms and jointly owned infrastructure allow cooperatives to innovate, develop new products and services, and scale impact.

Circumventing profit-seeking middlemen, cooperative value chains apportion more value to producers and consumers. Surpluses generated are recycled to support members and communities rather than extracted by external shareholders. Equitable value distribution lifts up disadvantaged groups through new livelihoods and capabilities.

In essence, cooperative value chains refashion economic relationships around mutual interests instead of capital versus labor. Reciprocal service provision replaces one-sided resource exploitation. Democratic accountability replaces autocratic, opaque governance. The logic of cooperation thus transforms value chains holistically to center on shared prosperity, ecological regeneration, human dignity, and real democracy.

The commons offers a model to rethink value creation in ways that remedy the social and environmental ills of capitalism. Constructing cooperative value chains provides a strategy to reorganize how we produce goods, deliver services, and meet common needs. Updating traditional commons stewardship of natural resources for the twenty-first century, commons principles allow envisioning enterprises, economies, and societies structured for the benefit of all members and the planet we inhabit together.

Sustainable Systems

In recent decades, the limitations and externalities of conventional profit-driven business models have become increasingly apparent. In response, alternative economic approaches centered on collective stewardship of shared resources are gaining traction. Two related paradigms with transformative potential are commons value creation and the promotion of the social and solidarity economy (SSE) through new public policies.

Proponents argue that expanding the commons sphere can foster more ecologically resilient, socially inclusive, and economically equitable modes of provisioning compared to capitalist markets (Chaves Ávila & Gallego-Bono, 2020). Some key potential benefits include:

- Economic resilience: Commons diversify economic production and activities. Reciprocity and exchange within commons communities build solidarity. Commons demonstrate viable alternatives to profit maximization.
- Social inclusivity: Participatory governance engages marginalized groups and democratizes decision-making. Needs-based access broadens essentials like food, energy, housing, and finance. Global digital commons enable open sharing of knowledge and technology.
- Ecological sustainability: Commons ties usage to resources' regeneration rates. Stewardship ethics embedded in communities align production with local ecosystem limits. Legal rights of nature need reinforcement.

However, commons face challenges scaling up within current economic systems. Supportive public policy and legal frameworks are generally lacking. Capitalist markets tend to enclose commons resources for privatization (De Moor, 2013). Still, public–commons partnerships and policy innovations to bolster commons show promise in spreading alternative provisioning models.

The social and solidarity economy (SSE) or social economy refers to private enterprises and organizations focused on social purposes and democratic governance rather than profit maximization (Utting, 2015). It includes cooperatives, mutuals, associations, foundations, and social enterprises. SSE organizations are value-driven and embedded in communities. The SSE is increasingly recognized as a distinct third economic sector besides the private, for-profit sector and the public sector.

A new generation of public policies aims to catalyze SSE growth and benefits through systemic, transformative approaches. Since the 2010s, such policies have spread at multiple government levels worldwide. Chaves Ávila and Gallego-Bono (2020) term these "transformative policies for the social and solidarity economy" (TPSSEs). They exhibit several interrelated features:

- Public–community partnership: Policies are co-constructed and implemented via multi-stakeholder collaboration between governments, SSE networks and other partners.
- Mainstreaming: The SSE is integrated across policy areas rather than isolated in marginal initiatives.
- Innovation: New governance tools, financing instruments, legal frameworks, and participatory processes modernize public action.
- Systematization: Complex, holistic policy ecosystems with strategic objectives replace fragmented, piecemeal efforts.
- Transformative aims: TPSSEs use the SSE as an engine to drive inclusive, sustainable, economic change.

Advocates contend this policy model can unleash the SSE's potential to tackle issues like poverty, social exclusion, unemployment, urban decay, and environmental degradation. It represents a new form of partner state thinking (Utting, 2015).

However, TPSSEs face implementation obstacles including bureaucratic resistance, scarce resources, and difficulties sustaining multi-stakeholder collaboration. They can appear threatening to existing interests and routines. Evaluating success also remains a challenge. Still, the widespread experimentation with TPSSEs points to their potential in steering economic systems in more socially and ecologically beneficial directions.

Both commons value creation and TPSSEs share core aims of transforming economies to be more equitable, ecological, and democratic. They offer pathways to re-embed economic activity within social and environmental limits through collective action and stewardship. However, achieving the scale required to drive sustainable development will necessitate growing these alternative practices within a still dominant capitalist system.

This requires building broad political support and mobilizing resources to foster commons and SSE growth. State power and capacity will need channeling to provide an enabling framework. Cross-sector partnerships can align interests and investments. Movement-building can help shift cultural narratives and behaviors. Further research should assess the impacts of existing initiatives and models that can be replicated and scaled up (Utting et al., 2014).

Commons and the SSE will not solve all societal challenges, but can serve as living laboratories innovating more holistic provisioning systems. By elevating solidarity over individualism and human thriving over profits, they offer concrete steps to build "development alternatives" centering well-being within ecological limits (Borzaga & Defourny, 2001; Johanisova et al., 2013). Continued experimentation with commons and TPSSEs thus provides grounds for hope in realizing more sustainable futures.

Practical Transformations

Alternative economic approaches such as the social economy and cooperative management structures offer pathways to transform society based on principles of abundance rather than scarcity. By utilizing strategies like community wealth building, place-based change, distributed manufacturing enabled by technology, skill sharing, and policies providing greater economic security, the social economy aims to build economies where all people can freely and accessibly obtain what they need to thrive (Dubb, 2016).

The social economy consists of organizations and enterprises focused on serving social aims and community interests rather than maximizing profits. It includes cooperatives, mutual associations, foundations, and non-profit groups working to address human and environmental needs often unmet by state or market sectors. Social economy entities are grounded in principles of solidarity, cooperation, reciprocity, and mutualism. They build community wealth and aim to equitably distribute resources based on needs, thereby embodying an economics of abundance (Raworth, 2017).

Cooperatives are a major component of the social economy based on shared member ownership and democratic governance. As member-serving organizations, cooperatives aim to provide sustainable livelihoods and meet members' needs. They enact cooperative principles like voluntary participation, member control, and concern for the community. By collectively organizing production, services, finance, and consumption, cooperatives demonstrate the viability of economic models maximizing societal well-being over profits.

Several strategies utilized by the social economy and cooperatives align with abundance-based economics and have transformative potential:

- Community wealth building: Community wealth building democratizes ownership and governance of economic assets like land, enterprises, infrastructure, financial institutions, and housing. Strategies like cooperatives, community development corporations, municipal enterprises, and land trusts aim to build an inclusive, place-based economic system that spreads wealth, power, and benefits more equitably (Dubb, 2016). For example, cooperatives root jobs and capital locally by broadening ownership. Community land trusts ensure housing access. Public banking provides affordable credit. Such pluralistic, community-centered models enact abundance by giving all residents a stake in the economy.
- Place-based approaches: The social economy utilizes place-based approaches recognizing the interdependence between economic, social, political, and environmental forces in a territory. Meeting a community's multidimensional needs requires holistic, localized strategies. Social economy entities like multi-stakeholder cooperatives and non-profit community development groups often lead participatory processes to set place-based development agendas. Mobilizing existing physical, natural, human, and social capital unlocks abundantly available but underutilized community resources. This place-consciousness cultivates solidarity and shared purpose.
- Distributed manufacturing: Technologies like computer-controlled fabrication, modular design, and collaborative digital platforms enable a distributed manufacturing model aligned with social economy values of cooperation and sustainability. Community-based maker-spaces and digital networks allow localized production of small batches in response to needs. Cooperatives utilizing shared machines, open-source design, and peer-to-peer collaboration demonstrate the potential for more democratic, regenerative manufacturing. By localizing production and replacing mass consumerism with on-demand fabrication using recycled materials, distributed making aligns consumption with real needs and community capacities.
- Online platform cooperative: Platform cooperatives utilize shared digital infrastructure to facilitate exchanges of goods, services, and knowledge between peers. While corporate sharing platforms like Uber often exacerbate inequities,

cooperatively owned platforms aim to fairly distribute value and power. Platform co-ops enable service providers to own and govern the platforms they rely on. Applications like cooperative ride-hailing, childcare, eldercare, and equipment sharing help mobilize underutilized assets for mutual benefit. Digital abundance thinking applied ethically opens new frontiers of shared prosperity.

The social economy cultivates multidimensional human development through skill sharing. Time banking initiatives allow community members to exchange services based on time contributions rather than money. Maker spaces facilitate peer-to-peer learning and collective tinkering. Open educational platforms widely distribute knowledge. Cooperative volunteer boards build leadership capacities. These skill exchanges aim to develop each person's full potential in service of community goals. They reflect an economics of abundance where human talents are recognized as plentiful, renewable assets to enrich lives.

Policies guaranteeing basic economic security provide foundations for people to fully access and contribute to social economy initiatives. Models like a universal basic income or guaranteed minimum income reduce vulnerabilities to poverty and precarity. Access to healthcare, childcare, education, and the internet expand capabilities. Supportive social policies enable engagement in socially transformative projects by freeing time and energy otherwise consumed by survival struggles. Once freed from structural scarcity, human talents can be contributed as abundant cooperative resources.

The social economy and cooperatives operationalize an economics of abundance by fostering equitable access based on needs, broadly sharing power and resources, and unlocking the full capacities of people and communities. Redirecting economic activity to nourish human development and social–ecological integrity supports more just, sustainable, and fulfilling lives. Actualizing models of authentic abundance can cultivate post-scarcity consciousness to transform society.

Managing Disruptions

The social economy encompasses organizations and activities with social objectives, such as cooperatives, mutual societies, non-profit organizations, social enterprises, and voluntary associations. Managing the social economy involves navigating possibilities as well as significant challenges. One key distinction is between innovation, which improves upon existing goods, services or systems, and disruption, which fundamentally transforms the status quo.

Innovation in the social economy often focuses on enhancing social value creation. This could involve tweaking an existing business model to better meet community needs, using new technologies to improve services and operations, or reconfiguring organizational processes to be more inclusive. While important, innovation works within existing frameworks and norms. It does not challenge the fundamental structure of markets, organizations, or society.

In contrast, disruption introduces something genuinely new that rewrites the rules of the game. For the social economy, disruptive innovations are systemic transformations that challenge dominant institutions, practices, and mindsets. Examples include the emergence of cooperatives and mutual aid societies as alternatives to traditional enterprises, sharing economies that question private ownership models, and degrowth proposals that confront the growth imperative.

Disruptive social innovations hold the promise of catalyzing progressive change. However, managing disruptive transformations also poses complex difficulties. Three key challenges are:

- Designing truly democratic and participatory processes for developing disruptive proposals, ensuring they reflect diverse needs and perspectives. Top-down implementation risks replicating existing power imbalances and exclusionary dynamics (Nicholls & Murdock, 2011).
- Building broad social legitimacy and acceptance for fundamentally new ideas. Disruption often meets initial resistance or skepticism, even from marginalized groups it aims to benefit. Careful awareness raising, coalition building, and inclusive governance are required.
- Ensuring strong sustainability in the rollout and institutionalization of systemic changes. Well-intentioned reforms sometimes spawn unintended consequences. Careful systems thinking and precautionary policies can help promote resilience (Seyfang & Smith, 2007).

To manage these challenges, social economy leaders need capabilities for "innovative disruption"—creative strategies to facilitate transformation while upholding inclusive, democratic principles. Examples include:

Open collaborative design platforms to crowdsource and refine proposals for disruptive social innovations.

Immersive simulations and participatory theater to viscerally engage diverse stakeholders in envisioning and experientially exploring systemic alternatives.

Phased implementation roadmaps that balance urgency for change with thoughtful sequencing that allows iterative learning and course correction.

Hybrid funding models blending market, public, and social resources to develop the ecosystems and absorptive capacity required for deep transition.

Proactive policies to compensate those negatively affected by disruptive reforms and retrain workers for new roles.

Reflexive governance processes with continuous multi-stakeholder monitoring, reflection, and adaptation.

Innovative disruption combines urgency for transformational change with thoughtful responsiveness to complex dynamics and unintended consequences. It fosters the mindset, methods, and mechanisms necessary to implement disruptive social innovations in ways aligned with inclusive, democratic principles.

Applying this approach to degrowth proposals highlights the possibilities. Degrowth aims to reduce environmental impacts and enhance wellbeing through more selective, small-scale, and self-determined economic activities (Seyfang & Smith, 2007). Realizing this disruption requires innovative strategies engaging diverse stakeholders in reimagining core societal institutions like work, technology, business, consumption, and governance. Creative policies, anticipatory transition planning, and new platforms for open collaboration and governance can help implement degrowth-aligned changes while attending to equity and democracy.

The social economy has always been a source of experimentation and disruptive innovation. As systemic crises like climate change intensify, the capability for innovative disruption—facilitating bold yet judicious transition—becomes ever more critical. This will be central to manifesting an economy oriented to abundance, ecology, and social justice.

Conclusion

This concluding chapter has surveyed pathways for implementing models that make cooperation the norm, democracy the process, and shared prosperity the goal. The aim has been equipping readers with conceptual resources and strategic knowledge to bring revolutionary visions to life.

The social and solidarity economy offers living examples of embedding care, reciprocity, and stewardship into economic structures. But inspiring examples alone are insufficient; actualizing systemic change requires skillful strategy and organizing. The chapter synthesized diverse cases and concepts into integrative recommendations for action.

Constructing cooperative value chains provides a strategy to reorganize production, services, and exchange around mutual interests instead of capital versus labor. Democratic governance and participatory decision-making redistribute power more equitably. Open innovation approaches mobilize collective creativity for common benefit. Circular business models align commercial activities with ecological limits.

However, the core emphasis must be on how citizens can create vibrant commons and cooperate at the grassroots. Tactics like leveraging anchor institutions, progressive municipalism, and participatory budgeting can expand community control. But enabling policies are insufficient without grassroots capacity-building and leadership development.

Through a people-centered approach, linking local alternatives into facilitated networks allows seeds of change to take root and blossom in fertile soil. Rather than waiting for system reforms, ordinary citizens can cultivate the communities they wish to inhabit. Diverse economic innovations demonstrate that alternative futures are possible. But realizing systemic change requires cultural shifts toward solidarity, sustainability, cooperation, and participation.

By learning from diverse experiments in equitable, ecological economics, citizens can begin laying the foundations of new systems today. The social and solidarity economy offers not fixed prescriptions, but adaptable principles and innovations to creatively apply based on local contexts and aspirations. The ultimate goal is embedding care, reciprocity, and stewardship into the practices, routines, and relationships of everyday life.

Though the destination remains uncertain, the path is clear: building participatory cultures of cooperation from the ground up through leadership development, capacity-building, and prefiguring desired futures in the present. Through foresight, strategy, and solidarity, an economy founded on abundance, mutual aid, and liberation can arise as today's utopia becomes tomorrow's reality. The social and solidarity economy provides a compass to guide the way. This concluding chapter aimed to synthesize its diverse lessons to steer readers on the journey ahead.

References

Amin, A. (2009). *The Social Economy: International Perspectives on Economic Solidarity*. London: Zed Books.

Bollier, D., & Helfrich, S. (eds). (2014). *The Wealth of the Commons: A World Beyond Market and State*. Amherst, MA: Levellers Press.

Borzaga, C., & Defourny, J. (2001). *The Emergence of Social Enterprise*. London: Routledge.

Chaves Ávila, R., & Gallego-Bono, J. R. (2020). Transformative policies for the social and solidarity economy: The new generation of public policies fostering the social economy in order to achieve sustainable development goals. The European and Spanish cases. *Sustainability*, *12*(10), 4059.

The Democracy Collaborative (n.d.). *Community Wealth Building*. Available at: https://www.democracycollaborative.org/community-wealth-building (accessed February 17, 2024).

De Moor, T. (2013). *Homo cooperans: Institutions for Collective Action and the Compassionate Society*. Utrecht: Utrecht University, Faculty of Humanities.

Dietz, R., & O'Neill, D. (2013). *Enough is Enough: Building a Sustainable Economy in a World of Finite Resources*. London: Routledge.

Dubb, S. (2016). Community wealth building forms: What they are and how to use them at the local level. *Academy of Management Perspectives*, *30*(2), 141–152.

Gibson-Graham, J. K. (2006). *A Postcapitalist Politics*. Minneapolis: University of Minnesota Press.

Johanisova, N., Crabtree, T., & Fraňková, E. (2013). Social enterprises and non-market capitals: a path to degrowth? *Journal of Cleaner Production*, *38*, 7–16.

Kallis, G. (2018). *Degrowth*. Newcastle upon Tyne: Agenda Publishing.

Nicholls, A., & Murdock, A. (eds). (2011). *Social Innovation: Blurring Boundaries to Reconfigure Markets*. London: Palgrave Macmillan.

Nyssens, M. (Ed.). (2007). *Social Enterprise: At the Crossroads of Market, Public Policies and Civil Society*. New York: Routledge.

Ostrom, E. (1990). *Governing the Commons: The Evolution of Institutions for Collective Action*. Cambridge: Cambridge University Press.

Raworth, K. (2017). *Doughnut Economics: Seven Ways to Think Like a 21st-century Economist*. White River Junction, VE: Chelsea Green Publishing.

Seyfang, G., & Smith, A. (2007). Grassroots innovations for sustainable development: Towards a new research and policy agenda. *Environmental Politics, 16*(4), 584–603.

Srnicek, N., & Williams, A. (2015). *Inventing the Future: Postcapitalism and a World without Work*. London: Verso Books.

Utting, P. (Ed.). (2015). *Social and Solidarity Economy: Beyond the Fringe*. London: Zed Books.

Utting, P., van Dijk, N., & Matheï, M. A. (2014). *Social and Solidarity Economy: Is There a New Economy in the Making?* United Nations Research Institute for Social Development.

Weeks, K. (2011). *The Problem with Work: Feminism, Marxism, Antiwork Politics, and Postwork Imaginaries*. New York: Duke University Press.

Wright, E. O. (2010). *Envisioning Real Utopias*. London: Verso.

About the Authors

Peter Bloom is a professor of management at the University of Essex. His research critically explores the radical possibilities of technology for redefining and transforming contemporary work and society. It focuses on better understanding the trans-human aspects of organizational existence and the potential for constructing more empowering cultural paradigms for organizing the economy and politics. He is the author of nine books and is regularly published in top international journals and media outlets. He is currently leading the development on a first of its kind community economy digital platform called "Shared Futures" and is the founding director of COVER (Centre for Commons Organising, Values, Equalities, and Resilience). Originally from the United States, he now lives in London with his family.

Rok Kranjc is a researcher in the fields of political ecology, alternative economies, and futures studies. He is also founder of Futurescraft, a research and development (R&D) studio that employs futuring, games, and performative methods as tools for collectively imagining, reflecting on, and prefiguring transition pathways aligned with post-capitalist perspectives. Notable projects include the modular board game and game show *Game-Changers: The Game* and public performance series Future 14B. Rok frequently collaborates with organizations like Aksioma—Institute for Contemporary Art Ljubljana, Maska Institute, Crypto Commons Association, P2P Foundation, and Participatory Futures Global Swarm. Rok has translated several books into his native Slovenian, including Escobar's *Designs for the Pluriverse*, Hajer's *The Politics of Environmental Discourse*, and Ostrom's *Governing the Commons*.

https://doi.org/10.1515/9783111080147-010

Index

https://doi.org/10.1515/9783111080147-011